D1406034

THE INCREDIBLE
SHRINKING
SON OF MAN

THE INCREDIBLE
SHRINKING
SON OF MAN

How Reliable Is
the Gospel
Tradition?

ROBERT M. PRICE

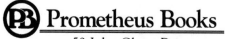 **Prometheus Books**

59 John Glenn Drive
Amherst, New York 14228-2119

Published 2003 by Prometheus Books

Inquiries should be addressed to
Prometheus Books
59 John Glenn Drive
Amherst, New York 14228–2119
VOICE: 716–691–0133, ext. 210
FAX: 716–691–0137
WWW.PROMETHEUSBOOKS.COM

16 15 14   9 8 7

Library of Congress Cataloging-in-Publication Data

Price, Robert M., 1954–
    The incredible shrinking Son of Man : how reliable is the gospel tradition? / Robert M. Price.
        p.   cm.
    Includes bibliographical references.
    ISBN 978-59102-121-6
    1. Bible. N.T. Gospels—Evidences, authority, etc. 2. Bible. N.T. Gospels—Criticism, interpretation, etc. 3. Jesus Christ—Historicity. 4. Church history—Primitive and early church, ca. 30–600. I. Title.

BS2555.52.P75 2003
232.9'08—dc22

                                                                    2003016868

Printed in the United States of America on acid-free paper

Dedicated to Grover Furr,

who finally convinced me I had enough to say on the subject to write a book!

CONTENTS

INTRODUCTION
CRITERIA

THE PIETY OF CRITICISM

As Paul Tillich has said, when anything is placed on a pedestal beyond criticism, it becomes an idol. Those who thus seek to screen an idol from criticism only betray their own suspicions about the worthiness of the totem they worship. The Bible has become, in the words of the Reverend Jim Jones, "a paper idol." Once, at the time of the sixteenth-century Protestant Reformation, champions of the Bible celebrated the Bible's being made available to any and all who might wish to read it. They insisted that the book be freed from the gilded chains of sacred hermeneutics, to be read by the same rules scholars use to make sense of any ancient text. The Bible was to them a newly discovered treasure that they rejoiced to behold glittering in the sun. But it was not long before they began to look about suspiciously and pile the riches back into the chest and replace it in the ground. Sacred scripture must be protected from the unworthy glance of impious outsiders and heretics after all. Not everyone was satisfied with this turn of events. The appearance of *historical-critical study*, or the "Higher Criticism," of the Bible,[1] beginning in the eighteenth century with men like Johann Salomo Semler, Johann Gottfried Eichorn, Johannes Philipp Gabler, and Hermann Samuel Reimarus, represented a return to Reformation vitality where the Bible was concerned. Once again, Bible students were unafraid to read the Bible without the lenses of official dogma, insofar as they could manage it. As these critics, many of them influenced by Rationalism, and their successors applied their critical tools to the text, their orthodox opponents could see only the vandalism wrought by infidel detractors of scripture. If it turned out that the Red Sea were really only the Reed Sea, if it eventuated that Daniel, Isa. 40–66, and the Pentateuch were not written by Daniel, Isaiah, and Moses, then the edifice of faith appeared to the conventional churchman to be collapsing.[2] The Bible had been carried off by the enemy, as when in 1 Sam. 4:11, the Ark of the Covenant had been seized off the battlefield by the victorious Philistines.

And it cannot be denied that some of the earliest biblical critics were looking to debunk and discredit the Bible. This was not necessarily because they thought the Bible a particularly evil book, or that they deemed themselves happy champions of evil. No, many no doubt shared the ambivalence of the great agnostic Robert Green Ingersoll,[3] who gladly admitted he should have nothing to say against the Bible, easily looking past the inevitable shortcomings of a Bronze Age document, if not for the powerful voices of fanaticism that demanded conscientious people accept this ancient book as the inspired Word of God and believe all within it uncritically. This Ingersoll could not brook. So he set himself the task of laying bare the absurdities of the Bible for the modern age. His task was much the same as that of the Christ in Col. 2:14–15, taking the supposedly divine law out of the hands of humanity's tormentors and publicly exposing it, so as to make it impossible for it ever to be so used again.

This task retains something of its importance today, when the Bible still functions as a warrant for the opinions of demagogues who hope, by brandishing it, to bypass rational argumentation and win assent to their opinions by cultivating superstitious fears. But mere negative apologetics, if we may call it that, can never be the real goal of the higher criticism of the Bible, for fundamentalists and demagogues are far from the only zealots for the Bible. Many more of us, whether Christians, Jews, Humanists, or just plain historians, have been bitten by the biblical bug and devote our efforts to elucidating the pages of a text we find consumingly fascinating for its own sake. We feel about the Bible as others do about the works of Homer and Shakespeare. We feel the need to explode misconceptions about the Bible (whether dangerous or merely quaint) primarily so that a better understanding of the text may come to replace them. The quest for the historical Jesus is a specific case, or subset, of this scholarly zeal. It may also be important to question a traditional picture of Jesus that has sometimes had nefarious political and spiritual effects, but the effort should be seen primarily as a positive one: given the cultural importance of the Jesus figure, how can it not be irresistibly fascinating to seek after whatever factual basis may lie at the root of it? And what data do not fall into the category of fact ought to prove equally interesting for the history of religious thought: what path does .a movement follow in creating a man-god to serve as its figurehead? What dynamics are involved in creating the very authority one meanwhile imagines to be creating and sustaining one's movement?

More specifically, it is incumbent upon higher critics of scripture to demonstrate the positive value of our approach that attracted us in the first place and that should win over others who mistakenly perceive us and our enterprise as a threat. Namely, we need to display the unparalleled utility of criticism in elucidating a sometimes dark and mysterious text. Criticism can be shown to unravel the riddles that perturb every Bible reader. As we show that criticism can make an intelligible sense of the conundrums of Scripture, the "apparent contradictions" that cause so many of the pious to scratch their heads, we will show the superiority of our approach, not in destroying the Bible, but in better understanding the beloved text. Granted, the price paid is a high one, for the notion of "biblical authority" can never again seem so simple, but then it will more readily be seen how unstable and logically contradictory was the old belief. And have not biblicists always claimed to prize the right understanding of the Bible over any particular doctrine whose validity might be called into question by means of biblical scrutiny? If, for example, one is willing to part with doctrines of Purgatory or Predestination should they not square with the biblical text, then presumably any doctrine of biblical authority that did not pass muster by an honest scrutiny of the text would be as easily jettisoned. In the long run, there is nothing more edifying than understanding the text.

Why Not

Having sought to make clear the positive character of biblical criticism, let us set forth a few of the major criteria that will guide us in this book, enabling us to set aside this saying or that story (or version of a story) as secondary and historically inauthentic. What appears here in skeletal form will quickly be fleshed out in the chapters to follow. Conversely, these criteria will help us to give shape to the great mass of textual data that we face. Consider them sculptor's tools, not weapons.

What if we discover a discrepancy between one gospel and another on the same point? Often the later document will have the more spectacular version of the story. For example, in Mark, it is Jesus who walks on the water (6:45–52), spectacular enough, one might think. But Matthew adapts the story (14:22–27), adding Peter (14:28–33) as a second defier of gravity. John (6:16–21) knows the story, too, but, like Mark, he has only Jesus stride the waves. The typical fundamentalist response is that of attempted harmonization: both Jesus and Peter walked on water that night, but for some reason, Mark and John decided to mention only Jesus. After all, neither one says *nobody but* Jesus walked on water. For that matter, presumably, the whole population of Galilee could have been walking on water that night, and Mark and John would still be accurate and inerrant because they reported that Jesus walked on water, leaving aside the question of anyone else who may have been similarly engaged in boardless surfing. To which we must reply, this is no different from the guilty husband who answers his wife's question, "Where were you tonight?" with the reply, "I was at the supermarket," strategically omitting his hours of dalliance with another woman in a cheap hotel downtown. After all, he didn't say, "I went to the supermarket and nowhere else." No one will be persuaded by such an argument whose conscience is not mortgaged to fundamentalist inerrantism. Is it not, by contrast, the most reasonable thing in the world to conclude that Matthew read a story depicting Jesus alone walking the sea and made an edifying expansion on it? "Keep your eyes fixed on Jesus, and you need not worry about succumbing to life's storms." And with this insight comes the implication that Matthew was simply *not trying to narrate history*, any more than was Jesus when he spun out his parables. The fundamentalist and the critic face the same puzzle; who can deny that the critic is able to offer a better solution? And from this example we derive a general rule of procedure: when a later gospel offers a more spectacular version of a story from the earlier, source gospel, then the less spectacular, if either, is the historical one. This is because it is always more natural to imagine the story growing in the telling, not shrinking. One might want to beef up a more modest version, but who, already possessing the spectacular version, would prefer a simpler or more mundane one? So *the more spectacular is always to be judged inauthentic.*[4]

Similarly, when the later gospel has a seemingly more theologically sophisticated version of a saying or story than its source and predecessor, we may conclude that the later version is the creation of the evangelist. Sometimes mere differences are explicable on a different basis. It may be that the later evangelist was very familiar with a different version of a story or saying from having heard it in the oral tradition and preferred it, or just inadvertently substituted the oral version he was more familiar with. In such a case, it may be the source gospel that had already innovated from oral tradition, the later gospel inadvertently restoring it. But this is more likely the case where there is no important difference between the two. By contrast, take the important story of Peter's confession of Jesus' messianic identity at Caesarea Philippi. Our earliest version has Jesus solicit Peter's opinion, "You are the Christ" (Mark 8:29). Luke modifies the title accorded Jesus: "You are the Christ of God" (9:20), a simple clarification: the anointed of God. Matthew wants a beefier Christology, so his Peter says a mouthful: "You are the Christ, the Son of the living God" (16:16). Merely "the Christ" is no longer good enough. Matthew piles on the theology: Jesus is also Son of God, and not just of some pagan Gentile god but "the living God," the God of Israel. For some reason, John has transferred something very much like Matthew's version of the confession over to Martha of Bethany (11:27), and to Peter he allows but the curt "You are the Holy One of God" (6:69), the acclamation of the demoniac to Jesus in Mark 1:24! Whatever is going on here, we can be sure of one thing: in the original circumstance, Peter did not say something like, "You are the Christ, the Holy One and Son of the Living God," with each evangelist picking and choosing whatever verbal fragments he liked best. The differences, at least among the Synoptics (Mark, Matthew, and Luke), do not lend themselves to that analysis. Instead, there is clear development from a "lower" Christology to a "higher" one. Thus, if any version is most likely to be historical, it is surely the earliest and simplest, the least theologized.

Suppose we find a great clustering of stylistically and/or thematically similar sayings in a single gospel, but pretty much unparalleled in others. We must regard the distinctive material as very likely the work of the particular evangelist in whose work the sayings appear. For if the Gospels were all random samplers of the teaching of Jesus, we would expect them all to have more or less the same range of types of sayings. For instance, John's gospel features numerous self-declarations of Jesus beginning with the revelation formula "I am. . . ." The Johannine Jesus announces himself as the light of the world, the bread from heaven, the true vine, the good shepherd, the door, the way, the truth, and the life, and so on. If Jesus indeed said such things, why on earth do we hear nothing of the kind in any of the other gospels? Isn't it rather because Jesus never made any such statements, but Christian devotion predicated all these things of him? John's Jesus is a crystallization of Johannine Christian devotion, and it has remained the favorite devotional gospel for that reason. This is an important distinction, ignored by C. S. Lewis and his imitators who like to bully the skeptic by asserting that "Jesus claimed to be God."[5]

We need to keep these principles in mind when we encounter similar disagreements *within a single gospel*. They may result from analogous contradictions between the various traditions the evangelist used to build his gospel. Sometimes we find more and less spectacular or theologically sophisticated versions of the same story or explanation of a problem. Again, we must disqualify the more spectacular, the more sophisticated. For instance, Mark seems to have juxtaposed two mutually contradictory traditional answers to scribal criticism: "If your Jesus were in fact the Messiah, why did no one see Elijah come first?" Since they were dealing with the same subject matter, albeit in a contradictory manner, Mark has clipped them together, as he did with sabbath controversy episodes in 2:23–3:6. Mark 9:13 preserves what was no doubt the earlier answer Christians thought of: Elijah *did* come—*figuratively*, in the person of John the Baptist. Mark 9:4 preserves a later attempt to solve the problem: Elijah himself did appear on earth but only briefly, and not publicly. You weren't there? Too bad. Perhaps both incidents are historically spurious, but if either is to be taken seriously, at least as earlier tradition, it must be the John the Baptist answer. If you knew Elijah himself had touched down to earth again, what would ever cause you to fabricate a lame excuse like his second coming being only figurative?

HISTORY VERSUS THE GOSPELS

It is obvious that we have a problem when discrepancies arise between gospel accounts of an event and accounts from some other source, whether archaeology or written histories, usually Flavius Josephus. For example, Mark attributes the death of John the Baptist to Herod Antipas, having been maneuvered by his wife and daughter, who wanted John removed since he was a public embarrassment, denouncing Herod Antipas for seducing his brother's wife, Herodias, away from him (Mark 6:17–28). Josephus (*Antiquities* 18.5.2) says Herod Antipas had John killed without a qualm because of his great influence among the people, fearing he might eventually prove a threat. While the two accounts can be harmonized with some imagination, why should they be? It is possible Mark is right and Josephus is wrong, but given the apparent similarity between Mark's version and the story of Esther, probability would seem to lie with Josephus's piece of *Realpolitik*. In addition, for what it may be worth, Mark also seems to have the wrong brother cuckolded. Josephus says it was Herod, not Philip as Mark has it (or Herod Philip, as harmonists have suggested—these are all separate historical characters, despite the close names!). Luke, too, is found to be in error when compared even with early Christian historians on the question of who ruled as Roman procurator in Galilee around the time of Jesus' birth: Luke has the later Quirinius, while in fact it was Sentius Saturninus, then Quintilius Varus.

A major collision between the gospel tradition and archaeology concerns the existence of synagogues and Pharisees in pre-70 C.E. Galilee. Historical logic implies there would not have been any, since Pharisees fled to Galilee only after the fall of Jerusalem. Sure enough, there is virtually no archaeological evidence for synagogue buildings in Galilee in Jesus' day, and this is a major blow to gospel historicity, since Jesus is depicted as constantly "entering" synagogues, or meeting halls. A similar problem is posed by the ill fit between the synagogue disputes with Jesus and the scribes and the actual opinions of the scribes as inferred from the Mishnaic evidence. The Gospels seem to caricature scribal opinion in such a way as to suggest they were not even familiar with their opponents' views. Thus, these stories can scarcely go back to the time they pretend to report.

Another type of anachronism occurs whenever Jesus is made to address some issue or situation that probably could not have arisen in his own day but more likely emerged only in the early Christian community after him. Two examples should make this clear. In the Gospel of Thomas, saying 53, we read, "His disciples said to him: 'Is circumcision profitable or not?' He said to them: 'If it were profitable, their father would beget them circumcised from their mother. But the true circumcision in spirit has become profitable in every way.'" Is it really possible to imagine the question of circumcision even coming up for discussion in the ministry of Jesus among Palestinian Jews? Who would have questioned the propriety of the ancient token of the Abrahamic covenant? No, the historical Jesus simply cannot have addressed this one. It must instead have come up in the later context of the Gentile Mission, as Christianity made its way into the Greco-Roman world. Circumcision was the iceberg-tip of the question so central to the Pauline Epistles: do Gentile converts from paganism have to embrace Judaism before they can become Christians? Some Jewish Christians thought so, while Paul believed imposing the alien cultural traditions of Judaism would prove a needless stumbling block to many who would gladly embrace the Christian gospel if they could remain Gentiles doing it. In precisely such a context, the same question finds its natural home: "Then what advantage has the Jew? Or what is the value of circumcision? Much in every way" (Rom. 3:1–2a). In fact, had Jesus addressed such an issue, we might ask how it could ever have become a matter of intra-Christian debate in the first place. Surely, then, it was in an effort to settle (i.e., win) the debate that someone first coined the saying we find in Thomas 53.

The same goes for a more familiar passage, the Great Commission to preach the gospel among the nations (Matt. 28:19, Luke 24:47, [Mark 16:15]). If Jesus had really said this, how can we imagine the controversy over Peter preaching to the Gentile Cornelius (Acts 10–11) ever having arisen? How can Peter have been initially reluctant? How can his colleagues in Jerusalem have called him on the carpet, questioning his orthodoxy? If the parting words of the Risen Christ were a command to preach to Gentiles, whence the dispute? Notice, too, that Peter is not simply stubborn: he is readily convinced by the vision of the animals and the sail-cloth (Acts 10:9–16) that he ought to heed Cornelius's invitation. But why did it take even this, if Jesus had not long before made it clear that the chief business of the apostles was to convert the heathen nations? Clearly, then, the Great Commission sayings were coined only once the great Gentile Mission debate began, as an attempt by the liberal pro-mission faction to win their point. It may be that Christian prophets arose in the assembly to adjudicate the issue with a communiqué from the Risen Lord, and it may as easily be that other prophets had clashing oracles, one such preserved in Matt. 10:5. Paul knew the difference between simple common sense and a "word of wisdom" from the heavenly Christ (1 Cor. 7:10, 12, 25), and he must have known which carried more clout.

We witness something very similar to the situation envisioned here among the Appalachian Holiness churches of our own day. Sociologist Nathan L. Gerrard describes their frequent theological debates: "Knowledge of the Bible is fragmentary, and passages are frequently cited out of context or in garbled form. Often there is no Bible in the church unless a member brings one, but this is not surprising since most members of the congregation are functionally illiterate. Nevertheless, the members enjoy doctrinal disputes, and the older men in particular fancy themselves as biblical authorities. . . . An outsider may sometimes get the impression that the cited 'quotations' have been improvised in the heat of debate—chapter, verse, and all."[6] The early Christians were not necessarily illiterate, but the situation is similar for the simple reason that there were no privately owned copies of Scripture at that time: Christians remembered what they could of what they had heard publicly read. And the same was no doubt true of sayings of Jesus: who knew precisely *what* he had and had not said? There is always the temptation to assume that, Jesus being at least as bright as oneself, he must have shared one's own views, and then it is just a short step to saying that he did, and in what words.

THE CRITERION OF DISSIMILARITY

We have been getting closer and closer to the controversial criterion of dissimilarity. According to this critical canon, the historian has no right to accept a saying as authentically dominical (i.e., coming from the Lord, *Dominus*, Jesus) if it has any parallel in either contemporary Judaism and Hellenism or in the early church. Why not? Simply because of the tendency to ascribe one's favorite sayings to one's favorite sage. For the same reason, we find a single saying ascribed to several different names in the Mishnah. Or, for a more contemporary example, once I found myself listening to Walter Bjork's fascinating radio program *Bible Questionnaire* (WFME, Orange, N.J.), and a caller asked where in the Bible one would find the statement "Neither borrower nor lender be." The poor host flipped like mad through his concordance without success. Naturally, since the quote is not from the Bible at all, but from Shakespeare's *Hamlet*! But it *sounded* biblical, so caller and host alike attributed it to scripture. Can it have been much more difficult to naively attribute wise sayings to Jesus?

We know from Galatians that there was a movement afoot to "Judaize" Christianity, to bring it into stricter accordance with the parent faith. It is thus natural to suspect that sayings might have been attributed to Jesus to reinforce observance of the Jewish Torah among Christians. We have such a saying in Matt. 5:17–19, "Think not that I have come to abolish the Law and the Prophets. I have come not to abolish them, but to fulfill them. . . . Whoever then relaxes one of the least of these commandments and teaches others to do so shall be called least in the kingdom of heaven; but he who does them and teaches them shall be called great in the kingdom of heaven." It is not hard to recognize here a polemical shot across the Pauline bow. The saying presupposes that there are Christians who hold the opinion that "Jesus came to abolish the Torah and the Prophets." The wording implies a particular interpretation of the redemptive mission of Jesus, what he "came" to do on earth; thus, we are not dealing with some sniping from Jesus' own enemies, charging him with antinomianism. In fact, we find a pretty close sentiment in Rom. 10:4, "Christ is the end of the law, that every one who has faith may be justified." Matt. 5:17–19 (building on a core of earlier material, verse 18) means to rebut such teaching, pulling rank by attributing the saying to Jesus himself, undercutting the rival view. This saying is thus secondary and Judaizing in tendency. We would then be well within our rights to wonder if *any* Jewish-sounding saying reflects Jewish or Judaizing Christianity rather than the historical Jesus.

For the same reason, any time Jesus sounds like a Cynic or Stoic or like Socrates, we may wonder if we have evidence of Gentile Christians coining sayings to distance Jesus from Judaism and thus to legitimate their own preferences. For instance, when Jesus is made to abandon fasting since the kingdom of God has arrived, and one cannot force the new spiritual reality into the outmoded forms of Jewish observance (Mark 2:21–22), we have to wonder: are we seeing here a religious revolutionary breaking with his own culture? Or are we seeing an excuse by Hellenistic Christians for why they do not intend to continue Jewish fasting practices? The same suggests itself when Jesus is seen quoting the Greek Septuagint (the original Hebrew would not fit the point at issue) of Isaiah in Mark 7:6–23 and "proves" that kosher laws are irrelevant. Surely this is theological propaganda for Gentile Christians repudiating alien Jewish norms. Was Jesus a radical, or has a later faction of his followers rewritten him in their own image?

If sayings of Jesus strongly echo Christian belief, practice, or wisdom, we have to wonder if someone is, again, attributing to him what they had come to believe on other grounds, providing a dominical pedigree once debate arose. We will see in the next chapter how this principle disqualifies virtually all the sayings of Jesus in the Gospel of John: they are unparalleled in other gospels, closely paralleled in the Johannine Epistles, and they explicitly state sophisticated Christology that seems to have formed through a complex process of Christian reflection, not just to have dropped from the lips of Jesus himself. Specifically, it seems much more likely that John developed his Christology from a long study of Philo's writings than that he just recorded it all from Jesus.

Often sayings of Jesus in the Synoptics find echoes in other New Testament texts, especially the Epistle of James and Romans, chapter 12. Apologists like to contend that all such Jesus-like maxims in the epistles are unattributed quotations of Jesus, but surely it is more likely that if one's point were to quote the Son of God and thus settle some issue, one would hardly neglect naming the source! And then it seems likely enough that the name of Jesus was eventually grafted onto such sayings in order to give them a force they might have lacked. Again, a word from the Lord outweighed Paul's opinion. And it may well be that the Cynic-sounding sayings of Q1 (the earliest stratum of the Q document underlying Matthew and Luke) gained their ascription to Jesus in order to legitimate and facilitate their circulation among Christians.

Many have objected to the criterion of dissimilarity that it is all-devouring, a universal solvent that does not and cannot by its very nature leave any Jesus-sayings as genuine. But is it the *method* or the *result* that is unacceptable here, as when President Nixon brusquely turned down the report of his own Commission on Pornography when it didn't return the verdict he wanted? The trouble with the criterion of dissimilarity is the basic operating assumption of the form-critical method: the early Christians passed down nothing they did not find usable.

Indeed, the material was passed down via the usage. This means that every individual saying or anecdote represents some aspect of the early Christian movement. None is simply an objective datum. Every single one thus fails, and must fail, the criterion of dissimilarity. Even a saying that offended later orthodoxy ("Why do you call me good? Only God is good," Mark 10:18; "Why do the scribes say the Christ is David's son?" Mark 12:35; "But of that day and hour no one knows, not even the angels in heaven, nor the Son, but only the Father," Mark 13:32) must have been amenable to some rival faction or at some earlier, less sophisticated stage—or we would not have it.[7] Even those sayings that command renunciation of self-defense and of property and family, as Gerd Theissen suggested,[8] must have been preserved (or created?) by those elite troops, the mendicant "itinerant radicals" who wandered the world preaching, seeking shelter beneath God's providential canopy (Mark 6:7–11, Matt. 25:34–40, 3 John 5–8, Didache 11:3–13:7). Sayings like these, though conscience-intimidating to rank-and-file believers, as they remain today, served as proud credentials for those few who had actually made the break. Thus, it is no surprise they kept the mendicancy sayings very much alive.

Do the strange-sounding healing stories with their spit-and-polish techniques (Mark 7:32–35, 8:22–26) go back to Jesus? They were enough of an embarrassment to Matthew that he omitted them, lest Jesus sound like a Hellenistic conjurer. But who's to say they were not fabricated by early Christian-era exorcists who sought to add the new divine name Jesus to their incantatory arsenal (Acts 19:13)? Again, some have suggested the historical Jesus must have been a political revolutionary, and that Mark has toned down the story of the raid on the temple to hide this.[9] But may not the earlier, suppressed version reflect some other faction of Christians, years earlier, when the agenda was different?

Again, some object that the criterion of dissimilarity ignores the obvious: wouldn't there be some continuity between Jesus and the religion of his own culture? He may have said all manner of things Jewish in character. And mustn't there have been some degree of continuity between Jesus and the religious community he founded? Of course, but no one is suggesting that the historical Jesus must have been an alien intruder with nothing in common with his environment or legacy. It is just that, for reasons already mentioned, it is no less apparent that sayings and stories were fabricated by his followers and borrowed from his contemporaries. Just because Jesus *might* have said something (echoing Judaism or early Christianity) does not give one the right to assume that he *did* in any given case. But suppose we did have some way of confidently ascribing to Jesus various sayings that mirrored Judaism and the early church? What would this leave us with? A Jesus who amounts to no more than one more instance of the common and the typical, at most the first Christian.

Norman Perrin and others who first employed the criterion of dissimilarity seemed to think they could arrive at a portrait of Jesus that might be minimalistic, missing some similarities he might actually have had with Judaism and early Christianity, but in the process catching what was most distinctive about Jesus. To cite a parallel to what they had in mind, consider Martin Luther. Here was a man who had repudiated significant elements of Roman Catholicism and yet whose faith still had a great deal in common with it, especially when compared to the Radical Reformation sects. Here was a bold innovator whose disciples followed in his steps in some instances (doctrines of salvation by grace through faith and of biblical authority) but blanched at others (reorganizing the canon of Scripture). Yes, Luther was a mix of conventionality and tradition on the one hand and of radicalism on the other. We can see what he selected from Catholicism and where he led that his compatriots feared to follow. It would not be surprising had Jesus been the same way. But we have a distinct advantage in the case of Martin Luther: he wrote books. Suppose we had no writings of the Great Reformer and no reliable contemporary witnesses. Suppose all we could do was to compare the general contours of Catholicism and Lutheranism and decide where Martin Luther fit in. We would be in the same boat as when we seek the historical Jesus. Perrin and his congeners were able to persuade themselves they had been able to "rediscover the teaching of Jesus" because they cheated, taking as echoes of Jesus' distinctive voice gospel texts that, by the criterion of dissimilarity, ought to have been dismissed as Jewish borrowings ("The sabbath was made for man, not man for the sabbath" was a rabbinical chestnut) or as Hellenist Jesus–retrofitting ("It is not what goes into a man that renders him unclean, but rather what emerges from him").

Despite these considerations, we will not proceed in a deductive manner, assuming at the outset that the various gospel materials must be inauthentic. We will examine specific cases, demonstrating in detail that a heavy burden of proof rests on anyone who would vindicate the material as genuine.

THE PRINCIPLE OF ANALOGY

By now New Testament critics are used to the libel that they classify gospel miracle stories as legendary solely because they are personally committed to philosophical naturalism and believe that miracles cannot occur, hence never have occurred. The charge is ludicrous and only betrays the apologists' failure to understand what they pretend to refute. Historians, like scientists, meteorologists, sociologists, and futurologists, use what is aptly called "methodological atheism," or "the surprise-free method."[10] No historian or scientist pretends to be an oracle, issuing infallible dicta about what once happened or what will one day happen. All historical and scientific judgments are *probabilistic* in nature, provisional and tentative, because they are inevitably based on analogy. When the market planner says, "If conditions continue as they are now," or "If present trends continue to hold," he admits there may be surprises that might falsify the projection he is about to make. The analogy is with the present state of things. Radiometric dating is based on the assumption of uniformitarianism, that natural processes would always have worked the same way they do now, so carbon 14 would presumably have the same rate of decay, enabling us to date objects by gauging their half-lives. Conceivably, some cosmic upheaval might have changed the rate of decay, though it is hard to imagine what might have done so. But unless there is good reason to think it did, isn't the only course open to us to assume things have always worked as they do now? *Probably* so. The humble weatherman is telling you what *should* happen if fronts and pressure zones continue to behave as they are doing at the moment. Of course, he is often wrong, but he never claimed to be the Oracle of Delphi. Anything unforeseen *might* throw a monkey wrench into our best calculations. We cannot factor in the unpredictable. That's why we call it the unpredictable! Even so, any wildcard from Merlin the magician to an act of God *might* have functioned as a cause of events in the past, but how is a historian to reckon with this? Merely because some ancient text says so? If we do not use the criterion of analogy with contemporary experience as our shibboleth for what *probably* did and did not happen in the past, we will be at the mercy of every medieval tale, every report that a statue wept, or that someone changed lead into gold or turned into a werewolf. If God really parted the sea as Cecil B. DeMille depicted, the historian is out of luck. His discipline's epistemology will not allow him to declare the Exodus story as "probably factual," even if it happened. He doesn't have a time machine at his disposal, only inference from analogy.

But how is any nonhistorian, or the religious believer in miracles, supposed to have any *better* epistemological access to the past? By faith? Here, it seems to me, one is dealing with a claim very close to that of Rudolf Steiner, Alice A. Bailey, and others, to be able to read the unknown events of the secret past by means of privileged psychic access to the Akashic (Etheric) Records, a kind of Cosmic Three Degree residuum of all that has ever happened. And all this has much more in common with "psychic archaeology" than with historical criticism. If miracles happened in the past, there is no way to detect them. If they are going to happen in the future, there is no way to predict them. Maybe they can happen. Maybe they did. Maybe they will. That is not at issue.

And the sword cuts both ways. If we cannot render "probable" a story of a man walking on water because we have no analogies in contemporary experience for it (and that's all it would take, even if we didn't understand how it were possible), we can consider a story of an exorcism or a faith healing likely enough. Scenes like those in the Gospels occur today. You can go out and with little difficulty find some healing rally or deliverance meeting. You can easily find people speaking in tongues, just as they did in Corinth. You may prefer a natural or a supernatural explanation of what you are seeing, but it will occur to you, "This is what it must have been like in New Testament times!" Even the supposedly archskeptical Bultmann forthrightly declared that the historical Jesus must have been a worker of what he and his contemporaries considered miracles.[11] But you will search in vain for a Pentecostal meeting where the rotting dead are revived (though we know of numerous cases where gagging followers kept macabre bedside vigils over the increasingly ripe corpses of their gurus who had promised to rise again),[12] where people walk on water (though we know how Jim Jones faked it).[13]

THE PRINCIPLE OF BIOGRAPHICAL ANALOGY

If some New Testament miracle stories find no parallel in contemporary experience, they do have parallels, often striking ones, in other ancient writings that no one takes to be anything other than mythical or legendary. The hero tales of the world abound in heavenly annunciations, miraculous conceptions, portents at birth, child-prodigy stories, divine commissionings, devilish temptations to leave the ordained path, miracles, gaining and losing the approbation of the crowd, literal or figurative coronation, betrayal, execution (often on a hilltop), resurrection or disappearance or ascension into heaven, postmortem appearances, and so forth. As Martin Dibelius pointed out,[14] such miracles always seem to punctuate the life stories of saints and heroes in order to cast a halo over their every moment. The Gospels come under serious suspicion because there is practically nothing in them that does not conform to this "Mythic Hero Archetype," no "leftover," secular information such as we do find in the case of Caesar Augustus and a few others,[15] which serves to tie them into the fabric of history.

In any event, when a gospel story fits easily into the category of typical herowonders, we have to have a pretty good reason for holding that, in this one case, *it really happened*. If the story fits the analogy of legend, then what is the historian to do but place it in that category? The principle of analogy is so simple, so natural, that everyone uses it in daily life. Imagine someone sitting down in front of the television after a long day at work. The first image he sees is that of a giant reptile squashing tall buildings. Is one's first hunch, "Oh! The *news* channel!"? Probably not. More likely one surmises the TV set had been left on the science fiction channel. Why? Because one's world of contemporary experience does not include newscasts of giant dinosaurs wreaking havoc in modern cities, but one has seen monster movies in which such disasters are quite typical. Which analogy does the TV screen image fit?

Those who claim that only a naturalistic bias prevents critics from accepting the biblical miracle stories as factual have to explain why they themselves are by no means willing to accept all the wonders of nonbiblical scriptures and legends. It is obvious that they are simply trying to substitute for historical method the old doctrine of the inerrancy of the Bible. Their real gripe is not that critics *hold* a theoretical bias, that of naturalism, but rather that they *fail* to hold one, namely the belief in the historical infallibility of the Christian Bible.

But if our judgments on gospel authenticity must be restricted to matters of mere probability, they must be *at least probable*. That is, we must ever keep in mind the dictum of Ferdinand Christian Baur that anything is *possible*, but that we must ask what is *probable*. This is important because of the very widespread tendency of conventional Bible students, even of otherwise sophisticated scholars, to weigh arguments for critical positions and then toss them aside as "unproven." The operative factor here would appear to be a deep-rooted inertia. The controlling presupposition seems to be, "If the traditional view cannot be *absolutely debunked* beyond the shadow of a doubt, if it still *might possibly* be true, then we are within our rights to continue to believe it." But scholarly judgments can never properly be a matter of "the will to believe." Rather, the historian's maxim must always be Kant's: "Dare to know."

NOTES

1. That is, "higher criticism" as distinguished from lower criticism. Lower criticism is textual criticism, weeding out scribal errors and textual corruptions. Even most fundamentalists have no objection to lower criticism, while opposing high criticism, the inquiry into authorship, integrity, historical accuracy, and other such matters. As a matter of lower criticism, I have placed in brackets references to New Testament texts that seem to be later interpolations, such as citations of the spurious Long Ending of Mark, 16:9–20, or the episode of the adultress, tacked onto John's gospel (7:53–8:11).

Throughout this book, I quote from the Revised Standard Version or else from my own translation.

2. Thomas Hardy, "The Respectable Burgher: On 'The Higher Criticism,'" poem 129 in *The Complete Poems of Thomas Hardy*, ed. James Gibson (New York: Collier/Macmillan, 1976), pp. 159–60.

3. Robert Green Ingersoll, *Some Mistakes of Moses* (Amherst, N.Y.: Prometheus Books, 1986 [orig. 1879]), pp. viii–ix.

4. As I was rereading this chapter I chanced upon a church newsletter containing a feature about Christmas poinsettias (Gwynne Elliott, "Poinsettia," *Scroll* [Goldsboro, N.C.: St. Stephen's Episcopal Church, December 2001], p. 10), which provides an excellent contemporary illustration of this critical axiom. The item compares two accounts of the origin of the bright red flower. One is a story set in Mexico, where cousins Pepita and Pedro are on their way to a Christmas service at church. Pepita is downcast: like the Little Drummer Boy, she has no gift to offer the Christ child. Pedro reassures her that it is the devotion of the heart that counts, so she gathers some miserable weeds and humbly places them at the altar, whereupon they sprout the distinctive blooms of the poinsettia, and thus the flower, which they called *Flores de Noche Buena*, "Flowers of the Holy Night," was born! In the other story, we learn how the ancient Aztecs already knew the flower and called it *cuetlaxochitle*, prizing it as effective against fever, as the source of a red-purple dye, and as a symbol of purity. Which of the two accounts is likelier to be historically accurate?

5. C. S. Lewis, *Broadcast Talks* (London: Geoffrey Bles: Centenary Press, 1942), p. 50–51.

6. Nathan L. Gerrard, "The Holiness Movement in Southern Appalachia," in *The*

Charismatic Movement, ed. Michael P. Hamilton (Grand Rapids: William B. Eerdmans, 1975), p. 165.

7. In his February 24, 1967, debate with Thomas J. J. Altizer, John Warwick Montgomery said, "The point is that you are selecting from His teachings this particular aspect—apocalypticism—and you're arguing that it is primary because it would have been offensive to a particular group within the early church. Now, as a matter of fact, practically everything Jesus said was offensive to somebody in the early church, and this is no criterion at all for selectivity" (*The Altizer-Montgomery Debate: A Chapter in the Death of God Controversy* [Chicago: InterVarsity Press, 1967], p. 64). Montgomery is quite correct, as is the hidden corollary of what he says, namely, that everything attributed to Jesus, however offensive to some in the early church, must have been amenable to others.

8. Gerd Theissen, "The Wandering Radicals: Light Shed by the Sociology of Literature on the Early Transmission of Jesus Sayings," in *Social Reality and the Early Christians: Theology, Ethics, and the World of the New Testament*, trans. Margaret Kohl (Minneapolis: Fortress Press, 1992), pp. 33–59.

9. S. G. F. Brandon, *Jesus and the Zealots: A Study of the Political Factor in Primitive Christianity* (New York: Scribner, 1967).

10. Peter L. Berger, *A Rumor of Angels: Modern Society and the Rediscovery of the Supernatural* (Garden City: Doubleday Anchor, 1970), pp. 16–17.

11. Rudolf Bultmann, *Jesus and the Word*, trans. Louise Pettibone Smith and Erminie Huntress Lantero (New York: Scribner, 1958), p. 173.

12. Jack Gratus, *The False Messiahs* (New York: Taplinger, 1975), gives a number of instances. Jemima Wilkinson, "the Public Universal Friend," told her followers not to bury her corpse when she died, because she would shortly rise again. They hid her body when the time came, in 1820, and they waited, but in vain (p. 162). In 1823, Swiss Messiah Margaret Peter and her sister Elizabeth insisted that their followers beat them to death without qualm, since they would rise again. Visitors were invited to witness the miracle of resurrection, but it didn't happen (pp. 167–70). Shortly before Joanna Southcott died in 1814, one disciple professed his faith that she would rise again. She herself ordered that her body be kept warm for four days with hot water bottles, then opened up, and a living, virginally conceived messianic child ("Shiloh") would be found. The reeking body did not rise, and no fetus was found, dead or alive (pp. 176–77). Sir William Courtenay, "the peasants' Messiah" and reincarnation of Jesus Christ, was killed in a hail of British army bullets, and his corpse was laid out for viewing. Multitudes crowded the parlor, expecting him to rise from the dead and hoping to witness it, but without success. One woman was even found trying to pour water between his inert lips (p. 192).

13. A former adviser of Jim Jones, Jeannie Mills, told me in 1980 how they had once contrived for Jones to appear to stride the waves. The congregation went to the beach for a retreat and slept out on the sand. In the first moments of dawn, Jones positioned himself as if walking back to the shore from the sea, but all he was doing was walking a couple of feet out into and back from the spreading surf. On cue, someone called out to wake the sleepers, "Look! Father's walking on the water!" All blearily beheld what they supposed was the conclusion of a miracle.

14. Martin Dibelius, *From Tradition to Gospel* (New York: Scribner, n.d.), pp. 104–108.

15. Alan Dundes, "The Hero Pattern and the Life of Jesus," in *In Quest of the Hero*, ed. Robert A. Segal, Mythos series (Princeton: Princeton University Press, 1990), pp. 179–223.

CHAPTER ONE
SOURCES

What quarry does the historical investigator start digging in to find materials to erect the pyramid of a life of Jesus? What sources did the ancient evangelists employ when they wrote their gospels? We must devote some attention to both questions, and, while related, they are not the same question. Our sources will of necessity be very different from those used by the traditional Christian believer to compose one's "personal savior," one's own Christ of faith. The preached figurehead of Christian devotion and dogma is a composite of a Christ who is little more than a mathematical integer in a theological formula, a figure seen in stained-glass windows and Sunday school illustrations, and, of course, an uncritical reading of the four canonical gospels. The last thing we as critical historians can do is to allow the party line of an institution (i.e., the creed of a church) to control our reading of the evidence. This is why the vast writings of Christian apologists hold no attraction at all for the critic. The historical critic is conscience-bound to explore the very real possibility that the Christian Jesus has been shaped by the dogmatic agenda of the religion that claims him as a warrant for everything it does. The critic must wonder if the "official biographies" of Jesus, the canonical gospels, are actually faithful reflections of what a historical Jesus of Nazareth, if there was one, did and said.

In some ways, the sources available to the critic are wider and fuller than those available to the believer, the dogmatician, the apologist, for the former risks looking into literary sources that the New Testament evangelists may have used. Since this implies the fictive character of at least some gospel elements, believers will not go venturing down those particular paths. Dogma tells them not to, since their official Jesus *must* have done and said thus-and-so. Other gospels, not included in the official canon of scripture, are available to the critic as well: may Jesus have said or done something reported there? Do such documents perhaps preserve more accurate transcriptions of what he did and said? The Gospel of Thomas and others are included in the vineyard of our labors.

But it is also true that the critic has fewer sources in another sense. This is because the historical critic, as R. G. Collingwood has made so clear,[1] sees his duty as very different from that of his premodern predecessor, the mere chronicler, the scissors-and-paste historian who approaches his task with the expectation that his sources present true facts almost all the time. His job is to preserve the data and harmonize it into a single coherent account. (Obviously, the Christian apologist for the entire accuracy of the Gospels is this sort of historian's modern heir.) He finds a place for everything, by hook or by crook. As much as possible must be preserved, and the premodern historian's ingenuity is devoted to reconciliation and harmonization of what his documentary "authorities" present him. Not so the critical historian, the historical critic, who demotes his documents from the status of "authorities" to that of mere "sources." He may or may not accept what they offer, recognizing that they offer him as much legend as history, propaganda as often as fact. He has to learn to tell the difference, and when he has done, most of the data are still useful to him, albeit for a variety of purposes, for, as Collingwood says, propaganda has its own history.[2] That is what redaction criticism of the Gospels is all about: by tracing the alterations made by the evangelists in the documents or traditions they used, one can trace their theological tendencies, the spin they placed on the material. In this way, we can begin to discern not just the facts about the historical Jesus, whatever they may turn out to be, but also the creative contributions of the evangelists, whose departures from objectivity must not be dismissed crudely as "errors," but rather appreciated as marks of authorial inventiveness. But insofar as we are trying to recover the facts about Jesus, we may find ourselves with precious little left to us that we may call fact, much less than the scissors-and-paste "historian," who hopes merely to combine all the canonical data into a single super-gospel, as Tatian did in the second century.

WHAT DID THEY KNOW AND WHEN DID THEY KNOW IT?

How did we get from Jesus to the Gospels? Beginning with the work of Martin Dibelius, Rudolf Bultmann, and Karl Ludwig Schmidt,[3] scholars have surmised that Christians circulated a great number of sayings attributed to Jesus and stories of what he had done. They may have passed them on faithfully, already feeling themselves bound by a kind of "oral canonicity." Or they may have freely added to the tradition various items that they thought Jesus might have, must have, or would have said or done. The oral tradition continued to grow and to be passed down, gradually crystallizing in several documents, gospels, at least four. Mark seems to have been the first, along with a collection of sayings scholars call simply Q (for *Quelle*, German for "source"). These two were somewhat later used and combined by two other authors independently, the evangelists Matthew and Luke. John has some similarities, but many more differences, with the first three gospels. He may have read some or all of the previous gospels, or he may simply have known a number of the traditional stories and sayings they had also used. More about these gospels in a moment. For now we must just note that their publication would not have stopped the continuing development and oral circulation of the Jesus tradition any more than it would have stopped the production of yet more gospels. Those like Irenaeus of Lyons and Eusebius, who argued on behalf of the canonical fourfold gospel, had to offer contrived rationalizations for excluding subsequent gospels as theologically spurious. It was by no means obvious the gospel well had dried up.

Bultmann, Dibelius, Dennis E. Nineham, and others were called "form critics" or "form historians" because they believed one could trace out an implied history of the various forms (or types) of sayings and stories. Brief stories told by Jesus issuing in a memorable punch line (variously called *apophthegmata*, pronouncement stories, or paradigms) would have served early on as something like modern sermon illustrations. Sentences of holy law[4] were prophetic pronouncements in the name of the Risen Christ to settle some issue of church governance. Miracle stories came from a subsequent stage of missionary penetration into the Mediterranean world, aping the mission propaganda of hero cults and mystery religions with their commercial-like stories of the wondrous deeds of their saviors. One might also speculatively reconstruct the *Sitz-im-Leben* (setting in life) for each bit of the tradition. On the assumption that everything passed down had a use, and was passed down by means of this use, one could usually surmise the use and thus reconstruct many aspects of early church life. For example, they would have used healing and exorcism stories as how-to-do-it paradigms or actual narrative incantations for their own attempts at healing and driving out devils.

Form criticism seemed a natural, almost inevitable, way of reading the Gospels since they are episodic collections of self-contained vignettes, each pretty much isolated and independent. The individual passages, or *pericopes* (a word originally denoting particular scripture portions abstracted for liturgical use), usually have no intrinsic connection. One does not naturally lead to the next (until we reach the Passion narrative, an interconnected whole, though various episodes have attached themselves to it like barnacles on a hull). They appear in a somewhat different order in each gospel, sometimes topically arranged, sometimes almost randomly. This means they were just assembled like tiny stones in a larger mosaic. And each one is brief, featuring only as much detail as is needed to make the point. Often there are no names. A person is described physically only if some plot element depends on it, Jesus himself never being described! Such streamlining again argues for an oral origin.

If the gospel material originated as oral tradition, who may we imagine passing down this tradition? There are two groups we may nominate as candidates. First, the circle of apostles, direct hearers and apprentices of Jesus. Second, *everybody else*. Apologists argue that the original disciples (the twelve disciples, minus Judas, plus other early companions) made it their business to oversee the passing down of the tradition of Jesus' sayings and deeds, clamping the lid on any emerging apocrypha. They might indeed have done this if their first concern had been to make things easy for apologists two millennia later, but otherwise it is hard to see how they would have either wanted to bother or been able to manage it. The Gospels envision Jesus himself as trying unsuccessfully to restrict the transmission of reports of his deeds! Mark makes clear that despite his teaching the crowds, they had grossly erroneous ideas about him. Despite his daily teaching of the disciples themselves, they continued to entertain the densest misconceptions of his teaching, for example, that they should inherit a worldly kingdom, or that the Son of man had come to destroy men's lives instead of saving them.

Harald Riesenfeld and Birger Gerhardsson[5] compared the transmission of Jesus' teaching to that of the rabbis and their disciples after Javneh (the Mishnaic reconstruction of Judaism after 70 C.E.): the faithful disciple was "like a plastered cistern that loseth not a drop" (*Mishnah Aboth* 2.8). Disciples rigidly memorized maxims and rulings of their masters. Might not Jesus' disciples have done likewise? They might have, but the model is an anachronistic one, and we might as well invoke the example of later Muslim traditionists who rampantly fabricated *hadith* (traditions) of the prophet Muhammad to lend weight to their own opinions. Who knows if either possible parallel applies? And even if Riesenfeld and Gerhardsson were right about the practice of the immediate disciples of Jesus, it remains wholly gratuitous to suppose that they remained the sole source for the material that wound up in the Gospels. It might have stemmed from the Twelve—or from anybody else!

If the Gospels were based on word-of-mouth transmission, how accurate would they be? Sometimes we are told that the Middle Easterner's memory, not having so ready a crutch in cheap writing materials as we have, is amazingly retentive, and that tradition-based Jesus material could be assumed accurate. But it is not so simple. Keep in mind that those Muslims who memorize the entire Koran have a written original to work from. We have nothing comparable in the case of Jesus. There the holy text comes at the opposite end of the process. Also, Albert Bates Lord's studies[6] of Balkan bards who "memorize" traditional epics rivaling the *Iliad* in length show that they do not in fact retain and repeat the same material verbatim but rather create a new version each time they perform it. They retain basic structures and "half-lines," which merely form the skeleton for improvisation. Again, this is nowhere near as strict as apologists would like gospel accuracy to be.

If one wants to compare the gospel tradition process with analogous developments in the cases of other religious heroes like Jesus, one finds again that religious enthusiasm causes the tradition to evolve new forms, some radically discontinuous with the original, and virtually overnight. In this way, for example, twentieth-century Congo prophet Simon Kimbangu,[7] languishing in prison, was unable to stop the burgeoning propaganda of his disciples that he was the new "God of the Blacks" or "Christ of the Blacks." Followers of seventeenth-century messiah Sabbatai Sevi gleefully passed around fabulous miracle stories despite the warning of the apostle Nathan of Gaza that the messiah would do no miracles![8]

As Bultmann and others suggested, we must also reckon with the likely contribution of early Christian prophets who imagined themselves to be speaking under the inspiration of the Risen Christ, as we witness taking place explicitly in Revelation, chapters 2–3, and as clearly anticipated in John 16:12–14 and Luke 21:15. Early Christians would have held prophetic words from the ascended Lord in equal esteem with any reports of what Jesus had said on earth, all the more since the new oracles would likely deal with new issues of pressing concern. There is no particular reason to think they would have had any reason to want to discriminate between what Jesus had said on earth and what he had said through prophets. Any collection of Jesus sayings might as easily have included both side by side. We cannot assume that the early Christians would have had any of our historical curiosity motivating them to keep the two categories apart. Anyone who deems it unlikely that mystical Christians should have larded the store of Jesus sayings with their own charismatic oracles need only look at the vast amount of Jesus-fabrication in Gnostic documents like the Pistis Sophia or the various Nag Hammadi gospels, not to mention orthodox gospels like the Epistle of the Apostles and the Gospel of Nicodemus. It is sheer theological arbitrariness to draw a line between canonical books and noncanonical, allowing early Christian imagination/inspiration free reign only outside the boundaries of the official list.

SPOTLIGHT ON THE EVANGELISTS

It was an implication of the whole form-critical approach to view the evangelists as scissors-and-paste compilers with little individual contribution to make. Only John seemed to have exercised more creative freedom, applying generous amounts of his own mortar between the traditional bricks. But closer scrutiny of the gospels by Willi Marxsen, Günther Bornkamm, Hans Conzelmann,[9] and others eventually made it clear that the evangelists had at least made frequent changes in detail that were more than stylistic polishing, much less mere mis-copying. No, the changes were intentional and made sense viewed altogether in patterns. One could discern the manner in which one gospel-writer would redact (edit) his predecessor, toning down this element, omitting that doctrine, changing the effect of Jesus' teaching here or there. What attentive precritical Bible readers had puzzled over as "apparent contradictions" revealed themselves to the new generation of redaction critics as clues for characterizing the individual view-points of the gospel writers. One could even make good guesses about what Mark had done to his own oral tradition sources by noting where his version departed from the narrative logic of a basic form. For instance, though miracle stories virtually always conclude with the cheers of the crowd, trying to prompt reader reaction like a laugh track in a modern TV sitcom, Mark occasionally has Jesus tell the healed person not to tell anyone of the miracle. This figures into the "Messianic Secret" theme[10] Mark has imposed onto earlier tradition. (To all these specifics we will return in later chapters.)

The next step in the evolution of gospel criticism was that of literary criti-cism proper. Scholars including Erhardt Güttgemanns, Robert M. Fowler, Frans Neirynck, and Werner Kelber[11] began to show that, despite their brief, episodic character, the gospel stories bear extensive traces of authorial creation, original, de novo storytelling. Earlier tradition may have played a role, but there is less and less reason to think so, the more "Markan," "Matthean," "Lukan," or "Johan-nine" a story appears. This is measured by the extent to which each gospel story employs the familiar themes and vocabulary of each writer as established by studying his redactional treatment of prior gospels. The resultant theory would see Mark as writing much or even most of his work (as the radical critic Bruno Bauer had said already in the nineteenth century) out of his imagination, with Matthew and Luke freely redacting Mark's work and adding much new material of their own invention. Critics had been in the habit of speaking of special "L" material in Luke's gospel, special "M" material in Matthew's,[12] and they meant that stories or sayings unique to Luke or Matthew had been drawn from separate collections of Jesus material unknown to Mark or the Q compiler. Now it seems more and more likely that Mark was as genuinely creative a writer as John, and that, where they have something to add to Mark, Matthew and Luke consulted their own imaginations, too.

The more we see the Gospels as genuinely literary creations, the less need there is to posit underlying oral tradition as their source. On the one hand, the various gospel tales look less and less as if they must be products of oral tradi-tion; on the other, if the Gospels are de novo literary compositions, the hypoth-esis of some kind of informational bridge between a historical Jesus and the creation of the Gospels becomes unnecessary. Bruno Bauer believed Mark had invented Jesus, just as Mark Twain created Huck Finn. In our own day, Walter Schmithals[13] sees no reason to reject a historical Jesus but denies there was a pre-Q, pre-Markan oral tradition and declares the Gospels almost an apocryphal development, a late growth in a Christian movement whose early stages are better represented by the Pauline epistles.

But even this estimate of their creativity does not mean the evangelists did not use prior sources. A new wave of critics suggest that the evangelists' sources were literary sources. Randel Helms, John Dominic Crossan, Earl Doherty, and others[14] have shown the surprising extent to which gospel narrative is simply rewritten Old Testament material. Doherty states most clearly the underlying logic. New Testament writers often say that so-and-so happened "according to the Scriptures," and we have supposed they meant that some gospel episode (whether in fact originating in history or legend) had occurred as a fulfillment of some scripture prophecy. Then the New Testament writer sought an appropriate prooftext: the virginal conception, no doubt borrowed from typical hero legends, receives an after-the-fact pedigree by invoking Isa. 7:14 ("Behold, the maiden/ virgin shall conceive and bear a son, and you shall call his name Emmanuel") grossly out of context. But, Doherty asks, what if they began with no stories or historical memories of Jesus but simply believed in a mythic Son of God, who must have secretly come to earth to redeem humanity? What if they for some reason subsequently decided to reconstruct his hypothetical incarnation: where would they derive the material for his biography? Where else but Scripture, read as a cipher? With esoteric methods of interpretation reminiscent perhaps of the Kabbalistic sages of another age, they read Scripture against the grain, looking for hints that any particular passage might have an encoded message about the Christ, the Son of God. Stories of earlier Jewish and Israelite heroes like Moses, David, Elijah, and Elisha would have been fertile sources. And usually it was the Greek version of the Old Testament, the Septuagint, that the Christians used. So when they said he visited Egypt or rose from the dead *according to Scripture*, perhaps what they meant was that they surmised he *must* have done these things because Scripture (read through esoteric lenses) said he did. Supposed prophecy would then have been translated directly into past-tense narrative.

Another major source would have been Homer. Dennis R. MacDonald has shown very effectively how many puzzling elements in Mark's gospel may be elucidated by the hypothesis that he was following the *Iliad* and the *Odyssey* as models.[15] Luke, too, I have argued elsewhere,[16] probably used Homer and certainly (in Acts) used Euripedes.

I'M LATE! I'M LATE! FOR A VERY IMPORTANT DATE!

When were the Gospels written? The conventional dates ascribed to the Gospels are controlled by the agenda of apologetics: the goal was to date the documents as early as possible so as to shorten the time span from Jesus to the Gospels, to make the oral-tradition period as short as possible, betraying an acknowledgment that oral tradition is not after all to be trusted. Interestingly, conservative gospel scholars like F. F. Bruce and I. Howard Marshall seem simultaneously to deny and to affirm the possibility of accurate oral transmission. This is because they accept the source hypothesis outlined above, that Matthew and Luke must have consulted and copied common written sources, that is, Mark and Q, *since mere common oral tradition alone could not have resulted in the close conformity in wording between Matthew, Mark, and Luke.* But then they argue that the oral traditions collected in Mark, Q, M, and L are verbally accurate to what Jesus really said! They can't have it both ways. Either oral transmission is verbally accurate and trustworthy or it isn't.

So they choose the earliest possible date as the most likely date of composition. No one denies that Mark 13, the so-called Little Apocalypse, has the immediate destruction of Jerusalem in its sights, so apologists admit Mark must have been written in the general neighborhood of 70 C.E., probably before, since who's to say Jesus' prediction of the destruction couldn't have been a genuine prophecy before the event? The trouble with this reasoning is that it violates the analogy of interpretation all scholars use when dating apocalypses. The whole genre is one of rationalizing and interpreting history *after the fact* in the manner of "theodicy," explaining God's purposes in allowing or causing a catastrophe. That the events are "predicted" fictively after the fact is a way of saying God's providence had foreseen them, and that everything, despite appearances, is under control. Thus, unless we have a good reason (other than theological preference) for treating the Markan apocalypse differently from all other members of the genre, we must make 70 C.E. (or shortly thereafter) the earliest possible date (not the *most probable* date) of writing. And if chapter 13 is a prior document taken over by Mark, as many think, then only the Little Apocalypse itself, and not the whole gospel, should be dated a bit after 70 C.E. (In the same way, many think that Revelation chapter 11, the "Little Scroll" that the angel bids the seer eat, is actually an earlier source document written in the wake of the destruction of Jerusalem in 70 C.E., though the surrounding document, our Book of Revelation, is of later date, perhaps from the time of Domitian, some thirty years later than the Little Scroll itself.)

A better clue to the date of Mark as a whole is found in Mark 9:1. "There are some standing here who will not taste death before they see the kingdom of God come with power." While all interpreters admit this prediction must have the Parousia in mind (the apocalyptic coming of the Son of man at the end of the age), Mark makes it issue immediately in the Transfiguration, as if this were the intended fulfillment. The unnatural juxtaposition means that Mark writes, like the author of John 21:20–23, after the death of the last of the original disciples. The promise had been that all would see the coming of the kingdom (Mark 13:30), but time went on and many died (1 Thess. 4:13–18). The scope of the promise was adjusted to fit new circumstances: now it would be only *some* who would survive to see the end (Mark 9:1). Eventually only *one* remained, then he died (John 21:20–23), and the promise became a cause of embarrassment (2 Pet. 3:4). Mark's solution, a desperate one, was to reinterpret the inconvenient prophecy as referring to something the disciples could have seen in the lifetime of Jesus. But then, in the version he knew, it was to be only "some" of the disciples, so he had to have Jesus arbitrarily restrict the circle of witnesses to Peter, James, and John. If, as most think, John the Apostle died only at century's end, this would place Mark in the early second century—at the earliest! And we might have to push the gospel even later in view of Hermann Detering's forceful argument[17] that Mark 13 reflects not the destruction of Jerusalem in 70 C.E., but rather that at the close of the Bar Kochba revolt in 132 C.E.!

Mark, by the way, was the most common male name in the Roman Empire, and if the first evangelist were actually named Mark (originally the Gospels were anonymous), it wouldn't much help in narrowing down his identity. Church fathers just took a guess that the evangelist Mark was the same as (one of) the character(s) Mark mentioned in the New Testament (Acts 12:12, 15:37, 39; 2 Tim. 4:11; 1 Pet. 5:13).

Most date Matthew about 80 C.E. because Matthew uses Mark, almost all of Mark. Essentially he was producing a corrected and expanded edition of Mark for the use of his own missionaries (analogous to the circle of missioners supervised by the Elder in the Johannine Epistles). Apologists figure they have to allow a decade from the early date assigned to Mark to give Matthew time to have gotten hold of Mark, become familiar with it, and worked up a new version. But this is way too early. We must allow more than a decade, in all probablility, for the Matthean revision of Mark to have gone through at least two stages. For instance, someone has added the regulation that missionaries not go among unwashed Samaritans and Gentiles (10:5), while a later Matthean redactor has opened up the evangelistic mission to all the nations (28:19). The original section contrasting true piety with hypocritical (6:1–6, 16–18) has been interrupted by verses 7–15, addenda on prayer that ruin the structure. And as Arlo J. Nau has demonstrated, an initial Matthean redactor must have rehabilitated Mark's insulting portait of Peter, while a later Matthean redactor has gone back and punctured Petrine pretensions anew.[18] How long before Matthew even got a look at Mark? Then how long had it been used in his church community before someone felt the need to revise it? And then how long, in how many stages, did it take? Matthew must *at the earliest* have appeared in the mid-second century. Whence its title? It is a pun on the word for "disciples," used often in this gospel, *mathetai*.

Luke's gospel seems to have appeared in two forms, an earlier, shorter version used by Marcion about 140 C.E. and a Catholic redaction padded out and supplemented with the Acts of the Apostles sometime later in the second century.[19] Genre affinities with surviving apocryphal gospels and Acts as well as the ancient novels that flourished in the second century make such a date even more likely. Indeed, a second-century date for Luke-Acts is increasingly common among scholars today.

John's gospel shares a number of points with Luke's. There are many details where Luke differs from the common reading of Matthew and Mark, and whenever John parallels either Luke or Matthew/Mark, he will virtually always agree with Luke's version. This means John either knew both versions and preferred Luke for some reason, or, without actually consulting Luke's or any other written gospel, he simply had access to the same stream of tradition Luke used. Or it may be more complicated still. John may have absorbed some elements from Marcion's Ur-Lukas (the predecessor to our canonical Luke). John (or an early version of it!) then came into the hands of the redactor of our present Luke, who borrowed some elements of it. Then canonical Luke may have influenced the redactor of our canonical John. Who knows? As to date, even conservatives have allowed a date of about 100 C.E. They are pretty much stuck with it since they want to uphold (apocryphal) patristic reports that Mark was based on Peter's preaching and Luke on Paul's, and these accounts also make John's gospel the last will and testament of the aged John dying at century's end. Other conservatives, like A. M. Hunter and John A. T. Robinson,[20] have seized upon the work of C. H. Dodd[21] to try to push John's gospel back earlier. Dodd argued that, though he had expanded and rewritten them almost past recognition, John had used a set of Jesus traditions not unlike those used by the Synoptic evangelists (Matthew, Mark, and Luke, who, contrasted with John, seem to share a similar viewpoint, which is what "synoptic" means). These stories and sayings, though a bit different in emphasis from their Synoptic counterparts, are nonetheless pretty close and might stand to be just as early. Though this argument makes the highly stylized and theologized Johannine discourses (as we read them today) the work of a much later mind, apologists refer to Dodd's work as if he had somehow vindicated an early date for the final content of John's gospel. In any case, apologists have happily pointed to the John Rylands Papyrus of a scrap of John as proof positive that the gospel can date from no later than 100, since the fragment itself dates, by comparative handwriting analysis (paleography) to about 125. But does it? As it happens, there are so few surviving specimens from that time that for all we know, the John Rylands Papyrus might just as easily date some fifty or more years later. It really provides no boundary line after all.

THREE AGAINST ONE

John's gospel, though it keeps the basic format shared by the Synoptic gospels, is well on the way to the Pistis Sophia and the Apocryphon of John in that it makes little effort to anchor the "Jesus" monologues and dialogues it presents in any earlier tradition or source at all. As with its Gnostic compatriots, John's gospel soars free into the heady atmosphere of mystical speculation and devotionalism. It represents a significant innovation in the tradition. David Friedrich

Strauss, followed by Albert Schweitzer, made clear long ago that if the researcher into the historical Jesus hopes to find any straw for his bricks in the Gospels, he has a much better chance of success with Matthew, Mark, and Luke. John is very much a different sort of document. Given the importance of John for Christian theology and the great desire of some to consider the Johannine Jesus as historical, it is important to show in some detail why this appeal must be ruled out.

For one thing, John 16:12–14 broadly hints that the readers of this gospel are the beneficiaries of teaching that would have been too advanced for the original generation of Christians. It even admits pretty overtly that Johannine teaching comes not from the historical Jesus (the narrative frame notwithstanding) but from the Paracletos, one sent after Jesus to clarify and update his doctrine. "I have yet many things to say to you, but you cannot bear them now. When the Spirit of Truth comes, he will guide you into all the truth; for he will not speak on his own authority, but whatever he hears he will speak." We do not need to think very hard to see that this Paracletos is none other than the gospel writer himself. And the literary, nonhistorical character of his gospel is evident from several factors.

First, there is the great difference between the *style* of Jesus' teaching here as opposed to the Synoptics. John has no real parables and uses a drastically different (much simpler) vocabulary. And while the style and vocabulary have little in common with Matthew, Mark, or Luke, they sound as if they are cut from the very same cloth as the Johannine Epistles. One hears the same voice there. In fact, if read out of context, it would be hard to tell whether a number of texts came from the gospel or the epistles ascribed to John. Note further that the similarity holds good not only between the Gospel and Epistles of John but also among all the characters in the gospel. We are not dealing with reporting here. Whether we are ostensibly listening to Jesus, John the Baptist, Thomas, Peter, Mary and Martha, the Sanhedrin—they each and all sound just like the evangelist! It is exactly like reading Kahlil Gibran's fictive collection of memoirs, *Jesus the Son of Man*.[22] There we read the (fictive) recollections of scores of witnesses of Jesus, all quite profound, like the Gospel of John itself. But all speak with the readily identifiable voice of Gibran!

William Temple, followed by George Eldon Ladd and others, adopted the desperate expedient of proposing that while both Johannine and Synoptic idioms go back to the historical Jesus, John preserves the language Jesus used in secret with the disciples.[23] Does it? How odd that John is the very gospel that has Jesus denying that he had any special private teaching (18:20)! This surprising attempt to make Jesus into an esoteric mystagogue will not fly, and one cannot imagine Temple or Ladd accepting it for one second if someone were to appeal to the same argument to vindicate something like the Pistis Sophia as authentic (as Margaret Barker[24] does).

Second, there is the vast difference in content between John and the others. Simply put, John has Jesus preach himself as the object of faith, while Matthew,

Mark, and Luke make Jesus a pointer to the Father. In the Synoptics, Jesus proclaims the coming kingdom of God, while in John he speaks instead of eternal life. For the Synoptic Jesus, one must believe in his news and repent, while the Johannine Jesus demands belief in himself. In the first three gospels, repentence is sufficient for salvation, unlike John, where, unless one accepts the Christological claims of Jesus, one will die in one's sins.

Third, the staged artificiality of the discourses and dialogues of Jesus in John make clear that they are purely the writer's own creation. They all share a structure in which carnal-minded opponents misunderstand Jesus' spiritual double entendres (sometimes existing only in Greek, 3:3, 6:33, as if we could imagine Jesus debating with Palestinian Pharisees in Greek!). This gives Jesus occasion to explain his point at greater length for the benefit of the reader. Examples would include John 2:13–22, especially verse 20; 3:1–15, especially verse 4; 4:7–26, especially verses 11 and 15; 6:25–60, especially verses 34, 42, and 52; 7:32–35, especially verse 35; 8:12–59, especially verses 22, 27, 33, 41, and 57; 11:11–15, 23–27, especially verses 12 and 24.

In the same way, note the artificial prompts put into the mouths of Mary the mother of Jesus (2:5) and Martha of Bethany (11:21–22). They have no possible meaning in the imagined historical circumstances and exist only to provide a drumroll anticipating the miracle Jesus will go on to work.

Fourth, the complete textuality of the work is clear from the way characters will make cross-references to other selected scenes earlier or later in the story, *as if it is a story* with but a few incidents that the characters have no more trouble remembering than the reader does. In this way, John 13:33 points backward to 7:33–34. John 7:21–23 points back to 5:1–18. John 5:33 ff. points back to 1:19, 29–34, which then points back even further to 1:15, almost as if to say, "As I said in chapter so-and-so. . . ."

Fifth, the chronology of John is so totally at odds with that of the Synoptics (not that they always agree among themselves) that we must suppose John's itinerary of Jesus to be governed solely by the theological demands of any particular scene. For example, Matthew, Mark, and Luke have Jesus, by implication, active for about a year's worth of ministry and teaching in Galilee, after which he embarks on the fatal visit to Jerusalem for Passover. But John has Jesus going to Jerusalem and back several times. For Matthew, the Jerusalem crowds on Palm Sunday have to inquire of the Galileans who Jesus is, but John's Jerusalemites know him well enough. And John has Jesus present at three Passover feasts, giving us our traditional estimate of a three-year ministry. But is John just constructing a Passover scene whenever he wants to have Jesus return to Passover themes in his teaching? Likewise, in the Synoptics, the Last Supper takes place on Thursday, the crucifixion on Friday, but not in John, where Jesus must die on Thursday, like the Passover lamb he typologically embodies.

A LIMIT TO LATENESS?

Traditionally, very late dates have not been assigned to the Gospels because external attestations seem to anchor them earlier. While Helmut Koester has demonstrated[25] that we have no clear or certain quotation from the canonical Gospels in the so-called Apostolic Fathers of the second century (*Epistle of Barnabas*, *1* and *2 Clement*, Ignatian Epistles, *Epistle to Diognetus*, *Martyrdom of Polycarp*, *Shepherd of Hermas*, the *Didache/Teaching of the Twelve Apostles to the Nations*), most agree that the second-century writers Papias and Irenaeus provide an upper dating limit for the Gospels. Papias was the bishop of Hierapolis, the third in a triangle of cities with Laodicea and Colossae (both mentioned in the New Testament). Papias was an antiquarian who researched as much as he could about the earliest Christians. He compiled what he could scrape up into a book, now lost, called *The Oracles of Our Lord*. The book appears, from the surviving quotations of it, to have been filled with gross legend, misattributed quotations, and misinformation. Writing about 130 C.E., Papias says this about the origin of the only two gospels he knew of, Matthew and Mark: "Matthew composed the sayings in the Hebrew dialect, and every one translated it as he was able" (quoted in Eusebius *Ecclesiastical History* 3.39).[26] "Mark, being the interpreter of Peter, whatsoever he recorded he wrote with great accuracy but not however, in the order in which it was spoken or done by our Lord, for he neither heard nor followed our Lord; but as before said, he was in company with Peter, who gave him such instruction as was necessary, but not to give a history of our Lord's discourses: wherefore Mark has not erred in any thing, by writing some things as he has recorded them; for he was carefully attentive to one thing, not to pass by any thing that he heard, or to state any thing falsely in these accounts" (in Eusebius *Ecclesiastical History* 3.39).[27]

But are we sure Papias is even referring to our familiar gospels of Matthew and Mark? From his description of the Peter-Mark document, he might as easily be talking about the Ebionite work *The Preachings of Peter*[28] And as D. E. Nineham notes, our Mark does not sound like anyone's table talk.[29] And Matthew? Our Matthew was certainly not originally composed in Hebrew or Aramaic, for the simple reason that most of it is the reproduced text of the Greek Mark! (For the same reason, this evangelist cannot have been the disciple Matthew, since an eyewitness of Jesus would scarcely crib from a book written by someone who *hadn't* been one!) We could just say, as many do, that Papias is all wrong about Matthew, but why suppose so? Isn't it just as natural to infer he is talking about a different document, attributed to Matthew, that *was* composed in Hebrew or Aramaic? Jerome and others testify to such. There seem to have been a number of writings attributed to Matthew, including the notorious Infancy Gospel of Matthew.

Irenaeus, bishop of Lyons in Gaul (southern France), wrote about 175 C.E., and he, too, relates information about the writing of the Gospels. "Matthew published his gospel among the Hebrews in their own tongue, when Peter and Paul were preaching the gospel in Rome and founding the church there. After their departure, Mark, the disciple and interpreter of Peter, himself handed down to us in writing the substance of Peter's preaching. Luke, the follower of Paul, set down in a book the gospel preached by his teacher. Then John, the disciple of the Lord, who also leaned on his breast, himself produced his gospel, while he was living at Ephesus in Asia" (Irenaeus *Against Heresies* 3.1; also quoted in Eusebius *Ecclesiastical History* 5.8). Irenaeus goes on to argue that these four gospels and no others belong in a Christian canon. He is talking about our four Gospels, so they must have existed and even been collected by his time, in the late second century C.E. Suddenly they are known, in the very time the emerging Catholic church was trying to co-opt the success of the Marcionite church by adopting its New Testament canon, padding it out with, among other things, three more gospels than Marcion had and a doctored version of the one he did have, Luke. On the other side of the Mediterranean, Tatian was trying to dilute Marcion, too, by taking these four gospels and weaving them into a single continuous narrative, the *Diatessaron*.

There remains one last consideration. It is striking to realize that we have no actual text of Papias, only a set of quotations in various ancient authors, and it seems rather strange that we do not have it. After all, it would seem to have been a widely respected and nonheretical repository of lore from the earliest days of Christianity. If it ever existed, that is. It seems worth asking if "Papias" simply functioned as a blanket attestation for any stray bit of lore or speculation about early Christianity and its heroes. In his inspired work on the attribution of sayings in the Mishnah, Jacob Neusner has shown[30] how name-citations, ascriptions to this or that famous name, must be understood not as evidence for what those worthies actually said or wrote but rather according to the name-citation's polemical significance in the document under consideration. In short, we cannot be sure Rabbi Johannon ben-Zakkai really said what the Mishnah attributes to him, but we can discern what point is being made by the Mishnaic compiler mentioning the name of Johannon ben-Zakkai where he does. There is in fact very little inherent likelihood that Rabbi Johannon ben-Zakkai said any of the things later attributed to him. How might we apply this lesson to the question of Papias and Irenaeus on the dates of the Gospels? Since we have no text of Papias at all and no manuscript of Irenaeus as old as Eusebius, it becomes reasonable to treat the passages we have quoted from Papias and Irenaeus as no older than Eusebius's *Ecclesiastical History*. For us, they are no more than apologetical garnishes to that fourth-century treatise and may be no older. The same holds good for the famous *Testimonium Flavianum* attributed to Josephus: it certainly did not appear in the edition of Josephus read by Origin in the early third century. Eusebius "quotes" it as from Josephus, and it appears in manuscripts of Josephus copied after that time. In precisely the same way, the Irenaeus passage on gospel origins may have originated with Eusebius and wound up subsequently interpolated into copies of Irenaeus's *Against Heresies*. Such a tactic would certainly not have been out of character for Eusebius, who did not hesitate to inflate both the extent and the antiquity of the antiheretical literature before his time so as to create the impression that the controversies of his day had already been as good as settled long before.[31] This would mean we ought to use as our upward limit for the date of the Gospels the date of writing for Justin Martyr's *Apologies*, which at least quote the Synoptics (late second century).

THE BOTTOM FALLS OUT

One last factor affecting any efforts to date the Gospels is our uncertainty as to when to date the historical Jesus. All today take for granted that Jesus was born at least two years before the death of Herod the Great in the year 2 B.C.E. and that he died by the sentence of Pontius Pilate. He would have been "about thirty" (Luke 3:23) when his ministry commenced, and he would have died a year or three years later, about 27 or 30 C.E. How well-founded are these dates? Not very.

As we will see in some detail, Herod the Great is associated with the birth of Jesus in Matthew's gospel for purely literary reasons: Matthew was copying Josephus's Moses nativity, and he needed a "modern-day" counterpart to the persecuting Pharaoh. There was one candidate for this role: Herod the Great, known by all as a ruthless butcher. The two years business comes, again, from fictive details of Matthew's story: the tyrant killed all the babies and toddlers of Bethlehem up to two years old since the Magi had seen the natal star rise two years previously. Luke places the birth of Jesus in the reign of Augustus Caesar, Herod's contemporary. He mentions Augustus for the sake of the empirewide census that took Joseph and the heavily pregnant Mary to Bethlehem. But this story, to which we shall return, is full of errors, placing the census under Quirinius a decade too early. We may accept with less difficulty Luke's estimate that Jesus was about thirty, though we have no idea how he knew it, and it is well to note that this was not the only estimate: Irenaeus thought Jesus lived to the age of fifty. After all, did not the temple elders reprove his rash words by pointing to his tender age? "You are not yet fifty years old!" (John 8:57). If he were thirty, why not make the point even stronger? "You are not yet *forty* years old!" And if he had been nearly fifty at this point in John's narrative, given his three-Passover chronology, he would have died at fifty. Irenaeus says that all the presbyters of Asia believed this (*Against Heresies* 2.22.4–5). Irenaeus figured that Jesus had died under the emperor Claudius. And such a dating must make us wonder how familiar Irenaeus can have been with the canonical gospels, perhaps not as familiar as Eusebius makes him, if he could so boldly reject the testimony of all four that Jesus was crucified under Pilate. Or did he imagine Pilate to have served under Claudius?

And the link with Pilate is more tenuous than one might think. Scholars have always choked on the implausibilities attendant upon the gospel trial scenes, with the Sanhedrin convening on Passover eve itself, and the Jew-baiting Pilate being so reluctant to hand Jesus over to death. But if one rejects these features of the stories, what is left? Many see the difficulties with the Sanhedrin trial as so insuperable that they erase all Jewish involvement from the record, placing the whole initiative and responsibility on the shoulders of the Romans. But isn't the Pilate story even more outrageous? Why retain it as evidence of any Roman involvement at all? It is a tenuous link.

More astonishing still is the widespread Jewish and Jewish-Christian tradition, attested in Epiphanius, the Talmud, and the Toledoth Jeschu (dependent on a second-century Jewish-Christian gospel), that Jesus was born about 100 B.C.E. and was crucified under Alexander Jannaeus![32]

The point is this: since we cannot really determine exactly when Jesus would have lived or died, it is useless to speculate upon how much or little time would have been necessary for the Jesus tradition to grow and mutate from fact to fancy. By our evidence, vague as it is, the Gospels might possibly have been written as late as the third century C.E., while the life of Jesus may have been over in the first century B.C.E.!

NOTES

1. R. G. Collingwood, *The Idea of History* (New York: Oxford University Press, Galaxy Books, 1957), pp. 234–38 ff.

2. Ibid., pp. 259–61.

3. Rudolf Bultmann and Karl Kundsin, *Form Criticism: Two Essays on New Testament Research*, trans. Frederick C. Grant (New York: Harper & Row, Torchbooks, 1962); Bultmann, *History of the Synoptic Tradition*, trans. John Marsh (New York: Harper & Row, 1972); Martin Dibelius, *From Tradition to Gospel*, trans. Bertram Lee Woolf (New York: Scribner, n.d.); Klaus Koch, *The Growth of the Biblical Tradition: The Form-Critical Method*, trans. S. M. Cupitt, Scribner Studies in Biblical Interpretation (New York: Scribner, 1969); Vincent Taylor, *The Formation of the Gospel Tradition* (London: Macmillan, 1957); Karl Ludwig Schmidt, "Jesus Christ," in *Twentieth Century Theology in the Making*, vol. 1, *Themes of Biblical Theology*, ed. Jaroslav Pelikan, trans. William Collins (London: Collins, Fontana Library [of] Theology and Philosophy, 1969), pp. 96–99.

4. Ernst Käsemann, "Sentences of Holy Law in the New Testament," in *New Testament Questions of Today*, trans. W. J. Montague (Philadelphia: Fortress Press, 1979), pp. 66–81.

5. Harald Riesenfeld, "The Gospel Tradition and Its Beginnings," in *The Gospel Tradition*, trans. Margaret Rowley and Robert Kraft (Philadelphia: Fortress Press, 1970), pp. 1–30; Birger Gerhardsson, *Memory & Manuscript: Oral Traditon and Written Transmission in Rabbinic Judaism and Early Christianity with Tradition & Transmission in*

Early Christianity, trans. Eric J. Sharpe, Biblical Resource Series (Grand Rapids: William B. Eerdmans, 1998); Gerhardsson, *The Origins of the Gospel Traditions* (Philadelphia: Fortress Press, 1979).

6. Albert Bates Lord, *The Singer of Tales*, Harvard Studies in Comparative Literature 24 (Cambridge: Harvard University Press, 1960); Lord, *Epic Singers and Oral Tradition*, Myth and Poetics (Ithaca: Cornell University Press, 1991); John Miles Foley, *The Singer of Tales in Performance* (Bloomington and Indianapolis: Indiana University Press, 1995).

7. Marie-Louise Martin, *Kimbangu: An African Prophet and His Church*, trans. D. M. Moore (Grand Rapids: William B. Eerdmans, 1975), pp. 72–78; G. C. Oosthuizen, *Post-Christianity in Africa: A Theological and Anthropological Study* (Grand Rapids: William B. Eerdmans, 1968), pp. 95–96.

8. Gershom Scholem, *Sabbatai Sevi: the Mystical Messiah 1626–1676*, Bollingen Series 93 (Princeton: Princeton University Press, 1973), pp. 252, 265.

9. Willi Marxsen, *Mark the Evangelist: Studies on the Redaction History of the Gospel*, trans. James Boyce, Donald Juel, William Poehlmann, and Roy Harrisville (New York: Abingdon Press, 1969); Günther Bornkamm, Gerhard Barth, and Heinz Joachim Held, *Tradition and Interpretation in Matthew*, trans. Percy Scott, New Testament Library (Philadelphia: Westminster Press, 1976); Hans Conzelmann, *The Theology of St. Luke*, trans. Geoffrey Buswell (New York: Harper & Row, 1961); Joachim Rohde, *Rediscovering the Teaching of the Evangelists*, trans. Dorothea M. Barton, New Testament Library (Philadelphia: Westminster Press, 1968); Norman Perrin, *What Is Redaction Criticism?* Guides to Biblical Scholarship, New Testament Series (Philadelphia: Fortress Press, 1969).

10. William Wrede, *The Messianic Secret in Mark's Gospel*, trans. J. C. G. Grieg, Library of Theological Translations (Altrincham: James Clarke & Co. Ltd., 1971).

11. Erhardt Güttgemanns, *Candid Questions Concerning Gospel Form Criticism: A Methodological Sketch of the Fundamental Problematics of Form and Redaction Criticism*, trans. William Guy Doty, Pittsburgh Theological Monograph Series 26 (Pittsburgh: Pickwick Press, 1979); Robert M. Fowler, *Let the Reader Understand: Reader-Response Criticism and the Gospel of Mark* (Minneapolis: Fortress Press, 1991); Frans Neirynck, *Duality in Mark: Contributions to the Study of the Markan Redaction*, Bibliotheca Ephemeridum Theologicarum Lovaniensium 31 (Louven: Louven University Press, 1972); Werner H. Kelber, ed., *The Passion in Mark: Studies on Mark 14–16* (Philadelphia: Fortress Press, 1976).

12. Burnett Hillman Streeter, "A Four Document Hypothesis," chap. 9 in *The Four Gospels: A Study in Origins* (London: Macmillan, 1951), pp. 223–70.

13. Walter Schmithals, *The Theology of the Earliest Christians*, trans. O. C. Dean Jr. (Louisville: Westminster John Knox Press, 1997), pp. 18–20; ibid., "The Parabolic Teachings in the Synoptic Tradition," trans. Darrell J. Doughty. *Journal of Higher Criticism* 4, no. 2 (fall 1997): 3–32.

14. Randel Helms, *Gospel Fictions* (Amherst, N.Y.: Prometheus Books, 1989); John Dominic Crossan, *The Cross That Spoke: The Origins of the Passion Narrative* (San Francisco: Harper & Row, 1988); Thomas L. Brodie, "Luke the Literary Interpreter: Luke-Acts as a Systematic Rewriting and Updating of the Elijah-Elisha Narrative in 1 and 2 Kings" (Ph.D. diss., Pontifical University of Thomas Aquinas, 1981); Earl Doherty, *The*

Jesus Puzzle: Did Christianity Begin with a Mythical Christ? (Ottawa: Canadian Humanist Publications, 1999).

15. Dennis R. MacDonald, *The Homeric Epics and the Gospel of Mark* (New Haven: Yale University Press, 2000).

16. Robert M. Price, "The Legend of Paul's Conversion," *Journal for the Critical Study of Religion* 3, no. 1 (fall/winter 1998): 7–22.

17. Hermann Detering, "The Synoptic Apocalypse (Mark 13 par): A Document from the Time of Bar-Kochba," *Journal of Higher Criticism* 7, no. 2 (fall 2000): 161–210.

18. Arlo J. Nau, *Peter in Matthew: Discipleship, Diplomacy, and Dispraise*, Good News Studies 36 (Collegeville: A Michael Glazier Book/Liturgical Press, 1992).

19. John Knox, *Marcion and the New Testament: An Essay in the Early History of the Canon* (Chicago: University of Chicago Press, 1942).

20. John A. T. Robinson, "The New Look on the Fourth Gospel," in *Twelve New Testament Studies*, Studies in Biblical Theology 34 (London: SCM Press, 1962), pp. 94–106; Archibald M. Hunter, *According to John: The New Look at the Fourth Gospel* (Philadelphia: Westminster Press, 1976).

21. C. H. Dodd, *Historical Tradition in the Fourth Gospel* (New York: Cambridge University Press, 1976).

22. Kahlil Gibran, *Jesus the Son of Man: His Words and His Deeds as Told and Recorded by Those Who Knew Him* (New York: Alfred A. Knopf, 1928).

23. William Temple, *Readings in St. John's Gospel*, First and Second Series (London: Macmillan, 1952), p. xiv.

24. Margaret Barker, *The Risen Lord: The Jesus of History as the Christ of Faith* (Valley Forge: Trinity Press International, 1997).

25. Helmut Koester, *Ancient Christian Gospels: Their History and Development* (Philadelphia: Trinity Press International, 1990), pp. 14–19. He rightly finds Gospel texts quoted in Polycarp's Epistle to the Philippians, but this is moot, since the letter is plainly a pseudepigraph, a cento of quotes and allusions from all over the late-second-century canon.

26. Christian Frederick Cruse, trans., *The Ecclesiastical History of Eusebius Pamphilus* (Grand Rapids: Baker Book House, 1955), p. 127.

27. Ibid.

28. David Friedrich Strauss, *The Life of Jesus for the People* (London: Williams and Norgate, 1879), vol. 2, p. 76: ". . . with regard to our Gospel of Mark, we cannot tell even whether it had any connection at all with the work of Mark of which Papias speaks."

29. Dennis E. Nineham, "Eye-witness Testimony and the Gospel Tradition—I," in *Explorations in Theology* 1 (London: SCM Press, 1977), pp. 24–37.

30. Jacob Neusner, *In Search of Talmudic Biography: The Problem of the Attributed Saying*, Brown Judaic Studies 70 (Chico: Scholars Press, 1984).

31. Walter Bauer, *Orthodoxy and Heresy in Earliest Christianity*, 2nd ed., ed. Robert Kraft and Gerhard Krodel, trans. a team from the Philadelphia Seminar on Christian Origins (Philadelphia: Fortress Press, 1971), p. 158.

32. G. R. S. Mead, *Did Jesus Live 100 BC?* (New Hyde Park: University Books, 1968), pp. 135–51, 302–23, 388–413; Hugh J. Schonfield, *According to the Hebrews* (London: Duckworth, 1937), pp. 101, 122, 146–47.

CHAPTER TWO
BIRTH
AND LINEAGE

NEWBORN SUN

I recall how astonished I was to learn, in my freshman year in college, that independence was declared by the Continental Congress on July 2, 1776, how John Adams wrote home to his wife, Abigail, that he did not doubt that future generations of Americans would celebrate with parades and fireworks this declaration of national independence—on July 2! Oh, yes, the patriots began putting their signatures on Thomas Jefferson's document two days later, a process that lasted some months before all eventual signatories could get around to it, but independence had been declared by vote, which is all it took, on the second of July. My professor, Robert Beckwith, delighted in scandalizing his students this way, because it showed us quickly that despite all we took for granted, we still had lots to learn! I mention it here because in the case of Jesus, too, where we think we know so much, we have much more to learn than we might imagine. In both cases, to get started, we may have to unlearn what we thought we already knew. And so it is with the supposedly obvious fact that Jesus was born on December 25. And that is only the beginning.

The birth of Jesus is, of course, celebrated on December 25. How was this custom established? Was it simply that people remarked and remembered the birth date of a famous man? Apparently not. It is an important clue that the date coincides with a major holiday celebrated throughout the Roman Empire, Brumalia, the eighth and greatest day of the Feast of Saturnalia. It was the (re-)birthday of the sun god Mithras. Mithras was a very ancient deity, first mentioned in the hymns of the Rig Veda in India as early as 1500 B.C.E. In Vedic Hinduism, he had been an assistant to the high god Varuna and functioned as a watcher over pacts (cf. Gen. 31:49–50, "He said 'Yahve watch between you and me, when we are absent one from the other. If you ill-treat my daughters, or if you take wives besides my daughters, although no man is with us, God is witness between you and me'"). When Varuna, known by the title Ahura Mazda ("Wise Lord"), became head of the pantheon in Persian Zoroastrianism, Mithras accompanied him to his new position and eventually overtook his Lord in importance, so that he became the chief object of worship. After that, Mithras was merged with the zodiacal god Perseus by the astronomers of Tarsus, who wanted to honor Mithridates, their king, by merging his patron deity with Perseus, the god into whose constellation the equinox had processed.[1] This version of Mithras, slayer of the bull (Leo, the previous constellation to host the equinox), was a virile warrior, and Roman legionaries encountered his cult while away on tours of duty at the eastern frontier. They liked what they saw and imported the worship of the macho savior throughout the empire when they returned home. Mithras would eventually become the official god of the empire (before that honor would pass to Jesus himself, that is!). Mithraeums, underground grotto sanctuaries, have been found all over Europe in great profusion. So just about everybody celebrated his birth with the ancient equivalent of office parties and holiday gift giving.

But in fact Mithras was never born at all. He was not a historical figure. Whence his birthday, then? Brumalia marked the winter solstice according to the old Julian calendar. This was the day when the days, having shrunk to their shortest, began to elongate again. This meant, in mythic-symbolic terms, that the sun god had spent his force, grown old and died, sunk beneath the sea on the horizon and entered his tomb in the caves beneath the earth, and he would rise from there, reborn and rejuvenated, on the solstice. As each new day was longer, by a modicum, than the one before it, stretching on into spring and summer, the sun god grew and grew to full manhood. December 25, then, was the start of that cycle.

For the same reason, December 25 was also celebrated as the sun god's birthday in Egypt, Persia, Phoenicia, Greece, and Germany. Dionysus, Adonis, and Horus shared the birthday. This is also the time when the constellation Virgo appears on the horizon. So on that date the pre-Christian Egyptians and Syrians would symbolize the sun as an infant and hold him up before his adoring worshipers with the words "Behold, the virgin has brought forth!"

As scholars have long noted, several biblical characters bear signs of solar mythology. Whether they originated as purely mythic characters like Mithras and Apollo or whether they were historical characters who gradually took on these sun god features as their legends grew, we do not know. Samson (whose name simply means "the sun") was surely just the Hebrew version of Shamash of Babylon. That he was the blazing sun is still evident in the Book of Judges despite the editor's attempts to reduce him to an ancient but mortal hero. After all, he burns the Philistine grain harvest (Judg. 15:4–5); his hair is plaited into seven long locks, symbolizing the sun's rays, and for this reason, when they are cut off, he is both blinded and weakened (Judg. 16:19–21). The sun, no? Elijah's trademark "hairiness" (2 Kings 1:8) likewise denotes the sun's rays. Elijah calls down fire from the sky on two separate occasions (1 Kings 18:36–38, 2 Kings 1:9–12). Finally, he rises up to the zenith of the sky in a flaming chariot, just like Apollo. Enoch, too, is the sun, God's walking companion around the circle of the sky, whose life span is a suspicious 365 years! And Esau is red and hairy like the sunset and shoots sunstroke arrows like Apollo (cf. Ps. 91:5–6, "You will not fear . . . the arrow that flies by day . . . nor the destruction that wastes at noonday;" also 2 Kings 4:18–20). And think of Moses, who, like the sun, emerges from the divine tent (cf. Ps. 19:4) with his countenance glowing (Exod. 34:29–35) and gives laws (cf. Ps. 19:7–11) as the sun god gave to Hammurabi. Like Apollo, he wields the healing Caduceus (Num. 21:8–9). Jesus, too, shines like the sun in its strength (Matt. 17:2; Acts 9:3, 17; Rev. 1:16). He is surrounded by twelve disciples, recalling (as do Hercules' dozen labors) the houses of the zodiac. So solar imagery attaches itself to the figure of Jesus already in the New Testament. Though no birthdate is assigned him there, it is natural that December 25 should eventually suggest itself.

The first Christian to refer to the Nativity occurring on December 25 is Hippolytus of Rome, about 200 C.E. Taking the date of March 25 as the date of the first Easter, he reasoned (somehow) that the birth of Jesus must have taken place nine months earlier on the calendar, albeit some thirty years before. The logic is far from clear and conveys the impression that he was desperately searching for some after-the-fact argument to provide a historical grounding for a birthdate originally assigned on different grounds altogether.

It makes sense that the birth of Jesus became a matter of interest to emerging Orthodox/Catholic Christianity only in the early fourth century, when the Roman Empire had newly welcomed Christianity and the emperor Constantine, eager amateur theologian that he was, convened the Council of Nicea to settle the vexed question of whether the divine Word incarnated in Jesus Christ had been fully divine with the very divinity of the Father (as Athanasius held) or rather the highest and mightiest of God's creations (as Arius argued). Constantine let his preference for the former opinion be known and, not surprisingly, it prevailed. This meant that when Jesus was born, God himself had been incarnated, and the birth took on a theological importance it had never before held. It was during this century that Christmas began to be celebrated. Previous to this, Christians (and not all of them; perhaps only the Gnostics) had celebrated Epiphany (January 6). They understood Epiphany, marking the baptism of Jesus in the Jordan, as the divine Nativity of Jesus, on the assumption that Jesus had been a righteous but mortal man up to that point, whereupon the Christ-Spirit descended into him (as Mark 1:10 has it), making him the Son of God. This understanding of the exaltation of Jesus to divine status during his earthly life (I will discuss it in more detail in the chapters on the Baptism and the Resurrection) is called "adoptionism," implying that a mortal Jesus only later became God's son in an honorific sense.

One may ask why this date was chosen for Epiphany. Simply because, according to a previous calendar, this, too, was the solstice and the nativity of at least one god, Aion, the Lord of Infinite Time. Thus, the Jordan baptism was early on understood as the "birth" of Jesus as God's son. Popular piety remembered this and would not give up the association (you know how stubborn people tend to be about their religious traditions!), even once Christmas (December 25) had been made the Christian Nativity, as we can see from the fact that January 6 continued as "Little Christmas," commemorating the visit of the Magi from the East.

So might December 25 have been the birthday of Jesus? There's about one chance in 365.

SON OF DAVID?

The issue of Jesus' birthplace, which one might expect to have been the very next topic under discussion here, is so closely intertwined with other aspects of the birth and lineage of Jesus that we cannot get to it directly, without taking what may seem a side trip into these other questions first. Let us proceed to our evidence for and against the traditional claim that Jesus was descended from King David. This claim, unlike the date of birth, is actually asserted in New Testament, but the Gospels are hardly univocal on the matter, as we will see. I believe we can trace a trajectory along which early Christian belief regarding Jesus' genealogical credentials evolved.

We start with Mark 12:35–37, "And Jesus said, as he taught in the temple, 'How can the scribes say that the Christ is the son of David? David himself said by the Holy Spirit, "The Lord said to my Lord, 'Sit at my right hand, until I put your enemies beneath your feet.'" David himself calls him "Lord," so how can he be his son?'" Whether this passage is a genuine recollection of Jesus or, as I think more likely, a piece of apologetics from the early church (see Mark 9:11, "Why do the scribes say Elijah must come first?" for another page from the same book), in either case this text has no other meaning than to prove that the Messiah, contrary to the expectations of many, is not supposed to be a descendant of King David. Though commentators, and even translators, commonly twist the text to assure the reader that all Mark means to say is that the Christ, in addition to being David's heir, must be more than that as well, namely, God's son, too, this is really out of the question. No one would treat the text in this manner if he did not find himself in a tight spot theologically.

This text is far from the only piece of anti-Davidic messianic propaganda in Jewish history. The same theme had already surfaced in connection with the Hasmonean royal house. Keep in mind that the "Messiah" commonly denoted the king of Judah once national independence should be restored in the providence of God. Most seem to have believed that the royal line of David would be restored, so that the first new king would be a Davidic heir (they had not all been exterminated). But, famously, independence was restored by Judah Maccabee ("Judah the Hammer") and his fighting brothers in the second century B.C.E. These men established the Hasmonean dynasty (of which Herod the Great posed as the last scion). The trouble was that the Hasmoneans were not descended from David and did not even belong to David's tribe of Judah. Instead, they were Levites, members of the priestly tribe. Thus new, alternate messianic credentials had to be created, old ones deflated. We find these in the pseudepigraphical text the Testaments of the Twelve Patriarchs, where we read that the future messiah will spring from Levi's line, not that of Judah: "Draw near to Levi in humility of heart, that you may receive a blessing from his mouth. For he shall bless Israel and Judah because the Lord has chosen him to be king over all the nations. And bow down before his seed . . . and [he] will be an eternal king among you" (T. Reuben 2:28–30). Other passages split the messianic role between Levi and Judah: "By you and Judah the Lord shall appear among men, saving every race of men" (T. Levi 1:14, cf. T. Judah 4:1–4, T. Isshachar 1:43, T. Naphtali 2:24–25, T. Joseph 2:77, T. Benjamin 2:26).[2]

Similarly, Géza Vermes, an authority on the Dead Sea Scrolls and contemporary Judaism, thinks that, in order to fit the slain Messiah Simon bar-Kochba (d. 136 C.E., fighting against Rome) into messianic history as a noble failure rather than a false Christ, wistful Jews created the category of a preliminary "Messiah ben Joseph," who should hail from the Northern tribes, not Judah.[3] His martyrdom in battle should pave the way for the ultimately victorious Son of David. Bar-Kochba hadn't been Davidic either, but he had established Jewish independence, at least for a time, so some could not help considering him the Messiah, or a messiah, and so a new position, one not requiring Davidic pedigree, had to be created for him. If Vermes is right, we would have a second, post-Jesus example of theological tinkering to accommodate a non-Davidic Messiah. It at least illustrates the logic of the matter. But it is important to note that many scholars think the idea of Messiah ben Joseph originated independent of Simon bar-Kochba and could have been earlier. It is never easy to date these things, since we cannot assume ideas are no older than their first attested appearances in texts available to us.

Mark 12:35–37 may itself be based on an old bit of Hasmonean messianism. The argument would have come in equally handy there. But whether Christians created or borrowed the passage, the implications are the same: there was a time when Christians knew quite well that their Christ was not a Davidic descendant and made the best of it. They knew many fellow Jews believed the Messiah had to be Davidic and simply denied the premise.

We have a modern parallel to the theological strategizing envisioned here in the case of Saiyid Ahmad, founder of an important Wahabi renewal movement in North India (another branch would set up the monarchy that survives today in Saudi Arabia), a pretender to the mantle of the Shi'ite Mahdi. Early on he attracted to himself two doctors of Islamic jurisprudence who helped design his apologetics. Stephen Fuchs explains the dilemma and how they met it. "Since the events amid which his career began could in no way be reconciled with the popular conception of this last struggle between good and evil, the two Doctors of the Law boldly attacked the established belief and asserted that the true Imam Mahdi was to come, not on the Last Day, but as an intermediate leader half-way between the death of Mohammed and the end of the world, which they calculated to be the thirteenth century of their era (1786–1886). Saiyid Ahmad was born in 1786!"[4]

One might suspect that the text, or the argument, of Mark 12:35–37 originated among Galilean Christians whose northern Israelite ancestors had given up any hope of a Davidic Messiah centuries before when they seceded from Judah and the Davidic dynasty (1 Kings 12:16). About the only way they would be able to bring themselves to believe in Jesus was to make him a Messiah in some non-Davidic sense. And indeed it may be to such Christians that we owe the preservation of the passage. But they cannot have originated it, since Mark 12:35–37 clearly envisions, explicitly states, that Jewish scribes, scripture experts, not Judean Christian rivals, are the polemical opponents in view: "When the scribes reply to us that Jesus couldn't have been the Messiah since everybody knows he wasn't Davidic, how do we respond to them?" This was their answer, until something better came along, that is.

Matthew and Luke represent the next stage of Christian apologetics dealing with the issue of Jesus' credentials for the job. Each has included an ostensible genealogy of Jesus, tracing him back, albeit by different hypothetical routes, to King David. Matt. 1:2 traces Jesus all the way back to Father Abraham, no doubt because he was writing in the face of a broad-ranging Jewish polemic that denied Jesus, hailing from "Galilee of the Gentiles" (Matt. 4:15), was even Jewish, a view National Socialist theologians would find rather handy centuries later. Luke, for his part, traces Jesus back even further, to Adam, perhaps because of the world missionary outlook so evident in his gospel and Acts.

Each genealogy has its problems. Matt. 1:11 has Jesus descended from King Coniah (or Jeconiah), despite the fact that the prophet Jeremiah had disqualified any heir of this king from ever taking the throne: "Record this man as 'childless,' a man who shall not succeed in his lifetime; for none of his offspring shall manage to sit on the throne of David, or rule again in Judah" (Jer. 22:30). Matthew (or his source, if he inherited the genealogy from someone else) had neglected to do his homework. Luke inserts into his genealogy several names unique to the priestly tribe of Levi (Heli, Matthat, Levi, Mattathias, Maath, Mattathias again, another Matthat, Mattatha). Is his based on a Hasmonean genealogy of some sort?

It is just impossible to reconcile the two tables, though the desperate have tried. For instance, some say that Luke's is really the family tree of Mary, but it is hard to see how, in view of the explicit pinning of the whole thing on Joseph (Luke 3:23). No doubt neither genealogy is genuine. If it were only that they contradict each other, one of them might still be authentic, but the point is that both alike are rendered spurious by the witness of Mark 12:35–37, considered just above. If Jesus were known to have been descended from David, would anyone have wasted time trying to show it was all right for him not to be?

If neither genealogy of Jesus is genuine, how did Matthew and Luke know Jesus was descended from David? No doubt they, or the sources they used, acted in good faith as modern genealogists do, making the best links they could between the known and the unknown. But the "known," or the Davidic origin of Jesus, was pure surmise. Eventually the apologetical argument of Mark 12:35–37 just didn't cut it. It persuaded no one, and even many Christians must have choked on the idea that the Messiah was not after all Davidic. So the new trend was to assume Jesus simply must have been Davidic and to connect the dots as best one could. (In the same way, as we shall see, the original argument that Elijah *did so* appear before Jesus, so to speak, in the form of John the Baptist, seemed lame and was replaced by the more spectacular version we read in the Transfiguration scene.)

Let no one miss another implication of Matthew's and Luke's lists: namely, that both take for granted that Jesus was the natural son of Joseph and Mary, contrary to the virgin birth stories that accompany them in both gospels. If Joseph is a scion of David, but Jesus is not the son of Joseph, the whole thing's to no purpose. To maintain, as Raymond E. Brown does,[5] that the mere legal technicality of Jesus being Joseph's adoptive son would be sufficient to secure Jesus' messianic credentials seems absurd. Thrones have been lost through such technicalities. It matters that the new king springs from the loins of the old king, as history shows. It would be a wretched bit of apologetics to prove Jesus was the adoptive or foster son of the heir of David!

I have mentioned in passing the possibility that Luke and Matthew were not themselves the compilers of the genealogies they have included. The reason for this suspicion is that in both cases there are clear hints of the gospel writer harmonizing the genealogy with his Nativity story only with some difficulty. Both evangelists have (at least on the usual reading—see below) a story of the miraculous conception of Jesus with no human father. We will examine them in a bit more detail below, but for the moment suffice it to point out that such a story is by no means compatible with a genealogy tracing Jesus to David through Joseph, and both Matthew and Luke noticed the difficulty. Both patch the genealogy into the narrative by means of a clumsy jog. "And to Jacob was born Joseph the husband of Mary, by whom was born Jesus who is called Christ" (Matt. 1:16). "And when he began his ministry, Jesus himself was about thirty years of age, as it was being thought, the son of Joseph" (Luke 4:23). In both cases, one receives the distinct impression we are not reading the original wording of a genealogy, since in both cases the mesmerizing pattern of "A begat B; B begat C; C begat D" is suddenly and jarringly broken. Interestingly, one important early manuscript of Matthew, the Sinaitic Syriac Palimpsest from about 200 C.E. (joined by a number of other ancient translations (mss. O; f13; 1547m; it. a, [b], c, d, g, [k], q; Ambrosiaster) preserves the reading at Matt. 1:16, "Jacob begat Joseph. Joseph, to whom was espoused Mary the virgin, begat Jesus, who is called Christ." If this should be the original reading, the way Matthew wrote it, then we would still have the contradiction between genealogy and Nativity story, but we would have no clumsy attempt to harmonize them. The harmonization would have been a very early scribal correction.

Do we have any independent evidence that there were early Christians who did not believe in the miraculous conception of Jesus? These would be Christians who held the belief about Jesus' parentage presupposed in the genealogies: Jesus the true son of Joseph and Mary. And there were some. Eusebius tells us that in the early-to-mid second century there were certain Jewish Christians who did not believe in the virgin birth. The Jewish Christian sect of the Ebionites ("the Poor"—see Gal. 2:10) "considered him a plain and common man, and justified only by his advances in virtue, and that he was born of the Virgin Mary, by natural generation" (*Ecclesiastical History* 3.27.2).[6]

Here we must remember one of our fundamental axioms: if we possess two versions of a story, one more and one less spectacular, if either is closer to the truth, it must be the latter. If the former, the more dramatic, were earlier, how can we explain the origin of the latter, the more conservative version? If the first story to be told were more spectacular, who would ever try to supplement it with a tamer one? But if the tamer tale were the first, it is easy to see how later on someone might think a juicier version desirable. This critical principle is indispensable here, since we cannot rest content, as some do, merely cataloguing the differences of beliefs among the early Christians. The existence of the belief in the natural conception of Jesus must be understood as the stubborn persistence of an earlier belief in the face of the popular growth of a subsequent belief, perhaps influenced by pagan myth: the virgin conception of Jesus. It is easy to imagine how a natural origin such as everyone else has should eventually be thought unimpressive, especially since rival savior deities could boast of supernatural origins. On the other hand, imagine a scenario in which Jesus was widely known to have had a miraculous birth and someone has it occur to him: "Hey, wouldn't it be great if Jesus was no different from anyone else? That's it! He had a . . . a natural birth!" Not likely.

Later, we will consider the rise of the virgin birth belief. For now it is enough to point out that when we compare Matthew and Luke on the one hand with Mark on the other, we notice two contrasts, each of which implies a stage of growth in the Nativity tradition. First, Mark, whether or not he realized the implications, has preserved a bit of apologetics that presupposed that Jesus was not a descendant of David, and that everyone knew it and tried to make the best of it. Then, Mark and Luke, simply by including Davidic genealogies as credentials for Jesus, demonstrate that Christian belief changed at this point when Christians themselves found the earlier version too inconvenient or otherwise unacceptable. But the fact that Matthew and Luke both combine a virgin birth story with the Davidic genealogy implies that they themselves represent a period when the belief in the natural conception of Jesus through Joseph and Mary was being superseded by the story of a miraculous conception. In this manner, they hoped to have their cake and eat it, too.

SON OF BETHLEHEM?

Our earliest gospel, Mark, appears to suppose that Jesus was born in Nazareth of Galilee: "Now after John was arrested, Jesus came into Galilee, preaching the news of the kingdom of God" (1:14). The rest of his story, till the final journey into Jerusalem, takes place there, as he goes from synagogue to synagogue. And in one such scene, Mark says Jesus was returning to "his own country" (1:6), implying he was a Galilean, a Nazarene. Of course, Jesus is often referred to as "the Nazarene," and Mark no doubt took this as a geographical reference (though we will see there might have been a different meaning). Thus, had anyone asked Mark point blank, "Where was Jesus born?" we can only infer he would have said, "Nazareth."

As Strauss demonstrated with inescapable lucidity many decades ago, the two nativity stories of Matthew and Luke disagree at almost every point, one exception being the location of Jesus' birth in Bethlehem. They spring apart like positively charged magnets, however, when it comes to how Jesus came to be born in Bethlehem. Briefly, Matthew assumes Jesus was born in the home of Mary and Joseph in Bethlehem, and that they only relocated to Nazareth in Galilee after taking off for Egypt to avoid Herod the Great's persecution. Luke knows nothing of this but instead presupposes that Mary and Joseph lived in Galilee and "happened" to be in Bethlehem when the hour struck for Jesus' birth because the Holy Couple had to be there to register for a Roman taxation census. I want to return to the gross improbabilities attaching to this feature of Luke's story below. For the moment, my point is to suggest that Luke and Matthew both seem to have been winging it, just as they did with their genealogies. They began with an assumption and tried to connect the dots. This time, their common assumption was that Jesus was born in Bethlehem. Whence this assumption? Was there historical memory that Jesus was born there? Hardly; if there had been, we cannot account for Mark's utter lack of knowledge of the fact. No, it seems much more natural, much less contrived, to suggest that Matthew and Luke alike simply inferred from their belief in Jesus' Davidic lineage that he must have been born in Bethlehem.

Whence, in turn, this assumption? It seems safe to say they had it from the early Christian (and perhaps contemporary Jewish) understanding of Mic. 5:2: "But you, O Bethlehem Ephratha, so little to be counted a clan of Judah, you shall bear me one destined to be ruler in Israel, whose origin is from old, from ancient days." Matthew actually quotes the text. It seems to me he has in this case derived the story from the prooftext, not dug up the prooftext later to justify the story. So did Luke, or the tradition he depends on. It may seem clear enough that the Micah passage is a messianic prediction, but I think it was not so intended. Rather, I deem it more likely Micah preserved one of many ancient Jewish birth oracles issued to herald the birth or coronation of a new king of Judah.[7] The Bethlehem reference denoted not the place of birth of the newborn scion (who would most likely have been born in the royal palace in Jerusalem), but rather the origin of the Davidic dynasty in Jesse's village of Bethlehem.

In short, Matthew and Luke both placed the birth of Jesus in Bethlehem because they mistakenly thought prophecy demanded it. They went to work trying to connect the dots with narrative or historical verisimilitude, but with limited success. But the point here is that they thought he was born in Bethlehem only because they first thought he was of David's dynasty. And Mark undermines both assumptions.

What of John's gospel? Though later than the other three, it seems to agree with Mark on this question. Scholars today tend to agree that John either knew the stories and sayings independently collected by the Synoptists or that he was actually familiar with their finished gospels, at least some of them. Sometimes he is manifestly trying to correct the earlier works. This is one of those places. In John, chapter 7, John creates a dialogue between Jesus and the crowd, then among the crowd. First Jesus says, "You know me, and you know where I come from. But I have not come of my own accord; he who sent me is true, and him you do not know" (7:28). The people react: "When they heard these words, some of the people said, 'This is in truth the prophet.' Others said, 'This is the Christ.' But some said, 'Is the Christ to come from Galilee? Has not the Scripture said that the Christ is descended from David and comes from Bethlehem, the village where David was?'" (7:40–42). The Pharisees concur with the latter opinion: "Search [the Scripture] and you will see that no prophet is to rise from Galilee" (7:52). The gist is that John knows quite well the tradition that the Messiah is to be born in Bethlehem, but he seems to reject it. This is evident from the fact that he has Jesus admit the crowd knows his place of origin, and that no one in the crowd, not even his supporters, is depicted as believing Jesus does come from Bethlehem. The point at issue is not whether Jesus hails from Bethlehem, but rather, assuming that he does not, does this fact disqualify him for the messianic role? Some say yes, some say no. John seems to be holding onto the primitive Markan or pre-Markan acceptance of a Galilean origin for Jesus.

SON OF NAZARETH?

Does this leave Nazareth the only candidate for the birthplace of Jesus? Should they redirect Christmas pilgrims in the Holy Land from Bethlehem in the South to Nazareth in the North? It is amusing to imagine Liberal Protestants making their Yuletide tourist trips to Nazareth instead, but that, too, might be premature. For it seems quite likely that this, too, is a misinterpretation, a false inference from the New Testament data.

Despite the rendering of many English Bible translations, Jesus is very seldom called "Jesus from Nazareth" in the Gospels. Mark calls him "Jesus the Nazarene," as does Luke twice (Mark 1:24, 10:47, 14:67, 16:6; Luke 4:34, 24:9), while Matthew, John, and Acts always call him "Jesus the Nazorean" (Matt. 26:71; John 18:7, 19:19; Acts 2:22, 3:6, 4:10, 6:14, 22:8, 26:9), with Luke using this epithet once (Luke 18:37, the Bar-Timaeus episode, where he has replaced Mark's "Nazarene" with it). Some critics have questioned whether the village of Nazareth even existed in the time of Jesus, since it receives no mention outside the Gospels until the third century. Whether that is important or not, the difference between "Nazarene" and "Nazorean" does give us reason to suspect that the familiar epithet does not after all denote Jesus' hailing from a village called Nazareth. "The Nazarene" would imply that, but not "the Nazorean." That seems to be a sect name, equivalent to "the Essene" or "the Hasid." Epiphanius, an early Christian cataloguer of "heresies," mentions a pre-Christian sect called "the Nazoreans," their name meaning "the Keepers" of the Torah, or possibly of the secrets (see Mark 4:11, "To you has been given the secret of the kingdom of God, but to those outside all is by way of parable"). These Nazoreans were the heirs, supposedly, of the neoprimitivist sect of the Rechabites descending from the times of Jeremiah (Jer. 35:1–10). They were rather like Gypsies, itinerant carpenters. "Nazorean" occurs once unambiguously in the New Testament itself as a sect designation, in Acts 24:5: "a ring leader of the sect of the Nazoreans." Robert Eisler, Hugh J. Schonfield,[8] and others have plausibly suggested that Jesus (and early Christians generally) were members of this Jewish pious sect. Many more modern scholars have followed Strauss in an equivalent theory, seeing Jesus as an apprentice and disciple of John the Baptist, in short, a member of his sect until John was arrested, at which time Jesus would have taken on his mantle as Elisha did Elijah's.

It should be clear that such a scenario, while quite natural historically, is offensive to the Christological beliefs of some, since it presupposes Jesus was a disciple, that he needed to learn religion. How could that be if he were the incarnate Son of God? Harold Bloom (*The Anxiety of Influence* [Oxford: Oxford University Press, 1997]) describes "the anxiety of influence' as the reluctance to acknowledge the degree to which one's "distinctives" are owed to one's predecessors. We can observe it in the way various early Christian documents deal gingerly with the baptism of Jesus by John the Baptist. Matthew, for instance, has John stop Jesus and ask him if he is sure he wants to go through with it (Matt. 3:14), while John's gospel skips the baptism altogether! We see the same unease displayed in a grosser fashion in some of the apocryphal Infancy Gospels where the child Jesus is taken to receive lessons from a schoolmaster. The divine boy already knows not only the letters of the alphabet but even their esoteric Kabbalistic significance. For this seeming effrontery, the tutor smacks young Jesus with a ruler, whereupon the petulant savior strikes him dead, being in no more a mood to accept guff from mere mortals than was the prophet Elisha when mocked by a band of delinquents, whom he dispatched two she-bears to devour (2 Kings 2:23–24). For some it smarts that Jesus should have been a member of a religion, and not just the superhuman founder of one, and here we may discern the reason some had for preferring to understand "the Nazorean" as if it meant "the Nazarene." Here I think we may borrow the text-critical axiom that the more difficult reading is likely to be the earlier and more authentic. I am betting that originally people spoke only of "Jesus the Nazorean," not of "Jesus the Nazarene," but the latter began to catch on when either some sought to suppress the original denotation of the epithet "Nazorean" or when others just no longer knew the original meaning and connection.

Such a reinterpretation of names and epithets was certainly nothing new in the Bible. For instance, Judges, chapters 17 and 18, seem to preserve a recollection of a time when *kohanim* were called "Levites" because of their trade as oracles or, to put it bluntly, fortune-tellers. The story concerns a man named Micah who is by tribal connection an Ephraimite but by profession a Levite, or one who knows how to manipulate the ephod, a sacred oracle of some kind. But elsewhere in the Bible it is presupposed that Levites were a separate tribe unto themselves. In the same way Micah the Levite would be thought in one period to mean "Micah the oracle," but in another "Micah from the tribe of Levi," Jesus the Nazorean would first be understood as "Jesus the Sectarian" and only later as "Jesus from Nazareth." And if this is the way the tradition developed, we have to discount even the "backup" alternative that Jesus was born in Nazareth. Thus, we have no more information about where Jesus was born than about when he was born.

SON OF THE VIRGIN?

I have already touched on the question of the virgin birth of Jesus, showing how it was most likely a subsequent stage of belief. There is a good deal more to be said about it. For one thing, if it is a later version of Christian belief, where did it come from? And how can we trace its evolution in the Gospels?

Mark seems not to have heard of any virgin birth of Jesus. Not only does he not mention any such belief, but what he does say militates against it. Mark

3:19b–21 and 31–35 preserve an episode that Mark has interwoven with a separate scene, the Beelzebul controversy, which seemed thematically parallel. To isolate the original, though, we get: "Then he went home. And the people mobbed him again, so that he could not even eat. And when his family heard of it, they went out to seize him, for they said, 'He is out of his mind.' And his mother and his brothers came; and, standing outside, they sent word to him, calling him. And a crowd was sitting around him, and they told him, 'Your mother and your brothers are outside, asking for you.' And he said, 'Who are my mother and my brothers?' And looking around at those who sat about him, he said, 'Here are my mother and my brothers! Whoever does the will of God is my brother and sister and mother.'"

One thing is clear from this passage: Mark cannot have believed in a virgin birth of Jesus, or if he did, he had an awfully strange way of showing it! Presumably, as in Luke and Matthew, a virgin birth would have been accompanied by a divine annunciation to Mary or Joseph, and they would have known to expect great things from the divine child. And then one may ask how Mary, however concerned about her dear son's welfare she might be, can have thought him insane! It can be no coincidence, surely, that both Matthew and Luke, who do supplement Mark's gospel story with virgin birth narratives, have also cut from Mark's story any note that the reason for Jesus' relatives' visit was that they feared for his sanity. In both later gospels, the scene arrives (Matt. 12:46–50, Luke 8:19–21), but Jesus' family has shown up from out of the blue, with no word said of the occasion for their journey. Luke has even softened the words of Jesus so as to imply Jesus' relatives are included among his disciples as those who perform the will of God and therefore qualify as his true kin after all. In short, both Matthew and Luke have seen how Mark's scene is incompatible with a virgin birth.

Thus, Mark's is the earliest version. Matthew's and Luke's are secondary. But then have we shown Mark's is historical fact? After all, there may be earlier fictions as well as later ones. And in this case it seems pretty clear that Mark (or some hypothetical source document) has created the scene based on a rewriting of the story of Moses, Zipporah, and Jethro in Exodus 18. "Now Jethro, Moses' father-in-law, had taken Zipporah, Moses' wife, after he had sent her away [for her own safety] and her two sons, the first named Gershom . . . the second Eliezer. . . . And Jethro . . . came with [Moses'] sons and his wife to Moses in the wilderness where he was encamped at the Mountain of God. And when one told Moses, 'Lo, your father-in-law Jethro is coming to you with your wife and your two sons with her,' Moses went out to meet his father-in-law, and bowed before him and kissed him, and they asked of each other's welfare and entered the tent. . . . On the morrow Moses sat to render judgment for the people, and people stood around Moses from morning to evening. When Moses' father-in-law saw all that he was doing for the people, he said. . . . 'Why do you sit alone and all the people stand around you from morning to evening?' And Moses said . . . ,

'Because the people come to me to inquire of God; when they have a dispute, they come to me and I decide between a man and his neighbor, and I make known the statutes of God, and his decisions.' Moses' father-in-law said to him, 'What you are doing is not good. You and the people with you will wear yourselves out, for the thing is too heavy for you; you are not able to perform it all by yourself. Listen now to my voice and . . . choose able men . . . such as fear God, men who are trustworthy and who hate a bribe; and place such men over the people as rulers of thousands, of hundreds, of fifties, and of tens. And let them judge the people at all times. Every great matter they shall bring to you, but any small matter they shall decide for themselves. This way it will be easier for you, and they will bear the burden with you.'" Moses heeds the advice, and this is the origin of the system of seventy elders, later called "the Great Synagogue."

Now isn't it interesting that just before Mark's story of the visit of Jesus' relatives, occasioned as it was by their fear of Jesus having a nervous breakdown from so heavy a schedule (no time to take for a simple meal!), we find the story of Jesus choosing "twelve to be with him, and to be sent out to preach and have authority to cast out demons" (Mark 3:14–15a), in other words, to divide the very work Jesus has been shown doing, to share the burden with him. I cannot resist the conclusion that Mark inherited some narrative that sought to explain the appointing of disciples by creating a Jesus version of the Moses story we have just reviewed. In it, Jesus was shown swamped by his eager fans who just cannot get enough of his teaching and healing. His relatives appear with good advice to ease his burden. He follows it and is relieved. He chooses twelve to do what he does. According to this version, it would have been the sage advice of Mary and the brothers and sisters of Jesus to choose the disciples.

Mark has decided to use this episode but to turn it all around. The choice of the Twelve becomes Jesus' own idea. (How can the Son of God have needed a cooler head to show him what to do? The anxiety of influence again.) Originally, the idea would have been that Jesus' family, like Moses' father-in-law, was afraid the press of work would drive him over the edge if something were not done. But the need has already been obviated by placing the choice of the Twelve before the mention of the family of Jesus, so that we are left with the unflattering picture of them just thinking he was crazy already.

But why would Mark do this? What we see here is a piece of the factional polemics of the early Christians, battles for and against various leadership groups and their followings (cf. 1 Cor. 1:11–13 ff.). The tactic was to try to undercut the credentials of rival groups by making it look like their relations with Jesus were sour. This is surely why in Mark's gospel, much more than the others, the Twelve themselves come in for such a drubbing. Mark makes them look like thick-headed dunces every chance he gets (Mark 4:13; 6:51–52; 7:17–18; 8:14–21, 33; 9:18, 28–29, 33–34; 10:35–41; 14:37–42). Granted, the disciples often perform a merely literary role as foils for Jesus, misunderstanding him in order to provide the narrator a chance to have Jesus provide a more complete explanation for the readers' benefit—but then why not do as John's gospel does and assign this role to the enemies of Jesus or to the ignorant among the crowd? One must conclude Mark was trying to undermine the credibility of the Twelve and the Christian factions who claimed them as their figureheads. He does the same with the women followers of Jesus (Mark 15:40–41), when he has them pointedly disobey the direction of the angel at the empty tomb, failing to deliver the tidings of the resurrection (Mark 16:8)! We know from various sources that James the Just, so-called brother of the Lord, followed by Simeon, another of these brethren (Mark 6:3), was chief ruler over Jewish Christians, and his claim was based on his blood relation to Jesus. He and his dynasty were known as "the Heirs of the Lord." Stories like Mark 3:19b–21, 31–35, John 7:1–9, and John 19:26–27 (probably even Luke 1:27) mean to tell us that the relatives of Jesus had no privileged claim to Christian leadership. Thus, the otherwise inexplicable downplaying of physical relationships to Jesus. (We will return to this matter in the next chapter, "The Childhood and Family of Jesus.")

So Mark's story of Jesus' cold-shoulder response to his visiting relatives undermines the historical credibility of Matthew's and Luke's later versions. (At least Matthew and Luke certainly thought so, seeing as how they both changed Mark at this point!) And the earlier version, flattering the relatives of Jesus, the version Mark turned upside down, was itself unhistorical, being an entire rewrite of an ancient Moses and Jethro story. And the pre-Markan version, while it lacked Mark's vitriol against the faction of "the Heirs of Jesus," still had nothing to say of any virgin birth.

Many have tried to find in Mark 6:3, the visit of Jesus to his home synagogue, a veiled and oblique reference to the virgin birth doctrine, a hint not that Mark himself promoted the doctrine, but only that a detail of the story presupposes the doctrine was already known and widely disputed by Jews prior to Mark. What detail can that be? We are supposed to see in the remark of the crowd, "Is not this the carpenter, the son of Mary and brother of James and Joses and Judas and Simon, and are not his sisters here with us?" (Mark 6:3), a reference to Jesus being illegitimate. How is that? Since he is called only "son of Mary," we are to infer that the crowd believed the identity of his father to be unknown. Presumably they would have heard long ago of Mary's becoming pregnant, but not by Joseph (Matt. 1:18–19), only they did not believe the news that quieted Joseph's anguish, that his fiancée was pregnant not by any rival's caresses but by the Holy Spirit's ectoplasmic injection (Matt. 1:20). In this case, we are to envision the crowd heckling Jesus' synagogue scripture exposition with rowdy catcalls of "You bastard!" This seems to me not only a grossly perverse reading of the text but a wholly gratuitous one as well.

First, the acclamation of the crowd must be intended as appreciative, as are the preceding words: "Where did this man get all this? What wisdom is given him! What mighty works are accomplished at his hands!" The point is "Local boy makes good." It is only after the praise of the crowd that Mark slams on the brakes and reverses the sense of the whole scene, making the crowd suddenly and arbitrarily turn ugly (for reasons we will see in a subsequent chapter).

Second, the argument I am rejecting here isolates the phrase "son of Mary" from the immediate context as well. The fact that his siblings are mentioned, even listed, in the same breath shows that Mark simply means the crowd to specify Jesus as the man they know to be related to a group of familiar locals. Perhaps Joseph (never mentioned by Mark anyway) is omitted because he is dead, just as Luke means no slur when he describes the dead man of Luke 11:12 as "the only son of his mother," because the whole point is that she is an abandoned widow. No one makes anything of the fact that Mark mentions only Jesus' mother, brothers, and sisters in Mark 3:32–34. Do Jesus himself and his disciples mean to cast doubt on his honorable paternity?

Interpreters like to fill in imagined gaps by informing us, given current Jewish idioms, customs, and the like, that the "real" issue in this or that passage is one never mentioned by the gospel writer explicitly. He would have expected you to know that for Jews to mention someone merely by his mother's name, not by the father's, implied bastardy. But this, as I have tried to show, makes nonsense of the passage. If such scholars are right about a Jewish custom of referring to bastards by a matronymic, then it is not modern readers but the evangelist Mark himself who failed to grasp the Jewish custom (as he does elsewhere!). True, later copyists of Mark 6, like the evangelist Matthew (Matt. 13:55, "Is this not the carpenter's son? Is not his mother called Mary?"), changed the text to read, "Is this not the son of the carpenter and Mary?" But this only shows that Mark's copyists and editors were sensitive to a nuance lost on him, or he would not have written the scene the way he did. This would be far from the only instance of later writers changing Mark because something that had seemed innocuous to him had become delicate in terms of later developments in doctrine.

It is easy for readers to overlook the Markan data just discussed because they cannot see past the long and colorful Nativity stories of Matthew and Luke, which do (at least on the traditional reading to be pursued here) ascribe a miraculous birth to Jesus. These now require our attention. At the outset it must be said that the two stories differ over most every detail save for the fact of the miraculous conception and locating the birth in Bethlehem. I said above that the two stories tend to cancel one another out, and that both alike are ruled out by Mark's earlier version, which shows no trace of such a miracle. We will shortly see that, even if we had no rival account with which to compare either one of the stories, each fails as history on its own account.

Luke has interspersed with an account of the nativity of John the Baptist (no doubt obtained from the rival sect of John) a parallel nativity of Jesus built on John's model. Not that Luke himself was the one who composed it; it, too, was most likely pre-Lukan material. The Jesus version occupies Luke 1:16–38, 2:1–40. The birth annunciation to Mary recalls those of Isaac (Gen. 18:9–15, "Sarah your wife shall have a son"; 17:19, "Sarah your wife shall bear you a son, and you shall call his name Isaac.") and Samson (Judg. 13:2–5, "Behold you are barren and have no children; but you shall conceive and bear a son . . . and he shall begin to deliver Israel from the hand of the Philistines"), on which it is probably based. In all three cases, the births of Isaac, Samson, and Jesus are announced by angels. But the story also owes a debt to the commissioning narratives of Moses and Jeremiah, in which God summons his chosen servant, the man objects, and God reaffirms his call. "'Come, I will send you to Pharaoh that you may bring forth my people. . . .' But Moses said to God, 'Who am I that I should go to Pharaoh . . . ?' He said, 'But I will be with you . . .'" (Exod. 3:10–12). "The word of Yahve came to me saying, 'Before I formed you in the womb I knew you, and before you were born I consecrated you; I appointed you a prophet to the nations.' Then I said, 'Ah, Lord Yahve! Behold, I do not know how to speak, for I am only a youth.' But Yahve said to me, 'Do not say, "I am only a youth . . . for I am with you to deliver you."'" (Jer. 1:4–8).

Less-familiar sources used for Luke's nativity include the Biblical Antiquities of Pseudo-Philo and an Aramaic version of Daniel only recently recovered among the Dead Sea Scrolls. As to the former, we read how, during Pharaoh's persecution of Hebrew babies, Amram planned to defy Pharaoh by having a son. God's will is made known when an angel appears to the virgin Miriam, and the Spirit of God overcomes her, inspiring predictions of the child Moses' great destiny. "And the spirit of God came upon Miriam one night, and she saw a dream and told it to her parents in the morning, saying, 'I have seen this night, and behold a man in a linen garment stood and said to me, "Go and say to your parents, 'Behold, he who will be born from you will be cast forth into the water; likewise through him the water will be dried up. And I will work signs through him and save my people, and he will exercise leadership always'"'" (9.10).

As to the latter, the Jesus Nativity has most certainly borrowed from an Aramaic Daniel the angel's prediction in Luke 1:32–33, 35. "[And when the Spirit] came to rest up[on] him, he fell before the throne. [Then Daniel rose and said,] 'O king, why are you angry; why do you [grind] your teeth? [The G]reat [God] has revealed to you [that which is to come.] . . . [Peoples will make war,] and battles shall multiply among the nations, until [the king of the people of God arises. He will become] the king of Syria and [E]gypt. [All the peoples will serve him,] and he shall become [gre]at upon the earth. . . . He will be called [son of the Gr]eat [God;] by his Name he shall be designated. He will be called the son of God. They will call him son of the Most High. . . . His kingdom will be an eternal kingdom, and he will be righteous in all his ways" (4Q246, The Son of God).[9]

Though Luke used prior sources, probably in Aramaic, for the nativities of John and Jesus, it appears he himself contributed bits of connective text to bring the two parallel stories into a particular relationship so that John should be subordinated to Jesus, whom Luke makes Jesus' elder cousin. This original, redactional material is Luke 1:36, 39–45, 56. It consists of a visit of Mary to her cousin Elizabeth, whereupon the fetus John, already in possession of clairvoyant gifts, leaps in the womb to acknowledge the greater glory of the messianic zygote. All this is blatantly legendary, or there is no such thing as a legend. Luke probably got the idea from Gen. 25:22, where according to the Greek translation of the Old Testament, the Septuagint, Rebecca is painfully pregnant with twins. The two little ones, Jacob and Esau, are already wrangling for precedence before birth: "And the babes leaped within her." This precedent Luke seeks to reverse by having the older cousin, John, deferring, already in the womb, to the younger, Jesus, by leaping when his fellow fetus approaches. In this way Luke tries to harmonize the competing traditions of Jesus and John, whose cousinhood is no doubt his own invention.

In chapter 3, Luke contrives to get the Nazarene couple Mary and Joseph down to Bethlehem in time for Jesus to be born there. He asks himself just what it would take to get the pair on the rough hilly roads this far into Mary's pregnancy. Surely no mere vacation. Perhaps influenced by the well-known story of Krishna's nativity, in which Krishna was born while his earthly father was away registering for taxation, Luke has a Roman census require Joseph's (and Mary's?) presence elsewhere, in Bethlehem, where King David once lived, Joseph being a remote descendent of David. The absurdity of this is manifest. No taxation census ever required individuals to register, not where they themselves live but rather where their remote ancestors once lived! What, after all, is the point of a census in any century? The government wants to know how much they can expect to collect and at what address. Imagine asking people to register where their forebears lived a thousand years previously! That is what Luke bids us imagine, but we cannot.

Even if we felt we could swallow a camel of such volume, there are gnats aplenty at which to strain. For one thing, the census Luke posits (2:1), levied at the command of Caesar Augustus, is unknown to any historian of the period. This is exceedingly strange, given the meticulous documentation of the era. (Moses of Chorene says this census had been carried out in his homeland of Armenia, but he wrote in the sixth century C.E. and was a Christian, perhaps trying to harmonize the biblical account by reference to some local census, much as apologists for Noah's Flood try to connect it with geological evidence of local flooding in the same region.)

According to both Matthew and Luke, Jesus was born during the reign of Herod the Great. He was a client king of Rome, ruling a satellite state of the Roman Empire, much like Poland before the 1989 breakup of the Soviet bloc. But since Palestine was not yet actually a province of Rome's empire, it would not have been included in any taxation of the empire proper. There was a census taken under the Roman governor of Syria, Quirinius. Luke is right about this (Luke 2:2). The trouble is, this census was conducted in the year 6 C.E., a full decade later than Luke supposes. Quirinius was not yet governor of Syria when Herod the Great ruled. As Tertullian tells us, this post was occupied by two men, Sentius Saturninus (4–3 B.C.E.) and Quintillius Varus (2–1 B.C.E.), during Herod's rule of Judea. Luke also knew good and well (Acts 5:37) that when Quirinius did tax Jews, in 6 C.E., it was an unprecedented outrage among Jews, who responded by rebellion at the instigation of Judas the Gaulonite, issuing in thousands of crucifixions all over the Galilean hills. This shows that Roman taxation of Jews could not have been taken for granted a decade earlier, no matter who we might imagine conducting it.

The attempt of apologist Sir William Ramsey to make Quirinius governor of Syria on an earlier occasion, though much cited by fundamentalists, is totally unfounded. All Ramsey discovered was an inscription saying Quirinius had been honored for his aid in a military victory, and Ramsey gratuitously guessed that Quirinius's reward had been a previous tenure as governor of Syria. Besides, there is no room for it. We know who occupied the post in Herod's time, and it was not Quirinius.

But suppose Luke was mistaken in associating Jesus' birth with Herod the Great. Could we then salvage the census of Quirinius as the context of Jesus' birth, albeit at the cost of having Jesus born in 6 C.E.? No, because under Quirinius the region of Galilee had been split off from Judea and remained outside direct Roman control. It was instead ruled by Herod's son Archelaus (Matt. 2:22). Thus, Mary and Joseph, living in Nazareth, as Luke supposes, would be unaffected by any census in Quirinius's domain. Luke seems to have imagined Palestine united as it was under Herod the Great but all under the jurisdiction of a Roman governor. (Luke falls victim to the same sort of confusion in Acts 9, where he has Saul sent by the Sanhedrin from Jerusalem to Damascus to arrest Christians, even though the Jerusalem authorities had no authority there and could not have imparted any to Saul. Luke just wanted to have Saul in Jerusalem for the death of Stephen and in Syria for his own conversion. He did his best to get him there, as he did to get Mary and Joseph to Bethlehem from Nazareth, but his skills as a travel agent were not up to the task.)

The visit of the shepherds, alerted by angels to the advent of the baby savior, is of a piece with current nativity myths. Shepherds attend the birth of Mithras, too, and the divine youth Longus was born in the open field as well. The sky-filling angels also bring to mind a close parallel to the Buddhist story of Asita, which in turn would appear to have suggested Luke's story of the oracle of Simeon (Luke 2:25–35). Prince Siddhartha has just been born, and his ostensible father, King Suddhodana, sought the aid of diviners to predict the destiny of the child.

And at that time on the side of a peak of the Himalayas dwelt a great sage named Asita. . . . At the moment when the Bodhisattva was born he beheld many marvelous wonders: the gods over the space of the sky making the word "Buddha" resound, waving their garments, and coursing hither and thither in delight. . . . So the great sage Asita . . . rose up and flew through the air to the great city of Kapilavatthu, and on arriving, laid aside his magic power, entered Kapilavatthu on foot, arrived at the abode of King Suddhodana, and stood at the door of the house. . . . Then the king taking the boy . . . in both hands brought him into the presence of the sage. Thus Asita observing beheld the Bodhisattva endowed with the thirty-two marks of a great man and adorned with the eighty minor marks, his body surpassing that of Sakra, Brahma, and the world protectors with glory surpassing a hundred and thousandfold, and he breathed forth this solemn utterance: "marvellous verily is this person that has appeared in the world," and rising from his seat clasped his hands, fell at the Bodhisattva's feet, made a rightwise circuit round, and taking the Bodhisattva stood in contemplation. [He then predicts the two possible careers of the child, as a world conqueror or a world redeemer.] And looking at him he wept, and shedding tears, sighed deeply. The king beheld Asita weeping, shedding tears, and sighing deeply. And beholding him the hair of his body rose, and in distress he hastily said to Asita, "Why, O sage, dost thou weep and shed tears, and sigh deeply? Surely there is no misfortune for the boy?" At this Asita said to the king, "O king, I weep not for the sake of the boy . . . , but I weep for myself. And why? I, O king, am old, aged, advanced in years, and this boy . . . will no doubt attain supreme complete enlightenment. And having done so will turn the supreme Wheel of Doctrine that has not been turned by ascetic or brahmin, or god, or Mara, or by any other in the world; for the weal and happiness of the world he will teach the Doctrine. . . . But we shall not see that Buddha-jewel. Hence, O king, I weep, and in sadness I sigh deeply, for I shall not be able to reverence him."[10]

Like Simeon, Asita embodies all the faithful of past centuries, having lived long enough to glimpse, but just to glimpse, the Desire of Ages finally come. Whereas Simeon rejoices to have gotten even this peek, Asita is sorrowful he will see no more than a peek, but the metaphor is the same. And it is not too much to suggest that the Christian story has been borrowed from the Buddhist. Ever since Alexander the Great, traffic and trade, not to mention missionary propaganda, had flowed freely between Greece, the Near East, and India. It is by no means unrealistic to suppose Christians and Jews were familiar with Buddhist and Hindu stories and liked what they heard.

Matthew's nativity story is woven from a series of formula quotations from the Old Testament supposedly fulfilled in Jesus. These quotations are all introduced by the formula, "This happened to fulfill the scripture, which said. . . ." We can recognize here the use of an apologetics manual like that in Mark 9:11 and 12:35, there introduced by the formula, "Why do the scribes say . . . ?" We find the same sort of introductory formula, and the same sort of esoteric interpretation of Scripture, in the Dead Sea Scrolls, specifically, 1QpHab, the Habbakuk Commentary. After the citation of each passage, the commentator introduces his gloss with the phrase, "Interpreted, this concerns . . . ," and the passage is made to anticipate events in the life and history of the sect. The use of such documents implies that our gospels stand not at the beginning but well along the way at some later stage of early Christian apologetics.

Matthew has also juggled the most favorable readings from various available editions and translations of the Old Testament to arrive at a reading of each prophecy that will best match the "fulfillments"! Sometimes he has created events on the assumption that if they were predicted they must have happened. Other times he has found a text to "predict" events in a story he has obtained from oral tradition.

Unlike Luke, Matthew has the angelic annunciation made to Joseph, not to Mary (1:20–21). Not only that, but here as elsewhere, Matthew has angels appear to characters in the story through the medium of dreams, whereas in Luke's Nativity story the angels appear in waking reality. A difference like this denotes a difference in fictional idiom, in storytelling.

On the whole, Matthew seems to have borrowed the Jesus Nativity from Josephus's story of Moses' birth and persecution. Whereas Exodus has Pharaoh institute a systematic butchery of Hebrew babies simply to remove the potential threat of a strong Hebrew fifth column in case of invasion, Josephus makes the planned pogrom a weapon aimed right at Moses, who in Josephus becomes a promised messiah in his own right. Amram and Jochabed, expecting baby Moses, are obviously alarmed. What should they do? Abort the pregnancy? God speaks in a dream to reassure them.

> One of those sacred scribes, who are very sagacious in foretelling future events truly, told the king that about this time there would a child be borne to the Israelites, who, if he were reared, would bring the Egyptian dominion low, and would raise the Israelites; that he would excel all men in virtue, and obtain a glory that would be remembered through all ages. Which was so feared by the king, that, according to this man's opinion, he commanded that they should cast every male child into the river, and destroy it. . . . A man, whose name was Amram, . . . was very uneasy at it, his wife being then with child, and he knew not what to do. . . . Accordingly God had mercy on him, and was moved by his supplication. He stood by him in his sleep, and exhorted him not to despair of his future favours. . . . "For that child, out of dread for whose nativity the Egyptians have doomed the Israelites' children to destruction, shall be this child of thine . . . he shall deliver the Hebrew nation from the distress they are under from the Egyptians. His memory shall be famous while the world lasts." (*Antiquities* 2.9.2–3).[11]

It is evident that Matthew has simply changed some names here, creating his own version in which Herod the Great takes the role of Pharaoh, warned by his own scribes of the birth of a savior, whereupon he determines to kill all the babies he has to in order to eliminate the child of prophecy. Joseph takes the place of the worried Amram, Mary of the dangerously pregnant Jochabed. A dream from God reinforces his resolve, along with a prediction of the child's future greatness.

Matthew quotes the Greek Septuagint translation of Isa. 7:14 ("Behold, the virgin shall conceive and bear a son, and you shall call his name Emannuel"), already a complex and redacted passage in Isaiah. In Isaiah's context the oracle evidently means to assure the chicken-hearted King Ahaz that God would inter-vene on behalf of Judah in a matter of a very few years, no more than required for a child, soon to be conceived, to grow to the age where he can decline baby food he doesn't like. Assyria will by then have wiped the allies Samaria and Syria off the map. Obviously Isaiah cannot have intended this prophecy to predict events in the life of Jesus more than seven centuries later. Matthew cannot have thought that he did. Like the authors of the Dead Sea Scrolls, he must have imag-ined the verse contained a hidden message, only newly discernible in light of the advent of Jesus the Messiah. Isaiah must have intended the imminent conception of his own son who, like his other two hapless sons Shearjashub ("a remnant shall return") and Maher-shalal-hashbaz ("the spoil speeds; the prey hastens"), no doubt little appreciated being named for dad's prophecies, as if he had named them Mark, for "Mark my words!" Chapter 8 is pretty much parallel to chapter 7 and serves to explain it.

And in this context, it is important to know that the word translated "virgin" in the King James and New International Versions is the Hebrew *almah* and means the same as the ambiguous word "maiden," not necessarily innocent of sexual intercourse, but a young woman in any case. If Isaiah intends his wife, he cannot mean a virgin in the technical sense. Matthew, though, chooses to quote not the Hebrew but rather the Septuagint Greek version where the word *parthenos* is used. This Greek word is usually thought to have the narrower meaning "sexually virginal." Since Matthew seems to want to tell us that Jesus was conceived virginally, miraculously, he prefers using a version of the Bible that seems to contain an appropriate prediction.

But it is still more complicated than that. Isa. 7:14 looks like an older birth or enthronement oracle originally issued for some king of Judah (cf. Isa. 9:6 and 11:1–10) and used by the compiler of the Isaiah collection in a new context. This is interesting because in that context almah did denote a virgin, namely, the virgin goddess Shahar, from whose womb the king sprang (Ps. 110:3b, "From the womb of Shahar [the dawn goddess] the dew of your youth will come to you"). In this case, as in several others, the New Testament quotation of Old Testament texts may not be so far off the mark. They are in effect rediscovering the forgotten royal ide-ology of the kings of Judah, which included painting the monarch in divine colors, and applying it to the divine king Jesus. (More of this in a later chapter.)

It is revealing that when Matthew's Magi (Zoroastrian astrologers from the Parthian Empire) learn from Mic. 5:2 that the Messiah must be born in Beth-lehem, we are implicitly shown how Matthew himself "knew" it, not from his-torical information, but by exegesis. Having honored the divine child, the Magi are warned by an angel in a dream (2:12), just as Joseph was (1:20) and shortly will be again (2:13) and again (2:19) and yet again (2:22)! They return to Parthia by another route.

The business of the moving star, surreal enough in its own right, also shows how Matthew has added to an original story of the Magi's visit. Originally, the point was that they, as astrologers, had assigned a particular significance to some star as the natal star of the king of the Jews. Its rising was enough to signal them to go to Jerusalem to seek the new king in the royal palace there. Where else would he be? They apparently imagine him to be Herod's own newborn son, only Herod hasn't any to show them. Where else might the king of the Jews be born? This brings in the prophecy (as it was then interpreted) of Micah about Bethlehem. Such a king would of course be Herod's rival, the real king, not Herod's heir. Up to this point in the story the star did not move. It had "led" them simply by its implications. But Matthew misunderstood this leading to imply that it moved across the heavens like a flair to guide them to Jerusalem, and that they only had to stop and ask Herod for directions because the star had mysteriously winked out, leaving them stranded. Now it reappears, moving through the night sky like Tinkerbell to rest over one particular Bethlehem hovel. Why did he clumsily tamper with the original Magi story? He wanted to connect it with the story of the slaughter of the innocents. Originally the Magi, in their own self-contained story, would have gone straight to Bethlehem, guided by the Micah prophecy, which they would have known if they knew enough to seek out a messianic King of the Jews. Originally, in the self-contained slaughter of the innocents story, Herod would have seen a star, just as the wicked king Nimrod saw the natal star of Abraham according to Jewish legend, and his scribes would have directed him to Bethlehem. Since both stories featured the natal star of Jesus as well as the Bethlehem prophecy, Matthew tied them together to avoid redundancy. The result was somewhat less than successsful.

The grisly episode of the slaughter of the innocents of Bethlehem, though buttressed by the out-of-context quotation of Jer. 31:15, has not grown from this text but rather owes its origin to the law of biographical analogy. The notion of the powers of evil being apprised of the birth of a child who is destined to overturn them and then seeking futilely to destroy him is a universal feature of the Mythic Hero archetype. We have seen that Matthew most likely borrowed it from Josephus's retelling of the nativity of Moses, but it would have inevitably suggested itself in any case. Romulus and Remus, Oedipus, Perseus, Cyrus the Great, Caesar Augustus, the prophet Zoroaster, the patriarch Abraham, and the god Krishna all escape the dread designs of the evil when still in their cribs, thanks to divine providence. To be sure, Herod the Great was just the sort of monster to kill all the children of a village if that were the only way of being sure he had eliminated an alleged messianic child who might be manipulated by rebels for their own purposes. (Perhaps Matthew had a scenario in mind, or thought Herod did, like that in 2 Kings 11, where a faction uses Joash, a young prince saved from death at the hands of a usurper, as a weapon to challenge the legitimacy of the new regime.) It would certainly not have been out of character for the paranoid Herod. But then no such deed is recorded of Herod, whose monstrosities are catalogued in fulsome detail by Josephus and others. It is more likely, I suggest, that the "fit" of the atrocity with Herod's character is more a matter of narrative verisimilitude than of history. It was because of Herod's well-known ruthlessness (including his extermination of numerous wives and progeny for fear of imagined threats and conspiracies) that Matthew has chosen him to play the villain.

The flight of the Holy Family into Egypt has been derived by Matthew, not from legend or early tradition, but rather from exegesis. He (or rather his scribal predecessors—cf. Matt. 13:51–52) chanced upon the reference to "my son" in Hos. 11:1 ("Out of Egypt I have called my son") and figured it must signal some sort of hitherto-unsuspected prediction of the life of Jesus the Son of God. The surface sense, as must have been quite as clear to Matthew as to us, refers to the exodus of God's "son," the nation of Israel, from Egypt. But Matthew decided Jesus, too, must have visited Egypt and returned therefrom. This also enabled Matthew to draw a parallel between the Joseph of Genesis and his own character Joseph, since now both go to Egypt.

But that is not all. I believe Matthew meant to foreshadow the death and resurrection of Jesus at this point in his story. Note that in the Old Testament, Egypt is sometimes connected with Rahab the sea monster, whose defeat at the dawn of time made Yahve king of all gods (Ps. 89:10, "You crushed Rahab like a carcass," and cf. Ps. 74:13b–14a, "You crushed the heads of the dragons on the waters; you crushed the heads of Leviathan"). Isa. 52:9–10 makes the exodus from Egypt a kind of historical replay of the primordial victory over the dragon, equating Rahab and Egypt: "Flex! Bend! Clothe yourself with strength, O arm of Yahve! Flex as in the old days, the generations of long ago. Was it not you who chopped Rahab to pieces, who skewered the dragon? Was it not you who dried up the sea, the waters of the great deep? You, who made the depths of the sea a road for the redeemed to walk on?" Matthew knew that Jonah was swallowed by a sea monster at Yahve's disposal (cf. Jon. 1:17; cf. Job 41:1–4 ff., "Can you draw out Leviathan with a fish hook [as I did]? . . . Will he make a covenant with you [as he did me] to take him for your servant forever?"). And he saw the swallowing by the fish as a prefiguration of Jesus' descent into the tomb: "For as Jonah was three days and three nights in the belly of the whale, so will the Son of Man be three days and three nights in the heart of the earth" (Matt. 12:40). The flight into Egypt has the child Jesus already going down into Rahab, the belly of the sea beast, Egypt.

In some ways the strangest of Matthew's formula quotations occurs in 2:23, where, in order to prooftext Jesus' residence at Nazareth (perhaps something of an embarrassment in light of all the Bethlehem business), he quotes a prophecy no one has ever been able to locate: "He shall be called a Nazorean." Can Matthew have been thinking of Judg. 13:7, "The boy shall be a Nazirite [devoted] to God from birth?" If so, he has inserted the perceived esoteric meaning right into the wording of the Scripture text, since "Nazirite" and "Nazorean" are not the same thing. (A Nazirite was one who for a short duration vowed to leave his hair unshorn, not to drink wine, nor to touch any unclean thing. There were no lifelong Nazirites; Samson is made one after the fact to find a different explanation for his long hair, originally the mark of his having been the sun god.)

It is quite clear that neither Matthew nor Luke had any historical memory or tradition to rely on to create their stories of the miraculous Nativity of Jesus. Instead, they wove their stories from Scripture passages reinterpreted or reapplied, as well as from similar stories from contemporary hero tales. And there were very many gods and heroes whom legend made the products of miraculous conception. The philosopher Plato was one such: "Speusippos, in his writing 'The Funeral Feast of Plato,' and Klearchos, in his 'Encomium on Plato,' and Anaxilaides, in the second book 'On the Philosophers,' all say that there was at Athens a story that when Periktione was ready [to bear children] Ariston was trying desperately [to impregnate her] but did not succeed. Then, after he had ceased his efforts, he saw a vision of Apollo. Therefore he abstained from any further marital relations until she brought forth a child." That is, Apollo's son Plato (Diogenes Laertius *Lives of Eminent Philosophers* 3.45).[12]

Alexander the Great, too, seemed to his admirers too great for human DNA alone to account for: "The bride, before the night in which they were to join in the bedchamber, had a vision. There was a peal of thunder and a lightning bolt fell upon her womb. A great fire was kindled from the strike. Then it broke into flames which flashed everywhere, then they extinguished. At a later time, after the marriage, Philip saw a vision: he was placing a seal on his wife's womb; the engraving on the seal was in the image of a lion. The men charged with interpreting dreams were made suspicious by this vision and told Philip to keep a closer watch on his marital affairs. But Aristander of Telmesus said her husband had impregnated her, for nothing is sealed if it is empty, and that she was pregnant with a child whose nature would be courageous and lionlike. On another occasion, a great snake appeared, while Olympias was asleep, and wound itself around her body. This, especially, they say, weakened Philip's desire and tenderness towards her, so that he did not come often to sleep with her . . . because he considered himself discharged from the obligation of intercourse with her because she had become the partner of a higher being." Alexander was the result (Plutarch *Lives of the Noble Greeks and Romans*: Alexander 2:2–3:2).[13]

Pythagoras was another product of divine impregnation. "The soul of Pythagoras came from the realm of Apollo, either being a heavenly companion or ranked with him in some other familiar way, to be sent down among men; no one can deny this. It can be maintained from his birth and the manifold wisdom of his soul. . . . He was educated so that he was the most beautiful and god-like of those written about in histories. After his father died, he increased in nobility and wisdom. Although he was still a youth, in his manner of humility and piety he was counted most worthy already, even by his elders. Seen and heard, he persuaded everyone, and to everyone who saw him he appeared to be astonishing, so that, reasonably, he was considered by many to be the son of a god" (Iamblichus *Life of Pythagoras* 8–109).[14]

"To his mother, just before [Apollonius] was born, there came an apparition of Proteus, who changes his form so much in Homer, in the guise of an Egyptian demon. She was in no way frightened but asked what sort of child she would bear. And he answered, 'Myself.' 'And who are you?' she asked. 'Proteus,' he answered, 'the god of Egypt.' . . . Now he is said to have been born in a meadow. . . . [J]ust as the hour of his birth was approaching, his mother was warned in a dream to walk out into the meadow and pluck the flowers; and in due course she came there and her maids attended to the flowers, scattering themselves over the meadow, while she fell asleep lying on the grass. Thereupon the swans who fed in the meadow set up a dance around her as she slept, and lifting their wings, as they are wont to do, cried out aloud all at once, for there was somewhat of a breeze blowing in the meadow. She then leaped up at the sound of their song and bore her child, for any sudden fright is apt to bring on a premature delivery. But the people of that country say that just at the moment of the birth, a thunderbolt seemed about to fall to earth and then rose up into the air and disappeared aloft; and the gods thereby indicated, I think, the great distinction to which the sage was to attain, and hinted in advance how he would transcend all things upon earth and approach the gods" (Philostratus *The Life of Apollonius of Tyana* 1:4–5).[15]

Though I have restricted myself here to parallel miraculous birth stories of historical figures, there are numerous others attached to overtly mythical demigods like Perseus, Horus, and Hercules, and it was these to whom early pagan critics derisively compared the Nativity of Jesus. (Justin Martyr admitted the aptness of the parallels: "As to his being born of a virgin, you have your Perseus to balance that," *First Apologia*.) I am holding open the possibility that Jesus was, like Pythagoras, Plato, Alexander, and Apollonius, a historical individual to whom mythical features rapidly became attached rather than a pure myth that later became historicized.

At any rate, it is evident how the nativity stories in Matthew and Luke are cut from the same cloth as these. We have the elements of divine annunciation, heavenly portents, the legal husband shunning sex with his wife once the deity's claim was understood, interpretative dreams, and of course the resulting belief that the *Wunderkind* was the son of a god. It should surprise no one who is familiar with the great degree to which even supposedly traditional Judaism was Hellenized since the time of Alexander the Great that these pagan mythemes entered the Jesus story.

SON OF PANDERA?

A few times I have hinted that there may be available to us an alternate way of understanding Matthew and Luke to the effect that the myth of the virgin birth of Jesus had not already crept into the Jesus tradition on their watch. Could they have intended something other than the virgin birth miracle we usually read them as relating? Jane Schaberg[16] thinks so. In her opinion, Matthew does not yet know of the virgin birth legend. He is much concerned with the irregular birth of Jesus, it is true, but he means only to make the best of a tradition, without denying it, that Jesus was the son of Mary and someone other than Joseph, perhaps a Roman soldier named Pandera ("the panther," in fact a widely attested name/epithet of Roman legionaries), as Jewish polemic always claimed. Presumably Mary would have been raped, possibly seduced, by this man.

Schaberg asks why Matthew should include only four names (actual or implied) in his genealogy of Jesus: Tamar (1:3), Rahab (1:5), Ruth (1:5), and Bathsheba (1:6, "her of Uriah"), and all of these sullied by reputations of sexual indiscretion. Tamar posed as a harlot in order to trick old Judah into giving her a child, her due by the custom of Levirate marriage (Gen. 38). Rahab was a Jericho harlot who sold out her people and sheltered the two Israelite spies (Josh. 2), and later, according to tradition, married no less than Joshua himself. Ruth appears to have seduced her kinsman Boaz, climbing into bed with him after the orgiastic harvest festival (Ruth 3:6–10 ff.). Bathsheba was the wife of King David's lieutenant Uriah the Hittite, whom David betrayed and disposed of in order to have Bathsheba for himself (2 Sam. 11). Jewish tradition, copiously quoted by Schaberg, honors all four women despite their dubious morals, because in each case God brought good out of their sin. These women all become foremothers of David, the sun-king Solomon, and the Messiah.

Various Targums (Aramaic paraphrases of the Hebrew text, incorporating popular interpretations current at the time, like Kenneth Taylor's *Living Bible* today) of Genesis have the voice of God sound forth to prevent the stoning of Tamar. "It is from me that this thing comes" (*Targum Pseudo-Jonathan*). "Both of you are acquitted at the tribunal. This thing has come from God" (*Fragmentary Targum*). "They are both just; from before the Lord this thing has come about" (*Targum Neofiti I*). "When Judah said, 'She is righteous,' the Holy Spirit manifested itself and said, 'Tamar is not a prostitute and Judah did not want to give himself over to fornication with her; the thing happened because of me, in order that the King Messiah be raised up from Judah'" (*Midrash Ha-Gadol I*, a medieval commentary). Schaberg suggests that this is what it means when Matthew has Mary vindicated in Joseph's eyes by the word of the angel, "That which is conceived in her is of the Holy Spirit" (1:21). That is, according to the will of God.

And the reference to a "virgin" conceiving? Schaberg observes that the Greek parthenos must have picked up the same sexual ambiguity as the Hebrew almah, since the Septuagint translators would have had no reason to understand it in the context of Isa. 7:14 to imply technical sexual virginity. Perhaps Matthew didn't intend the technical sense, either. His answer to the "Jesus ben Pandera" slur would have been to take the bull by the horns and make the best of it, as Christians had once done in the case of Jesus' lack of Davidic credentials. The only miracle Matthew had in mind, on this reading, was that of the providence of God whereby the bad may be turned to good.

There are quite different reasons to wonder if Luke had actually intended to tell a story of a virginal conception. Here the argument is text-critical. There is a stray manuscript (Old Latin manuscript b) that omits Mary's question in Luke 1:34, "How shall this be, since I know not a man?" If this verse were in fact not part of the original text, it would make better sense of the passage. For one thing, the inspired song of Gabriel, like his recital to Zechariah (Luke 1:14–17) and those of Zechariah (Luke 1:68–78), Mary (Luke 1:47–55), and Simeon (2:2–35), would then proceed uninterrupted by prose insertions. For another, verse 34 makes Mary counter the angel with a skeptical objection precisely parallel to Zechariah's in 1:18, "How shall I know this? For I am an old man, and my wife is advanced in years." Gabriel strikes him deaf and mute until the child John is born, in punishment for daring to doubt his word. Would Luke so easily attribute the same incredulity to Mary, and if he did, would he let her off with no angelic reprisal?

Note that without this verse there is nothing in Luke that even implies a supernatural conception or birth. Everything else anyone says about the Nativity simply concerns the great identity and destiny of the child Jesus. For the angel to tell Mary that she will at some future time conceive a child would be nothing to doubt as Mary does in verse 34. She is after all betrothed to be married! The very unnaturalness of the question implies again that it is a clumsy invention designed precisely to inject the foreign notion of a virginal conception. And if this is so, the whole notion of the virgin birth enters Luke's gospel by the way of later scribal alteration, to square the text with the emerging doctrine of the virgin birth. Such textual funny business should not surprise us. Tertullian wanted to find a reference to the virgin birth of Jesus in John's gospel, where, according to all extant manuscripts, it has no place. But he quoted a manuscript that read at John 1:13, "who *was* born, not of blood nor of the will of the flesh nor of the will of a husband, but of God," where all our copies of John have "who *were* born, not of blood, nor of the will of the flesh, nor of the will of a husband, but of God." The point of the original seems to be believers' birth "from above," birth "of the Spirit" as in John 3. But Tertullian's source transformed this text into a prooftext for the virginal conception of Jesus with the stroke of the pen. Has the same thing happened in the case of Luke's gospel? It makes a lot of sense, but the evidence is too meager for us ever to be able to settle the question.

Speaking of John's gospel, it is worth noting in conclusion that, just as this latest of the Gospels seems to reject the Bethlehem tradition of Matthew and Luke, sticking with Mark's implied understanding that Jesus was a Galilean, so does John seem to reject the virgin birth idea he found (as most readers still do, even if Schaberg is right!) in Luke and Matthew. In John 1:45, John has one of his trustworthy characters, not a foil spouting erroneous ideas, call Jesus "the son of Joseph." He never corrects the impression given that "son of Joseph" is just as true of Jesus as that he is the one "Moses in the Law and also all the prophets wrote about."

SON OF JOSEPH?

So we would seem to be left with little reason to believe that Jesus was produced by miraculous conception. The irreducible historical datum would have to be that Joseph was his father (or perhaps Pandera). But I fear we are not on secure ground even here. For the possibility remains that for Jesus to have been called "son of Joseph" may be another historicizing reinterpretation of an obsolete messianic title, namely, that of Messiah ben-Joseph, the northern Messiah. I have already cautioned that Vermes might be wrong about the Messiah ben-Joseph being a reflection of Simon bar-Kochba. If he is, then we would have to look for a different origin for the whole conception, and it would not be too hard to find. The two-Messiah doctrine would just be a harmonization of rival Galilean and Judean Messiah expectations. The north, too, had ample traditions of a powerful monarchy led by such kings as Omri and Jeroboam. It is no surprise that the Assyrian conquest should have long ago bred in the Galileans a hope for a restoration of a throne in Samaria. And the Genesis traditions of Joseph as one day destined to rule all the tribes (Gen. 37:5–10) would have fed this flame of messianic (but non-Davidic) hope.

We have already seen how there was an early stage in which Christians regarded Jesus as a non-Davidic Messiah. He was thought to have been a Galilean, so presumably at this stage of belief he would have been Messiah ben-Joseph. We might even have a fossil remnant of that Joseph-messianism surviving in one of the Christian interpolations (as most scholars reckon it) into the Testament of Benjamin, one of the Old Testament Pseudepigrapha: "Jacob cried out, 'My child Joseph, you good child, you have won your father's heart.' And he embraced him and kissed him for two hours, and said, 'In you shall be fulfilled the prophecy of heaven about the Lamb of God and Savior of the world— that one without blemish shall be offered up on behalf of sinners, and one without sin shall die on behalf of the ungodly, in the blood of the covenant, for the salvation of the Gentiles and of Israel, and he shall destroy Beliar and those who serve him'" (3:8).[17] Elsewhere in this fascinating document we hear that Levi or Judah or some combination of the two tribes will provide the seed of the coming Messiah, but here, all of a sudden, the Messiah is to stem from Joseph, that is, either Ephraim or Manasseh. I submit that this text demands an origin in circles where a Messiah-ben-Joseph was hoped for.

But what would have happened once Christians abandoned the non-Davidic messiahship notion and sought instead to secure a Davidic genealogy for their Lord? Obviously, Jesus' earlier status as Messiah son of Joseph would have to be forgotten or reinterpreted, just as "Jesus the Nazorean" was reinterpreted after "Nazorean" as the understanding of a sectarian tag was left behind. It came to be imagined that Jesus was the son of a man named Joseph. But as for the real name of Jesus' own biological father, none can say.

NOTES

1. David Ulansey, *The Origins of the Mithraic Mysteries: Cosmology and Salvation in the Ancient World* (New York: Oxford University Press, 1989).

2. The translation is that of M. de Yonge in H. F. D. Sparks, *The Apocryphal Old Testament* (New York: Oxford University Press, 1984).

3. Géza Vermes, *Jesus the Jew: A Historian's Reading of the Gospels* (Glasgow: Collins/Fontana, 1977), p. 140.

4. Stephen Fuchs, *Rebellious Prophets: A Study of Messianic Movements in Indian Religions* (New York: Asia House, 1965), p. 183.

5. Raymond E. Brown, *The Birth of the Messiah: A Commentary on the Infancy Narratives in Matthew and Luke* (Garden City: Doubleday, 1977), p. 64.

6. Eusebius, *Ecclesiastical History*, trans. Isaac Boyle, Twin Books Series (Grand Rapids: Baker Book House, 1969), p. 112.

7. Sigmund Mowinckel, *He That Cometh: The Messiah Concept in the Old Testament and Later Judaism*, trans. G. W. Anderson (New York: Abingdon Press, 1954), pp. 102–22. Mowinckel himself (p. 19) sees the Micah passage as a genuine prediction of the restorarion of the Davidic dynasty, which, in its redactional context, it no doubt is, but as a simple matter of form-criticism, I make Mic. 5:2 a pre-Exilic fossil, one of the old birth oracles, which Micah reapplies to his situation.

8. Robert Eisler, *The Messiah Jesus and John the Baptist*, trans. Alexander Haggerty Krappe (New York: Dial Press, 1931), pp. 234–35; Hugh J. Schonfield, appendix 2, "North Palestinian Sectarians and Christian Origins," *The Passover Plot: New Light on the History of Jesus* (New York: Bernard Geiss Associates/Random House, 1965), pp. 207–14.

9. Translation of Robert Eisenman and Michael Wise, *The Dead Sea Scrolls Uncovered* (Rockport: Element Books, 1992).

10. Edward J. Thomas, *The Life of Buddha as Legend and History* (London: Routledge & Kegan Paul, 1927), pp. 39–41.

11. *The Works of Flavius Josephus*, trans. William Whiston (London: Ward, Lock & Co., n.d.), pp. 64–65

12. David L. Dungan, trans., in *Sourcebook of Texts for the Comparative Study of the Gospels*, ed. David L. Dungan and David R. Cartlidge, 4th ed., Sources for Biblical Study 1 (Missoula: Scholars Press, 1974), p. 9.

13. David R. Cartlidge trans., ibid., pp. 7–8.

14. David R. Cartlidge trans., ibid., pp. 33–34.

15. Philostratus, *The Life of Apollonius of Tyana*, trans. F. C. Conybeare, vol. 1. Loeb Classical Library 16 (Cambridge: Harvard University Press, 1912), pp. 11, 13.

16. Jane Schaberg, *The Illegitimacy of Jesus* (New York: Harper & Row, 1987), pp. 20–77.

17. M. de Yonge, trans., in *Apocryphal Old Testament*, p. 595.

CHAPTER THREE
CHILDHOOD
AND FAMILY

GOSPEL OF THE INFANCY

W hat do we know of the childhood of Jesus? The answer would depend entirely upon whom you asked and when. Today, most readers of the Bible would admit, regretfully, that we know virtually nothing of the days when Jesus was growing up. They say this because they are reading only the four canonical gospels, and of these, only Luke offers us even a single anecdote from the childhood of Jesus. But through much of Christian history, at least in earlier centuries, you would have received a very different answer from any Christian you might have asked, for many knew the tales of the young savior collected in gospels like the Infancy Gospel of Matthew, the Infancy Gospel of Thomas, and the Arabic Infancy Gospel. They probably wouldn't have had ready access to these particular texts, but the stories circulated widely, and most people would have known (and believed) them. The state of things today, with Christians and unbelievers alike admitting agnosticism as to the formative years of Jesus, represents, though we are not used to thinking of it this way, a major step in the direction of historical-critical skepticism about the Jesus tradition, which was once commonly imagined to cover a lot more territory than it is now! For some centuries now, Christians have accommodated themselves to knowing much less than their ancestors thought they knew about the life of Jesus. It is analogous to the way things might be generations from now should the historical revisionism represented by the Jesus Seminar (and the present book!) prevail among Christians: people would have adjusted to knowing a lot less about a historical Jesus but would find it unproblematic. That is something to keep in mind: no matter how much of the canonical gospels you believe literally, many of your forebears in the faith would consider you half a skeptic.

Here are some sample tales from the Infancy Gospel of Thomas:

> Now when Jesus was five years old, there was a great rain upon the earth, and the child Jesus walked about in it. And the rain was very terrible, and he gathered the water together into a pool and commanded with a word that it should become clear, and immediately it did.
>
> Again, he took some of the clay from that pool and fashioned it into twelve sparrows. Now it was the Sabbath day when Jesus did this among the Hebrew children, and the Hebrew children went and said to his father Joseph, "Lo, your son was playing with us, and he took clay and made sparrows, which it was not right to do on the Sabbath, and he has broken it." And Joseph went to the child Jesus and said to him, "Why have you done this which was not right to do on the Sabbath?" But Jesus spread forth his hands and commanded the sparrows, "Go forth into the sky and fly! You shall not meet death at any man's hands." And they flew and began to cry out and praise Almighty God. But when the Jews saw what was done, they marveled and departed, proclaiming the signs Jesus did.
>
> But a Pharisee who was with Jesus took a branch of an olive tree and began to empty the pool Jesus had made. And when Jesus saw it, he was annoyed and said to him, "O man of Sodom, ungodly and ignorant, what harm did the fountain of water I made do you? Lo, you shall become like a dry tree with neither root, leaf, nor fruit!" And immediately he shriveled up, fell to the earth, and died. His parents carried him away dead and reviled Joseph, saying, "Look what your son has done! Teach him to pray, not to curse!"
>
> And after some days, as Jesus walked with Joseph through the city, one of the children ran and struck Jesus on the arm. But Jesus said to him, "Come now to the end of your road!" And at once he fell to the earth and died. But when those present saw this wonder they cried out, "Where does this child come from?" And they said to Joseph, "It is not right for such a child to live among us!" As he departed, taking Jesus with him, they called out, "Leave this place! Or else, if you must stay with us, teach him to pray and not to curse; for our sons lose consciousness!"
>
> And Joseph called Jesus and began to admonish him: "Why do you call down curses? Those who live here are coming to hate us!" But Jesus said, "I know these words are yours, not mine, but for your sake I will be silent from now on. Only let them see [the result of] their own foolishness." And immediately those who spoke against Jesus were made blind, and as they wandered about they said, "Every word from his mouth is fulfilled!"
>
> And when Joseph saw what Jesus had done, he took hold of his ear in

anger. But Jesus was annoyed and said to Joseph, "It is enough for you to see me, not to touch me. For you do not know who I am, and if you knew it, you would not grieve me. Although I am with you now, I was made before you."

There was a man named Zacheus who heard all that Jesus said to Joseph, and he marveled silently and said, "I have never seen a child who spoke this way." And he approached Joseph and said, "You have a wise child. Bring him to me to learn the alphabet." . . . And Joseph took the child Jesus and brought him to the house where other children also were taught. But the teacher began to teach him the letters with sweet speech and wrote for him the first line, from A to T, and began to flatter him and to teach him. But the child remained silent. Then the teacher hit him on the head, and when the child felt the blow, he said to him, "I ought to be teaching you, rather than you teaching me! I know the letters you would teach me." . . . And beginning with that line he pronounced all the letters from A to T well and swiftly. Then he looked at the teacher and said, "But you do not know how to interpret A and B; how do you propose to teach others? You hypocrite! If you do know A and can tell me about it, then I will teach you about B." But when the teacher started to explain A, he was speechless.

Now one day Jesus climbed up on top of a house with the children and began to play with them. But one of the boys fell down through the door to the upper room and immediately died. And when the children saw it, they all fled, leaving Jesus alone in the house. And when the parents of the boy who had died arrived, they accused Jesus, saying, "Truly, it was you who made him fall!" But Jesus said, "I never made him fall." Nevertheless they went on accusing him. So Jesus came down from the house and stood over the dead child and shouted, calling him by name, "Zeno! Zeno! Arise and tell whether I made you fall." And immediately he arose and said, "No, Lord." And when his parents saw this great miracle which Jesus did, they glorified God and kneeled before Jesus.

And after a few days one of the boys in that village was chopping wood and struck his foot. And when a crowd of people came out to see him, Jesus accompanied them. And he touched the wounded foot, and immediately it was made well. And Jesus said to him, "Rise, and chop the wood, and remember me." But when the crowd with him saw these signs, they kneeled before Jesus and said, "Truly, we surely believe you are God!"

And Jesus came to be eight years old. Now Joseph was a builder and made ploughs and ox yokes. One day a certain rich man said to Joseph, "Sir, make me a bed, both sturdy and beautiful." But Joseph was dismayed when he saw that the beam he had prepared was too short. Jesus said to him, "Do not be dismayed. You take hold of one end of the beam and I will take the other, and let us stretch it out." And so it happened, and at once he found it suitable for the job. And he said to Joseph, "Make it any way you want." But when Joseph saw what happened, he hugged him and said, "Blessed am I that God has given me such a son!"

The recurrent motif throughout these stories is that Jesus is a child in appearance only. Thus, as Strauss pointed out, they are docetic in character. "Docetism" ("apparitionism") is, among other things, used to denote an only apparent humanity. He was God or a heavenly being, an angel perhaps, but not really human. Some stories portray Jesus (or the Buddha, of whom such stories are also told) as not even having flesh and blood, so that one's hand might fail to touch him. In others, he might be depicted as physically solid but being inwardly a heavenly messenger already possessed of more than human wisdom and knowledge. Either way, the humanity of Jesus is only an apparent, outward show. And that is what the infancy gospel tales are. In them Jesus is shown again and again to be wiser than the adults around him. Their stupidity is often heightened to bring the contrast into starker relief. The point is the same as the frequent skepticism motif in miracle stories, whether of the child or of the adult Jesus: the unbelief or obtuseness of the bystanders only increases the glory of the feat performed (see chapter 5, "The Miracles").

Why am I spending such an amount of space discussing material that does not occur in the New Testament gospels? But in fact this infancy gospel tradition does seem to have managed to gain a toehold within the canon. There are two passages that seem to have been culled from the larger mass, or possibly they are among the earliest instances of what would eventually swell into the large body of Jesus *Wunderkind* stories we read in the infancy gospels. The first canonical example is Luke 2:41–52: "Now his parents visited Jerusalem every year for the Feast of the Passover. And when he was twelve years old, they went up [to the city] as they always did. When the feast was concluded, as they were returning home, the boy Jesus stayed behind in Jerusalem. His parents did not know it and continued on for a whole day, assuming he was somewhere in the caravan. They looked for him among their relatives and acquaintances, and when they failed to turn him up, they returned to Jerusalem looking for him. After three days they found him in the temple, sitting among the teachers, listening to them and asking them questions. And all who heard him were amazed at his understanding and his answers. And when they saw him, they were astonished, and his mother said to him, 'Son, why have you treated us this way? Look, your father and I have been frantic searching for you!' And he said to them, 'Why did you have to search? Did you not know I must be in my Father's house?' And they did not understand the saying he spoke to them. And he went down [from Jerusalem] with them and came to Nazareth, and was obedient to them; and his mother kept all these things in her heart. And Jesus increased in wisdom and in stature and in favor with God and man."

Note, as in the stories from the Infancy Gospel of Thomas, the young Jesus acts sovereignly, and it is left for his hapless parents to catch up with him as best they can. He doesn't ask permission to stay. Why should he? Their understandable concern once they find him, as fully understandable as that of Joseph in the Thomas stories, is shown to be misplaced simply because they have failed to grasp that Jesus is not the sort of being they imagine. He is no child who needs their clumsy supervision. Jesus seems surprised at their anxiety, that they would not know where to find him at once: "Where else would I be?" The comedy implicit in the scene is rich: here is Jesus, engaged in midrashic dialectic with scribal colleagues who can appreciate his wisdom, suddenly being taken in hand, as if a mischievous brat, by his dull-witted parents who still do not get it! And as Strauss said,[1] the scene is nothing if not docetic in coloring. The point is not that Jesus is just precocious; no, he is the Son of God trapped for the time being in the largely useless form of a child no one will listen to. He must mark the time till he reaches adulthood and can begin his ministry. One can almost hear him already muttering, "Faithless generation! How long must I stay with you? How long am I to put up with you?" (Mark 9:19).

By the way, Strauss and G. A. Wells[2] both suggest that this story presupposes no annunciation or miraculous Nativity stories, since such preparation would make it implausible (whether in real life or in fictional narrative) for Mary and Joseph to be so surprised at finding Jesus in the temple. But there are two responses to this. First, the dim-wittedness of the parents is simply a compositional theme. It is going to be there for the sake of the buildup to the climax whether it makes sense outside the bounds of the anecdote or not. Second, Jesus rebukes his parents precisely because they *should have known* he would be about his Father's business, not in the video arcade and the comic-book store where they had wasted three days looking for him. So some previous acquaintance with his divine origins is presupposed.

Raymond E. Brown is surely correct to see the story of the Cana wine miracle in John 2:1–10 as another stray bit of infancy gospel material. John has simply placed it in a chronologically later context and inserted the disciples (superfluously) into the story (at verse 2, "with his disciples") as a tack pinning it in place.[3] Note again the ineptitude of the adults and how the divine youth gets them out of a tight spot, just as he saved Joseph from having to waste that miscut beam. "On the third day there was a marriage at Cana in Galilee, and the mother of Jesus was there. Jesus, too, had been invited to the wedding. . . . When the wine gave out, the mother of Jesus said, 'They have no wine.' And Jesus said to her, 'O woman, what have you to do with me? My hour is not yet come.' His mother said to the servants, 'Do whatever he tells you.' Now six stone water jars stood there, ready for the Jewish rites of purification, each having a capacity of twenty to thirty gallons. Jesus said to them, 'Fill those jars with water.' And they filled them to the brim. He said to them, 'Next, dip some out and take it to the master of ceremonies.' So they took it. The master of ceremonies tasted the water, now changed to wine. He did not know where it had come from, though the servants knew. So he called over the bridegroom and said, 'Usually one serves the good wine first and puts out the cheap wine once people have drunk enough not to know the difference. But you have kept the good wine until now!'"

Adults have mismanaged things, like Joseph in the carpenter shop. Jesus saves the day, even though the "salvation" is again merely a matter of convenience. But that is the premise of this whole subgenre of miracle stories: Jesus is not fully engaged in public ministry yet. So his powers, which piety cannot imagine him ever having been without, must have been spent on domestic tasks.

We can be sure this story belonged to a larger catalogue of them because Mary is quite confident that whatever the problem, her son can take care of it. Readers of John 2:3, "They have no wine," must have often asked themselves, "What can she have expected Jesus to do about it?" That's just the point. She expects him to do something, to save the situation. She does not know exactly what he will say to do, but she knows he will cook something up. (In the same way Zeller[4] pointed out how Acts 9:38 must be legendary, as it presupposes a conception of Peter as a miracle-working superman whom one may call to "fix" an annoying death among the brethren!) Again, the comedy is apparent: Jesus dislikes to waste his power on such trivialities, waiting instead for his proper hour to come (whether the cross or his adult ministry). His brusque words betray his pique. And yet he cannot resist his mother, as she knows, sweeping his irritated remark aside: "Do whatever he tells you."

Wunderkind stories are nothing new to Hellenistic Judaism, and there are other stories that supply ample background for the child prodigy tales of Jesus. The longer rescension of Ignatius's Epistle to the Magnesians (3:16–19) preserves Jewish tradition about the virtues of various Old Testament worthies at the age of twelve years, the same age as Jesus in Luke. "For the wise Daniel, at age twelve, became possessed of the divine Spirit, and he revealed the elders, who wore their gray hair in vain, as false accusers, and as desiring the beauty of another's wife. Samuel, too, when he was but a small child, rebuked Eli, who was ninety years of age, for honoring his son rather than God . . . Solomon also . . . becoming king at age twelve, rendered that awful and severe judgment in the case of the two women concerning their children."

Moses, like his latter-day counterpart, suffered the instruction of his elders but quickly surpassed them. Philo tells us that "young Moses had all kinds of teachers, one following another, some volunteering from the surrounding countries and the various districts of Egypt, and some being procured even from Greece by the inducements of large gifts. But in a short time he exceeded all their knowledge by the surpassing endowments of his own genius, so that everything he learned seemed instead to have been recollected. At the same time, he himself comprehended many difficult matters by virtue of his own genius" (*Life of Moses* 1.21).

Josephus tells much the same story. "Moses' understanding grew superior to his age, nay, far beyond that standard; and when he was instructed, he displayed greater quickness of apprehension than that characteristic for his age" (*Antiquities* 2.9.6). In fact, Josephus sang his own praises in much the same terms: "When I was a child, about fourteen years old, I was universally commended for my love of learning, on account of which the high priests and the chief men of the city frequently visited me in a group, to ask my opinion about the accurate understanding of points of the law" (*Life of Flavius Josephus* 2). Not likely.

With all these parallels, we may not be dealing with direct borrowing (though it is clear that Luke has the story of young Samuel in mind, since he has manifestly based Luke 2:52 directly on 1 Sam. 2:26: "Now the boy Samuel continued to grow both in stature and in favor with the Lord and with men"). But we have to think also of the law of biographical analogy. That is, the mythmaking imagination being what it is, proceeding from the same universal brain structure the world over, we can expect that the lives of heroes and saints will be glorified in essentially the same fashion in religion after religion, culture after culture. And this in fact is what we do find. In Arnold Schulman's 1971 memoir/study of Hindu seer Sathya Sai Baba, a contemporary miracle worker (since exposed as a sleight-of-hand artist!), we find another of these stories, parallel to Luke's. "One day, a number of teachers from the high school came to expose the boy. If he were in some way holy, as he claimed, he should have no trouble answering the questions they proposed to ask him. And so, for several hours they cross-examined him on Vedanta and philosophical matters. To their amazement, he not only answered all their questions but asked them questions they could not answer and then proceeded to tell them what the answers were. He also asked them to ask him questions, all speaking at the same time. After a few minutes of babble, which none of the witnesses present could understand, the boy proceeded to answer each question that had been shouted at him, taking each teacher, one by one, in turn."[5]

But, since this one actually stems from the lifetime of the subject of the story, do we not have here reliable historical reportage? And if so, is not the historical character of Luke's report of the twelve-year-old Jesus made more probable? No, because Schulman admits it was already too late to know for sure what actually happened: "For every story about Baba's childhood there are any number of conflicting stories and, at this point, the writer discovered, it is no longer possible to sift out the facts from the legend."[6]

SIBLINGS OF GOD

Did Jesus have brothers and sisters? This question was hotly contested long before, centuries before, the rise of historical criticism of the Bible. Protestants and Catholics debated this one, as had earlier factions in the ancient church, and though all shared the conviction that the Bible's statements on the subject were to be accepted, they could not agree on just what it said or what it meant. And even if we are asking deeper critical questions, we will have to start where they did. Does the New Testament at least *say* that Jesus had siblings?

Protestants like to point to two passages that seem to them effectively to establish that Jesus had siblings, Luke 2:7 and Matt. 1:24–25. Both seem to them to imply that Mary and Joseph had other children after Jesus' birth. Luke 2:7 reads: "And she gave birth to *her firstborn* son and wrapped him in swaddling bands, and placed him in a feeding-trough, because there was no vacancy for them in the inn." If Jesus was her firstborn son, Protestants reason, mustn't there have been others to follow? Actually, as Catholics reply, no. Not at all. Surely the point is the virginity of Mary: the emphasis is on the fact that she had not had any children *before* Jesus. What may or may not have happened subsequently is simply not an issue in this passage. And besides, we have a Roman tombstone from this period (5 B.C.E.) that commemorates poor Arsinoe: "In the pains of giving birth to a firstborn child, Fate brought me to the end of my life." She obviously did not have any more children, and the point of mentioning the status of the fatal child as first in order was to note that the mother had approached the otherwise happy prospect of childbirth oblivious of what might and did happen to her. She had had no previous difficulties to warn her. The Matthean text is no less equivocal in implication. "When Joseph awoke from sleep, he did as the angel of the Lord commanded him; he took his wife, but he did not know her *until* she had borne a son; and he called his name Jesus." Does Matthew mean somehow to tell us about the private life of Mary and Joseph after the birth of Jesus? Of course not. Again, the whole and only point is that *Jesus cannot* have been Joseph's son, not that *anyone else was*.

But since neither passage is concerned with events following the birth of Jesus, one can hardly say they militate against Jesus having had siblings, either. Are there passages that do address that issue? Mark 6:1–6 has Jesus return to his (unnamed) hometown to preach in the synagogue there. He impresses the crowd, who recognizes him as one of its own: "Is not this the carpenter, the son of Mary and brother of James and Joses and Judas and Simon, and are not his sisters here with us?" It is not surprising, given the pandemic chauvinism of the era, that we do not hear the number or names of the sisters. That the brothers are listed by name (and it is a *list*, not merely a mention) is significant, but we will have to return to that. For the moment it is enough to ask what relation these individuals are understood to bear to Jesus. It seems safe to say that any natural reading of the passage would yield the conclusion that these are the natural siblings of Jesus. Complications arise only if one brings to the text the theological assumption that Jesus cannot have had brothers and sisters, and many readers do just that. As anti-sexual asceticism began to prevail in Christian ethics of the second century, the pious began to shudder with revulsion at the very notion that Mary could ever have "known a man," even Joseph, even after the birth of Jesus. Mary was understood as a consecrated virgin not only before but after she gave birth to Jesus. If a standard of superior, virginal holiness was obtained among Christians, how could the mother of Jesus have adhered to anything lower? As the holiest of womankind, she, too, must have remained perpetually a virgin. And then she cannot have had those other children Mark mentions in 6:1–6 (and also in 3:31–32: "Your mother and your brothers are outside asking for you"). Of course it may be that the first advocates of Mary's perpetual virginity had never heard of this Markan text or the family arrangements implied in it; they weren't necessarily ignoring it. And, as we will see, it is possible, as Catholic interpreters maintain today, that the apparent references to the siblings of Jesus meant something else.

Catholic theologians have made various suggestions as to the relationship of James, Joses, and the others to Jesus. The most difficult is that they are intended as cousins of Jesus, and that the words "brothers" and "sisters" are stretched in meaning to imply kinfolk. But such usage was not common, and the suggestion amounts to saying that the words "brothers" and "sisters" cannot mean what they seem to mean. Less lexical violence is done if one adopts an alternative Catholic approach, that the siblings are stepbrothers and sisters of Jesus, being the natural sons of Joseph but not of Mary. According to the requisite scenario, we must understand Joseph as a much older man and a widower with a houseful of children, mentioned in Mark 6:1–6. He married young Mary to safeguard Jesus from the charge of illegitimacy, but the marriage was and remained a legal fiction.[7] Again, this arrangement is a reflection of the second- and third-century *virgines subintroductae*, or spiritual marriage partners who never had sex.[8] (They are discussed in the anachronistic and post-Pauline 1 Cor. 7.) The age difference would, as a bonus, account for Joseph not being mentioned in Mark 6. He is dead by this time. And by implication, Jesus would be the youngest of the family, not the oldest sibling, as Protestants picture him.

Though this sketch of family relationships would fit the text if it were true, that is quite different from saying the text really suggests it. That is, Mark nowhere suggests anything of the kind, and the picture he draws makes perfect sense without any such assumptions. The Catholic view might still be true, and Mark might have been unaware of the intricacies of the situation, which he would then have oversimplified. That is possible, but we still have to ask ourselves whether there is anything but second-century asceticism behind the reluctance to see real brothers and sisters behind the list of names in Mark 6. If it is only theological convenience that motivates the suggestion, then we might think twice before accepting the Catholic view as a historical reconstruction.

FRATERNAL FACTIONALISM

Sometimes the death of the founder of a religious community eventuates in a succession dispute: who has the right to succeed him as pontiff of the faithful? The successor may be entitled to the same degree of authority the founder had, or it may be a delegated, lesser authority, that of a vicar or caretaker. In either case, it is not unusual for conflict to emerge between partisans of the founder's relatives on the one hand and of his disciples on the other. It is one of the messiest aspects of what Max Weber called "the routinization of charisma,"[9] whereby the followers of a charismatic founder have to do the best they can to hold things together after the death of the leader. He was a tough act to follow, and no one can quite fill his shoes, so no one particular effort to claim to do so passes unchallenged. Islam, the Baha'i Faith, the Nation of Islam (Black Muslims), and the

Mormon Church (Latter-day Saints) all furnish us examples of such succession disputes. In Islam, the contest was over who should become caliph, political caretaker of the Islamic commonwealth. Some boosted the family of the Prophet Muhammad, Ali (his cousin, son-in-law, and adopted son) and, later, his daughter Fatima's descendants. Others supported the claims of the Prophet's Companions, his first and closest disciples: Abu Bekr, Umar, and Uthman. After uneasy coexistence during the reigns of the first three of these Companions, Ali's partisans rejoiced when Ali became caliph, but he was assassinated, and civil war ensued. The resulting schism bequeathed us Sunni Islam (loyal to the memory of the Companions) and Shi'a Islam (partisans, which is what "Shi'a" means, of the house of Ali).

When Mirza Ali Muhammad, the Bab (the Gate), was executed by Persian authorities (1847), who should have replaced him? The Azalis claimed the Bab had designated that his brother Subh-i-Azal should take over, but then surprisingly one of the disciples of the Bab, a man named Hussein Ali, called Bah'a'ullah (the Glory of God), stepped forth (1853) and announced that he had been divinely chosen as (no mere caretaker, but as) the next Manifestation of God like unto the Bab himself. Most Bab'is followed Bah'a'ullah, becoming Baha'is, but the Azalis still exist alongside them.

When the prophet Joseph Smith was martyred for his polygamous convictions, his church split over whether he should be succeeded by his son, Joseph Jr., or by a council of twelve apostles. Even today, the two mammoth denominations, the Church of Jesus Christ of Latter-day Saints (cleaving to the Twelve) and the Reorganized Church of Jesus Christ of Latter-day Saints (partisans of the prophet's progeny) grow side by side.

When Elijah Muhammad, recipient of the revelations of the divine incarnation master Farad, passed away, he left the reins of leadership in the hands of his son Wallace (later Wareeth Deen) Muhammad. The latter promptly began revising the eccentric doctrines of the sect toward greater compatibility with the tenets of Sunni Islam, whereupon Louis Farrakhan, an early disciple and evangelist for Elijah Muhammad, led a schism to return to the old ways, which were now being changed. The result is a lingering breach between the Bilalian Muslims or American Muslim Mission (led by the son) and the Nation of Islam (led by the disciple).

There are a number of hints here and there in the New Testament that imply such a succession dispute ensued upon the death of Jesus, leading to the establishment of at least two rival factions within early Jewish Christianity. The new religion soon passed over into Gentile country and culture, where it began to mutate into new forms and to face new questions. Pauline Christianity and Gnosticism were among the results, and the New Testament is mainly the product of this latter stage. So it is only in a glass darkly that we may try to discern the struggles and the tensions of that earlier, more Jewish phase. We have no clear picture of those days, so any reconstruction is bound to be tentative and provisional. That said, however, it does seem that a number of New Testament passages make the most sense as fossils of an internecine struggle between two Jewish-Christian factions, one championing the claims of the Twelve (companions and disciples of Jesus in his lifetime), the other partisans of the Heirs of Jesus (his surviving relatives, the Holy Family). Let us try to chart the trajectory of each through the New Testament, and then we will be in a position to evaluate the scanty gospel traditions that bear on the relatives of Jesus.

1 Cor. 9:5 argues that Paul ought to be considered a genuine apostle deserving of the prerogatives of others in that category: "Are we not entitled to be accompanied by a sister as wife [again, celibate, spiritual marriage] like the other apostles and the brothers of the Lord and Cephas?" If these "brothers of the Lord" are intended as the same characters listed in Mark 6:3, then we can see they had attained to an exalted state in the higher circles of early Christianity. It would then make sense of the fact that Mark 6:3 does not simply toss off a reference to Jesus' brothers still living in town but goes to the trouble of naming them, listing them. We begin to take the hint that the list functions like that of the Twelve in Mark 3:16–19. Each list is a miniature canon, intended as much to exclude some names as to include others. (Paul, Barnabas, and Apollos, for instance, do not make it into any of the lists, though in the Manichean Psalm-Book Paul actually becomes one of the Twelve, and in the Western text of Acts, Barnabas becomes a runner-up to replace Judas Iscariot.) This implies the lists might have been somewhat fluid at an earlier stage, with various factions venturing to add names of this or that favorite, to increase the clout of favorite apostles and the congregations they founded. The promulgation of the lists was an attempt to stop this. Perhaps as a result of the earlier fluidity, there is some confusion as to which of the two categories certain names properly belong in. For example, the trio James, John, and Peter familiar from the Gospels would seem to be the same as the three Jerusalem Pillars (see below) James, John, and Cephas, but the latter James is also supposed to be "the Lord's brother," and many exegetes have understood John son of Zebedee with his brother James to be cousins of Jesus! Thomas "the Twin" was popularly imagined to be Jesus' brother Judas (Acts of Thomas 1.1, Gospel of Thomas colophon, Book of Thomas the Contender 1.1 call him "Judas Thomas"), which would place him in both lists. Similarly, Philip, one of the Twelve, has often been confused with the Hellenist Philip, one of the Seven (Acts 6:5).

Besides the bare list itself, there are extrabiblical traditions, albeit fragmentary and equivocal, that the Jerusalem church was led by these brothers (sometimes, in the interest of Mariology, made cousins of Jesus). James led the church until he was martyred by the priest Ananas. Simeon bar Cleophas (Simon) then took over and was crucified at the (symbolic) age of 120 (the supposed age of Moses and Johannon ben Zakkai when they died), to be followed by Jude. Another Pauline text, Gal. 1:18–19, 2:9 ff., depicts James as a brother of the Lord and as an apostle along with Cephas, as in 1 Corinthians: "Then after three years

I went up to Jerusalem to consult Cephas, and I stayed with him fifteen days. But I saw none of the other apostles except James the Lord's brother"; "And when they perceived the grace that was given to me, James and Cephas and John, who were reputed to be pillars, gave to me and Barnabas the right hand of fellowship."

1 Cor. 15:5–7 offers a traditional list of Christian leaders commissioned as such by resurrection appearances vouchsafed them by the Risen Jesus (another canonical list, excluding, for example, Mary Magdalene). The list again classifies James as among the first rank of apostolic leaders, though, pointedly, not one of the Twelve: "And that he appeared to Cephas, then to the Twelve. Then he appeared to more than five hundred brothers at one time. . . . Then he appeared to James, then to all the apostles." As Adolf von Harnack argued long ago,[10] this list itself appears to be a patchwork of snippets that originally constituted lists or parts of lists of resurrection-commission credentials used by different, rival parties. The assertion of an appearance "to James, then to all the apostles" must originally have served as a counter to the claim that "he appeared to Cephas, then to the twelve," each of these men having been championed by their partisans as Prince of Apostles, one the brother of Jesus, the other the chief disciple of Jesus.

Another, fuller version of the appearance to James is preserved in the Gospel according to the Hebrews: "And when the Lord had given the linen cloth to the servant of the priest, he went to James and appeared to him. For James had sworn that he would not eat bread from that hour in which he had drunk the cup of the Lord until he should see him risen from among them that sleep. And immediately . . . he took the bread, blessed it and broke it and gave it to James the Just and said to him, 'My brother, eat your bread, for the Son of man is risen from among them that sleep'" (Jerome *De viris inlutribus* 2). In this scene, Jesus has appeared to Malchus or some other functionary of the high priest, giving him his burial shroud (possibly an etiological story for a cherished relic). Next, he apprehends James, startling him from out his fasting vigil. James, we must gather, had been present at the Last Supper and swore, like Jesus himself, to abstain till the resurrection: "Amen: I say to you, I shall not drink again of the fruit of the vine until that day when I drink it new in the kingdom of God" (Mark 14:25). The pledge must have begun as a piece of Christian apocalyptic asceticism, an oath taken by radical Christians, then placed into the mouth of Jesus, where it makes no real sense: how much chance is he going to have for another glass of wine before he gets arrested? Transferred to James, as in the Gospel according to the Hebrews, it at least makes some sense: James is going on a hunger strike till Jesus rises, a radical statement of faith that it is going to happen. Thus, James is seen here as a great saint and devotee of his brother even before the cross. One commonly hears the remark that it must have been Jesus' appearance to his brother that converted him from the unfaith attested in John 7, but this is a lame harmonization of two mutually exclusive views of the brother of Jesus: was he a believer or wasn't he? His partisans said he was, his enemies said he wasn't.

James appears in a number of the Nag Hammadi texts (Apocryphon of

James, 1 Apocalypse of James, 2 Apocalypse of James) as a unique revealer and apostle of Jesus, sometimes as the leader of the apostles, the same function performed symbolically by the character Thomas in other texts. But in one of these, the Gospel according to Thomas, where Thomas has been proclaimed by Jesus as his own spiritual equal, Thomas still yields to James as leader of the movement: "The disciples said to Jesus, 'We know that you will leave us. Who is it who shall be great over us?' Jesus said, 'Wherever you have come from, you will go to James the Righteous, for whose sake heaven and earth came into being" (saying 12). "Wherever you have come from, go to James" probably refers to the practice of early Jewish-Christian missionaries who filed a report with James about their activities upon returning to Jerusalem, which is just what Paul is shown doing in Acts 15:4, 12; cf. Gal. 2:1, 6–10.

Julius Africanus imagined the blood relations of Jesus making a tour of Palestine (maybe farther), boasting of their own messianic connections. "For the relatives of our Lord, according to the flesh, whether to display their own illustrious origin, or simply to show the fact, but at any rate adhering strictly to the truth, have also handed down the following accounts . . . [Herod the Great had the genealogical records at Jerusalem burnt so as to cancel the advantage of old and renowned Jewish aristocrats over him, an upstart Idumean outsider among Jews.] A few, however, of the careful, either remembering the names, or having it in their power in some other way, by means of copies, to have private records of their own, gloried in the idea of preserving the memory of their noble extraction. Of these were the above-mentioned persons, called *desposynoi*, on account of their affinity to the family of the Saviour. These coming from Nazara and Cochaba, villages of Judea, to the other parts of the world, explained the aforesaid genealogy from the book of daily records [i.e., the biblical Book of Chronicles], as faithfully as possible" (Eusebius *Ecclesiastical History* 1.7).[11]

But I believe Africanus has fallen victim to a case of mistaken identity. For one thing, he cites these alleged relatives of Jesus as if they held the key to harmonizing the genealogies of Matthew and Luke, when the bit of tradition he passes on has no evident connection with such apologetics. For another, I think he has erred in associating these individuals with the family of Jesus. He takes *desposynoi* to mean "those belonging to the Lord," even though this word does not properly refer to human beings, only to material possessions. Alternately, we know the word was sometimes used simply as synonymous to "Lords," which is probably what it originally meant in this case. Another thing: the use of genealogies stretching back into the Old Testament, not to mention the Book of Chronicles itself, is utterly irrelevant to itinerant would-be aristocrats trading on their supposed connections to Jesus of Nazareth. The trick would be to demonstrate one's connection to *him*, not to King David, unless of course one sought to prove that one were oneself the Messiah. No, Africanus had heard of a group of people precisely like Acts's "Seven sons of a Jewish high priest named Sceva," who traveled about performing miracles for the gullible (Acts 20:13–16), or the

Jewish fortune-teller described by Juvenal: "a palsied Jewess, parking her haybox outside, comes round soliciting alms in a breathy whisper. She knows, and can interpret, the Laws of Jerusalem: a high-priestess-under-the-trees, a faithful mediator of Heaven on earth. She too fills her palm, but more sparingly: Jews will sell you whatever dreams you like for a few small coppers" (*Satire* 6.542–48).[12]

Jewish mountebanks took advantage of the mystique Judaism had as an attractive "Oriental religion" in the Hellenistic world, sometimes claiming ancient and venerable priestly descent, which is how they supposedly had access to the ancient mysteries they claimed to trade in. If Africanus's *desposynoi* did denote "those belonging to the Lord," as most scholars say, then certainly it meant, in this case, those serving before the face of the Lord as high priests (hence the references to 1 Chronicles's priestly genealogies), fictitious though the claim must have been. We can imagine their schtick: sent wandering by the destruction of the Temple, these elite thaumaturges now made their acumen available to the masses, much like the "Hebrew" charismatic medicine-show men discussed by Dieter Georgi in *The Opponents of Paul in Second Corinthians*. And this business about Herod torching the Jerusalem genealogies? It is a fictive claim precisely analogous to the frequent claims among Islamic jurists to possess variant readings of the Koran on which to ground their proposed *hadith*. Of course, Uthman had (supposedly) destroyed all variant texts so their claims could never be corroborated—conveniently![13] It is likewise with the bogus priestly credentials of Sceva and his sons and their latter-day counterparts in Africanus, with their imaginary linkages to the hieratical genealogies of Chronicles.

But there remains enough New Testament evidence to secure the picture drawn long ago by Harnack and Ethelbert Stauffer of a "caliphate of James"[14] as one pole of Jewish-Christian leadership, as opposed to that of Peter and the Twelve. It would make sense to understand the gospel depictions of the relatives of Jesus in this light.

Mark and John tend to abuse the relatives of Jesus, presumably because they rejected the leadership claims from this group. Pauline texts damn these Pillars with faint praise ("And from those who were reputed to be something—what they were makes no difference to me; God shows no partiality" Gal. 2:6; "James and Cephas and John who were reputed to be pillars" Gal. 2:9). Mark and John make their polemical points (or the traditional tales they used did) by telling pointed stories. We saw in the previous chapter how Mark (in 3:19b–22, 31–35) reversed the point of a story that had earlier depicted the family of Jesus suggesting to him, as Jethro had to Moses, that he ease his workload by appointing assistants, in this case the Twelve. This implied the subordination of the Twelve to the Heirs in the politics of the early church, though it is at least a platform of coexistence. In the first version, the concern of the relatives of Jesus was similar to that of the mother of Sathya Sai Baba: "Why don't they leave him alone? Look how they make him work. He doesn't sleep, he doesn't eat enough. All they care about is themselves."[15] But Mark has turned it around, with the result that Jesus' choice of the Twelve owes nothing to his relatives; therefore neither do the Twelve. And the Heirs come off looking like obtuse obstacles to Jesus' mission, thinking him devil-possessed and insane.

Mark, not a Jewish Christian, was no friendlier to the Twelve, whom he vilifies even more seriously than he does the Heirs. Thus, he is not taking sides in the original conflict. But as a Gentile non-Torah Christian of some sort, he repudiates both leadership factions of his Jewish-Christian rivals. Mark's attitude is "A plague on both your houses!" The story he twisted, subordinating the Twelve to the Heirs, could be viewed as a compromise document once circulated in order to facilitate the coexistence of the two Jewish-Christian factions, much in the manner of the list taken over into 1 Cor. 15:5–7, where, as Harnack argued, the formerly competing James and Cephas appearance-assertions have been harmonized into one ecumenical creed, albeit a bit bumpily.

According to John 7:1–7, "His brothers did not believe in him." Mocking him as a limelight-seeking charlatan, they show themselves loyal members of that world of spiritual darkness from which Jesus has redeemed the Twelve (John 17:9, 14, 16). On the cross, Jesus entrusts his aging mother not to his brothers, surely available to take care of her, but to one of his disciples (John 19:25–27). If, as seems hard to deny, we are in any measure to see the church symbolized here by the mother of Jesus, this scene certainly rebuffs the claims of the relatives of Jesus as custodians of the church in favor of the Twelve (or some faction therein!).

Matthew pretty much ignores the family of Jesus except as characters in the birth story. He does soften Mark's story of Jesus rejecting his relatives in favor of those who do the will of God (Matt. 12:46–50) by omitting the reason for their visit (that is, deeming him mad), but he does this only because of the virgin birth, which he sees is incompatible with it, not because he especially wants to spare them embarrassment. In fact, Matthew makes his advocacy of Petrine claims to leadership crystal clear (16:16–19).

For Luke, Jesus' relatives are truly the Holy Family with a definite right to wield authority in the church, nor is this at the expense of the Twelve. True to his catholicizing agenda, whereby he ever seeks to paper over the cracks in the early church, Luke shows the two factions sharing power in Acts. Luke has Peter serving as the initial leader after Jesus' ascension, but after his miraculous escape from the murderous designs of Herod Agrippa I, Peter flees Jerusalem and is replaced at the helm by James. The way for James's ascendancy has already been prepared by Luke's Pentecost scene, which explicitly includes the mother, brothers, and sisters in the Upper Room alongside the Twelve, no coincidence to be sure. As far as Luke is concerned, or at least the way he wants us to think of it, Jesus' relatives were among his disciples all along. In his version (Luke 8:19–21) of the story where Jesus repudiates his family, Luke not only omits the madness business because of its conflict with the virgin birth story (as Matthew does) but also cuts out the ironic words "'Who are my mother and my brothers?'

And looking around at those who sat about him, he said, 'Here are my mother and brothers.'" The resulting text of Luke seems to make Jesus commend his physical mother and brothers standing by outside as themselves being "those who hear the word of God and do it" (cf. Luke 1:28). The element of contrast between the two groups has been completely eliminated. Both are disciples. Luke thus represents the same sort of reconciling perspective we saw in the pre-Markan story of the choosing of the Twelve.

In any of this, do we find any reliable information about the family of Jesus? I fear we do not, with the bare exception that there were relatives who vied with other leadership factions for authority in the emerging Christian communities. Indeed, this scenario is the strongest factor anchoring the Jesus figure into contemporary history. If he left relatives behind, occasioning a succession dispute, he must have been as historical as Joseph Smith, the Bab, Elijah Muhammad, or the prophet Muhammad, whatever else we do or do not know about him. But is it possible that the faction of the Heirs did not have a historical, flesh-and-blood link with a historical Jesus?

THESE MY BRETHREN

As we saw in the previous chapter, certain apparently historical data in the gospel life of Jesus seem to have originated as historicized versions of phrases or titles that originally had an entirely different meaning: was Jesus from Nazareth, or was he a Nazorean? Was his father named Joseph, or is that a vestige of a Galilean messianism that saw Jesus as Messiah ben Joseph (from the tribe named for the Patriarch Joseph)? In the same way, it is entirely possible that references to the "brothers" of Jesus, or of the Lord, originally meant something other than flesh-and-blood siblings.

First, the brothers of Jesus may originally have been understood as missionaries, perhaps a special group of them. The parable of the Sheep and the Goats (Matt. 24:31–46) warns of the terrible fate of those among the nations who do not extend adequate charity toward "my brethren," and these appear to be preachers of the gospel (cf. Matt. 24:14), not the homeless, as contemporary preaching would have it. Similarly, the itinerant missioners of the Johannine community were called "the brothers" (3 John 3, 5, 10). With these passages in mind, take another look at 1 Cor. 9:5, "Do we not have the right to be accompanied by a sister as wife, like the other apostles, and the brothers of the Lord, and Cephas?" Similarly, Gal. 1:19, "I saw none of the other apostles except James the brother of the Lord," which might mean to include James in both categories of missionaries, perhaps even implying the two groups overlapped. Being a brother of the Lord was like being an apostle. It may well be that the list of names of the brothers of Jesus in Mark 6:3 was originally the (or a) list of these particular missionaries. In that case, to make them a group of actual siblings of Jesus would have been another subsequent spinning out of a theological datum into a biographical one, a metaphor being literalized.

If that possibility were to prove out, what about all the factional disputes between the Twelve and the Heirs? Actually, little need change. For, though we would no longer be reckoning with a succession dispute between the Twelve and a group of Jesus' blood relatives, we can still readily imagine strife between two factions, one having chosen the number of the twelve tribes to distinguish them, the other choosing for themselves the image of brethren of the Messiah (cf. Heb. 2:11, "That is why he is unashamed to call them brothers, saying, 'I will proclaim your name to my brothers; amid the congregation I will praise you'"). By the time of Mark's and John's gospels, the historicization would have been accomplished, the original meaning no longer understood. Another possibility is that some in the early church may have taken advantage of the historicization (or caused it!) precisely in order to trace their own lineage (spuriously) to King Jesus. Such fictive claims would be no different in principle from the tendentious claims of apostolic succession made by this or that bishop and church in the second and third centuries.

Another neglected possibility for understanding the status of the "brothers" of Jesus, especially James the Just, is that the designation denotes the attempt to merge or reconcile two disparate or rival movements by means of fictively making their figureheads brothers. As Hermann Gunkel pointed out long ago,[16] this was a common technique of ancient "history" writing, whereby, for instance, the confederacy of twelve Hebrew tribes was associated together by making their tribal names into personal names of imaginary eponymous ancestors, all of whom are made brothers, then positing the mythic hero Jacob/Israel as their common eponymous ancestor. The nations of Ammon and Moab, traditional enemies of Israel, are nonetheless associated with Israel in Israelite folklore by tracing them back to (imaginary) bastard, inbred sons, Ben-Ammi and Me-Ab, of Lot (Gen. 19:30–38), himself linked to Abraham for this very purpose by being made Abraham's nephew (Gen. 12:5). Such fictive ancestral linkages were made when trade or political relations had to be established between formerly hostile groups.

New Testament scholars commonly recognize the same phenomenon in the case of Luke's making John the Baptist, originally a wholly separate historical figure with no connection to Jesus at all, into the herald, then actually the very cousin of Jesus. The point is to subordinate the figurehead of the John the Baptist sect to that of the Jesus sect, especially since it is the fetus John who defers to the zygote Jesus (Luke 1:41), not the other way around (cf. Matt. 3:14). It seems quite likely that James, around whom a separate hagiographic legend revolves (see Robert Eisenman's great book *James the Brother of Jesus*),[17] was the founder of a competing Jewish sect, perhaps the sect who originated the Dead Sea Scrolls. James the Just may have been, as Eisenman claims, the "Essene"

Teacher of Righteousness. The second-century Jewish Christian historian, Hegesippus, in the fifth book of his *Commentaries* (reproduced in Eusebius *Ecclesiastical History* 2.23), tells us how James was some sort of high priest allowed into the Inner Sanctum of the Jerusalem temple, that he prayed day and night for his people till he had thick calluses on his knees. He wore only linen and was called "Oblias," the bulwark, meaning that Jerusalem was safe as long as his holy presence lingered there. And the Jewish authorities who martyred him had no idea of his having any Christian allegiance (which, I am suggesting, like John the Baptist, he did not have). Just as John and Luke (see the next chapter, "Jesus and John the Baptist") seem to be aiming some remarks at members of the John the Baptist sect, trying to refute their claims and/or to entice them to abandon John's sect and come over to Jesus', there may have once been an effort to co-opt the sect of James. To make James the Just the brother of Jesus was very likely the same sort of maneuver as making John the Baptist the cousin of Jesus.

But does not Josephus also, independently, call James "the brother of Jesus called Christ"? There is no way to know, since, whenever Josephus overlaps New Testament subject matter, there is always the likelihood of Christian interpolation. Josephus's account of the martyrdom of James parallels the versions given in Hegesippus, as reproduced by Eusebius (*Ecclesiastical History* 2.23), and in the Nag Hammadi text 2 Apocalypse of James. Is the similarity enough to lead us to posit a Christian origin for the Josephus passage? Who knows? And besides, Josephus himself is plenty late enough for the trick to have been performed and forgotten. He may have followed the then generally accepted assumption that James was literally the brother of Jesus.

So did Jesus have brothers and sisters? We cannot know for sure.

THOSE MISSING YEARS

We have already seen how early Christian imagination felt impelled to fill the space between Jesus' Nativity and his maturity by creating a raft of divine child stories. These, in the form available to us in the Infancy Gospels, have been made to end at age twelve, the age of Jesus in Luke's story of Jesus in the temple. But that left the gap between age twelve and Jesus' first public appearance as a preacher at around the age of thirty (a figure that comes solely from Luke 3:23). Over the centuries, there have been various attempts to fill in that blank as well, as legend-mongers have sent the young man Jesus to Egypt, to be initiated into ancient mysteries and magic; to Britain, with his uncle, Joseph of Arimathea (who, according to the same legends, would return there with the Holy Grail some years afterward); and to India, Persia, and Tibet, to learn the ways of various yogis and mahatmas. (These modern legends must be distinguished from still others that have Jesus traveling far and wide after his resurrection.)

Of these "missing years" stories, the only one worth dealing with here is that underlying Nicholas Notovitch's *Unknown Life of Jesus Christ*, since this one claims an ancient documentary basis, and it has its partisans even today. In 1887, Notovitch, a Russian Jew and a war correspondent (and possibly a spy), visited the city of Leh, capital of the district of Ladakh, a district on the border of India and Tibet. He had a toothache and sought treatment at a Moravian mission station there. But his imagination got the better of him, and in 1894, his book told a new and much improved version of the story. Now it seemed he had visited the Tibetan lamasery (monastery) of Hemis (also spelled Himis). Here he mentioned folk legends he had picked up about a prophet named Issa, who sounded strikingly like Jesus. He was informed, he said, that the Hemis monastery itself housed a two-volume manuscript called *The Life of Saint Issa*! He hesitated to ask for access to the sacred book but announced he would return. This happened sooner than expected, however, as he fell from his horse and broke his leg. Carried back to the monastery, he was able to arrange to have *Saint Issa* read aloud and translated for him as he recuperated. As the story unfolded, his initial suspicions were confirmed: this could be nothing less than a hitherto-unknown chapter in the career of Jesus! He listened carefully and made copious notes. Reorganizing much of the material to make it suitable for Western readers, he finally produced *The Unknown Life of Jesus Christ*, and the book created an international furor.

The book did not escape the scrutiny of scholars. For one thing, Notovitch could offer no manuscript for examination, only an excuse for lacking one (he could not take it from the monastery). The great Orientalist Max Müller, editor of the epoch-making Sacred Books of the East series of translated Eastern scriptures, took an interest in the *Unknown Life*, unfortunately for Notovitch. He pointed out that such an honored work, as Notovitch made it, would inevitably have been included in the great canon lists of Tibetan books, the *Kanjur* and the *Tanjur*—but it wasn't. It is as if Notovitch had claimed a certain biblical book described the Buddha, but then there turned out to be no such book in the Bible!

Plus, Notovitch's frame story itself smacked too much of the legendary, the fictive. For the Russian maintained that the *Life of Saint Issa* was first compiled when Jewish merchants, having journeyed to India, told the recent news of Jesus' fiery preaching and crucifixion in Judea. By a Dickensian stroke of luck, the hearers of this tale just happened to include the very Asians who had themselves met Jesus in India a few years before! And these people were somehow certain that this Jesus was the same as the Issa whom they had known. Worse yet, Müller shared a letter (dated June 29, 1894) from an English woman who had visited Leh in Ladakh, including the Hemis lamasery, where she checked out Notovitch's story. It happened that, according to the abbot, "There is not a single word of truth in the whole story! There has been no Russian here. No one has been taken into the Seminary for the past fifty years with a broken leg! There is no life of Christ there at all!"[18]

If that weren't enough, two years later, Professor J. Archibald Douglas of Agra visited the Hemis monastery, near his university, and interviewed the abbot, reading him Notovitch's *Unknown Life*. The abbot was outraged at the hoax and asked why such crimes as Notovitch had perpetrated could not be punished! As abbot for the past fifteen years, he knew no one had been given shelter with a broken leg, and as a lama for forty-two years, he could attest there was no such document as Notovitch claimed to have used.

After Müller's attack, Notovitch began to backpedal, changing his story in the preface of the 1895 edition. This time it seemed that there had been no single two-volume work as he had first claimed, but that he had assembled his *Unknown Life* from fragmentary notices scattered among many Tibetan scrolls. This didn't help when Douglas's revelations appeared a year later. He was exposed as a fraud, and that was the end of it—for a while.

Swami Abhedananda (a disciple of the great Vedanta sage and mystic Ramakrishna) had read Notovitch's book and determined to find the truth of the matter. He was an admirer of Jesus but skeptical of Notovitch's account. So in 1922 he, too, traveled to Hemis. In the late 1970s, Dick and Janet Bock (devotees of Sathya Sai Baba) traveled to India and interviewed Swami Prajnananda, a disciple of Swami Abhedananda, now dead, who declared that his master "found the scrolls and he translated all the writings, all the life incidents of the Christ. He narrated those incidents in his book 'Kashmiri O Tibetti.'"[19] "Years afterwards he inquired but they said the scrolls were no longer there. I also requested to see the scrolls, but there is nothing. There are no scrolls. They have been removed, by whom we do not know."[20]

But this is not quite what Swami Abhedananda said in his book, translated into English as *Journey into Kashmir and Tibet* in 1987. There we read that "he requested to be allowed to see the book. . . . The lama who was acting as our guide took a manuscript from the shelf and showed it to the Swami. He said that it was an exact translation of the original manuscript which was lying in the monastery of Marbour near Lhasa. The original manuscript [as per Notovitch] is in Pali, while the manuscript preserved in Himis is in Tibetan. It consists of fourteen chapters and two hundred twenty-four couplets (*slokas*). The Swami got some portion of the manuscript translated with the help of the lama attending on him."[21] The excerpt that follows closely parallels, though not exactly, the corresponding section of Notovitch's book, also included in full as an appendix. It reads as if it might be a summary or abridgment of Notovitch. Note that in *Journey into Kashmir and Tibet*, we read not that Swami Abhedananda himself translated the text but that he managed to get someone to translate for him from a Tibetan text he could not read. And note that the Saint Issa gospel is once again a scroll, a single document, a version of the story that Notovitch himself had since abandoned!

Nicholas Roerich, a Theosophist and painter whose evocative work has its own museum today in New York City, and whose canvases influenced H. P. Lovecraft (see especially his novella *At the Mountains of Madness*), visited central Asia in search of the lost city of Shamballah and other mysteries. In the 1920s he, too, visited Ladakh and later (1925) recorded what he claimed were gleanings from popular tales about Saint Issa as well as related material from a fifteen-hundred-year-old Tibetan manuscript (too young by some four hundred years to be Notovitch's manuscript). But, as Per Beskow[22] notes, the texts Roerich quotes are simply an abbreviated set of verses from Notovitch and another set from *The Aquarian Gospel of Jesus the Christ*, a 1908 "channeled" life of Jesus, inspired by Notovitch, written by Levi Dowling (Leo W. Dowling).[23]

In 1926, a reprint edition of Notovitch's *Unknown Life* stirred up the same old furor among a credulous public that knew not Müller and Douglas. Five years later, Edgar J. Goodspeed wrote an invaluable book called *Strange New Gospels*[24] and outlined the refutations so as to put the matter to rest a second time.

In 1939, Dr. Elisabeth Caspari, a member of the Mazdaznan sect,[25] having journeyed into Tibet with some friends, attended a festival at the Hemis lamasery. One day during their stay, "the librarian and two other monks approached the ladies carrying three objects. Madame Caspari recognized them as Buddhist books made of sheets of parchment sandwiched between two pieces of wood and wrapped in brocades—green and red and blue seeded with gold. With great reverence, the librarian unwrapped one of the books and presented the parchments to Mrs. Caspari: 'These books say your Jesus was here!' . . . Mrs. Caspari tucked her precious treasure away in her memory, only volunteering it many years later at a Summit University Forum interview after having heard [apparently for the first time] of the beautiful verses about Jesus copied by Nicholas Notovitch from ancient Tibetan manuscripts at the monastery of Himis."[26]

It remains quite clear that Notovitch's *Unknown Life of Jesus* was a hoax. It is proof enough of this that Notovitch, intimidated by Max Müller's attack, backed down and changed his story, pulling the rug out from under his subsequent defenders, who were apparently ignorant of his revisionism. And the vehement denials of the original Hemis abbot echo loud and clear. So what are we to make of the testimonies and assertions of Swami Abhedananda, Nicholas Roerich, and Mrs. Caspari? First, following Per Beskow, we must conclude Roerich's literary imagination ran away with him, especially since we can actually identify his unnamed sources. His is no independent corroboration. In the cases of Swami Abhedananda and Mrs. Caspari, we are not even dealing with people who claim to have read the manuscript! Both were shown impressive volumes that they could not read, and someone else assured them that it was the Notovitch manuscript (or something corresponding to it). The solution is simple: the monks of Hemis had become familiar with Notovitch's book through Douglas's efforts to debunk it, and in later years, some of them told visitors what they wanted to hear, actually reading or paraphrasing from Notovitch's hoax-text itself. Even though Swami Abhedananda initially feared Notovitch's story was too good to be true, it is obvious that, if true, it would have delighted him, given his Vedanta-inspired esteem for Jesus. This would be no less true for Mrs. Caspari, a member of a pseudo-Zoroastrian syncretic religion that also happened to cherish the notion of Jesus having sojourned in India.[27] A handful of Tibetan monks, welcoming a theological agenda that made Christianity a derivative subset of Buddhism (Jesus having been trained in Tibet, after all), were happy to take up Notovitch's ball and run with it. Though not for long, since, as we have seen, some years later, Abhedananda's disciple was told there were no such books to be found.

But a good hoax will not go down easily, and the Notovitch gospel began to appear again under the auspices of New Age publishers in the 1980s. The text is reprinted, for example, in Janet Bock's *The Jesus Mystery: Of Lost Years and Unknown Travels* (1980) and Elizabeth Clare Prophet et al., *The Lost Years of Jesus: Documentary Evidence of Jesus' 17-Year Journey to the East* (1987). Paramahansa Yogananda's Self-Realization Fellowship, the Sathya Sai Baba movement, the Hare Krishna sect, and the Church Universal and Triumphant (or Summit Lighthouse), all Eastern and/or New Age groups, accept the Notovitch gospel as authentic, because it seems to them to incorporate Jesus into their own religious system. There is a precise parallel in the widespread Muslim embrace of the spurious late-medieval Gospel according to Barnabas, which makes Jesus the forerunner to Muhammad as the Messiah. For Muslims, this is the true and original gospel because it comes in mighty handy. (Even Notovitch eventually made it into Islam after a fashion, since his *Unknown Life of Jesus Christ* seems to have inspired Leo Dowling's *Aquarian Gospel*, which in turn was pirated to become the main substance of Noble Drew Ali's *Holy Koran of the Moorish Science Temple!*)[28]

IF HE WERE A CARPENTER

Most mainstream scholars believe that during the unrecorded years, Jesus was simply plying his inherited trade as a village carpenter, and much is then inferred about his social status, possible literacy, and class interests. But whence is the belief derived, and how firmly? The notion of Jesus working with hammer and saw comes from one place: the now-familiar story of Jesus preaching in his hometown synagogue (never mind that archaeologists have failed to provide any evidence for there having been Galilean synagogues in the first century). The crucial element is found in Mark 6:2–3, and again, somewhat revised, in Matt. 13:54–56. Mark has the hometown crowd exclaim, "Is not this the carpenter, the son of Mary?" Matthew, with some manuscripts of Mark, has them say, "Is not this the son of the carpenter and Mary?" If Matthew and the similar Markan manuscripts should happen to preserve the original wording, the evidence for Jesus as a carpenter would disappear at once. But even if the Markan reading, "Is not this the carpenter?" is original, we still do not necessarily have an indication of Jesus' day job.

As Vermes has pointed out,[29] Mark and Matthew may both be alluding to a contemporary scribal proverb. When the scribes found themselves stumped on a particularly difficult Torah passage, they would exclaim, "This is something that no carpenter, son of carpenters, can explain"; "There is no carpenter, nor a carpenter's son, to explain it." In such a context, "carpenter" is a metaphor for "skilled expert," in this case, skilled in expounding Scripture. And Mark's story provides exactly this sort of context, since the scene is one of synagogue preaching, which took the form of the speaker commenting on the daily Scripture lection. The crowd praises Jesus as a gifted interpreter, which is how John took it. In his version, he has the hearers say, "How is it this man has learning, when he has never studied?" (John 7:15). In Mark and Matthew, for Jesus to be hailed as either a carpenter or a carpenter's son seems intended as parallel in meaning to the immediately adjacent phrase, "Where did he get this wisdom?" And thus vanishes our sole basis for thinking we knew the trade of Jesus in Nazareth. The carpenter from Nazareth may have been a literalizing, historicizing transformation of the Scripture scholar from the Nazorean sect.

It is interesting that another ancient source, the third-century *Book of Baruch* by the Gnostic Justin, makes Jesus a shepherd before his ministry began: "In the days of King Herod Baruch was sent again by Elohim, and he came to Nazareth and found Jesus, the son of Joseph and Mary, feeding sheep, a boy of twelve years, and he told him everything which had taken place from the beginning, from Eden and Elohim and everything that will take place after this. He said, 'All the prophets before you were seduced; but Jesus, son of man, try not to be seduced, but proclaim this message to men and tell them about the Father and about the Good and ascend to the Good and sit there with Elohim, the Father of us all.'"[30] Might this text preserve ancient tradition that Jesus had been a shepherd? Most likely not; here again, a metaphor, this time, that of Jesus the Good Shepherd, has been literalized and historicized.

FILLING IN THE BLANKS

Why do we have such scant information on the childhood of Jesus and his life before his ministry began? Because at the stage of Christian preaching represented by the Gospels, Christians were not concerned with what Jesus may or may not have done before his public career began. That is to say, for them the gospel of Jesus began when the divine Spirit descended upon him (Matthew and Luke) or into him (Mark). It is not going too far to say that Jesus was not yet the Son of God before this happened. Matthew and Luke, with their Nativity stories, have begun the process of modifying this understanding, but it is plain the process is just beginning, and they have individually added miraculous birth stories onto a gospel template, that of Mark, which began with the descent of the

Spirit into Jesus at the Jordan. As C. H. Dodd showed,[31] Acts describes the preaching of the gospel beginning at the same point: "beginning from the baptism of John until the day when he was taken up from us" (Acts 1:22). "You know the message which he sent to Israel, preaching good news of peace by Jesus Christ . . . the message which was preached throughout all of Judea, starting from Galilee, with the baptism that John preached; how God anointed Jesus of Nazareth with the Holy Spirit and power; how he went about doing good and healing all that were oppressed by the devil, for God was with him. . . . They put him to death by hanging him on a tree, but God raised him on the third day and made him manifest" (Acts 10:36–41). "God has brought to Israel a savior, as he promised. Before his coming John had preached a baptism of repentance to all the people of Israel. And as John was finishing his course, he said, 'What do you suppose? That I am he? I am not he. Nay, but after me one is coming, the sandals of whose feet I am not worthy to untie'" (Acts 13:23–25). Though the wording of these passages is all redactional, not genuine quotation but the creation of the author of Acts himself, it is clear he presupposed a Markan-type adoptionistic gospel template—one that began with the baptism at the Jordan and the descent of the Spirit.

Looking at the gospel this way, it is not surprising these Christians would have nothing to say about whatever may have preceded the baptism. But, as we just saw, Matthew and Luke represent a trend whereby the boundaries of the gospel form were stretched: Jesus is *born* the Son of God, making the baptism somewhat anticlimactic. This opened the door for those infancy-childhood gospel traditions we reviewed before. Naturally, if Jesus were already the Son of God, he must have been a divine miracle worker even as a child. If I may be allowed an analogy from today's popular culture mythology, think of Jerry Siegel and Joe Schuster's character Superman. When Siegel and Schuster first told tales of the Man of Steel, he was said to have developed his powers only once he reached maturity. But Superman's adventures proved so phenomenally popular that the publisher suggested moving the origin of his powers, and hence of his superhero career, back one stage to his adolescence. So the adventures of Superboy premiered and continued for decades. Why not go a step further? The legend was revised again, so that the infant Superbaby was already helping out with farm chores using his superstrength, for example, lifting the tractor single-handedly. Even so, when Jesus' divine sonship was thought to have stemmed from his Spirit-baptism at the Jordan, his adult activities formed the content of the gospel. But once his sonship was believed to have started at his physical birth, his miraculous "adventures" had to be extended backward to fill the gap.

Raymond E. Brown observed[32] that even the Jordan baptism was not the first stage of the process, however. The New Testament preserves another version of adoptionism whereby Jesus was made the Son of God by virtue of his resurrection: "the gospel concerning his son, who was descended from David according to the flesh and designated Son of God in power according to the Spirit of holiness by his resurrection from the dead" (Rom. 1:3–4). "Let all the house of Israel therefore know assuredly that God has made him Lord and Christ, this Jesus whom you crucified" (Acts 2:36). "This he has fulfilled to us . . . by raising Jesus, as also it is written in the second Psalm, 'You are my son. Today I have begotten you'" (Acts 13:33). That is, being raised from the dead is seen as the fulfillment of the promise of sonship, so the two must be coincident. Brown traces the same complex of themes (Spirit-power-sonship) back from the resurrection to the baptism to the conception of Jesus. At his conception, Mary is overshadowed by the power and Spirit of the Most High (Luke 1:35). At his baptism, he is filled with the Spirit and power (Luke 4:1, 14). On Easter he is raised in power according to the Spirit (Rom. 1:4). But the last shall be first. The Spirit-power-sonship triad moved backward along the trajectory as the biography of Jesus was filled in by the Christian imagination in reverse.

And then we find ourselves facing a prospect Brown did not consider. If the youth of Jesus was filled in fictively only once the sonship was pushed back to physical conception and birth, mustn't the stories of the ministry have been similarly fabricated only once the sonship had been pushed back from the resurrection to the baptism? This was exactly the suggestion of Paul Couchoud, to which we shall return.

NOTES

1. David Friedrich Strauss, *The Life of Jesus Critically Examined*, trans. George Eliot, Lives of Jesus Series (1835; repr., Philadelphia: Fortress Press, 1972), p. 193.

2. Ibid., pp. 194–95; George A. Wells, *The Jesus of the Early Christians: A Study in Christian Origins* (London: Pemberton Books, 1971), p. 16.

3. See Rayond E. Brown, *The Gospel of John: Introduction, Translation, and Notes*, vol. 1, Anchor Bible 29 (Garden City: Doubleday, 1966), comments on John 2:1–11.

4. Edward Zeller, *The Contents and Origin of the Acts of the Apostles Critically Investigated*, trans. Joseph Dare, vol. 1 (London: Williams and Norgate, 1876), p. 271.

5. Arnold Schulman, *Baba* (New York: Pocket Books, 1973), pp. 130–31.

6. Ibid., p. 119.

7. John McHugh, "The Brothers of Jesus (II): The Epiphanian Theory," in *The Mother of Jesus in the New Testament* (Garden City: Doubleday, 1975), pp. 208–22.

8. Peter Brown, *The Body and Society: Men, Women, and Sexual Renunciation in Early Christianity*, Lectures on the History of Religions Sponsored by the American Council of Learned Societies, New Series 13 (New York: Columbia University Press, 1988); Dyan Elliott, *Spiritual Marriage: Sexual Abstinence in Medieval Wedlock* (Princeton: Princeton University Press, 1993); Susanna Elm, *'Virgins of God': The Making of Asceticism in Late Antiquity*, Oxford Classical Monographs (Oxford: Clarendon Press, 1994).

9. Max Weber, *The Sociology of Religion*, trans. Ephraim Fischoff (Boston: Beacon Press, 1964), pp. 60–62, 75, 78–79, 104.

10. Adolf von Harnack, "Die Verklärungsgeschichte Jesu, der Bericht des Paulus 1 Kor 15, 3 ff. und die beiden Christusvision des Petrus" (*Sitzungsberichte der Berliner Akademie der Wissenschafter*, Phil.-hist. Klasse, 1922): 62–80.

11. Eusebius *Ecclesiastical History* 1.7. Cruse trans., pp. 33–35.

12. Juvenal, *The Sixteen Satires*, trans. Peter Green (New York: Penguin Books, 1974), pp. 147–48.

13. John Burton, *The Collection of the Quran* (New York: Cambridge University Press, 1977), pp. 201–34.

14. Ethelbert Stauffer, "The Caliphate of James," trans. Darrell J. Doughty, *Journal of Higher Criticism* 4, no. 2 (fall 1997): 120–43.

15. Schulman, *Baba*, p. 116.

16. Hermann Gunkel, *The Legends of Genesis: The Biblical Saga & History*, trans. W. H. Karruth (1901; repr., New York: Schocken Books, 1964), pp. 25–27.

17. Robert Eisenman, *James the Brother of Jesus: The Key to Unlocking the Secrets of Early Christianity and the Dead Sea Scrolls* (New York: Viking Penguin, 1997).

18. Edgar J. Goodspeed, *Famous Biblical Hoaxes, or Modern Apocrypha*, Twin Brooks Series (Grand Rapids: Baker Book House, 1956), p. 11.

19. Janet Bock, *The Jesus Mystery: Of Lost Years and Unknown Travels* (Los Angeles: Aura Books, 1980), p. 21.

20. Ibid., p. 22.

21. *Swami Abhedananda's Journey into Kashmir and Tibet*, trans. Ansupati Dasgupta and Kunja Bihari Kundu (Calcutta: Ramakrishna Vedanta Math, 1987), p. 119.

22. Per Beskow, *Strange Tales About Jesus* (Philadelphia: Fortress Press, 1983), pp. 62–63.

23. Levi [Leo W.] Dowling, *The Aquarian Gospel of Jesus the Christ* (London: L. N. Fowler, 1943).

24. Edgar Johnson Goodspeed, *Strange New Gospels* (Chicago: University of Chicago Press, 1931).

25. The Mazdaznan sect was founded around 1900 by a German immigrant to America, Otto Hanisch, who styled himself Otoman Zar-Adusht Ha'nish. Mazdaznan disciplines include vegetarianism and breathing exercises. A racist group, it allowed that only true Aryans could be enlightened.

26. Elizabeth Clare Prophet et al., *The Lost Years of Jesus: Documentary Evidence of Jesus' 17-Year Journey to the East* (Livingston, Mont.: Summit University Press, 1987), pp. 348, 353.

27. O. Z. Ha'nish, *The True Story of Jesus Christ entitled Yehoshua Nazir* (London: Mazdaznan Call, 1917), pp. 46–47: "He decided to go to India to gather a few more blossoms of wisdom. It was in India that Yessu became much impressed with the wisdom-religion and concluded to use the sum and substance of its philosophy in His own country, but to simplify it, however, to suit the conceptions of the Jewish mind."

28. Drew Ali, *The Holy Koran of the Moorish Science Temple of America* (reprint; New York: African Islamic Mission, 1988). Sayyid al Imaam Isa al Haadi al Mahdi, in his *Who Was Noble Drew Ali? 1886 A.D.–1929 A.D.* (Nubian Islaamic Hebrew Mission/ Ansaaru Allah Publications, 1988), pp. 54–58, demonstrates the use of the *Aquarian Gospel* by the Moorish Science Koran.

29. Géza Vermes, *Jesus the Jew: A Historian's Reading of the Gospels* (Glasgow: Fortean/Collins, 1977), pp. 21–22.

30. Robert M. Grant, *Gnosticism: An Anthology* (London: Collins, 1961), pp. 98–99.

31. C. H. Dodd, "The Framework of the Gospel Narrative," in *New Testament Studies* (Manchester: Manchester University Press, 1967), pp. 1–11.

32. Raymond Edward Brown, *Birth of the Messiah: A Commentary on the Infancy Narratives in Matthew and Luke* (Garden City: Doubleday, 1977), pp. 312–14.

CHAPTER FOUR
JESUS AND JOHN THE BAPTIST

DOWN BY THE RIVERSIDE

John the Baptist, or Baptizer, is introduced in Mark 1, Matthew 3, Luke 3, and John 1. He is depicted as a desert ascetic having emerged from his eremetic retreat to announce the soon-coming Final Judgment of mankind. It should be carried out, he says, by the Coming One, by which epithet he may very likely have intended the eschatological prophet Elijah, whose return at the end of days had been prophesied in Mal. 3:1, 4:5. His purifying fire should burn up the wicked and purify the saved with an outpouring of the Holy Spirit. John's own role was to make available a new way of salvation before the end should arrive: a baptism of repentance that would mark the baptized as one of the elect when the Coming One arrived for his own. We read that he was "preaching a baptism of repentence for the forgiveness of sins" (Mark 1:4), which implies he was announcing a new plan of salvation: one's sins could be washed away all at once, a necessity given the shortness of the time remaining before the end. One might think here of the analogous position of the early Christian prophet Hermas. The Shepherd, or Angel of Repentance, sent him forth to proclaim a "second repentance" to ease the consciences of Christians who had slipped up and sinned again since baptism (*Shepherd of Hermas* Mandates 4.6; Similitudes 8.5.6, 11.1–4,

10.2.2–4). Again, think of the Oglala Sioux shaman Black Elk, who, after being so commanded in a vision, designed a ritual garment and proclaimed to his people that wearing it would magically expel the white man. And just as Black Elk's new way was superseded by the similar Ghost Dance movement, so was the movement of the Baptist eclipsed historically by that of Jesus Christ.

Many of those who heeded John's revivalist preaching became his disciples with their own sectarian prayers (Luke 11:1, 5:33) and regimen of fasting (Mark 2:18). This Baptist sect long outlasted its founder. We can catch glimpses of the early Christian polemic against this rival movement already within the New Testament itself, but it emerges into full sunlight in the Clementine *Recognitions*, a second-century Apocryphal Acts novel. There we read of a public debate between all the notable contemporary Jewish sects in Jerusalem, including Pharisees, Sadducees, Christians, and John the Baptist followers. We learn of the clever arguments the Baptists mounted against Jesus, demonstrating that John must be the true Messiah. The sect seems to have continued to evolve over the centuries and still exists today in Iraq and over the borders of neighboring states. They call themselves the Nasoreans, though scholars have become accustomed to referring to them as the Mandaeans (Aramaic, which they speak, for "Gnostics"). They continue to baptize (by having the initiate kneel in the water and bend over facefirst into it), and they teach that the true Messiah was the Primal Man Enosh Uthra (the transfigured Gen. 4:26 patriarch Enosh). His prophet on earth was John the Baptist, and Jesus was naught but a false Messiah sent to deceive.[1]

The mere fact of John's sect continuing on side by side with that of Jesus, as the Gospels themselves tell us, implies that John can hardly have been what Matthew and John make him, just the front man announcing the coming of Jesus. If that were the case, why continue to have a sect of disciples who followed different customs? If one nominated a contemporary as the Messiah, would one continue to operate one's own sect in utter disregard of the ostensible Messiah's well-known teachings (Mark 2:18)? As we will shortly see, it is clear that John had no witting connection with the rival Jesus movement. The bond between them was a piece of subsequent Christian propaganda, as when the Koran (61:6) has Jesus predict the coming of Muhammad.

SON OF NONE?

If we consider John the Baptist as an important religious figure in his own right, what can we say of him? Not surprisingly, there is the possibility that he was not originally a historical figure. Arthur Drews floated the possibility that John (Greek: *Ioannes*) was a historicized version of the ancient fish god Dagon or Oannes, who was believed to have emerged from the waters (as John preaches beside the Jordan) to impart wisdom to humanity.[2] The biblical Joshua, son of

Nun, goes back to a mythic god. "Nun" is not an attested proper name, but means "fish," Nun evidently being the same as Oannes. Is it an accident that the New Testament Joshua (Jesus) is, religiously speaking, the son of Ioannes? If this speculation were correct, it would mean that the Baptist sect was already very ancient in New Testament times, a popular survival of the worship of gods long-ago interdicted by the Jerusalem hierarchy. And, just as the ancient Joshua cult had been forced to demote its deity to the status of a mere hero in the face of growing Israelite monolatry, much later the Oannes cult thought it wiser to transmute its lord into a human preacher, at least for public consumption. (And who can guess what connection the Oannes cult might have had with the early Christian "*ichthus*" sign of the fish?)

It might be thought a demerit against this theory that Josephus treats John the Baptist as a historical figure of the recent past. But it is worth asking if the passage (*Antiquities* 18.5.2) is perhaps an interpolation, as some have suspected. I see two reasons to regard it so. First, the writer deems it a matter of disproportionate urgency to correct a sacramental interpretation of John's baptism: he "commanded the Jews to excercise virtue, both as to righteousness toward one another, and piety towards God, and so to come to baptism; for that the washing would be acceptable to him, if they made use of it, not in order to the remission of some sins, but for the purification of the body; supposing still that the soul was thoroughly purified beforehand by righteousness."[3] What is this doing in the present context? Why would Josephus care about such niceties any more than Gallio did (Acts 18:14–15)? It sounds like sectarian theological hair-splitting, more at home in a Baptist or Christian setting. John Meagher[4] believes that it came from the former, that Josephus derived this information from the Baptist sect of his own day, which had spread out into the Hellenistic world (cf. Acts 19:1–7). These latter-day Baptists had begun to reflect on the nature of baptism, their hallmark ritual, and they had come to rationalize it, precisely as Christian Baptists do today: baptism is not of itself a saving rite. That would be magic. Rather, it denotes a change of mind and heart, which is what really saves. These concerns came along with the rest of the information, says Meagher, from a Baptist source, hence their irrelevance in their present context in Josephus.

But I rather imagine Josephus would have edited out such extraneous information. I prefer to see the whole passage as an interpolation into Josephus by a Christian (or Baptist) who was trying to correct Mark by interpreting what he said about a "baptism for the forgiveness of sins" in a nonsacramental direction. (He may also have repudiated Mark's version of John's death, thinking that it let Herod Antipas off the hook, blaming the death on the scheming Herodias, and so offered a contrasting version, seen here.) My second reason for seeing it as an interpolation is the apparent presence of a redactional seam, a telltale sign of a copyist stitching in new material. Often an interpolation may be detected by parallel opening and closing sentences. This results from the copyist having to re-create the peg from which the continuation of the original narrative first hung.

In this case, the passage begins with the words, "Now, some of the Jews thought that the destruction of Herod's army came from God, and that very justly as a punishment of what he did against John." I am suggesting that this passage is the interpolator's paraphrase of the closing words of the passage: "Now, the Jews had an opinion that the destruction of this army was sent as a punishment upon Herod, as a mark of God's displeasure against him." The latter version would have been the original, speaking of Herod's general impiety, the former being the paraphrase that introduces John the Baptist by name, making the military defeat the punishment for John's ill treatment. So it may be that Josephus did not originally mention John at all.

But suppose John was a historical figure, as he very likely was. Even if one should hold to the view that Jesus was not a historical figure, he would not necessarily take John down with him, so to speak. Any way one views it, the connection between Jesus and John is secondary, an attempt to co-opt John's sect and absorb it into the early church by subordinating John to Jesus, as we shall soon see. Once it reached this point, it would scarcely matter if the figurehead of one sect were historical, the other mythical.

ON JORDAN'S STORMY BANKS I STAND

A historical John would no doubt have looked a great deal like the Qumran sect, keepers of the Dead Sea Scrolls. Most scholars identify them as Essenes (an ascetical brotherhood dwelling in towns and in a Dead Sea retreat, as we learn from Pliny the Elder and Philo of Alexandria, both of whom visited and interviewed them). Cecil Roth[5] and others have seen the Qumran sect as belonging to the militant Zealot party, the dynastic movement of freedom-fighters descended from Judas the Gaulonite. But, with Robert Eisenman,[6] we may wonder if there was much of a difference between these parties of *Schwärmerei*, as Luther would have dubbed them, perhaps as little as between the People's Front of Judea and the Judean People's Front.[7]

There are striking similiarities between John the Baptist as the Gospels depict him and the writers of the Dead Sea Scrolls. Like the Qumran covenanters, John shunned wine and ate locusts (Luke 1:15, Mark 1:6). Both used Isa. 40:3–5 as a prooftext for their ministries as "voices crying in the wilderness." Both are said to have predicted judgment by fire as well as the purifying dousing with the divine Spirit. The *Manual of Discipline* says, "God will purge all the acts of man in the crucible of His truth, and refine for Himself all the fabric of man, destroying every spirit of perversity from within his flesh and cleansing him by the holy spirit from all the effects of wickedness. Like waters of purification He will sprinkle upon him the spirit of truth to cleanse him of all the abominations of falsehood."[8] A Qumran hymn says, "When the rivers of Belial burst their high banks /—rivers that are like fire / devouring all that draw their waters, / rivers whose runnels destroy / green tree and dry tree alike, / rivers that are like fire / which sweeps with flaming sparks / devouring all that drink their waters."[9] Such an outpouring of the Spirit had been predicted in Joel 2:28–29, Ezek. 39:29, and Isa. 32:15. The winnowing and burning of chaff (Matt. 3:12//Luke 3:17) comes from Mal. 3:2, 4:1. Like the sectarians of the Scrolls, John, of course, administered baptism. Theirs was daily repeated for ritual purity's sake. One ancient source, the Clementine *Recognitions*, makes John, too, a "hemerobaptist," or daily baptizer. Perhaps his followers made the trek out to the Jordan every day, if they lived close enough. Could John have been a member of the Dead Sea Scrolls community or the Essene Monastery at some point? It is certainly possible. In fact, Julius Schousboe and Robert Eisler,[10] followed today by Barbara Thiering,[11] went so far as to identify John with the enigmatic Teacher of Righteousness, the founder or reformer of the Scrolls sect. (Others[12] finger Jesus or his brother James the Just as the Teacher's alter ego, or leave the space blank.) But it is not as if this type of ascetical spirituality was so rare that the Essenes or anybody else had a corner on the market. John would not have had to belong to them in order to look and talk like them.

A related possibility, also broached by Robert Eisler in his neglected treasure trove *The Messiah Jesus and John the Baptist* (1931), is that a historical John might have been closer to the Zealot end of the spectrum than the Essene. He might have been a fomentor of *jihad* against the Roman occupation. Eisler takes seriously the puzzling Slavonic recension of Josephus's *Jewish War*, which contains what appear to be greatly expanded sections on John the Baptist and Jesus, roughly corresponding to the more familiar passages in his *Antiquities of the Jews*. Though most scholars ignore the Slavonic Josephus, dismissing it as a product of the Judaizing movement in sixteenth-century Russia, there is no compelling reason to do so, and Josephus translator G. A. Williamson thought the Slavonic version quite likely authentic, representing a later amplification by Josephus himself. Here is Williamson's translation of the passage:

> At that time a man was going about Judea remarkably dressed: he wore animal hair on those parts of his body not covered by his own. His face was like a savage's. He called on the Jews to claim their freedom, crying: "God sent me to show you the way of the Law, so that you can shake off any human yoke: no man shall rule you, but only the Most High who sent me." His message was eagerly welcomed and he was followed by all Judea and the district around Jerusalem. All he did was to baptise them in the Jordan and dismiss them with an earnest exhortation to abandon their evil ways: if they did so they would be given a king who would liberate them and master the unruly [the lawless, Gentiles?], while himself acknowledging no master. This promise was derided by some but believed by others.
>
> The man was brought before Archelaus and an assemblage of lawyers, who asked who he was and where he had been. He replied: "I am a man called by

the Spirit of God, and I live on stems, roots and fruits." When he was threatened with torture if he continued living and talking like this, he retorted, "It would be more to the point if you stopped acting so disgracefully and submitted to the God you profess to worship."

Simon, a scribe of Essene origin, sprang up and exclaimed angrily: "We study Holy Writ every day; you have just come out of the forest like a wild animal; and do you dare put us right and mislead the people with your damnable nonsense?" Simon then rushed at him to tear him to pieces. But the man replied with a warning: "I will not reveal to you the secret that is in your midst, as you have refused to listen and so have brought immeasurable disaster upon your own heads." Then off he went to the other side of Jordan, where he resumed his work unmolested.[13]

Eisler drew a number of interesting connections not only with the Gospels but with the Mandaean writings as well. He connects John's nameless self-declaration, "a man," with the Primal Man soteriology/mythology of the Nasoreans/Mandaeans, inferring that John saw himself as something like the Nasorean messiah, concealing the "secret among them" of his own messianic identity. The text literally has the man say he eats "wood-shavings," something we may readily connect with the fact that the pre-Christian Nasorean sect comprised itinerant carpenters.[14] The secrecy motif would also fit the Gnostic character of the Nasoreans, not to mention the Clementine tradition that John the Baptist was the teacher of both Gnostic messiahs Simon Magus and Dositheus.

But the Slavonic Josephus's Baptist was a contemporary of Archelaus, brutal son and successor of Herod the Great. Matthew has Joseph the father of Jesus quail at returning with the baby Jesus from Egypt since Archelaus had taken his father's throne. Doesn't this paint a picture of John the Baptist as active earlier than Jesus by some decades? Eisler suggests that this was most likely the case. Once we discard Luke's tendentious attempt to make John only half a year Jesus' elder (to which we shall soon return), we can suddenly recognize the neglected meaning in another gospel saying, Matt. 11:12, "From the days of John the Baptist until now the kingdom of God has suffered violence [or, has been advancing by violence], and violent men take it by force." For one thing, the saying seems to look back on the period of John the Baptist as long over with ("Ever since . . ."). For another, it associates John with revolutionary violence, as one of the violent men seizing the kingdom of God to drag it into earthly reality.[15]

JOHN'S DOCTRINE

What did John teach? We have already seen that Mark understands John to have offered salvation in the time of tribulation by means of repentance and baptism, in anticipation of One to Come for salvation and judgment. Q material adds more apocalyptic embellishment: the Coming One even now hefts his axe and is about to swing it for a stroke of judgment against sinners. Like Dionysus, he holds a winnowing fan to shake out the sinners from the company of the righteous. Q has John sound almost like Paul, rejecting one's Jewish heritage as useless baggage in the final hour. Physical descendants of Abraham are no better than stones (a pun, *beni*, sons, and *ebeni*, stones) in God's eyes. What he needs to see is repentence and its fruit, a changed life. It is Luke who has John get down to specifics. In Luke, the crowd asks the Baptist precisely what he has in mind; and he responds. All who have spare food and clothing must share them with the destitute (Luke 3:11). Tax collectors are told, surprisingly, not to leave their jobs (as Roman lackeys!), but not to extort more than the minimum required amount (3:13). Soldiers (Herodian? Roman?) are told, again, not to abandon the army, but, again, merely not to extort money from the cowed populace (3:14). The mildness of this advice is perhaps surprising compared with Mark's story of the tax collector Levi renouncing his trade to follow Jesus (2:14), and with the refusal of second-century Christians to take Roman military oaths. But there are various ways of understanding John's words.

Hans Conzelmann[16] contends that Luke is trying to downplay the eschatological enthusiasm of the early church, toning down such elements in his story. Thus, he does not want John to appear as a herald of the imminent end of the world, which Luke, writing many decades later, knows did not happen. So, Conzelmann reasons, Luke put into John's mouth these fairly conventional moralisms that are purposely not very radical, a liveable stance in a world that is going to continue as far as we can see into the future before Christ returns. And Conzelmann, whose case for an antiapocalyptic Luke is certainly very strong, may be right about these particular verses. If they are Luke's creation (only he has them, remember), we are probably to read them as Conzelmann suggests. But suppose they predate Luke and should actually be ascribed to the Baptist? Then they might mean something different, for they remind us of the advice dispensed in 1 Cor. 7:17–24, 29–31, where, precisely because the present world is already passing into oblivion, one might as well remain in the position he occupied when he was called by God, practice business as usual. Any serious attempt to reform life and the world on the eve of destruction would be like rearranging the furniture aboard the *Titanic*. John could have seen it the same way. "The time is near! Let the evildoer still do evil, and the filthy still be filthy, and the righteous still do right, and the holy still be holy! Behold, I am coming soon, bringing my recompense, to repay every one for what he has done!" (Rev. 22:10b–12).

Eisler offered still another reading, calling these verses John the Baptist's "field sermon"[17] delivered to those rebelling against Archelaus, in whose time there was already a kind of run-through for the disaster of 70 C.E., the temple being set afire and pitched battle erupting. (Luke makes a garbled reference to these conflicts, substituting Pilate for Archelaus, in 13:1.) Eisler notes that the word used for those John addresses is not that for soldiers (στρατιωται) but rather στρατευομενοι, those actually going off to war. John is issuing stipulations for a truly holy war (cf. 2 Cor. 10:3–4), in which God's soldiers will not exploit and brutalize those they are sworn to protect. Likewise, the austerity of the conditions in which the proud owner of a second coat is urged to supply one for a refugee utterly despoiled implies wartime depredation. And the question of the tax collectors would have been prompted by the demands of the Jewish rebels that Archelaus abolish taxation. John says to continue it, for the rebellion needs funds, too, but no longer to oppress the taxpayer. Eisler compares the sermon of John, understood this way, to that of Josephus himself, when he addressed the insurgents of Galilee in the war against Rome: "If you thirst for victory, abstain from the ordinary crimes, theft, robbery, and rapine. And do not defraud your countrymen; count it no advantage to yourselves to injure another. For the war will have better success if the warriors have a good name [*according to the Slavonic text:* and their souls are conscious of having purified themselves from every offense]. If, however, they are condemned by their evil deeds, then will God be their enemy and the aliens will have an easy victory" (*Jewish War* 2.576.581).[18]

As all the gospel texts read, John is already a Christian before Christ. He is Old Testament man as Christians have always fancied him: fully conversant with New Testament events, only in the future tense. Critical scholars admit that passages in which John endorses Jesus must be spurious Christian creations. But some scholars wonder if perhaps some of John's recorded preachments might be authentic once one removes the Christian "spin" the evangelists have placed upon them. We have already seen the comparison between John's prediction of a purifying bath of the Spirit with the same expectation in the Dead Sea Scrolls. Bultmann will have none of this, dismissing the Spirit passages as mere Christian ventriloquism, comparing John's water baptism with their own superior Christian spirit baptism.[19] He may be right. Accordingly, it may be that the whole notion of John predicting the Coming One is simply a Christian attempt to make him predict Jesus, instead of a genuine prediction of some eschatological figure whose name and form John could not have anticipated. But either is reasonable. Raymond E. Brown[20] goes even further in the direction of reclaiming canonical sayings of John as genuine with a pre-Christian meaning. In John's gospel, the Baptizer designated Jesus as the very "lamb of God who takes away the sins of the world" (1:29). John the evangelist certainly means to have John the Baptist announce Jesus as the Christian savior from sin who will die as a human Passover lamb. Brown knows that cannot be historically true, but he wonders if perhaps John was remembered as speaking of a rather different sort of coming lamb of God to do away with the world's sin (cf. 1 John 3:5, 8). In Rev. 5:4–5 ff., *Testament of Joseph* 19:8, and *1 Enoch* 90:38 we find the image of a warrior lamb or ram who stands for the conquering Messiah. He does away with sin by obliterating the sinners, the wicked enemies of the people of God. Could something like this have been the subject of John's preaching? Could this Ram of God have been the same as the Coming One? No one can say.

THE SUN BLACK AS SACKCLOTH

Who did John the Baptist understand himself to be? That is, did he identify with some predefined role marked out by scripture or contemporary belief? His dress, a tunic of camel's hair, recalls the distinctive dress of Elijah. "He wore a garment of haircloth, with a girdle of leather about his loins" (2 Kings 1:8). Compare Mark's description of John: "Now John was clad in camel's hair, and had a leather girdle around his waist" (1:6). One might readily think, from the wording, that Mark means the reader to think of Elijah in the 2 Kings passage. Thus, for Mark, John was Elijah. But it is not so simple. Zech. 13:4 implies the hair shirt was the trademark garb of prophets, not just Elijah. Would John have been dressing like a prophet, or dressing like Elijah in particular? We have seen that John preached the arrival of the Coming One, the fulfillment in all likelihood of Malachi's promise of Elijah's return. If this is what John had in mind, then he did not see himself in the role of Elijah, unless, of course, he had his own "messianic secret" up his sleeve and eventually intended to announce himself as the one whose eager expectation he had already whipped up. Ali Muhammad, the Bab (Door) to the Hidden Imam in nineteenth-century Persia, first preached the imminent coming of "Him Whom God Shall Make Manifest," then announced himself as that one, the Mahdi.

Mark applies to John a conflated text ("Behold, I send my messenger [αγγελον] before your face, who shall prepare your way"), a splicing together of Mal. 3:1 ("Behold, I send forth my messenger [αγγελον], and he shall survey the way before me") and Exod. 23:20 ("And behold, I send my angel [αγγελον], that he may keep you in the way, that he may bring you into the land which I have prepared for you"). Mark erroneously ascribes the hybrid text to Isaiah, but it was not he who first combined the two passages; they already appear in the spliced form in rabbinic writings.[21] Matt. 11:10//Luke 7:27 (Q) has Jesus himself apply the double text to John. The Malachi element, if we are meant to recall its context, implies the text refers to the coming of Elijah. Thus, the Synoptics seem to regard John as Elijah returned, and to make Jesus share that view. Matt. 11:13–14, 17:13//Mark 9:13 have Jesus implicitly or explicitly identify John with Elijah. Luke lacks both these texts, available to him from his sources Mark and Q—why? We will shortly see.

JOHN'S SECT AND ITS REMAINS

Who is the real Messiah? The Baptists seem to have had three major arguments on their candidate's behalf. First, since John had appeared on the scene before Jesus (whether by years or months does not matter), he must be the more important (in the same way Christians recognize Jesus as superior in dignity to Paul).

Second, since it was Jesus who had applied to John for baptism (as the Synoptic gospels admit), John must be the superior of the two. Third, Jesus himself was on record as proclaiming John the greatest man in history ("Amen: I say to you, among those born of women there has risen none greater than John the Baptist" Matt. 11:11a//Luke 7:28a). We will shortly see how Christians endeavored to deal with these points. But first, we might ask just how John's devotees came to believe their master was the Messiah. In any case, we seem to be able to discern in the pages of the New Testament several vestiges of the sacred traditions of the Baptist sect. They bear an uncanny resemblance to the gospel tales of Jesus, and that is probably no accident.

First, Luke preserves what is in all likelihood the sacred *nativity story* of John the Baptist: Luke 1:5–25, 46–55, 57–80 (omitting "in the house of his servant David" from verse 69, as this interrupts the poetic meter and is thus an interpolation by Luke into a preexisting hymn). Luke (or a previous source) has interwoven the nativity of John with a closely parallel nativity of Jesus, the latter perhaps modeled upon the former. But originally the two had naught to do with each other, as attested by how easily they may be disengaged by source analysis. By the way, the Magnificat was originally Elizabeth's, not Mary's, as the earliest Old Latin manuscripts and quotations from the church fathers attest. The context, too, implies it, as no shame attached to a young woman like Mary not yet having conceived, while Elizabeth's long barrenness brought reproach upon her. In addition, the Magnificat is obviously based on the Song of the barren Hannah, now impregnated with Samuel (1 Sam. 2:1–10), and both versions are concerned with the removal of barrenness, Elizabeth's problem, not Mary's.

Second, we have John's *Passion narrative* in Mark 6:17–29, with a shorter version in Matt. 14:3–12. Like Jesus, John is done in by a wicked tyrant. It is hard to know just what to make of the fact that the story tries to exonerate Herod Antipas by having him forced into the execution through the manipulative wiles of his wife, Herodias. All the Gospels try to whitewash Pontius Pilate, shifting the blame for Jesus' death completely onto the Jews. Presumably this happened because, as time went by, Christians cared little what Jews thought but were anxious to curry Roman favor. But what led to a whitewashing of Antipas? We might infer that over the years, the surviving Baptists were trying to avert the hostility of subsequent Herodian rulers such as Herod Agrippa I (Acts 12:1–23) and Herod Agrippa II (Acts 25:13–26:32), who we may imagine viewed Herodias as another Yoko Ono (it was further scheming of hers that eventually led to Antipas's disgrace and deportation).

Third, there is the Baptist *resurrection kerygma* (preaching) barely discernible in Mark 6:14b, "Some said, 'John the Baptizer has been *raised from the dead*! That is why these *powers* are at work in him!'" Compare this with the creedal formulation quoted in (or perhaps interpolated into) Rom. 1:3b–4, "who was descended from David according to the flesh and designated Son of God in *power* according to the spirit of holiness by his *resurrection from the dead*, Jesus

Christ our Lord." One is tempted to believe that the Markan sentence about John's resurrection first circulated the same way as that about Jesus now embedded in Romans. Mark has borrowed the resurrection proclamation formula one would have heard chanted among the Baptist sectarians on their own Easter morning. Even the note at the close of the Baptist passion story, "When his disciples heard of it, they came and took his body, and laid it in a tomb" (Mark 6:29), sounds suspiciously like Mark 15:47, "Mary Magdalene and Mary the mother of Joses saw where he was laid." Do not both sound like anticipations of a resurrection? Otherwise, why even note what would, by itself, be an utterly insignificant detail? Mark has not preserved an empty tomb story for John (why would he, as a Christian?), but we must suspect there was one. He has, then, taken the resurrection kerygma of John and explained it away as a case of mistaken identity (as Hugh J. Schonfield would do with Jesus himself).[22] Some may have thought they were seeing a risen John, but in fact it was the miracle-working Jesus.[23]

It was, then, in all probability the belief that John had been raised from the dead that led his disciples to conclude that he himself was the Coming One whom he had predicted. The Christological importance attached to John by his followers shines forth clearly from a pair of sayings in the Q source, misattributed to Jesus. "The law and the prophets prophesied/were until John" (Matt. 11:13//Luke 16:16a). As Schonfield pointed out,[24] there is nothing here to say the Scriptures became outmoded upon John's advent (a kind of Pauline twist); rather, the point is that John is the very goal of scriptural prophecy, of salvation history! And again, we read, "Among those born of women, none has risen greater than John the Baptist" (Matt. 11:11a//Luke 7:28a). That's pretty self-explanatory.

WATER FELLOWSHIP, WATER JOY DIVINE

Just as F. C. Baur made new sense of Acts and the epistles by placing them on either side of the polemical Pauline/Petrine divide in the early church, so scholars have illuminated the Gospels, especially Luke and John, by placing them in their proper historical context as part of the propaganda war against the rival sect of John the Baptizer. Here, too, we can recognize Christian anti-John texts that give way to "catholicizing" texts tending to co-opt John for Christianity.

Very early on, someone added a severe qualification of the praise of John as the very best of men. Already in Q and in Thomas we read: "Amen: I tell you, among those born of women, none has risen greater than John the Baptist; nevertheless, he who is least in the kingdom of God is greater than he" (Matt. 11:11//Luke 7:28//Thomas 46: "From Adam until John the Baptist there is among those who are born of women none higher than John the Baptist, so that his eyes will not be broken.[25] But I have said that whoever among you becomes as a child shall know the kingdom, and he shall become higher than John"). The Christian comment nullifies John's supposed greatness by relegating him to the sphere of mere nature, not of grace, where the one born again of Christian baptism is automatically higher in rank than the highest in this world. It is truly to damn John with faint praise since he is implicitly dismissed as a worldling. The implied contrast is the same as in Luke 16:8b, "For the sons of this age/world are wiser in their own generation than the sons of light."

That the encomium on John once circulated without the put-down modification is implied in the debate scene in the Clementine *Recognitions*, already referred to. The Baptist spokesman there refers only to what I am saying was the original version: "And, behold, one of the disciples of John asserted that John was the Christ, and not Jesus, inasmuch as Jesus himself declared that John was greater than all men and all prophets. 'If, then,' said he, 'he be greater than all, he must be held to be greater than Moses, and than Jesus himself. But if he be the greatest of all, then must he be the Christ.' To this Simon the Canaanite [i.e., the Zealot], answering, asserted that John was indeed greater than all the prophets, and all who are born of women, yet that he is not greater than the Son of Man. Accordingly, Jesus is also the Christ, whereas John is only a prophet: and there is as much difference between him and Jesus, as between the forerunner and Him whose forerunner he is; or as He who gives the law and him who keeps the law" (chapter 60).[26] That is not much of an argument. A much better one would have been that the Baptist apologist had flagrantly taken the statement out of context—had it had such a context at the time, which I say it did not. By the same token, the praise of John had already been attributed to Jesus, as Simon the Apostle takes that for granted. We may guess that it was not Christians but Baptists who first attributed to Jesus the encomia on John as the greatest son of the human race and the goal of all biblical prophecy. In the same way, the Koran attributes to Jesus bald-faced endorsements of Islamic doctrines about Jesus in order to cut the ground from Christian opponents (5:16–18; 61:6).

Another early Christian canard (unless it was true, which it might well have been!) against John was that he had been the guru of the Samaritan heresiarchs Simon Magus and Dositheus. "There appeared a certain John the Baptist. . . . [T]here gathered about John thirty eminent persons according to the reckoning of the lunar month. . . . Of these thirty Simon counted with John as the first and most distinguished." He would have been John's successor except that he was away in Egypt when the Baptist died, and Dositheus took over the sect (Clementine *Homilies* 2.23.1–24.1).[27] This made John, from the Christian standpoint, the very fountainhead of heresy. Subsequent Christian writers would make Simon Magus the father of Gnosticism, but originally it was John the Baptizer who held that distinction—until Christians deemed it better to rehabilitate and co-opt John for their own purposes.

Baur saw the Pauline epistles, John, Mark, and Hebrews, as representing Paulinism, Matthew, James, and Revelation as Petrine, with Acts, the Pastorals,

1 and 2 Peter, and Rom. 14:13–15:33 as catholicizing documents reflecting or trying to effect the reconciliation between Judaizing and Pauline factions of the church. In the same way, there are a number of New Testament passages we may point to as pro– or anti–John the Baptist and as effecting or attesting a rapproachment between the John and Jesus factions.

Not only that: we also have a freeze-frame of the debate as seen by disgusted outsiders. "It is like children sitting in the market places and calling to their playmates, 'We piped to you, and you did not dance!' 'We wailed, and you did not mourn!' For John came neither eating nor drinking, and they [Christians] say, 'He is a demoniac.' The Son of Man came eating and drinking, and they [Baptists] say, 'Behold a glutton and a drunkard, friend of tax-collectors and sinners!' Best leave it to history to decide (literally, "But wisdom is vindicated by her children," the outcome)" (Matt. 11:16b–19). The scene here is a dispute between a group of girls and a group of boys, all of whom are willing to play, but the boys insist on the male pursuit of dancing, while the girls only want to play at public mourning, the province of women. They should be playing together, but each group insists on its own way, so nothing happens. In the same way, someone ironically observes how the Jesus and John sects criticize each other, one too strict in the other's eyes, the other too lax for its rivals. The criticism is not directed against the indifferent public of both sects, as is usually assumed, but rather is aimed by that public at both warring sects!

Is the conflict situation envisioned here merely paper speculation? Sometimes we can do no better than impose a paradigm on the data of the text and see how well everything fits. But there is at least a bit more to it in this case. We can recall a possible historical analogy, that of the Bab'i and Baha'i sects after the death of Ali Muhammad, the Bab. In view of his coming execution, the Bab designated his brother Subh-i-Azal as caretaker of the Bab'i community. The next Manifestation of God (like the Bab himself) should appear many thousands of years in the future. Till then the laws newly promulgated by the Bab were to hold good. But suddenly, shortly after the Bab's death, one of his disciples, Hussein Ali, came forth as the next Manifestation of God and took the name Baha'ullah (the Glory of God). If early Christianity were wracked by the delay of the Parousia of the Messiah, the Bab'is were thrown into confusion by their Messiah's arriving way *ahead* of schedule! Many, eventually most, Bab'is followed Baha'ullah, and they became the Baha'i Faith. A minority clung to Subh-i-Azal and is known today as the Azal'is. Here I think we have a close analogy to the sectarian competiton posited between the John and Jesus sects. John predicted the unidentified Coming One. Jesus was preached as the fulfillment of that prediction, and after John's death, some Baptists accepted it (John 1:37, 3:26; Acts 19:1–7). Others were die-hards and held out, at least into the second century, when the author of the Clementines became familiar with their propaganda, and maybe even till today, if the Mandaeans are actually John's sect.

FORERUNNER AFTER THE FACT

Strikingly, both Luke and John have John the Baptizer deny that he is the Messiah. Luke merely adds to his Q material a question that slants the "answer" in a new direction. "As the people were in expectation, and all men were wondering in their hearts about John, whether he were the Christ, John answered them all, 'I baptize you with water; but he who is mightier than I is coming, the thong of whose sandals I am not worthy to untie'" (Luke 3:15–16a). Note that the "answer" is Q material, only there it is not an answer to anything. It is simply an assertion by the preacher. Luke reads into the contrast a denial that John is the Messiah. He does the same sort of thing in Acts 19:1–7, when he has Paul redirect the allegience of Baptist sectarians. Paul reiterates that John had preached that people should "believe in the one who was to come after him, that is, Jesus." Luke does not have Paul say John predicted or acknowledged Jesus by name, only that the one he predicted later turned out to be Jesus. It is left at an inference that Christians draw, but which others might not draw.

John's gospel is more overt. He has John the Baptist asked point-blank, "'Who are you?' He confessed, he did not deny, but confessed, 'I am not the Christ.' And they asked him, 'What, then? Are you Elijah?' He said, 'I am not.' 'Are you Elijah?' And he answered, 'No'" (John 1:19–21). The scene is fictive, artificial, based on the Caesarea Philippi confession scene of Mark 8:27–30. In Mark, it is Jesus whose identity is in question, and he rejects three options offered him: he is not John the Baptist, nor Elijah, nor one of the old prophets, but rather the Christ. Now it is John who is asked, is he the Christ, or Elijah, or the Prophet, but he is none. He is rather the prophesied voice in the wilderness. Obviously, the "Christ" and "John the Baptist" options have switched places. But the point is, he has John deny the very thing his followers believed about him, that John was the Christ.

We saw how Mark and Matthew gave John the status of the returned Elijah, but Luke and John will not grant him even that consolation. John the evangelist has the Baptist asked if he is Elijah, as we have just seen, and he denies that, too! And as Conzelmann observed,[28] Luke considers John simply one more prophet in the long (and continuing) course of salvation history. He is for Luke no harbinger of the end of the age, and for this reason Luke, like John, omits any mention of John's hair-shirt costume. No one should think of him as a second or returned Elijah! And Luke pointedly does not have Jesus explain that John is the returned Elijah as he does in Matt. 11:14, 17:13, and Mark 9:13. If John's sect pushes him a notch higher than Elijah, Luke and John are pushing him a notch lower.

In all likelihood, as Bultmann suggested,[29] the Logos hymn of John, chapter 1, was originally written about the incarnation of John the Baptist and subsequently applied to Jesus by the evangelist who had previously been himself a (Gnostic) Baptist. Note that John the evangelist has made a less-than-subtle correction, adding to the poem the note that no one should any longer imagine that John the Baptizer had been what his sect still claimed he was: the light of the world (John 1:6–8). Why go to all this trouble to deny up and down that John was the Christ, Elijah, the light of the world, unless there were people who believed he was and you wanted them to think someone else was? And yet these passages are not exactly anti-John. No, they are "catholicizing" in tendency in that they are attempting to carve out an appropriate place for John in the Christian scheme of things, other than hell.

Luke and John also seem to be trying to put to rest Baptist gripes against Jesus by turning the tables on the priority argument. Must John have been first in importance because he showed up first? Not if he were the forerunner, and this is what Luke (or his source) makes John by juxtaposing the nativity stories of the two saints, especially in Luke 1:39–44, where he connects the two stories, making Mary and Elizabeth, and therefore Jesus and John, cousins. As Elizabeth enters Mary's room, she feels the fetus leap in the womb in fealty to the embryonic Messiah! Luke seeks not only to subordinate John to Jesus in this way but also to reconcile the two sects, since the ancient reader would have recognized here an ingenious reversal of Gen. 25:22, "The children struggled (Septuagint 'leaped') together within her." Where such gestational gymnastics signaled perpetual enmity between Jacob and Esau and their seed, it means the opposite for the heirs of John and Jesus.

Did it matter so much which prophet had arrived first? To the ancients it did, so John the evangelist has John the Baptist pedantically explain how, even though Jesus appeared in public after he did, Jesus actually preceded him by virtue of heavenly preexistence (1:15, 29–31).

Both Luke and John make an unfavorable comparison between John's baptism and that of the Christian Church. In Acts 19:1–7, Paul stumbles upon a cell of Baptist sectarians in Ephesus. The passage first makes clear that these twelve men were disciples of some type, then reveals that they were still sadly lacking the seal of the Spirit. The poor wretches had undergone the paltry baptism of John but nothing since. Paul urges them to upgrade to Christian baptism, since only that kind brings the Spirit. He baptizes them, lays his hands upon them, and imparts the Spirit, as evidenced by their speaking in tongues. Here the two brands of baptism are contrasted side by side for the sake of Luke's readers, like a television commercial demonstrating which cleanser gets the stain out. Any Baptists reading Acts 19:1–7 are to take away a clear message: get rebaptized. (Incidentally, one must think again of Bultmann's suggestion[30] that the gospel pictures of John predicting Spirit baptism are anachronistic, because in Acts 19:3, Baptist followers profess never to have heard of such a creature as the Holy Spirit!)

John 3:22–30, 4:1–2 set up an object lesson by means of another anachronism. In order, again, to compare Johannine and Christian baptism side by side for the sake of Baptist readers, John the evangelist retrojects the baptismal competition into the days of Jesus and John themselves. The improbable result is that

Jesus himself is overseeing the baptism of new disciples and in great numbers. The fact that it is his disciples doing it, not, strictly speaking, Jesus himself, is a dead giveaway (as it will be in many another gospel passage) that it is not the historical practice of Jesus himself but rather that of the church in the evangelist's day that is being depicted.[31] John's intended reader becomes a character, or rather characters, in the text: "Now a discussion arose between John's disciples and a Jew over purifying. And they came to John, and said to him, 'Rabbi, he who was with you beyond the Jordan, to whom you bore witness, here he is, baptizing, and all are going to him'" (3:25–26). The self-effacing Baptist assures his anxious disciples that he is not worried; he only ever intended to prepare the stage for Jesus, and now he is happy to retire to the wings. "He who has the bride is the bridegroom; the friend of the bridegroom, who stands and hears him, rejoices greatly at the bridegroom's voice; therefore this joy of mine is now full. He must increase, but I must decrease" (3:29–30). The story is a fiction from beginning to end, not least because it would seem to be based on Mark 2:18–22, "Now John's disciples and the Pharisees were fasting; and people came and said to him, 'Why do John's disciples and the disciples of the Pharisees fast, but your disciples do not fast?' And Jesus said to them, 'Can the wedding guests fast while the bridegroom is with them? As long as they have the bridegroom with them, they cannot fast.'" In both cases, there is a debate about some ritual of purification/penitance, and Jesus' practice is contrasted with John's, and there is a third Jewish party involved, too. In both cases, the bridegroom image is invoked to explain the situation in which something seems untoward. In both cases, Jesus is the bridegroom. In Mark, the disciples of Jesus are the groomsmen, while in John it is John the Baptist who is the best man. He was not in the wedding party at all in Mark's version. But in John's version, the Baptist reader knows what he has to do next: drop his outmoded loyalty to John and get with the program.

THE BAPTISM OF JESUS

The theological tensions between the sects of Jesus and the Baptizer provide the necessary context for understanding the various stories of Jesus' baptism and why they differ as they do. We must examine the growing tradition stage by stage. We begin with Mark and Q. This is one of the thorniest patches of gospel source criticism, for though we usually say Q is the second source used by Matthew and Luke in addition to Mark, and that it constituted the material Matthew and Luke have in common that is not in Mark, there is in fact a good case to be made that Mark knew Q, paraphrased a few sayings from it, and just copied a couple sections.[32] Specifically, Mark's versions of the Baptism and Temptation episodes, as well as the Beelzebul Controversy, appear to be abbreviated editions of the versions we read in Matthew and Luke. This doesn't mean Mark is the abbreviator of the other two Synoptics, as some claim. It need mean no more than that Mark used a bit less of Q than did Matthew and Luke at these points.

At any rate, according to Mark 1:9–11, John baptizes Jesus simply as one more face in the crowd. There is no hint that he recognizes him or knows who he is. Jesus alone sees the vision of the opening of the sky and the descent of the Spirit. Only he hears the heavenly voice. If Mark is based here on a slightly longer Q baptism account, there was little additional in Q. Later in Q (Matt. 11:2–6//Luke 7:18–23), however, we find John in prison after his arrest by Herod Antipas. He hears of the miracles of Jesus and hope begins to dawn: could it be the Coming One has arrived? He sends a delegation of disciples to Jesus to ask. Jesus returns a somewhat equivocal answer, and we never hear what John made of it or of him. As Strauss observed,[33] chipping away the harmonizing mortar that held this text together with the baptism scenes of Matthew and John, this Q scene in no way implies that John had lost an initial faith in Jesus as the Coming One as he marked time in solitary, only to have his hopes rekindled. No, rather it is clear John has not before heard of this remarkable man of whom he now hears intriguing reports. For the earliest sources, then, Q and Mark, John did not know Jesus when he baptized him, and he only later heard of him and wondered if this man, unknown to him, might be the Coming One. And, remarkably, Mark and Q leave it open whether John the Baptist ever became a believer in Jesus. No doubt this means he didn't, or we would certainly hear of it.[34]

Luke 3:19–22 seeks to minimize John's involvement in the baptism, apparently so as to provide as little occasion as possible for Baptist readers to seize upon the fact and declare, "See? Your man was baptized by our man! What does that tell you?" Luke actually has John arrested and jailed before he relates the baptism of Jesus in a flashback tucked away in a subordinate clause! "When all the people were baptized, and when Jesus also had been baptized and was praying" (3:21), and then ensues the vision and the voice, all still the private experience of Jesus. The reader might be forgiven for asking, "Who baptized him?" Of course, it had to be John, but the convoluted character of the sentence seems intended to put as much distance as possible between the two. Even here, however, note that Luke has no hint of John already knowing Jesus, despite the implication of his own double-nativity story that the two cousins would have been acquainted. But that, too, was a fiction, and it does not occur to him to modify the tradition of the baptism that way, when he has this way in mind. They are two alternative ways of saying the same thing: Jesus is not subordinate to John. Again, even in Acts 19:1–7 Luke is careful not to give the impression that John proclaimed Jesus as the Coming One, even though Luke himself believes he was.

Matthew (3:13–17) has a very different story. John immediately recognizes Jesus as the Coming One and protests that it is not his right to baptize Jesus, who should instead be baptizing him! That is, of course, the way Matthew and other early Christians wish it had happened! In addition, now the voice from heaven speaks to all present ("This is"), and we do not read that "Jesus saw" the dove descending, only that it did descend, implying this, too, was for public consumption. The fictive character of Matthew's dialogue between the flustered John and the self-assured Jesus is evident not only from its tendentiousness but also from its arbitrariness: how did John know Jesus was the Coming One? The later evangelist of the Gospel according to the Ebionites recognized the problem here, so he borrowed from Paul's vision on the Damascus Road in Acts 9: "And immediately a great light shone around the place; and John, seeing it, said to him, 'Who are you, Lord?' And again a voice from heaven said unto him, 'This is my beloved Son in whom I am well pleased.' Then John, falling down before him, said, 'I beseech you, Lord, baptize me!' But he forbade him, saying, 'Let it be so; for thus it is fitting to fulfill all things" (preserved in Epiphanius *Against Heresies* or *Panarion* 30.13.7–8).[35] John's gospel (1:29–34) takes the most drastic approach to the embarrassment of Jesus having been baptized by John—it doesn't happen! Yes, John sees the Spirit descend upon Jesus, but this happens offstage, and John merely says he has seen it at some previous point, and this is what tipped him off to Jesus being the Elect of God (unlike Matthew, where John knows Jesus *before* the Spirit descends upon him). In John's gospel, there is no voice from heaven proclaiming Jesus as God's Son. It is John the Baptist himself who proclaims the news! And if these two versions of John's recognizing and endorsing Jesus as Messiah did not contradict one another, they both contradict the earlier Mark-Q-Luke version. The controlling factor is the increasing urgency of satisfying the qualms of Baptist sectarians and attracting them to the Christian camp.

But that is not the only trajectory along which the baptism narrative grew and evolved. The Markan version itself began to afford new embarrassments as Christian history progressed. After all, John's was a baptism for repenting sinners! What on earth was Jesus doing there? In modern terms, this is like Jesus going forward in a Billy Graham rally! Apparently, Mark saw nothing amiss. After all, it is a good thing to repent, isn't it? The same humility that led Jesus to wade into the Jordan that day also bade him deflect the polite flattery of a well-wisher in Mark 10:17–18. "Why do you call me good? No one is good but God alone!" Needless to say, the thought never entered Mark's head that Jesus might be an incarnation of God. That is a later stage of Christology, and when theologians arrived there, Mark 10:17–18 became a headache for which no cure has yet been found.

But Matthew does represent a more advanced stage of Christological reflection, and it is interesting to see what he does with this element of the baptism story. In 3:1, introducing the Baptist, he omits from his Markan text the description of the rite as a baptism of repentence for the forgiveness of sins, as if there might possibly be some other reason for showing up. Again, there is the panicky reluctance of John, who seems to fear it would be blasphemy to baptize Jesus; Jesus sets his mind at ease, telling him, "It behooves us in this way to fulfill all righteousness," which is Matthean lingo for "to perform all acts of piety." That isn't much of an explanation for poor John (or for the reader, for whom he stands), but the point is, "Don't worry; at least he wasn't there to have his sins forgiven!" We can be pretty sure we are correctly gauging Matthew's intention here because of what he also does to Mark 10:17–18. There, a polite inquirer has addressed Jesus with the honorific "Good teacher" and asked, "What must I do to inherit eternal life," causing Jesus to recoil with the pedantic denial, "Why do you call me good? No one is good but God alone!" Matthew alters this interchange so that it reads, "Teacher, what good deed must I do to have eternal life?" "Why do you ask me concerning what is good? One there is who is good" (Matt. 19:16–17). So Jesus is not flattered and need not repudiate it. Nor does he deny his own good-ness, which is for Matthew the operative concern. The trend here is evident.

The Gospel according to the Hebrews deals in its own way with the embar-rassment. "The mother of the Lord and his brothers said to him, 'John baptizes for the forgiveness of sins; let us go and be baptized by him.' But he said to them, 'In what have I sinned that I should go and be baptized by him? Unless, perhaps, what I have just said is a sin of ignorance" (preserved in Jerome *Against Pelagius* 3.2).[36] One feels sure the scene must have ended with something like this: "And they did not understand the saying which he spoke to them. And he went down with them . . . and was obedient to them" (Luke 2:50–51a). Once we see how this trajectory spins itself out, it becomes easier to recognize the tendency in passages where it has not gone quite so far.[37]

Another trajectory we can plot through the development of the baptism story is a Christological one dealing with the sonship of Jesus. The average reader of the New Testament reads Matthew before Mark and then goes on to Luke and John. Matthew gives him the impression that Jesus was born God's Son in a miraculous fashion. Mark begins only with the baptism, but the reader will think little of this: perhaps Mark begins in medias res. With Luke we are back to a miraculous nativity for one born the Son of God. In John the reader learns that Jesus had already been God's Son from all eternity. But suppose one read Mark by itself, as its first readers did. What impression would one receive? Surely in a book where the main character shows up as an adult and, right off the bat, expe-riences a vision of divine calling in which he and no one else is told that he is God's Son, the natural inference would be that the baptism was the beginning of an honorific Sonship. If he were already God's son, wouldn't he have known it? And then why should God tell him what he already knew? It seems that Mark might believe what others in the early church did, namely, in Jesus' *adoptive* Son-ship. Ebionite Jewish Christians and Cerinthian (also Jewish) Gnostics were adop-tionists, rejecting any miraculous generation of Jesus Christ from the deity. Epiphanius of Salamis tells us the Cerinthians believed "that after Jesus, who had been engendered from Joseph's seed and Mary, had grown up, Christ, that is the Holy Spirit in the form of a dove, came down into him in the Jordan from above, from the God above, and revealed to him and through him to those with him the unknown Father. And for this reason, because power from above came into him, he worked deeds of power" (*Panarion* 1.314.5–6).[38] Once we know this was a popular, though eventually controversial, option among early Christians, it begins to make a new sense that the earliest gospel, Mark, sounds adoptionist but is flanked and overwhelmed by subsequent gospels that have moved the Sonship further and further back, attributing to Jesus some degree of divine nature in the process. In fact, this looks to be why Mark has the baptismal Spirit descend "into" (εις) Jesus instead of "upon" (εν) him as Matthew and Luke both have it. They seem to want to avoid the implication that, as Basilides and others believed, Jesus was thenceforth possessed by some heavenly entity alien to his original nature.

God Quotes God

One of the prophetic experiences of Jesus at his baptism was the hearing of God's voice from heaven. Mark and Luke have Jesus alone as its audience, while Matthew turns it aside to speak to all the dripping crowd, and John omits it entirely. What does it say, and why? Mark 1:11 and most manuscripts of Luke 3:22 have the voice say, "You are my beloved Son, in whom I am well pleased." The fictive character of this brief speech is evident from its scribal nature. Short though it is, it has been cobbled together from three Old Testament passages. The author thought it right to make a new utterance of God sound authentic by synthesizing it from old texts. The first of these is Ps. 2:7, where Yahve announces to the newly crowned king of Judah, "You are my son; today I have begotten you." The Psalm in question was a coronation anthem repeated as part of the enthronement liturgy every time a new king took the throne (or perhaps every year at the enthronement festival). All alike were God's sons by virtue of the Davidic succession (2 Sam. 7:11b–16). After the fall of the monarchy to Babylon, Psalms like this were reinterpreted as referring in predictive fashion to the future king from David's line, the Messiah.

The second scripture fragment is Isa. 42:1, where God says of Israel (or its priestly aristocracy), about to return from the Exile, "Behold my servant, whom I uphold, my chosen, in whom my soul delights." (Matthew goes on to quote the whole of verses 1–4 in another context, also referring to Jesus, in Matt. 12:18–20). The third is Gen. 22:12, in the Greek Septuagint, where a voice from heaven calls to Abraham, telling him not to sacrifice his "beloved son" after all. Here the intended parallel is with Isaac, whose near death was counted in rabbinic theology as atoning for the sins of Israel. According to the Targums (freely interpretive Aramaic paraphrased versions of Scripture), Isaac, bound on the altar, looked up into an open heaven and saw angels and the Shekinah glory cloud of God, and a voice said, "Behold, two chosen ones."[39]

The theological point of this rich mosaic of conflated texts is to combine in Jesus Christ the roles of king, servant, and sacrifice. It is both clever and profound. But it is not historical, unless one wishes to imagine God sitting with his Hebrew Psalter, Greek Septuagint, and Aramaic Targum open in front of him, deciding what to crib. Only then does it come to seem ridiculous.

SOMETHING AT THE BOTTOM?

When you strip away the layers of edifying legend and controversial mythology, was Jesus baptized by John? A poll among New Testament scholars would no doubt yield a near-unanimous "yes" vote. The only item in the life story of Jesus considered equally secure is his crucifixion. And the reason for this is perfectly clear by now: the baptism was so embarrassing to Christians, both because it seems to subordinate Jesus to John and because it seems to cast Jesus as a repentant sinner, that the early church would never have fabricated it. Such reasoning is understandable, but it is also easily refuted, as long as one recalls that what offended one generation did not offend another. Mark seemingly had little enough trouble with a repenting Jesus. He appears not to have regarded himself "stuck" with the notion. Anyone who saw nothing amiss in it could have made it up if there were something useful in the story and there was. As some have suggested, the story may simply have originated as a cultic etiology to provide a paradigm for baptism: "Are you able to be baptized with the baptism I am baptized with?"

And originally, Christians may have seen baptism by John as a credential, an authorization, even without an explicit endorsement of Jesus by John, in much the same way President Clinton cherished the videotape showing a youthful version of himself shaking hands with President Kennedy. There may well have been a period (or geographical areas) in which no Christians perceived the followers of John the Baptist as rivals, a period in which both men were venerated side by side in a larger "Essene" community. And, as we will shortly see, there is a comparative religion parallel to the baptism of Jesus in the calling and temptation story of the Prophet Zoroaster. It would be easy to see in the parallel yet another example of the law of biographical analogy, or of outright borrowing, as Judaism and Christianity appear to have borrowed so much important material from Zoroastrianism.

IF YOU ARE THE SON OF GOD . . .

The Synoptic gospels agree that after being baptized, Jesus was driven by the Spirit, to which he was newly sensitive, out into the desert to be tested or tempted (same Greek word) by Satan. According to popular belief (Matt. 12:43), the demons lived in the desert, hence Jesus goes there to find the devil. (John's gospel has neither the story of the temptation nor any room for it. Remember, in that gospel Jesus is not baptized and leaves the Jordan to return home to Galilee after only a few days in John's vicinity.)

The role of tempter, by the way, was entirely in keeping with the historic role of the Satan figure in the Old Testament. "Satan," originally not a proper name but a title, "the Adversary," was a servant of God, a kind of security chief who occasionally urged the Almighty to take a second look at his favorites about whose character the Satan harbored some doubts. In the prose prologue added to the drama of Job, he has no interest in victimizing Job; he suspects Job is making a fool of God, his piety a pretense in order to keep the divine largesse coming. Job passes the test the Satan puts him through. In Zech. 3:1–5, the Satan hauls the high priest Joshua before the judgment bar, where his guilt is revealed before God but forgiven. In 1 Chr. 21:1, the Satan carries out God's own plan (cf. 2 Sam. 24:1) to catch David in a sting operation to see if he will abandon the traditional rules of Holy War and take an inventory of his troops. David fails with disastrous consequences. Thus, in the Gospels it seems only natural that Jesus, newly commissioned as God's Son, should be put through his paces by the Satan to determine whether he is really up to the job. That is the point of the taunt, "If you are the Son of God. . . ." Does Jesus understand what that entails? In the same way, Luke will later (22:31–32) portray Satan, again in character, as demanding, as is his right, to sift the twelve disciples like wheat, the same task as the Baptist ascribes to the Coming One, and they fail the test. Peter unwittingly acts the role of the Adversary when he tests Jesus' resolve to go forward with the crucifixion (Mark 8:32–33). Satan becomes the enemy of God and the champion of evil only insofar as he becomes mixed with other ancient characters like Beelzebul the Ekronite oracle-god (Matt. 12:24, 26; 2 Kings 1:2), Leviathan the Chaos Dragon (Ps. 74:13–14; Rev. 12:3 ff.), and Ahriman the Zoroastrian antigod (2 Cor. 4:4; Luke 10:17–19).

HE BIDS HIM COME AND DIET

Q and Mark agree that Jesus spent forty days in the desert. Mark does not picture Jesus fasting, as he says "the angels served him," presumably bringing him food as the angel fed Elijah in 1 Kings 19:5. Matthew and Luke (therefore Q) have Jesus fasting the whole time, like Moses (Exod. 34:28; Deut. 9:9, 18) and Elijah (1 Kings 19:8), who each fasted forty days. It is pretty clear, however, that for Q the forty days in the wilderness are intended to stand for the forty years Israel wandered in the wilderness with Moses. As Old Testament Israel was God's son (Hos. 11:1), so is Jesus. Will he do better, be more faithful, than Israel, who tried God's patience with all its murmuring? The key is the series of Scripture quotations with which Jesus is made to parry the temptations of Satan.

Matthew and Luke differ over the order of the temptations, and it is more likely Matthew who has preserved the original order in Q, whereby the greatest temptation comes at the end as a climax. Luke may have thought it more likely that Jesus should proceed from desert to mountain (if this is what he pictured; Luke does not actually say there was a mountain as Matthew does, only that Satan "took him up"), then to Jerusalem. Then again, Matthew may have left the offer of the world's kingdoms for last to *make* it the climax. Who knows? Matthew makes Jesus view the world map from the top of a very high mountain, presupposing a flat earth as well as a fairy-tale mountain, not one on any natural map.

The first temptation: *Change these rocks to loaves!* (Matt. 4:3–4//Luke 4:3–4). The picture is that of changing round, smooth stones into similar-looking barley loaves, which looked like modern dinner rolls. Jesus is, after all, quite hungry! "If you are the Son of God, prove it!" Jesus rebuts the proposition by quoting part of Deut. 8:3, "And he humbled you and let you hunger and fed you with manna, which you did not know, nor did your fathers know; that he might make you know that man does not live by bread alone, but that man lives by everything [or every word] that proceeds out of the mouth of Yahve."

The second temptation: *Leap tall buildings in a single bound!* (Matt. 4:5–7//Luke 4:9–12). If Jesus is so sure of God's fatherly providence, why not put it to the test? Jump off a building and see if the angels will catch you! But Jesus, unlike modern Charismatic television preachers, realizes God is not a genie one may command. (Note, however, the element of magical teleportation: we are not to imagine Jesus *walking* to Jerusalem and managing to climb to the topmost ledge of the temple without anybody trying to stop him!) Jesus this time quotes Deut. 6:16, "You shall not put Yahve your God to the test, as you tested him at Massah." Again, Jesus succeeds where old Israel failed.

The third temptation: *Sell me your soul!* (Matt. 4:8–10//Luke 4:5–8). Here, as in the previous scene, Satan magically teleports Jesus through space. This time Jesus is essentially being offered the option to "gain the whole world and lose his own soul" (Mark 8:36), since he must bow to Satan, or swear fealty, not become a Satanist in the modern sense of "worshiping Satan." It is interesting that Luke adds to the speech of Satan, apparently in order to explain how Satan can be in the position to make such an offer in the first place. Is it a bluff? No, for he has been entrusted with the kingdoms of the world, and he doles them out like a spoils system to his cronies! This smacks of extreme world-alienated apocalypticism or Gnosticism, almost like the belief of the Yezidi sect, which does worship Satan, at least placates him, because it believes God has put him in charge of the earth! Does Luke intend such drastic implications? In any case, Jesus banishes Satan, successfully completing his tests, with the citation of Deut. 6:13–14, "You shall fear Yahve your God; you shall serve him, and swear by his name. You shall not go after other gods, any of the gods of the peoples who are round about you."

The whole narrative is a midrash (narrative commentary) upon Deuteronomy and the wilderness stories it deals with. The contrast, again, is between Jesus and Israel. He proved faithful where they proved faithless. It is therefore fictive, which is no strike against it.

The temptation story is also another choice instance of the law of biographical analogy at work. The hero myth regularly has the hero prove his worth early on by passing some test. Hercules had twelve labors to perform. Oedipus had to decipher the riddle of the Sphinx, then kill it. Closer to home, the story is highly reminiscent of a story in *Gemara Sanhedrin* where Abraham is thrice tempted by the devil and the two trade Scripture quotes. Here is a similar one from *Midrash Hag-gadol*: "When Abraham was on his way to Mount Moriah to sacrifice his son Isaac, Satan met him and said, 'Old man, where art thou going?' He answered, 'I am going to fulfill the will of my Father in Heaven.' Then Satan said unto him, 'What did he tell thee?' Abraham answered, 'To bring my son to him as a burnt-offering' Thereupon Satan said, 'That an old man like thee should make such a mistake! His intention was only to lead thee astray and to tire thee! Behold, it is written, "Whoso sheds man's blood, by man his blood shall be shed." Thou art the man who bringest mankind under the wings of the Shechinah. If thou wilt sacrifice thy son, they will all leave thee and call thee murderer.'"[40]

IT IS NOT YOUR LOT TO SHOO FLIES

The story is also strikingly similar, though not in any specific detail that would suggest direct borrowing, to that of the temptation of Prince Siddhartha. Mara the Tempter, king of the material world (much as Luke describes Satan), becomes aware that Siddhartha is about to discover his secret, the trick whereby Mara keeps his dupes the human race enslaved to him, addicted to the suffering inherent in the material world. He knows he must put a stop to it before it is too late. Siddhartha has taken his seat in the shade of the Bodhi Tree (tree of enlightenment), where he has resolved to remain till the truth dawns upon him (as it will that very night). Mara tries every trick in the book to distract him from attaining Enlightenment (Buddhahood). First, he disguises himself as a messenger from the royal court of Siddhartha's father, King Suddhodana: can he not come home? His cousin Devadatta (the Buddhist Judas) has usurped the throne and abducted Siddhartha's wife! But Siddhartha sees through the ruse. Second, Mara sends his three voluptuous daughters to bump and grind before Siddhartha, but this is just the sort of diversion that had so grown to disgust the prince in the first place. Third, Mara sends whirlwinds, rainstorms, a flood, but the Naga king comes up from the ground and shelters the lone contemplative beneath his multiple cobra hoods. Fourth, Mara directs a shower of boulders, a rain of poisoned weapons, but the prince is untouched. The gods change the dangerous objects into blossoms that fall harmlessly around him. Fifth, Mara challenges Siddhartha's right to the piece of ground where he sits, but he calls upon the earth itself, who answers, affirming his right won through many lifetimes of accumulated karma. Despite all these interruptions, the prince then receives Enlightenment, becomes the Buddha in truth. But Mara sees one more chance: he approaches the Buddha, congratulates him, and says he might as well go ahead and attain final Nirvana right now, since none of the thick-headed human race will even be interested in a cure of what ails them! Of all the temptations, this one comes closest to success! For the Buddha is under no illusions about human nature (John 2:25). But upon a moment's reflection he decides, "Some will listen," and goes in search of his first converts. Mara has lost.[41]

THE ILLUMINATOR COMES TO THE WATER

Zoroaster was also tempted as he embarked on his mission. He began as a priest of the old Vedic religion. One day when he was thirty years old (Luke 3:23), he waded out into a river to obtain water for the *haoma* ceremony. Returning to the riverbank in a state of ritual purity from having immersed himself in the sacred element of water, he beheld in a vision the archangel Vohu Mana (Good Thought) sent from Ahura Mazda. The angel instructed him concerning the true God (Ahura Mazda, "Wise Lord," was apparently the same as Varuna, who had been the high god of the Aryan pantheon before the warrior Indra displaced him) and commissioned him prophet of the new Zoroastrian faith (*Dinkard* 3.51–61).[42] The archangel swept him up into heaven to confer with Ahura Mazda. Later, after a period of study and meditation in the countryside, Zoroaster found himself face to face with the evil Ahriman, seeking to avert him from his mission: "Do not destroy my creatures, O holy Zarathustra! Renounce the good law of the worshippers of Mazda, and thou shalt gain such a boon as the murderer gained, the ruler of the nations." Zoroaster's reply: "No! Never will I renounce the good law of the worshippers of Mazda, though my body, my life, my soul should burst!" (*Fargard* 19.1.6–7).[43]

   This history-of-religions parallel is perhaps the most important, because in it we find the whole baptism-and-temptation complex seen in the Synoptic gospels. As suggested in the previous chapter, it is not at all unlikely that we find right here the whole basis for the Synoptic story of both baptism and temptation. Like so much else, it may have come straight from Zoroastrianism. There, and in the New Testament and adjacent literature, we can detect an archaic mytheme whereby a divine virgin and/or pregnant woman is menaced by a dragon or other evil forces and is spirited away to safety, sometimes from the water, to a remote (desert or mountain) place of refuge. The original version is that of Rhea's deceiving the hungry Kronos and hiding baby Zeus from his father's wrath. We find one version of it in the *Liqqute Midrash*, set in the days of great wickedness before the Flood: "In those days only one virgin, Istahar by name, remained chaste. When the Sons of God made lecherous demands upon her, she cried, "First lend me your wings!" They assented and she, flying up to Heaven, took sanctuary at the Throne of God, who transformed her into the constellation Virgo."[44]

We find it again in the Gnostic text The Hypostasis of the Archons, also a variation on the Genesis primordial history. This time, Eve is the divine virgin, a heavenly entity, and something of a mother to Adam, as to the rest of humanity: "And the spirit-endowed woman came to him and spoke with him, saying, 'Arise, Adam.' And when he saw her, he said, 'It is you have given me life; you will be called "Mother of the living."—For it is she who is my mother. It is she who is the physician, and the woman, and she who has given birth.' Then the authorities came up to their Adam. And when they saw his female counterpart speaking with him, they became agitated with great agitation, and they became enamored of her. They said to one another, 'Come, let us sow our seed in her,' and they pursued her. And she laughed at them for their witlessness and their blindness; and in their clutches, she became a tree, and left before them her shadowy reflection resembling herself; and they defiled it foully" (89:11–25).[45] The spiritual Eve then fled away and used the trick of Daphne to escape Apollo's lustful embrace, turning into a tree. Note that Eve bears the same epithet as Aruru, another version of Ishtar, "Mother of all living" (as in Gen. 3:20). Istahar, obviously, is also another version of Ishtar.

Another Nag Hammadi text preserves what may be the original version of the myth.[46] It is a Sethian Gnostic document called *The Apocalypse of Adam* and purports to be an ancient revelation received by Seth from his father, Adam, on his deathbed. The document embodies heavy Zoroastrian imagery and may even be a Sethian edition of an older Zoroastrian work. Most of it is taken up with a review of the twelve incarnations of Zoroaster, one each in one of the twelve successive kingdoms (historical periods) of mankind. The first is that of the historical Zoroaster, founder of the Zoroastrian religion. The second sees him reappear in the form of the Iranian hero Zal (also called Dastan), brought up in the mountains by the mythic Simurgh bird. Zal reappeared from concealment to perform his heroic exploits. The Apocalypse of Adam says of him: "He originated from a great prophet. And a bird came, took the child who was born, and carried him to a high mountain. And he was nourished by the bird of heaven. An angel came forth there and said to him, 'Rise up, God has given you glory!' He received glory and strength. And thus he came upon the water."[47] The last two sentences are a repeated refrain throughout the document, and they refer to the Zoroastrian belief in the Saoshyant, or Benefactor, a descendant or reincarnation of Zoroaster, who would appear again and again as needed through the ages till his eschatological Parousia. The water image refers to the detail that each rebirth of the Saoshyant would be occasioned by a virgin bathing in the Lake Hamun and becoming impregnated by the living sperm of Zoroaster hidden there. The Apocalypse of Adam proceeds this way with all twelve incarnations of "the Illuminator," Zoroaster, and then adds a thirteenth kingdom, of the sons of Shem. The Illuminator appears in this kingdom, too: "And the thirteenth kingdom says of him that every birth of their ruler is a word. And his word received a mandate there. He received glory and power. And thus he came to the water, in order that the desire of those powers might be satisfied."[48] The point of this less-than-obvious wording seems to be to refer to the Word Jesus Christ as the rebirth of Zoroaster the Illuminator. His coming to the water seems to be his baptism, and there he received the call of God to messiahship.

It is interesting to trace the progress of the mytheme further, for the explicit Christian stories of Jesus' baptism seem to reflect it. In Mark, Jesus is designated Son of God as he came up from the water. The descending dove preserves the mythic element of the wings. According to Justin Martyr, "When Jesus went down to the water, fire was kindled in the Jordan" (*Dialogue with Trypho* 88:3).[49] The Gospel of the Ebionites has, "And immediately a great light shone around the place."[50] Two Italic manuscripts of Matt. 3:15 have, "and when he was baptized a huge light shone from the water so that all who were near were frightened."[51] He is, thus, so to speak, the Illuminator. Jesus is then driven by the Holy Spirit into the desert, where he is harassed by Satan. From thence he returns to perform great deeds. According to the Gospel According to the Hebrews, a second-century Greek gospel used by Jewish Christians in Egypt, Jesus, looking back on the baptism, recalls, "Even so did my mother, the Holy Spirit, take me by one of my hairs and carry me away on to the great mountain of Tabor" (Origen *Homily on Jeremiah*, 15:4).[52] Here are the Illuminator at the water, his rebirth as the Son, the divine wings, the spiriting away by the divine Mother, the retreat to the desert and pursuit by the evil one.

Finally, the Revelation of John repeats the myth, "And a great portent appeared in heaven, a woman clothed with the sun, with the moon under her feet, and on her head a crown of twelve stars; she was with child, and she cried out in her birth pangs, in anguish for delivery. And another portent appeared in heaven; behold a great red dragon with seven heads and ten horns, and seven diadems upon his heads. His tail swept down a third of the stars of heaven, and cast them down to the earth. And the dragon stood before the woman, who was about to bear a child, that he might devour her child when she brought it forth; she brought forth a male child, one who is to rule all the nations with a rod of iron, but her child was caught up to God and to his throne, and the woman fled into the wilderness, where she has a place prepared by God, in which to be nourished for one thousand two hundred and sixty days. . . . And when the dragon saw that he had been thrown down to the earth, he pursued the woman who had born the male child. But the woman was given the two wings of the great eagle that she might fly from the serpent into the wilderness, to the place where she is to be nourished for a time, and times, and half a time. The serpent poured water like a river out of his mouth after the woman, to sweep her away with the flood. But the earth came to the help of the woman, and the earth opened its mouth and swallowed the river which the dragon had poured from his mouth" (Rev. 12:1–6, 13–16).

The woman stands for the constellation Virgo, "pursued" across the starry sky by the dragon Draco, just as God turned the fleeing virgin Istahar into the constellation Virgo. Here again are the wings, the water, the mother, the birth of

the hero, the refuge in the wilderness, the pursuit by the evil one. The only difference between this Jesus version of the myth and the baptism version is that the
former is stated in more raw mythic terms, while the latter has fleshed it out and
historicized it. (Matthew has historicized the same myth another way, too. At
Jesus' physical birth, he is at once pursued by the evil one in the role of Herod
the Great and carried away by his mother into Egypt.)

It therefore appears that the baptism of Jesus is a concretization of a very
ancient myth.

NOTES

1. One of the greatest authorites on Mandaeanism, Edwin M. Yamauchi, *Pre-Christian Gnosticism: A Survey of the Proposed Evidences* (Grand Rapids: William B. Eerdmans, 1973), p. 125, follows Wayne Meeks and others in denying any historical connection to John the Baptist and suggests that the Nasorean sect fictively attached itself to his
name in the seventh century to avert the persecuting wrath of Muslims by claiming status
as a "People of the Book," like protected Jews and Christians. The only biblical prophet
who might be considered neither a Jew nor a Christian was John, so they chose him for
that reason. That may be true, but then why the sheer animosity toward Jesus, whom Islam
reveres as the true messiah?

2. Arthur Drews, *The Christ Myth*, trans. C. Leslie Burns, Westminster College–Oxford:
Classics in the Study of Religion (Amherst, N.Y.: Prometheus Books, 1998), pp. 120–22.

3. William Whiston, trans., *The Works of Flavius Josephus* (London: Ward, Lock
& Co., n.d.), p. 478.

4. John C. Meagher, *Five Gospels: An Account of How the Good News Came to Be*
(Minneapolis: Winston Press, 1983), pp. 37–38.

5. Cecil Roth, *The Dead Sea Scrolls: A New Historical Approach* (New York:
W. W. Norton, 1965).

6. Robert Eisenman, "Maccabees, Zadokites, Christians and Qumran: A New
Hypothesis of Qumran Origins," in *The Dead Sea Scrolls and the First Christians: Essays
and Translations* (Rockport: Element Books, 1996), pp. 3–21 ff.

7. Graham Chapman et al., *Monty Python's Life of Brian (of Nazareth)* (New York:
Ace Books, 1979), p. 39.

8. *The Dead Sea Scriptures in English Translation*, trans. Theodor H. Gaster
(Garden City: Doubleday Anchor, 1957), p. 45.

9. Ibid., p. 139.

10. Robert Eisler, *The Messiah Jesus and John the Baptist* (New York: Dial Press,
1931), p. 254.

11. Barbara Thiering, *Jesus and the Riddle of the Dead Sea Scrolls: Unlocking the
Secrets of his Life Story* (San Francisco: HarperSanFrancisco, 1992).

12. Jacob L. Teicher nominated Jesus as the Teacher of Righteousness in a 1951
series of articles in *Journal of Jewish Studies*; see Robert M. Price, *Deconstructing Jesus*
(Amherst, N.Y.: Prometheus Books, 2000), p. 72, for a listing. And of course Robert
Eisenman makes James the Just the Teacher.

13. Josephus, *The Jewish War*, trans. G. A. Williamson (Baltimore: Penguin Books, 1959), p. 397.

14. Eisler, *Messiah Jesus and John the Baptist*, p. 235; Hugh J. Schonfield, *The Passover Plot: New Light on the History of Jesus* (New York: Bernard Geis/Random House, 1965), pp. 63–64.

15. Interestingly, the film version of *The Passover Plot* (by Millard Cohan and Patricia Knop, directed by Michael Campus, Cannon Video, 1989) by Hugh J. Schonfield, a not uncritical admirer of Eisler's work, depicts John as Jesus' colleague and confidant, but as a much older man, a graybeard as opposed to Jesus' youthful vigor.

16. Hans Conzelmann, *The Theology of St. Luke*, trans. Geoffrey Buswell (New York: Harper & Row, 1961), p. 102.

17. Eisler, *Messiah Jesus and John the Baptist*, pp. 262 ff.

18. Ibid., p. 265–66.

19. Bultmann, *History of the Synoptic Tradition*, trans. John Marsh (New York: Harper & Row, 1972), p. 246.

20. Raymond E. Brown, "John the Baptist in the Gospel of John," in *New Testament Essays* (Garden City: Doubleday Image, 1968), pp. 179–81.

21. Meagher, *Five Gospels*, p. 61.

22. Schonfield, *Passover Plot*, pp. 175–79. Though unfashionable, the "mistaken identity" theory is quite attractive given the astonishing and persistent business about the Risen Jesus not being recognizable at first sight: Matt. 28:17b ("but they doubted"); [Mark 16:12]; Luke 24:16; John 20:14).

23. Mark has done exactly the same thing as the J redactor, who, as a Judean, could not countenance the cult etiology of Dan and Bethel, whereby the priests used to tell the pilgrims that they had known to symbolize Yahve as a young bull because in the days of Moses, Aaron had passed the gold into the fire and let divine providence determine the emergent icon's form. But J, the Yahvist, hated to toss aside a piece of tradition, so he made the miracle into a pathetic excuse by Aaron, trying to evade responsibility for designing the (to Judeans) idolatrous Golden Calf (Exod. 32:1–6, 22–24).

24. Hugh J. Schonfield, trans., *The Authentic New Testament* (New York: New American Library, 1958), p. 104, n. 77.

25. "That his eyes should not be broken"— blinded by John's glory? Or does it mean *John's* eyes will not be broken, that he alone might look upon the face of God and live?

26. *The Writings of Tatian and Theophilus; and the Clementine Recognitions*, trans. B. P. Pratten, Marcus Dods, and Thomas Smith, Ante-Nicene Christian Library: Translations of the Writings of the Fathers Down to A.D. 325, ed. Alexander Roberts and James Donaldson, vol. 3 (Edinburgh: T. & T. Clark, 1880), p. 182.

27. J. Irmscher, trans., "The Pseudo-Clementines," in *New Testament Apocrypha. Volume Two: Writings Relating to the Apostles, Apocalyses and Related Subjects*, ed. Edgar Hennecke, Wilhelm Schneemelcher, and R. McL. Wilson (Philadelphia: Westminster Press, 1965), p. 547.

28. Conzelmann, *Theology of St. Luke*, p. 101.

29. Bultmann, *The Gospel of John: A Commentary*, trans. A. R. Beasley-Murray, R. W. N. Hoare, and J. K. Riches (Philadelphia: Westminister Press, 1971), pp. 17–18.

30. Bultmann, *History of the Synoptic Tradition*, p. 246.

31. Ibid., pp. 16–19.

32. Harry T. Fleddermann, *Mark and Q: A Study of the Overlap Texts* (Leuven: Leuven University Press, 1995).

33. David Friedrich Strauss, *Life of Jesus Critically Examined*, trans. George Eliot, Lives of Jesus Series (1835; repr., Philadelphia: Fortress Press, 1972), pp. 219–22.

34. By the way, John 1:35–39, where the Baptist sends Andrew and another of his disciples to follow Jesus, is probably a rewrite of this Q story of John sending two disciples to Jesus. In Q, John sends the pair to ask if Jesus is the Coming One; in John, he is so sure Jesus is the Messiah, he tells the pair to stop wasting their time with him and to join Jesus instead!

35. Burton H. Throckmorton, *Gospel Parallels: A Synopsis of the First Three Gospels*, 3d. ed. (New York: Thomas Nelson, 1949), p. 11.

36. Ibid., p. 10.

37. James M. Robinson and Helmut Koester, "The Intention and Scope of Trajectories," in *Trajectories Through Early Christianity* (Philadelphia: Fortress Press, 1971), pp. 269–79.

38. *The Panarion of St. Epiphanius, Bishop of Salamis: Selected Passages*, trans. Philip R. Amidon (New York: Oxford University Press, 1990), p. 87.

39. William R. Stegner, "The Baptism of Jesus: A Story Modeled on the Binding of Isaac," in *Abraham and Family: New Insights into the Patriarchal Narratives*, ed. Herschel Shanks (Washington, D.C.: Biblical Archaeology Society, 2001).

40. In Solomon Schechter, *Some Aspects of Rabbinic Theology* (New York: Macmillan, 1910), pp. 251–52.

41. I have streamlined and paraphrased the story of Mara tempting the Buddha. There are several versions of it in Buddhist Scripture, including the *Acts of the Buddha* (*Buddhacarita*) of Asvaghosa, Canto 13; the *Mahavastu* 2.281; and the *Lalita-vistara* 18–21.261–263.

42. W. E. West, trans., "Marvels of Zoroastrianism," *Pahlavi Texts*, Part V, Sacred Books of the East, vol. XLVII, ed. Max Müller (1897; repr., Delhi: Motilal Banarsidass, 1969), pp. 47–50.

43. James Darmesteter, trans., *The Zend-Avesta*, Part I, The Vendidad Sacred Books of the East, vol. IV, ed. Max Müller (1887; repr., Dehli: Motilal Banarsidass, 1974), p. 206.

44. Robert Graves and Raphael Patai, *Hebrew Myths: The Book of Genesis* (New York: Greenwich House, 1983), p. 101.

45. "The Hypostasis of the Archons," trans. Bentley Layton, in *The Nag Hammadi Library in English*, ed. James M. Robinson (San Francisco: Harper & Row, 1988), p. 164.

46. James M. Robinson, "Basic Shifts in German Theology," *Interpretation* 16 (January 1962): 76–97 already contains the basis of our discussion here, linking most of these texts to reconstruct the mytheme underlying the baptism of Jesus.

47. Andrew Welburn, *The Beginnings of Christianity: Essene Mystery, Gnostic Revelation and the Christian Vision* (Edinburgh: Floris Books, 1991), p. 45.

48. "The Apocalypse of Adam," trans. George W. MacRae, in *Nag Hammadi Library*, ed. Robinson, p. 285.

49. Throckmorton, *Gospel Parallels*, p. 11.

50. Ibid., p. 11.

51. Ibid., p. 10.

52. Ibid., p. 13.

CHAPTER FIVE
THE MIRACLES

PRODIGY AND PROBABILITY

A s we try to make sense of the numerous miracle stories of the Gospels, we must keep in mind an array of important critical criteria. They do *not* include the philosophical presupposition that miracles cannot, therefore do not, happen. They do include the principle of analogy, whereby reported events cannot be judged as "probably" having occurred unless they find some counterpart in contemporary experience. They include the equally important law of biographical analogy, whereby we may expect piety to have embellished the careers of similar heroes in similar ways and that such embellishments are legendary. And we must remain mindful that whenever we can compare a more and a less extravagant version of the same claim or story, the more modest has the greater claim to authenticity.

SEEKING SIGNS

The strongest objection to the notion that a historical Jesus performed miracles is no naturalistic assumption brought to the text but rather something much nearer at hand. Two pieces of New Testament evidence seem to attest an early stage of belief when Jesus was simply not remembered/regarded as a wonder-worker. The first (and earliest, according to conventional dating) is 1 Cor. 1:18–25, "For the cross is folly to those who are perishing, but to us who are being saved it is the power of God. For it is written: 'I will destroy the wisdom of the wise, and the cleverness of the clever I will thwart.' Where is the wise man? Where is the scribe? Where is the debater of this age? Has not God made foolish the wisdom of the world? For since, in the wisdom of God, the world did not know God through wisdom, it pleased God through the folly of what we preach to save those who believe. For Jews demand signs and Greeks seek wisdom, but we preach Christ crucified, a stumbling block to Jews and folly to Gentiles, but to those who are called, both Jews and Greeks, Christ the power of God and the wisdom of God. For the foolishness of God is wiser than men, and the weakness of God is stronger than men." As George A. Wells notes, this text comes awfully close to explicitly denying that Jesus did miracles.[1] If this writer thought Jesus had performed miracles, why would his preaching seem so disappointing to those who "seek signs"? A harmonist might possibly want to suggest that, though Paul knew Jesus did perform miracles (something we have no evidence for, as Paul never mentions any miracles of Jesus), he might have feared seeming to cater to credulous and superficial belief had he preached the miracles. Maybe he just wanted to keep his existentialist priorities in order. But then one wonders why Jesus, presumably no less theologically perceptive than Paul, would have made the mistake of performing miracles and risking creating the wrong sort of faith. (John 14:11 already embodies an implicit critique of the Synoptic tradition's miracle propaganda.) And such a harmonization fails to grasp the nature of the contrast, which is really one of apparent powerlessness paradoxically conveying the true power of God, a power to save rather than to destroy, a power made perfect in weakness (2 Cor. 12:10), a power that speaks in a still, small voice, not in the cyclone or the earthquake. The compulsion of belief entailed in performing miracles to drive home one's point is what 1 Corinthians repudiates, no doubt making virtue of necessity—since the writer had no knowledge of any miracles that might have satisfied his disappointed Jewish hearers.

The second major text tending to undermine the likelihood of any miracles having been performed by Jesus is Mark 8:11–13. When asked for an authenticating sign from heaven, Jesus flatly refuses: "Amen: I say to you, no sign shall be given to this generation." The sense of this saying is painfully clear: "I'm not doing any miracles for anybody alive today." Strauss put it well: "Jesus would appear to have here repudiated the working of miracles in general. . . . This then is the question: Ought we, on account of the evangelical narratives of miracles, to explain away that expression of Jesus, or doubt its authenticity; or ought we not rather, on the strength of that declaration . . . to become distrustful of the numerous histories of miracles in the gospels?"[2]

An apologist might try to slip out of this one by pointing to the motives of the Pharisees as Mark describes them. They were insincere and sought to embarrass Jesus, and he would not play their game. Fair enough, but isn't that just the point in any case? Performing miracles would ipso facto be sinking to the level of such critics. Admittedly, the comment of Jesus assumes his ability to perform miracles (because it assumes anything is possible for God to do through his prophet, hence the "divine passive"), but it equally declares a permanent moratorium on them.[3]

One must ask: if such a statement stands astride the gospel tradition, where could the great number of miracle stories have come from? Well, of course, they would be fabrications of faith, attempts to enshrine the founder behind a stained-glass curtain of wonders. But would early Christians have tried this, given the clear warning of this saying? Would it have gone so completely unheeded? Why not? It did in other religious traditions. The Koran seems to be pretty clear on the matter: "Those who disbelieve say, 'If only a portent were sent down upon him from his Lord!' Lo, Allah sendeth whom he will astray, and guideth unto Himself all who turn unto him" (13:27). The point is the same: the skeptical heckling of the prophet's opponents who challenge him for a sign prompts only the disgusted abandonment of a sinful and adulterous generation to its fate. And yet subsequent Islamic tradition credits the Prophet with all manner of marvels, some copied from the New Testament.

Nathan of Gaza served as an apostle for messiah Sabbatai Sevi in the 1660s. Nathan sent out word to the burgeoning faithful, warning them that Israel would have to believe in her messiah without benefit of miracles. This, however, did nothing to prevent a flood of evermore spectacular miracle tales, and that within his lifetime.[4]

Nor is it as if modern scholars were the first to recognize the problem for the miracle tradition created by Mark 8:11–13. It is plain that the gospel writers saw the trouble and tried to mitigate it by reinterpreting and embellishing the verse. Matt. 16:1–4 adds to the stunning dictum of Mark the words "except the sign of Jonah" (which he derived from Q's version, see just below) plus some separate Q material about signs *and* heaven, as if it were relevant to the Markan signs *from* heaven. (In Luke 12:54–55, we see the same Q material but not connected with the sign of Jonah.) Q does know the saying preserved in its original form in Mark 8:11–13, but Q adds the "sign of Jonah," then vaguely explains what it is: incisive preaching that moved the ancient Ninevites to a reformation for which Jesus' contemporaries are too stiff-necked (Matt. 12:38–39//Luke 11:29–32). But this hardly fits. Matthew's own suggestion is more apt in one sense, but even farther-fetched in another. He adds a comment to Q, making the sign of Jonah a prediction of Jesus' resurrection: "For as Jonah was three days and three nights in the belly of the whale, so shall the Son of man be three days and three nights in the heart of the earth" (Matt. 12:40). Notice that by planting this statement here, in a reply to Jesus' enemies, Matthew has prepared the way for his scene to come in 27:63, where the Jewish authorities will tell Pilate they know Jesus predicted he would rise. Matt. 12:40 is where the Jewish authorities find this out. All this redaction of the original saying is pure back-pedaling. Often the preference of ancient scribes was not to omit old material that clashed with new but rather to harmonize and keep them both.

Saying So

Some have deemed it strong evidence that Jesus at least believed he had worked miracles that he is heard referring to them in passing, not exactly claiming to have done them, but taking them for granted. The first of these sayings is Matt. 12:27–28//Luke 11:19–20, the Q version of the Beelzebul controversy. Charged with expelling demons by gaining magical control over their diabolical chief, Jesus says, "If I cast out demons by Beelzebul, by whom do your sons cast them out? Therefore they shall be your judges. But if it is by the finger of God that I cast out demons, then the kingdom of God has come upon you." Universally prized as one of the few bedrock sayings of the historical Jesus, this text seems rather to represent a post-Jesus midrash, comparing him and his situation to that of Moses in Pharaoh's court, his miracle competition with the sorcerer-priests who reproduced most of Moses' miracles but finally had to give up in defeat when they could not copy the gnats. Exod. 8:18–19 says, "The magicians tried by their secret arts to bring forth gnats, but they could not. So there were gnats on beast and man. And the magicians said to Pharaoh, 'This is the finger of God.'" Jesus' accusers correspond to Pharaoh, while their "sons" who repeat Jesus' own miracles must correspond to the Egyptian magicians. (We have no other evidence of Pharisee exorcists; they have been posited in the Q saying simply for the sake of the Moses parallel.) If asked, they would surely reiterate the verdict anciently returned on Moses' miracles: Jesus casts out devils by the finger of God. This is not historical material, but apologetical midrash.[5]

The second saying is Matt. 11:5//Luke 17:22, Q's reply of Jesus to John the Baptist's emissaries. The messengers are to report what they see and hear of his miracles. This narrative is confused, since John has already heard these reports; they are what prompted him to send the messengers in the first place. Jesus' reply is pretty much a quotation of Isa. 35:5–6 and Isa. 61:1. Of course, there would be nothing stopping the historical Jesus from quoting Scripture. That is in itself far from improbable. But, as Bultmann pointed out,[6] who remembers the great man quoting someone else? He may have done it, but it is unlikely to be remembered. It seems more likely a striking saying from one source might be mistakenly attributed to another. Or that, as with the heavenly voice at Jesus' baptism, if a writer were trying to come up with something that would sound natural for someone like Jesus to say, he would glue together pieces of Scripture to get the appropriate ring. This text is simply a Christian affirmation that Jesus fulfilled Isaianic prophecy.

The third saying is another bit of Q (Matt. 11:21//Luke 10:13), a denunciation of towns unresponsive to gospel preaching: "Woe to you, Chorazin! Woe to you, Beth-saida! For if the mighty works done in you had been done in Tyre and Sidon, they would have repented long ago, sitting in sackcloth and ashes. But it shall go easier for Tyre and Sidon in the judgment than for you. And you, Capernaum! Will you be exalted to heaven? You shall be brought down to Hades!" Here the midrashist has combined the judgment oracles of Ezek. 28 (against Tyre) and Isa. 14 (against Babylon), especially likening Capernaum to Babylon in its overweening hubris: "You said in your heart, 'I will ascend to heaven!' . . . But you are brought down to Sheol, to the depths of the Pit" (14:13a, 15). Again, Jesus quoting Scripture? Likely we would never hear of it. One rather suspects what we have here is after-the-fact gloating over the destruction of these towns in the Jewish War (66–73 C.E.), in a voice reminiscent of the Son of God, whose eyes are as a flame of fire, whose voice is as the thundering of the cataract (Rev. 1:12–16), breathing threats against unrepentant churches in Asia Minor. It is the voice of Christian prophecy we are hearing here.

Fourth, Luke 13:32 makes Jesus refer to his habits and plans of healing and exorcising: "Behold, I cast out demons and perform cures today and tomorrow, and the third day I finish my course [or 'am perfected']; for it cannot be that a prophet should perish away from Jerusalem." This has the look of an editorial summary statement to catch readers up on the progress and direction of the plot, like the specious Passion predictions of Mark (Mark 8:31, 9:31, 10:33). It also contains distinctive Lukan themes, such as Jerusalem being the center of salvation history and Jesus being a prophet (Luke 7:16, 39; 24:19). We owe the saying not to Jesus but to Lukan redaction.

We have referred more than once to the Beelzebul controversy, where Jesus' enemies admit he draws upon supernatural powers but ascribes them to sorcery. Doesn't this, however, enshrine the ancient concession by his foes that Jesus did in fact do miracles? Or that he thought he did? To cite a modern parallel, if one wanted to verify whether Pentecostals speak in tongues or at least think they do (even if they themselves are generating it by sheer theatrics), one would not need Pentecostal affirmations of it. The claims of their enemies (Calvinists and Dispensationalists) that Pentecostals were really dupes of Satan, parroting his unintelligible blasphemies, would be enough. Where there's smoke, there might not be fire, but at least there must be a smoke bomb. Isn't that what we have in the scribal charge that Jesus casts out demons by compelling the Prince of Demons? That is an entirely reasonable interpretation, but it is not the only one.

We may instead have a piece of intra-Christian, intracharismatic polemic here. I believe we can isolate an earlier form of this pericope by bracketing the two very different hypothetical questions of Jesus, both Mark's ("How can Satan cast out Satan?") and Q's ("If I cast out demons by Beelzebul, by whom do your sons cast them out? Therefore they shall be your judges. But if it is by the finger of God that I cast out demons then the kingdom of God has come upon you").

What would we have left? "If a kingdom be divided against itself, that kingdom cannot stand. [The following 'house divided' doublette is redactional to tie the episode in with that of Jesus' own household.] And if Satan is risen up against himself and is divided, he cannot stand, but is coming to an end. But no one can enter a strong man's house and plunder his goods, unless he first bind the strong man; then indeed he may plunder his house." This sounds to me like a rationale for binding the power of the strong man, the ruler of devils, precisely in order to turn his power against him and ruin his kingdom, using his own authority to set his hostages free. The two "hypotheticals" posed by Jesus in Q and Mark seem designed to negate what follows them, the text just quoted. It appears that, in the interests of advanced Christology, someone is trying to disassociate Jesus from the albatross image of being a magician, something quite unembarrassing to an earlier generation to whom we owe the pre-Q, pre-Markan pericope in the first place. The setup with the Pharisees accusing Jesus of sorcery (something in the original version he did not deny) is secondary, of a piece with the two "hypotheticals." And as Morton Smith documented,[7] there was a time when early Christians affirmed the image of Jesus as a magician, but they changed their minds once it became a point of attack by people like Celsus. (This is also why Matthew and Luke both omitted the Markan passages 7:31–35 and 8:22–26, where Jesus uses well-known magical techniques to heal.)[8]

So we have no historical evidence after all of Jewish opponents of Jesus admitting he did supernatural feats. The Beelzebul controversy has been built around an earlier pericope endorsing, explaining, and defending religious magic. Nor is there adequate reason to attribute the original version to Jesus when it may as easily have come from any ancient Christian or Jewish magician. And it may be worth noting that the Beelzebul controversy and the request for a sign in Mark 8:11 are incompatible. The Beelzebul charge implies that Jesus' critics have seen miraculous signs but explain them away. The request for a sign implies they are still waiting to see anything at all. "He did no really miraculous works; otherwise, the demands for a sign would be incomprehensible."[9]

Gerd Theissen[10] thinks it remarkable that though, as we will see, many gospel miracles have particular parallels to other Jewish and Hellenistic stories, nowhere else do we see such a sudden and diverse flood of miracle stories told of one man. One infers that Theissen means to argue that with Jesus there must have been some truth to the rumor. But this will not pass muster. Surely there is a parallel to Jesus as to the number of miracle stories: Asclepius, the healing demigod. He had walked the earth in mortal form, son of Apollo and the mortal maid Coronis, healing the sick. Once he raised a dead person, whereupon Zeus decided he had blasphemously usurped the prerogative of true gods and killed him. But then Father Zeus raised him from the dead to dwell among the Olympians. Asclepius (called "the Savior") continued to manifest himself on earth, however, in fact for centuries, as sick suppliants would flock to his shrines, making reservations to partake of the spa waters and to sleep in a nocturnal chamber in which the form of the god would appear in one's dreams and suggest an appropriate cure or penance. Many of these miraculous visitations have been recorded as testimonials by satisfied pilgrims (or fabricated by money-hungry staff priests). We still have a great number of them, in the original tablets or in literary transcriptions by ancient authors. The number easily matches or surpasses Jesus' healings.

Why were there so many stories of Asclepius's wondrous healings? The shrines attracted many customers and coveted many more. Healing stories functioned as effective propaganda, as they did for the new Jesus cult. For there were many who traveled about offering healing in his name, both Christians (1 Cor. 12:9) and non-Christians using Jesus' name as a magical charm (Acts 19:13–14, Mark 9:38). Origen tells us that in his day the gospel episodes of healing and exorcism were recited verbatim as part of the healing or exorcism ritual. (Medieval Jewish exorcists did the same thing: "The efficacy of the ritual is ensured by reciting the first occurrence of a similar rite, performed by a mythical hero, [sometimes] the prophet Elijah" (Raphael Patai).[11] Christian exorcists used "the name of Jesus with the recital of the histories about him. For when these are pronounced they have often made demons to be driven out of men" (Origen *Against Celsus* 1.6).[12] This is no doubt why the original Aramaic words *Talitha cumi* ("Little girl, get up!") and *Ephphatha* ("Be opened!") are retained or supplied in two Markan stories, Mark 5:41, 7:34, so that subsequent would-be healers using these stories might use the very words they imagined that Jesus used on the same occasion. They have become magic words. "We would say . . . of the word Sabaoth, which is frequently used in spells . . . if we translate the name into 'Lord of the powers' or 'almighty' (for its interpreters explain it differently) we would effect nothing: whereas if we keep it with its own sounds, we will cause something to happen, according to the opinions of experts in these matters" (*Against Celsus* 5.45).[13]

THE GRAMMAR OF MIRACLE STORIES

Literary critics speak of a story being like an individual sentence: it can be diagrammed, laying bare the narrative grammar. The story, like the sentence, can be plotted along two axes, the *syntagmic* and the *paradigmatic*. The syntagmic axis refers to the linear plot structure of the story, the unfolding action and the reasons for it, how one plot element leads to another. The various occurrences in the plot may be told in various orders (say, with flashbacks or anticipations), but they will be understood as having occurred in a particular way, one thing leading to another. We may picture the syntagmic axis horizontally, like an English sentence stretching across the page. The paradigmatic axis is, so to speak, vertical, like the pull-down menu on a computer. It is a set of options the storyteller uses to fill in the blanks. Who is the hero? James Bond? Superman? The Lone Ranger? Robin Hood? What is the nature of the problem to be set right? A kidnapping? A theft? A murder to be solved or avenged? What does the hero do to stop it? What relation do the hero and the villain bear to other characters? Why and how do they come to be involved in the story? What weapons or stratagems does each use? Why does each succeed or fail? How many attempts will be made by the hero before one succeeds? When he encounters the villain, will he kill him? Let him go? See to his reformation? The paradigm of options is the storyteller's resource, his artist's pallet, for deciding what will happen to whom and why. The syntagm is a particular map he has chosen to use to get to the end. We speak of "genre fiction" or "formula fiction" when we know the author will have made familiar and predictable paradigm choices, and when the unfolding plot is going to narrow itself down to fewer and fewer well-trod paths, until one finally becomes evident when we reach the end.

The New Testament miracle stories share a formula with other ancient wonder stories. They all follow the same syntax, varying only the paradigmatic options, and that not by much. The narrative syntax of the miracle story is as follows. Note that every single element need not appear in every single miracle story, but most do most of the time, and the logical relation between the elements, or the stages, is the same.

First, there is the *setting*, described in brief strokes, only as much as we will need for the action to make sense. Jesus is surrounded by a crowd, or on the open sea, or is separated from the disciples, or is with a crowd in a wilderness.

Second, the *case history* indicates the severity of the plight from which the miracle will rescue the sufferer(s), perhaps the duration of an illness. Jairus's daughter was cut off at the tender age of twelve. The old woman had a twelve-year menstrual flow and has wasted all her savings on quack doctors. The lame man can't get anybody to help him to the healing bath. The crowd hasn't eaten in days. The disciples are about to be capsized in the storm. The man's son has had his demon since childhood. The dead man was the only support of his widowed mother.

Third, we hear the *announcement by the miracle worker* (or there is some equivalent signal) that he will act to save the day. "Our friend Lazarus sleeps, but I will go and wake him up." "You give them something to eat." "She is not dead but asleep." "Where is your faith?" "Do you want to be healed?" "Roll away the stone from the tomb."

Fourth, we hear the *skepticism of the bystanders*, an element designed to raise the bar, to heighten dramatic tension and increase the odds the hero must meet. "They laughed him to scorn." "How are we to feed such a multitude with these?" "Teacher, do you not care if we perish?" "Lord, by this time he stinketh!" "What do you mean, 'Who touched me?' The whole crowd presses upon you!" The point of this device is to anticipate the hearer's skepticism and to say, "Wait and see!" Sometimes the skepticism element is turned around, and it is the hero who raises the bar for the suppliant, in order to test his or her faith. "Too bad! I was sent only to the wandering sheep of Israel." "What do you mean, 'If you can?'" "You people just will not believe unless you see miracles!" "Do you believe I can do this?"

Fifth, the miracle worker *does something*, some discrete word or gesture to do the trick. Jesus puts his fingers into the deaf man's ears, pulls them out, and yells, "Be opened!" He takes the hand of Jairus's daughter and says to her, "Get up, little girl." He takes the hand of the widow's son. He rebukes the storm or the fever. He calls, "Lazarus, come forth!" He smears mud on the blind man's eyes and sends him to wash it off.

Sixth, the *miracle occurs*. The dead rise, the lame walk, the blind see, the hungry are fed, the water becomes wine.

Seventh, the narrative offers *concrete proof*, or what would have been accepted as such had you been there, a distinction it is hoped you will not think to draw (1 Cor. 15:6, John 20:26–29). Jairus's daughter walks and eats lunch (hence no ghost). There are baskets of the miraculous food left over. The possessed pigs stampede over the cliff. The formerly lame man walks home, carrying his pallet. The blind man tells what he sees.

Eighth comes the *acclamation of the crowd*. "We have never seen anything like this!" "God has visited his people!" "A great prophet has arisen among us!" "He does all things well!" "A new teaching! And with authority, for even the demons obey him!" The intent here is to cue the hearer to the desired reaction, like the laugh track on a television sitcom.

Here are a few extracanonical miracle stories, with the number of each element inserted where appropriate.

Our rabbis say: [1] once upon a time [2] a poisonous snake was injuring people. They went and made it known to Rabbi Hanina ben Dosa. [3] He said to them, "Show me its burrow." They showed him its burrow and [5] he put his heel upon the mouth of the hole. It came forth and bit him—and [6] it died. [7] He put that snake on his shoulders, went to the House of Study, and said to them: "See, my sons, it is not the snake that kills but sin that kills!" [8] Then they said, "Woe to the man a snake attacks and woe to the snake which Rabbi Hanina ben Dosa attacks!" (Babylonian Talmud *Berakoth* 33a).[14]

Our rabbis say: [1] once upon a time [2] Rabban Gamaliel's son got sick. He sent two men of learning to Rabbi Hanina ben Dosa to beg mercy from God concerning him. He saw them coming and [3] went to a room upstairs and [5] asked mercy from God concerning him. When he had come back down he [3] said to them, "Go, the fever has left him." [4] They said to him, "What? Are you a prophet?" He said, "I am not a prophet nor am I the son of a prophet. But this I have received from tradition: if my prayer of intercession flows unhesitatingly from my mouth, I know it will be answered [cf. Mark 11:24], and if not, I know it will be rejected." [7] They sat down and wrote and determined exactly the moment he said this, and when they came back to Rabban Gamaliel he said to them, [8] "By the Temple Service! [cf. Matt. 23:16–22] You are neither too early nor too late but this is what happened: [6] in that moment the fever left him and he asked for water!" (Ibid., 34b).[15]

A man [2] whose fingers, with the exception of one, were paralyzed, came as a suppliant to the god [Asclepius]. [1] While looking at the tablets in the temple [4] he expressed incredulity regarding the cures and scoffed at the inscriptions. But in his sleep [3] he saw a vision. It seemed to him, as he was playing at dice below the temple and was about to cast the dice, the god [5] appeared, sprang upon his hand, and stretched out his fingers. [6] When the god had stepped aside, it seemed to him that he bent his hand and stretched out all his fingers one by one. When he had straightened them all, the god asked him if he would still be incredulous of the inscriptions on the tablets in the temple, [8] he answered that he would not. "Since, then, formerly you were incredulous of the cures, though they were not incredible, [7] for the future," he said, "your name shall be 'Incredulous.'" When day dawned he walked out sound (Epidaurus votive tablets 1.3).[16]

A man came as a suppliant to the god. [2] He was so blind that of one of his eyes he had only the eyelids left—within them was nothing, but they were entirely empty. Some of those [1] in the temple [4] laughed at his silliness to think that he could recover his sight when one of his eyes had not even a trace of the ball, but only the socket. As he slept [3] a vision appeared to him. It seemed to him that the god [5] prepared some drug, then, opening his eyelids, poured it into them. When day came [7] he departed with the sight of both eyes restored (1:9).[17]

Gorgias of Heracleia [came afflicted] with pus. [2] In a battle he had been wounded by an arrow in the lung and for a year and a half had suppurated so badly that he filled sixty-seven basins with pus. [1] While sleeping in the temple [3] he saw a vision. It seemed to him the god [5] extracted the arrow point from his lung. When day came [6] he walked out well, [7] holding the point of the arrow in his hands (1:30).[18]

[1] When the plague began to rage in Ephesus, and [2] no remedy sufficed to check it, they sent a deputation to Apollonius, asking him to become physician of their infirmity; and he thought that he ought not to postpone his journey, but said, "Let us go." And forthwith he was in Ephesus. . . . He therefore called together the Ephesians, and [3] said: "Take courage, for I will to-day put a stop to the course of the disease." And with these words he led the population entire to the theater, where the image of the Averting god has [since] been set up. And there he saw what seemed an old mendicant artfully blinking his eyes as if blind, and he carried a wallet and a crust of bread in it; and he was clad in rags and was very squalid of countenance. Apollonius therefore ranged the Ephesians around him and said: "Pick up as many stones as you can and hurl them at this enemy of the gods." [4] Now the Ephesians wondered what he meant, and were shocked at the idea of murdering a stranger so manifestly miserable; for he was begging and praying them to take mercy upon him. Nevertheless Apollonius insisted and egged on the Ephesians to launch themselves on him and not let him go. [5] And as soon as some of them began to take shots and hit him with their stones, the

beggar who had seemed to blink and be blind, gave them all a sudden glance and [6] showed that his eyes were full of fire. Then the Ephesians recognised that he was a demon, and they stoned him so thoroughly that their stones were heaped into a great cairn around him. After a little pause Apollonius bade them remove the stones and acquaint themselves with the wild animal they had slain. When therefore they had exposed the object they thought they had thrown their missiles at, they found that he had disappeared and [7] instead of him there was found a hound who resembled in form and look a Molossian dog, but was in size the equal of the largest lion; there he lay before their eyes, pounded to a pulp by their stones and vomiting foam as mad dogs do. Accordingly [8] the statue of the Averting god, namely Hercules, has been set up over the spot where the ghost was slain (Philostratus *The Life of Apollonius of Tyana* 5.10).[19]

THE HAUNTED MAN

A number of the miracle stories in the Gospels and Acts are exorcisms. Exorcism was a form of faith healing widely practiced in the ancient world. Most often, it seems, demon possession was marked by stubborn disease, not by the more overt and theatrical signs familiar from movies like *The Exorcist*. The closest we come to that is the superhuman adrenaline strength of the mad, as with the Gadarene demoniac of Mark 5:1–20 and the wildman of Ephesus (Acts 19:13–17), and these are exceptions, as we will shortly see. Epilepsy was the perfect example of demon affliction. The word itself is Greek for being "seized upon," and it seemed reasonable to conclude that some invisible entity had one in its cruel throes. But other diseases were ascribed to pesky devils as well. As J. Ramsey Michaels demonstrates,[20] for Mark possession and sickness were separate categories, while Matthew seems to have considered possession one more type of sickness. Michaels sees Luke as tilting in Matthew's direction, but it is not hard to construe Luke as tending to subsume all sickness as Satan's bondage (Acts 10:38) and caused by "spirits of infirmity" (Luke 13:11) under his control.

Several magical handbooks survive from the New Testament period, and by comparing them[21] (and other contemporary sources), we can see how the gospel exorcism stories have presupposed standard technique and then altered it in view of their Christological agenda. That is, these stories, as Origen tells us, were themselves exorcism formulae, and this may explain why they try less to depict his technique as a model than to glorify Jesus himself.

How did ancient exorcists ply their trade? The protocol seems to have run something like this. First, one attempts to get the demon to name itself, since knowing its name imparted power over it, just as in magic one might invoke the demon by calling its name. This is why Jesus is shown demanding the name of the demon(s) infesting the Gadarene demoniac (Mark 5:9).

Second, one silences the demon from further speaking, since you don't want it to wheedle your name out of you and thus gain power over you! Jesus is shown silencing the demons (Mark 1:24–25, 33; 3:11–12), but Mark has transformed this traditional exorcistic motif into a Christological one: the messianic secret. It is that the demons, as invisible spirits, can recognize Jesus' own supernatural character and are threatening to blow his cover.

Third, the exorcist orders the demon to come out and not to enter the victim again, as in Mark 1:25b, 9:25, and Josephus's *Antiquities* 8.2.5. "I have seen a certain man of my own country whose name was Eleazer, releasing [2] people that were demoniacal [1] in the presence of Vespasian, and his sons, and his captains, and the whole multitude of his soldiers. The manner of the cure was this: [5] He put a ring that contained a root of one of those sorts mentioned by Solomon to the nostrils of the demoniac, after which [6] he drew out the demon through his nostrils; and when the man fell down immediately, he adjured him to return into him no more, making still mention of Solomon, and reciting the incantations which he composed. And when Eleazer would persuade and demonstrate to the spectators that he had such a power, [7] he set a little way off a cup or basin full of water, and commanded the demon as he went out of the man to overturn it, and thereby to let the spectators know that he had left the man."[22]

Fourth, one must adjure the demon by appeal to some authority, as Eleazar does in the example just given. Apollonius, too, "addressed [the possessing demon] with anger, as a master might a shifty, rascally, and shameless slave . . . and he ordered him to quit the young man and show by a visible sign that he had done so. 'I will throw down yonder statue,' said the devil. . . . But when the statue began by moving gently, and then fell down, it would defy anyone to describe the hubbub" (4.20).[23] In the Gospels, the adjuration element has been reversed. Jesus is no longer shown appealing to any particular authority, since implicitly he has become the authority, and the whole story is an appeal to his authority by the exorcist reciting the story. So instead we hear the demons adjuring Jesus: "I adjure you by God, do not torment me!" (Mark 5:7).

Fifth, and closely related, one may have to threaten the demon. Legion anticipates such a threat, "Do not torment me!" Iarchus, a miracle-working colleague of Apollonius, hands a letter to the mother of a possessed man: "the letter, it appears, was addressed to the ghost and contained threats of an alarming kind" (3.38).[24] Lucian of Samosata has a character describe a Syrian exorcist at work on his patient: "he levels oaths at him, but if the demon is not persuaded, he threatens, and expels the demon. I actually saw one coming out, black and smoky in color" (*The Lover of Lies* 16).[25]

Sixth, one may have to bargain with a particularly fierce demon. As Jesus allows the fleeing legion of demons to take up temporary residence in the nearby herd of swine (Mark 5:10–13), so did Rabbi Hanina ben Dosa bargain with Agrath the Queen of demons. "'I decree that you shall never again pass through an uninhabited place.' She said to him, 'Please allow me in for a limited time.' He then left to her Sabbath nights and Wednesday nights" (Babylonian Talmud *Pesahim* 112b).[26]

recognize what is going on in the story, what kind of story it is, we
hat are the chances of it being historically true? All such tales,
have any connection with a historical figure, seem designed to
ipse of an older hero by the reputation of one more recent. In the
ase, such a story would have to have arisen after the lifetime of the
me have not even this tenuous connection to historical characters,
s best to admit that the Mark and 2 Kings stories, by analogy, are
me fictive cloth.

cast out demons? That is, whether one believes in the reality of
did Jesus? And did he try to exorcise them? Analogy warns us not
ossibility too quickly. A historical Jesus would surely have shared
is contemporaries on such matters, and exorcists were certainly
. There are still a number of them active today, and one need not
nd wide to come upon scenes of "deliverance ministry" highly
the gospel scenes. So it is certainly plausible to suggest Jesus
an exorcist. But is it probable, especially when one recalls that
ividual pieces of evidence, the actual exorcism stories, passes
ical? True, a general reputation of Jesus as an exorcist might have
rise to fictional iterations, scenes of the sort of thing Jesus *must*
where is our evidence for Jesus as an exorcist *in general*? One
e Markan summary statements, for example, 3:11, "Whenever
ts beheld him, they fell down before him and cried out, 'You are
' And he would order them not to make him known." But these
ns based on the specific stories already considered. Thus, they
able.

re else might the gospel picture of Jesus as an exorcist have
is no mystery. As soon as Jesus was venerated as a god, exor-
added him to their pantheon of powerful names with which to
s. As a patron of exorcists, he would naturally come to be fea-
er in an ideal narrative used by exorcists as part of their ritual
s us Christians did in fact do). The reciter is assuming the very
ing Jesus by telling his story. But historically, the development
the opposite direction: the Jesus character would have been
he nameless individual exorcists who projected their activity
of strengthening their works.

IN

stories that do not seem to assume a demonic etiology, we
two lessons learned already. First, all these miracle stories
w of Mark 8:11–13, the preemptive denial of all miracles.

POINTED TALES

Before trying to answer the question of whether Jesus was an exorcist, as Morton
Smith and Rudolf Bultmann (certainly no fundamentalist apologists) believed,
we should take a look at the specific exorcism stories of the Gospels, starting
with Mark 1:21–28, the exorcism in the Capernaum synagogue. The whole point
of the story is to showcase the Markan theme of the messianic secret,[27] a har-
monistic device whereby the evangelist sought to reconcile the beliefs of two
Christian factions. One said that Jesus became the Christ only as of his resurrection, while the other believed his messiahship had already been secure, at least
from the Jordan baptism. Mark tried to have his cake and eat it, too, by having
Jesus already brimming with messianic power and glory from the baptism on, but
hiding his identity till the resurrection. Anyone who threatened to give the secret
away beforehand had to be silenced, demon (as in this pericope) or disciple (e.g.,
Mark 8:29–30, 9:9). Take out the secrecy motif and you don't have much of a
story left. Add to that the uncomfortable fact that we have no real evidence for
the existence of synagogues in Galilee till after the supposed time of Jesus, and
the story disappears from history.

Mark 5:1–20 is the story of the Gadarene demoniac, a miserable wretch possessed by an eponymous legion of demons. Here the principle of analogy poses
no problem, since one may compare the story with a case history from China,
1883, written by one Mrs. Liu, a participant. Here is just a bit of it.

> The demon replied: "I acknowledge the power of Jesus but I am not afraid of
> you. You have not faith enough to cast me out. You have not faith as much as a
> mustard seed." We replied: "We came trusting in Christ, and in his name we will
> cast you out." The possessed person replied by a contemptuous smile, followed
> by a fit of weeping. We then proceeded to hold a religious service. We first sang
> the hymn "The judgment day will surely come," and read the tenth chapter of
> Matthew. Then each of us in succession prayed, after which we sang. When we
> had finished the service, the woman was lying perfectly quiet, apparently
> unconscious or asleep. . . . About this time, just before dark an extraordinary
> commotion occurred among the fowls, which rushed and flew about in great
> consternation without any apparent cause, the family and servants having diffi-
> culty in quieting them, and restraining them from running away. After a while
> they cowered up in the corner of the yard in a state of fright. The swine also
> belonging to the family, more than a dozen in number, occupying a large pen or
> walled enclosure near by, were put into a singular state of agitation rushing
> about the enclosure, running over each other and trying to scrabble up the walls.
> The swine would not eat, and this state of disquiet continued until they were
> exhausted. These manifestations naturally excited a great deal of interest and
> remark, and were accounted for by the supposition that the demons had taken
> possession [of] the fowls and swine.[28]

What are we to make of the adventure of the Gadarene demoniac? Anything is possible, but what is probable? Theissen's reading of the story as a political allegory[29] of the Jewish will to drive the Roman legions, unclean swine, into the sea and out of the Holy Land is already enough to cast doubt on the historicity of the passage. The same goes for the geographical setting of the tale, as the nearest ledge or shore for the demoniac pigs to rush over lies some thirty miles from Gadara![30] But the most serious consideration against historicity must be the plain derivation of the whole tale from Homer's *Odyssey* 10, the episodes of Circe changing Odysseus's soldiers (legionaries) into swine and of their escape from the giant Cyclops Polyphemus (usually depicted naked).[31] The Gadarene demoniac is based on Polyphemus, hence mythical. Plus, where did he get the new clothes (Mark 5:15)?

Incidentally, once we recognize the fictive nature of the Gadarene, we find we must exorcise his counterpart in Acts, the Ephesian wildman, from history, too, for the latter seems to be a doublette based on the former. Luke has borrowed from Mark the elements of great strength, applied here as in Mark to the madman, and of nakedness and wounding, which Mark ascribes to the demoniac but Acts has the demoniac inflict on his victims (Acts 19:16).

Mark 7:24–30 briefly relates a contest of wits between Jesus and the Syro-Phoenician woman, whose daughter (offstage, back home) is possessed by an unclean spirit. Jesus appears reluctant to grant her request, but her clever rejoinder wins the day. (Was Jesus being Socratically ironic so as to prompt her?) Jesus assures her that her daughter's affliction is relieved, as Mark assures the reader. Of course, even if we knew that the scene between Jesus and the woman were historically accurate, we would have no way of corroborating Mark's claim that the girl had been healed. But is the scene historical? It is safe to say it is not. The reason is the obvious symbolic sense of the passage. It is hardly insignificant that Jesus performs this miracle on Gentile soil. The healing at a *geographical* distance stands for the *historical* distance between Jesus' ministry, pictured as in Palestine around 30 C.E., and the inception of the Gentile Mission some years later. For Jesus to mandate her healing over some miles of distance means that he is authorizing the spreading of the gospel among the Gentiles at a distance of some years. The point is the same in the Q story of the Centurion's servant (Matt. 8:5–13//Luke 7:1–10). These are the only two Gentiles Jesus is ever said to heal, and both healings take place at a distance. These stories were later supplanted by the overt and explicit postresurrection Great Commission scenes, since for some, apparently, the point was not clear enough. Most likely the character of the Syro-Phoenician woman was based on the widow of Zarephath, similarly concerned for her son (1 Kings 17:8–24).

Mark places another exorcism story just after the Transfiguration, since he needs to have Jesus rejoin the disciples, who are floundering on their own. They have been asked to cast out a demon and are not up to the task. The passage (Mark 9:14–29) seems to have conflated two earlier exorcism stories. One fea-

tured a deaf-mute demoniac, the othe (verses 15 and 25). One demon appear to leaving) as soon as he beholds Jesu vulsion occur once Jesus commands t of the two stories are different as well the difficulty of casting out certain typ the preparation of prayer (verse 29). cient, so some manuscripts have add strength even further. The implicit theme further, abandoning the eff(invoking him against the demon. N(disappointed disciples that their f fasting), and yet Jesus is easily ab prayer (or fasting). Why? Because fictive, mythic character of the sto verse 19, "O faithless generation! I I endure you?" These are the word patience with puny humans: "Wha

This places the exorcism story acle stories designed to demonstra greater than his master but can ne story of the resurrection of the sor show one thing: no one but Elisha one disciple, wielding his master's no less than Elisha to do the j(demonstrated in a story quoted i "A woman had a tapeworm and Then she came to Epidaurus and ailment that lived within her. The however, made the woman lie (suppliants. And the woman reste god made the preparations for th stretched down his hand and pul together and attach her head to approached and was provoke(beyond their wisdom. But w attached her head to her body

Even the famous story o Lucian's *Lover of Lies*, is anot apprentice to the sage Pancra life to do his housework. Fe Eucrates tried it one day in hi return of Pancrates saved the

KING OF P

Moving to healing must keep in min(stand in the shad(

Once we have to ask insofar as the reverse the ec nature of the earlier hero. S and it is perha cut from the s

Did Jesus demons or not to dismiss the the beliefs of not uncommon search too far reminiscent of might have bee *none* of the in muster as histor eventually giver have done. But might point to t the unclean spiri the Son of God! are generalizatio are even less reli

And yet wh come from? Tha cists would have intimidate demor tured as a charac (as Origen inforr role of the exorci may have run in made to emulate onto him as a way

Second, what holds true in general for the exorcism stories will very likely prove out here, too, namely, that they may well have been created by those who used them as patterns and even as ritual recitals to be used in Christian healing ministry. That is, instead of these stories enshrining a historical memory of Jesus as a faith healer, they may instead have created that impression by deciding to feature the god Jesus as an incantatory name.

First, Jesus is shown healing the blind in Mark 8:22–26. This episode is especially remarkable in that it has Jesus employ common magical healing techniques ("Here's mud in your eye!"), something Matthew and Luke did not care for and so omitted. Equally notable is the fact that the healed man does not recover his sight all at once. Jesus has to try again before sight is fully restored. Some critics have understood this detail as symbolic of the two stages of the awakening of the disciples' faith. They see the truth clearly enough to heed Jesus' call to follow, and yet they have no understanding of his divine fate till the end. Their spiritual blindness, then, would have cleared up in two stages. If we accept this interpretation, we are pretty much saying Mark created the detail. Others see the two-stage sequence, along with Jesus' diagnostic question, "What do you see?" as mere narrative coloring, trying to portray Jesus as a physician (just as the Four Noble Truths of the Buddha seem to reflect contemporary medical diagnosis-and-prescription formulae). This would also be fictive. My guess is that it is a Markan creation, drawing upon magical techniques that were common-enough knowledge in order to make it seem authentic. He thought no more of having Jesus have to try again than he did of having him repent in baptism. His Christology was not "high" enough for any of this to be an embarrassment, so we cannot point to what some call the embarrassment criterion and declare the text authentic because it embarrassed later New Testament writers or readers. Matthew would never have created such a story, true, but Mark saw nothing wrong with it. Where did he get the idea for the story? Mark was inspired by Q's denunciations of Chorazin, Capernaum, and Bethsaida for their failure to repent at gospel preaching (Matt. 11:20–34//Luke 10:12–15). Here is a man from Bethsaida, a sinful town doomed as Sodom was. The man is singled out like Lot as the one innocent in Sodom (deserving help). He is blind, as the angels visiting Sodom struck the wicked populace blind. And like Lot he is being warned to flee the city in advance of its inevitable destruction. The scene is Markan midrash.

Mark looks to have drawn upon the *Odyssey* for the story of Bar-Timaeus (Mark 10:46–52). Like Tiresias, the blind prophet, it is only blind Bar-Timaeus who can see, amid the "sighted" crowds, that it is the royal Son of David passing by. The crowd attempts unsuccessfully to silence him, recalling in a peculiar way the exorcism scenes where the afflicted demoniacs have supernatural recognition of Jesus and shout it out in titular form ("Son of the Most High God!" "Holy One of God!"), only to be rebuked and silenced. It is almost as if Jesus asks the price of his silence and is glad enough to pay it. No more of this "Son of David" business, okay? The beggar's name seems either to be an ideal name identifying the character by his function (based on the Aramaic *bar-teymah*, "son of poverty")[33] or another tip of the hat to a Classical source, Plato's *Timaeus*, where we read of the true vision, the mind's grasp of truth as opposed to the opinions of the crowd.

John's story of the nameless man born blind (9:1–41) is very likely a fictive, theological expansion of Mark 8:22–26, especially as it repeats the magical healing technique. He also "sends" the man off, to wash in Siloam's pool this time, not out of the city. The story, though excellently written, is vitiated with anachronism. Besides having Jesus throw the messianic secret to the wind (9:35–37), since it is no more a secret in the evangelist's day, the author also has the newly sighted man excommunicated from the synagogue on account of his faith in Jesus (verse 34), something his parents fear as well (verse 22) in light of the general excommunication that had been decreed. But such witch-hunts all transpired decades later, as John knows the reader knows (16:1–4). The Pharisees in John 9 even view Jesus as the founder of a rival religion (verse 28, cf. 1:17), a development much too late for the lifetime of Jesus.

Matt. 12:22 adds the blindness element to Q's introduction to the Beelzebul controversy (still found in Luke 11:14). Q had Jesus casting out a spirit of silence, but Matthew makes it a blind-mute spirit. Matt. 9:27–31 is another Matthean embellishment, a superfluous doubling of the healing of Bar-Timaeus.

Mark 1:40–45 has Jesus cure some skin eruption (in our usage, "leprosy" has come to refer strictly to Hanson's Disease, a much more devastating affliction than biblical "leprosy," or excema and psoriasis). Much has been made of the fact that Jesus tells the cured man to go and show himself to the priest for ritual authentication of the cure (enabling him to return to normal society). Is it a mark of the story being pre-70 C.E. in origin? Not at all. The point is simply to provide the objective verification of the miracle, like Jairus's daughter eating or the Gadarene swine plunging over the cliff. Is the pericope evidence, as many claim, that the historical Jesus repudiated all laws of ritual purity, embracing the Untouchables as God's true children, as Gandhi did, since he reached out and touched the yet-unclean leper? Here is a complete failure to grasp the nature of the story, which is by no means a datum about the life of Jesus but an anecdote about an invulnerable divine man (θειος ανηρ). He is a superman summoned to do a superhuman job. If for the narrator there is no doubt Jesus can cure the leper, there can be no chance he will be infected by the leper.

Luke has created a second leprosy cure (actually ten more!) in Luke 17:11–19. Jesus pronounces ten self-segregated lepers clean, and they depart in faith. As the healing manifests itself, only one man, a Samaritan, is moved to return to Jesus, glorifying God. Jesus comments acerbically on the rudeness of the nine ingrate Jews. Luke has elsewhere included in his special material or added to Markan miracle stories the note that the people "glorified God" (2:20; 5:25, 26; 7:16; 13:13; 18:43; 23:47). It is a Lukan signature mark, and in this story it is central. There is no story without it. Thus, Luke has created it. There is also the Lukan preference for Samaritans and the supercession of indifferent

Jewry, evident in Luke's Good Samaritan parable (Luke 10:30–37) and his account of the evangelization of Samaria (Acts 8).

Mark 1:29–31, where Jesus cures Simon Peter's mother-in-law of a fever so she can get back into the kitchen and cook them a meal, has the flavor of a piece of folklore apocrypha. John's fever cure (John 4:46–54) is superfluous, an addition to the Q story of the centurion's servant, whom Jesus cured at a distance from paralysis (Matt. 8:5–13//Luke 7:1–10). The transformation of the Gentile centurion into a Herodian royal official is a similar variation.

As for paralysis, we have already noted that the Q tale of the centurion's paralyzed servant (Matt. 8:5–13//Luke 7:1–10) must be dismissed as a piece of theological polemic on behalf of the Gentile Mission, the geographical distance between Jesus and the suffering Gentile lad being symbolic of the historical distance between Jesus and the Gentile Mission. The centurion is a gospel version of Naaman the Syrian general who petitions Elisha's help for his own leprosy. He was persuaded to do so by his Israelite slave-girl, who in the New Testament version has taken the role of the sick one (2 Kings 5).

Mark's tale of paralysis, Mark 2:1–12, is the wonderful story of the paralyzed man whose friends, unable to press to the front of the crowd, instead hoist the invalid's pallet up onto the thatched roof and tear a hole in it to let him down by ropes in front of Jesus. Their dogged efforts attest their faith, and Jesus rewards their outrageous behavior by forgiving their friend's sin, whichever it had been that led to such an affliction as God's punishment. Can it have happened? Well, one has to ask how long it would have taken the men to remove sufficient of the thatch, fit ropes (why did they have them along, anyway?) onto the ends of the pallet and lower him. Did no one notice the ruckus until they were done? Wouldn't they have been prevented long before their purpose could be accomplished? And let's not pass by too quickly the fact that Jesus knew just what his opponents were thinking without their saying anything. The story, in short, reads too much *like* a story, not at all like a report. It seems to be based on another story, one from 2 Kings 1:2–17a. In this one, the Israelite King "Ahaziah fell through the lattice in his upper chamber in Samaria, and lay sick." He sends messengers to inquire of the oracle of the god Baal-zebub ("Lord of Flies," because his soothsaying priests would claim to hear a buzzing in the ear, like the buzzing of flies, and the priests would decipher it as your fortune). Will he recover? Yahve, jealous that a king of Israel should resort to a second-rate Philistine deity, sends Elijah to intercept the emissaries. He tells them not to bother going any further. He can tell them right now, by the word of Yahve, that Ahaziah is doomed because of his lack of faith. The Markan story is a happy reversal of this one. We have a man, already afflicted for some sin, being forgiven. He, too, *descends through the ceiling,* but it is on his way to healing, not to illness. And his friends' faith is rewarded, just as Ahaziah's lack of it was sorely punished.[34]

A similar story with a similar origin is that of the healing of a man's withered hand (Mark 3:1–6), apparently based on the 1 Kings 13:1–6 story of an unnamed prophet who prophesies the deaths of the priests of the heathen high places at the hand of the future king Josiah.[35] King Jeroboam hears this and likes it not, so he gestures toward the man of God and orders him seized. Instead it is only his own pointing arm that withers. He pleads for mercy, and the prophet heals his arm. The 1 Kings story takes place in the temple, the Mark story in a synagogue. Mark's story ends with the note that the scribes were so incensed by Jesus' defiance of their petty legalism that they resolved on the spot to see him dead. This seems both a bit drastic and strangely premature, since Mark will not get around to Jesus' arrest for another eleven chapters, and then the Pharisees will have nothing to do with it. Someone has suggested that Mark 3:1–6 had earlier served as the direct introduction to the Passion narrative in some pre-Markan form of the gospel, perhaps an oral one. But it might make more sense to suggest that the anomalous timing and disproportionate rage of Jesus' opponents stem from the rewriting of the Old Testament original, where Jeroboam orders the death of the man of God (though he rescinds the command). If this item in the original were not going to be simply cut off, it had to be transformed into a premature lead-in to the Passion.

Luke 13:10–17, the story of the woman with a bent spine, is unique to Luke's gospel and yet redundant. It appears to be a pastiche of earlier, Markan stories of controversy occasioned by Jesus' healing on the sabbath (Mark 2:23–28; 3:1–6). Likewise, Luke 14:1–6 is a Lukan creation in order to provide a narrative context for the Q saying Matt. 12:11//Luke 14:5 (which Matthew has inserted into the Markan story of the withered hand).

John 5:2–18 has Jesus come to the aid of a man who has been lame for thirty-eight years and whiles away his time kibitzing at the porticoes of the Pool of Bethzatha. We may disregard the Johannine dialogue and monologues and deal with the basic story, which we may accept as pre-Johannine. It is a healing story of a particular kind. We have another in Philostratus's *Life of Apollonius of Tyana* 1.9.

> An Assyrian stripling came to [the temple of] Asclepius, and though he was sick, yet he lived the life of luxury . . . and finding his pleasure in drunkenness took no care to dry up his malady. On this account then Asclepius took no care of him, and did not visit him even in a dream. The youth grumbled at this, and thereupon the god, standing over him, said, "If you were to consult Apollonius you would be easier." He therefore went to Apollonius, and said: "What is there in your wisdom that I can profit by? for Asclepius bids me consult you." And he replied: "I can advise you of what, under the circumstances, will be most valuable to you; for I suppose you want to get well." "Yes, by Zeus," answered the other, "I want the health which Asclepius promises, but never gives." "Hush," said the other, "for he gives to those who desire it, but you do things that irritate and aggravate your disease, for you give yourself up to luxury, and you accumulate delicate viands upon your water-logged and worn-out stomach, and as it were, choke water with a flood of mud."[36]

The point of such stories is advertising propaganda on behalf of one source of healing at the expense of another. John 5:2–18 and this episode from Apollonius both glorify their respective heroes by showing them triumphant where an already-established healing shrine was ineffective.[37] We can now recognize still another of these in Mark's story of the woman with the flow of blood (Mark 5:24b–34). The improbable and grotesque ailment ascribed to her is already reminiscent of Asclepius testimonials (like poor Cleo, pregnant for five years!). Note the withering estimate of conventional medicine: "She had suffered much under many physicians, and had spent all that she had, and was no better for it, but only grew worse" (Mark 5:26). Notice, too, that the story is not even about Jesus! He does not even initiate the healing but only functions as a dynamo of divine energy, which she is able to access, via her great faith, by simply touching the hem of his prayer shawl. Jesus only learns what has happened after he has felt power escape from him. This structure is important, since it portrays Jesus as a source of healing. It is all up to the initiative of the sufferer: will she avail herself of Jesus' power? The same is hinted in John 5:6, "Do you *want* to be healed?" A good question, given the length of time the man has spent there in an ostensible healing shrine. The question is to the hearer/reader; it is up to him to make the "health-care choice" available to him, and after this commercial, the right choice should be obvious. Such tales presuppose the wide availability of Christian healers, and it is they whom we have to thank for creating these episodes.[38]

Mark 7:31–37 must have started out as another "how-to" paradigm for Christian healers. It is a recipe, using conventional magic techniques, for healing deaf mutes. It is a piece of what we would call *sympathetic* magic by *imitation*, since one imitates the blockage of the ears by inserting one's index fingers into the ears, then quickly withdrawing them and yelling, "*Ephphatha!* Be opened!" One sees the mute as "tongue-tied," so one lubricates the knot with spittle. (By contrast, the story of the bleeding woman depends upon *contagious* magic: touching the object charged with sacred *mana* does the trick.) Again, Jesus has evolved from the name invoked to the exemplar who reinforces the healer's procedure by posing as the originator and perfect practitioner of it.

The strongest argument in favor of Jesus actually having been a faith healer is that virtually all the ailments he is said to have cured have a place on the list of psychogenic maladies or somatization disorders in today's diagnostic manuals: loss of voice, deafness, double vision, blurred vision, blindness, seizures or convulsions, trouble walking, paralysis or muscle weakness, urinary retention or difficulty urinating, painful menstruation, menstrual irregularity, excessive bleeding. The apparent exceptions, cases where Jesus raises the dead or restores missing body parts, need not be taken as serious exceptions, as we will shortly see. Luke's report of Jesus restoring the servant's severed ear (Luke 22:51) is, as George A. Wells has shown,[39] the result of a misunderstanding of the Gethsemane arrest story. As soon as a zealous disciple tries to defend Jesus by taking a whack at the high priest's servant and misses, merely slicing off his ear, Jesus nips the violence in the bud. Jesus, in some oral version, must have said, "Let it be restored to its place." This was ambiguous. Mark therefore dropped what Jesus said. Matthew and John, however, paraphrased it: "Put your sword back into its place" (Matt. 26:52). "Put your sword into its sheath" (John 18:11). Luke guessed that Jesus meant not the sword but the ear! Thus: "And he touched his ear and healed him." We will wait till later to deal with the various resurrections Jesus is said to have effected.

In the meantime, what are we to make of the fact that Jesus' healing miracles fall well within the range of known somatization disorders, presumably susceptible to psychosomatic healing? Does it mean that, having modern medical analogies, they do not rest simply upon myth and fiction? If there hadn't been some kind of reality check, wouldn't the scope of Jesus' miracle stories be much wider than it is? No doubt. And it is true that the miraculous healing stories are not simply and completely fiction. Keep in mind that they are narrative magnifications of healings that early Christian healers actually tried to perform. This condition is what limited the scope of the healings. It is not necessarily Jesus who performed psychosomatic healings, but the early Chrstian healers did, or tried to. And any story of Jesus restoring rotting corpses or giving rationality to someone congenitally retarded simply could never have survived. No healer would have had success in such attempts, no matter how much prayer and fasting they engaged in. Any stories ascribing such feats to Jesus would have proven useless to the tellers of the stories, and so they would have been discarded. There are other gospel miracles much more spectacular than the healings, for example, walking on water and multiplying food, but there is no reason to think any early Christians tried to act these stories out. The sky was the limit when the point was just to magnify Jesus. And not even the sky is the limit, since Jesus eventually ascends into the heavens.

PREMATURE BURIALS?

There are three canonical stories of Jesus raising the dead. One of these is just one more variant of a story that circulated around the ancient world, attributed to various heroes. Another is a historicized version of a gospel parable. The third is a rewrite of an Old Testament miracle story.

Mark 5:22–23, 35–43 is the story of Jairus's daughter. Immediately we ought to catch the hint that it is fictional, as the name "Jairus" means "He will awaken." It is not really clear whether Jesus is supposed to be raising the dead. When Jesus, hearing that she is dead, comments, "She is not dead but only sleeps," he might mean that she is dead but not for long. But it is just as natural to suppose that he means the pronouncement of her death is premature, and that he is going to save her from premature burial. This story, like the next two we will consider from Luke and John, as well as Peter's resurrection of Tabitha in Acts 9:36–42, belongs with a whole group of popular tales in which an apparently dead person is brought back to consciousness on the very lip of the grave.

Here, too, is a miracle which Apollonius worked: [2] A girl had died just in the hour of her marriage, and the bridegroom was following her bier lamenting as was natural his marriage left unfulfilled, and the whole of [1] Rome was mourning with him, for the maiden belonged to a consular family. Apollonius then witnessing their grief, [3] said: "Put down the bier, for I will stay the tears that you are shedding for this maiden." And withal he asked what was her name. [4] The crowd accordingly thought that he was about to deliver such an oration as is commonly delivered as much to grace the funeral as to stir up lamentation; but he did nothing of the kind, but merely [5] touching her and whispering in secret some spell over her, at once [6] woke up the maiden from her seeming death; and [7] the girl spoke out loud, and returned to her father's house, just as Alcestis did when she was brought back to life by Hercules. [8] And the relations of the maiden wanted to present him with the sum of 150,000 sesterces, but he said he would freely present the money to the young lady by way of a dowry. Now whether he detected some spark of life in her, which those who were nursing her had not noticed—for it is said that although it was raining at the time, a vapour went up from her face—or whether life was really extinct, and he restored it by the warmth of his touch, is a mysterious problem which neither I myself nor those who were present could decide (4.45).[40]

Once, when [Asclepiades the physician] returned to the city from his country house, he saw a great funeral pile in the outskirts of the town, and around it a vast multitude, who had followed the funeral, all in great grief and soiled garments. He went up to the spot, as is the nature of the human mind, that he might know who it was, since no one answered his enquiries. Or, rather, he went that he might notice something in the deceased by means of his art. At all events, he took away death from that man who was stretched on the bier and nearly consigned to the tomb. The unfortunate man's body was already bedewed with perfumes, and his face was anointed with odorous ointment. Having carefully contemplated the man thus anointed and made ready for the funeral banquet, he noticed in him certain signs, handled the body again and again, and found life latent in it. Instantly he cried out that the man was alive, that they should take away the torches, put out the fire, pull down the pile, and carry back the funeral banquet from the tomb to the table. Meanwhile, a murmur arose, some saying that the physician should be believed, others making a mock of medicine. Finally, against the will of all the relations, whether it was that they were disappointed of the inheritance, or that they did not believe him, Asclepiades, with great difficulty, obtained a brief respite for the defunct, and so, in the end, he took him back to his house, snatched from the hands of the undertakers, and as it were from the infernal regions, and immediately revived his spirits, and called forth, by some medicine, the vital breath that was lurking in the recesses of his body (Apuleius *Florida* 14).[41]

The same early second-century author, Apuleius, tells another version of the tale in his *Metamorphosis* or *The Golden Ass*. A prominent physician exposes a scheme whereby some family members sought to manipulate the inheritance by murdering one son. He learned of it when he was approached by one of the conspirators desiring to obtain a subtle poison to fake the death by sickness. He pretended to cooperate, knowing that if he refused, another should do as the villain asked, and this way he might mount a counterplot to rescue the youth.

> "Wherefore I gave him no poison, but a soothing drink of mandragora, which is of such force that it will cause any man to sleep as though he were dead. . . . But if it be so that the child hath received the drink as I tempered it with mine own hands, he is yet alive and doth but rest and sleep, and after his sleep he shall return to life again. . . ." The opinion of this ancient physician was found good, and every man had a desire to go to the sepulchre where the child was laid: there was none of the justices, none of any reputation of the town, nor any indeed of the common people, but went to see this strange sight. Amongst them all the father of the child removed with his own hands the cover of the coffin and found his son rising up after his dead and soperiforous sleep: and when he beheld him as one risen from the dead he embraced him in his arms and he could speak never a word for his present gladness, but presented him before the people with great joy and consolation, and as he was wrapped and bound in the clothes of his grave, so he brought him before the judges (44).[42]

There are other versions besides these, and in all of them the feat of the hero is to save the victim from premature burial. The burden of proof ought to be borne by anyone who sees the story of Jairus's daughter as that of a genuine resurrection. The Lukan story (Luke 7:11–17) is clearly yet another version of the same story: the hero brings a funeral to a halt and retrieves the guest of honor back alive. It is more difficult to tell whether Luke wanted his readers to suppose the widow's son was truly dead, though, as his ultimate model was the 1 Kings 17:8–24 story of Elijah raising up the only son of a poor widow. Like Elijah (1 Kings 17:10), Jesus met the widow "at the gate of the city" (even though historical Nain, the village of Ain, had no city gate!). And, again like Elijah (1 Kings 17:23), after raising up the youth, "he gave him to his mother." Whether Elijah the prophet ever actually raised the dead is not our subject here, but it appears that Luke 7:11–17 is not a historical report of a resurrection, but rather a literary creation based on 1 Kings.[43]

Likewise, the literary sources of the Lazarus story in John, chapter 11, are too obvious for us to consider the story historical. First, John has used Luke 10:38–42, where Jesus visits the home of Mary and Martha. There is no mention of a third sibling, and we gain the definite impression that these two "spinster ladies" (Henry J. Cadbury)[44] live alone. One is serving, one is listening. Where is Lazarus? Note that in Luke 10:40, Martha upbraids Jesus, just as she does in John 11:21. Second, John has borrowed the Lukan parable of Lazarus and the rich man (Luke 16:19–31), in which a man named Lazarus dies, and someone proposes that he be sent back to the land of the living to urge people to repent. Jesus says it would be fruitless, as no one who does not already heed the biblical warnings to repent will change their mind, no matter what miracles they behold. What was a parable in Luke has become a miracle in John. A man named Lazarus is no longer just a character Jesus creates but rather a friend of his. Lazarus actually does die, and the truth of Jesus' rueful skepticism is demonstrated when the resurrection of Lazarus does nothing but further harden the hearts of Jesus' enemies. This is not history but a conflation of two earlier stories, one of them an admitted fiction.

OBEDIENT NATURE

The principle of analogy allowed us to consider the miracles of exorcism and healing as likely candidates for actual deeds in the life of Jesus, since there are faith healings and exorcisms today, whether one understands them as supernatural manifestations or as instances of abnormal psychology and psychosomatic healing. As it happened, however, there was the initial problem of weighing these stories against what appear to be earlier New Testament statements that Jesus did no miracles. And, examined each in turn, the stories all swarmed with problems of anachronism, narrative confusion, and marks of borrowing from outside sources. None appeared historically credible, and in no case was this simply because the story contained a miracle. But now we proceed to stranger, more exotic territory, that of the so-called nature miracles, divine feats unparalleled in contemporary experience but amply paralleled in ancient, non-Christian legends.

First, let us consider sea miracles. That of Jesus calming the storm (Mark 4:35–41) seems to be based pretty straightforwardly on the story of Jonah, especially on these elements: "But Yahve hurled a great wind upon the sea, and there was a mighty tempest on the sea. [Jonah 1:4] . . . But Jonah had gone down into the inner part of the ship and had lain down and was fast asleep. So the captain came and said to him, 'What do you mean, you sleeper? Arise, call upon your god! Perhaps the god will give a thought to us, that we do not perish' [1:5b–6]. . . . And the sea ceased from its raging. Then the men feared Yahve exceedingly [1:15b–16a]." Pythagoras, too, is said to have effected "tranquilization of the waves of rivers and seas, in order that his disciples might easily pass over them" (Iamblichus *Life of Pythagoras* 28),[45] but we really need look no further than Jonah for the basis of this story.[46] Why create a Jesus version of the tale? Perhaps it was someone's attempt to supply the answer to the enigmatic "sign of Jonah." At any rate, it functions as a lesson of faith in God's protective providence, such as Madame Guyon had. "We all of us came near perishing in a river which we found it necessary to pass. The carriage sank in the quicksand. Others who were with us threw themselves out in excessive fright. But I found my thoughts so taken up with God that I had no distinct sense of danger. It is true that the thought of being drowned crossed my mind, but it caused no other sensation or reflection in me than this—that I felt quite contented and willing it were so, if it were my heavenly Father's choice."[47]

Jesus not only stills the storm on the Sea of Galilee but also walks on the waves in Mark 6:45–51. This miracle is found in other traditions, too, and no one is especially urgent to defend any of these as historical reports. "After enlightenment, the teacher [Gautama Buddha] went to Varanasi on foot. In this journey he wanted to cross [the] river Ganga, but being unable to pay the fare to [the] boatman, crossed it through [the] air" (*Mahavastu* 3.328.6; *Lalitavistara* 528).[48] Again, Asvaghosa says the Buddha "walked in the air; on water as if on dry land" (*Saunerananda* 3.23).[49]

Because of the similarity to John 21:4, 7 and Luke 24:36–37, some have suggested that Mark 6:45–51 is based on a (slightly misinterpreted) resurrection appearance story. When verse 48 depicts Jesus περιπατων επι της θαλασσης, one can, as the old Rationalist Protestants used to point out, translate that Jesus was "walking *by* the sea." The preposition επι can mean "on top of" or "on the edge or verge of." Which option would have frightened the disciples, making them think they were seeing a ghost? Either one, depending on when they saw it. If they saw Jesus walking on top of the sea while he was still alive, as Mark 6 now has it, they would have concluded it was a ghost, since no substantial human being can defy gravity, while a ghost would be lighter than the water. But suppose they knew Jesus was dead and then saw him walking on the nearby sea shore? They would think they had seen a ghost, even though he appeared to be treading solid ground. Has Mark misplaced and therefore misunderstood a resurrection story? If he did, then we would still have a resurrection story to deal with, but even this would not feature a stroll on the waters.

Matthew has added an adjunct to this story, in which Peter, too, walks on the water (Matt. 14:28–33). Mark knows nothing of this sequel, nor does John (6:16–21). No one can imagine Mark and John neglecting to mention such an event had they known of it. And if it had happened, they certainly would have heard of it. Who would omit it? The narrative graft is clumsy; Peter asks, "Lord, if it is you, bid me come to you on the water!" (If the figure is not Jesus but someone else, will he *not* bid Peter? Or if he does, how will sharing his gift of antigravity prove it is Jesus?) And then he takes the plunge! If he has this much faith, what room was there for his initial doubts? Matthew's story is confused. But the point of his midrashic expansion is quite clear, as it has been to every preacher who has ever sermonized on the text: if you as a follower of Jesus will only keep your eyes fixed on him, in the midst of life's turbulent sorrows, you will rise above them, but if you begin to worry about them instead and take your eyes off Jesus, you will sink. And even then, the merciful savior will restore you. The point is exactly the same in a story of a lay disciple on his way to hear the

Buddha preach: "He arrived at the bank of the river Aciravati in the evening. As the ferryman had drawn the boat up on the beach, and gone to listen to the Doctrine, the disciple saw no boat at the ferry, so finding joy in making Buddha the object of his meditation he walked across the river. His feet did not sink in the water. He went as though on the surface of the earth, but when he reached the middle he saw waves. Then his joy in meditating on the Buddha grew small, and his feet began to sink. But making firm his joy in meditating on the Buddha, he went on the surface of the water, entered the Jetavana, saluted the Teacher, and sat on one side" (*Introduction to Jataka Tale* 190).[50]

The story of the coin in the fish's mouth (Matt. 17:24–27) must be the most obviously legendary tale in the Gospels, despite the fact that plenty of others are more spectacular. The core of the story is an attempt to settle an early Christian halachic dispute over whether Jews who are Christians are under any obligation to pay the annual half-shekel tax for the maintenance of the temple in Jerusalem. The story need not be earlier than the destruction of the temple, since, as with the halachic debates of the Mishnah, much later sages debated proper protocol to apply when the temple should be restored, as they believed it must be, and business returns to usual. The original conclusion, ferreted out of Peter by Jesus with Socratic questioning, is that Christian Jews stand higher than their kinsmen according to the flesh, closer to God as his children, not mere subjects like the rest of Jewry. Thus, they are exempt. And yet such a stance would obviously appear arrogant (as it may to us), so someone has "corrected," that is, reversed the original pronouncement story by adding, "Nonetheless, lest we offend them, go to the sea and cast out a hook, and take the first fish to come up, and when you open its mouth you will find a shekel. Take that and give it to them for me and for yourself." Jesus could have just taken a shekel out of the common purse. The reason he sends Peter to fish is to make clear that his teaching is the will of God. A miracle will provide the money for the tax, implying that God does indeed want them to pay it, since he has providentially provided the wherewithal to do it.

To be pedantic, one might point out that the story cannot be historically true for the simple reason that the fish could not retain a coin in its *mouth* after being hooked! But this is worth pointing out, since we have made it our policy never to discount a story merely because it involves the supernatural. There have always proven to be ample other reasons. And, once again, that for which we can find no analogy in contemporary experience finds its parallel in ancient and admitted legend, such as the story of Joseph-who-honors-the-Sabbath, from *Mishnah Shabbat* 119a. "Joseph-who-honors-the-Sabbath had in his vicinity a certain Gentile who owned much property. Some Chaldeans [i.e., soothsayers] said to him: 'Joseph-who-honors-the-Sabbath will consume all your property.' He went and sold all his property and bought a precious stone with the proceeds, which he set in his turban. As he was crossing a bridge, the wind blew it off and cast it into the water; a fish swallowed it. The fish was hauled up and brought [to market] on the Sabbath eve toward sunset. They said: 'Who will buy at this hour?' They said to them: 'Go and take them to Joseph-who-honors-the-Sabbath, as he is in the habit of buying.' So they took it to him. He bought it, opened it, and found the jewel therein, and sold it for thirteen roomfuls of gold denarii. A certain old man met him and said, 'He who lends to the Sabbath, the Sabbath repays him.'"[51] (Of course, Joseph's aim was to encourage sabbath observance by the merchants by not leaving them stuck with perishable merchandise as the sabbath began.)

Jesus causes a miraculous catch of fish in two passages, Luke 5:1–11 and John 21:4–13. This one has been borrowed from the lore of Pythagoras. Here is one version of the Pythagoras story. "At that time also, when he was journeying from Sybaris to Crotona, he met [1] near the shore with some fishermen, who were then drawing their nets [2] heavily laden with fishes from the deep, and [3] told them he knew the exact number of the fish they had caught. But the fishermen [4] promising that they would perform whatever he should order them to do, if the event corresponded with his prediction, he ordered them, [5, 6] after they had numbered the fish, to return them alive to the sea; and what is yet more wonderful, [7] not one of the fish died while he stood on the shore, though they had been detained from the water a considerable time. Having therefore paid the fishermen the price of their fish, he departed for Crotona. But [8] they everywhere divulged the fact, and having learnt his name from some children, they told it to all men" (Iamblichus *Life of Pythagoras* 8).[52]

John's version retains unassimilated marks of the Pythagorean original, namely, the fact that the fishermen counted the fish as well as the specific number of them, 153. Can one really picture these men carrying on inventory as usual if they now realized their crucified master had risen from the dead? "The rest of you fellows go have breakfast with the resurrected Son of God. I'll count the fish." Not likely. The element of counting the fish makes sense only in the Pythagorean original, where the vegetarian sage's supernormal wisdom enabled him to intuit the exact number. And the number itself? It turns out to be one of the "triangular" numbers venerated by the mathematically astute Pythagoreans. But Christians were not opposed to eating fish, so the original point of the miracle meant nothing to them. Why should Jesus challenge fishermen to such a game, when he couldn't have bemoaned the cooking and eating of fish? So in the Christian version, the miracle is the large catch of fish itself, caused by Jesus. Luke's version has effaced the more obvious marks of its Pythagorean origin, but it is the same story. As with the premature burial preventions, this story has simply attached itself to Jesus as it floated around the religious world of the Mediterranean.

With the miraculous catch of fish, we have already arrived at our second category of nature miracles, namely, food miracles. Another is the feeding of the multitude with scant loaves and fish. Mark gives us two separate versions of the story, 6:32–44 and 8:1–10. They are essentially the same in every detail except the precise numbers of people present and food left over. Such figures are, of course, the easiest details to lose and confuse (unless, as with the "triangular" 153, there is some special reason to remember them). It seems that Mark heard two versions of the story, differing in number, and like a good scribe, he decided to keep both of them, separating them by a couple of chapters, just as the Genesis redactor did with the three versions of the patriarch and his wife entering a foreign kingdom and lying about being married, in Genesis, chapter 13, with Abram and Sarai in Mizraim (Egypt), chapter 20, with Abraham and Sarah in Gerar of the Muzrim, and chapter 26, with Isaac and Rebecca in Gerar of the Philistines. And just as one might have expected Abraham to have learned his lesson after the first incident, one might have expected the disciples of Jesus not to be so flabbergasted by the suggestion that they feed the crowd with what they've got the second time! The first time, admittedly, skepticism would be inevitable, but the second? How obtuse can they have been? This is an unintended result of the redactional decision to retain both versions instead of choosing between them.

But did it happen even once? There is no reason not to understand the story as a Jesus version of the 2 Kings 4:42–44 story of Elisha multiplying food. "A man came from Baal-shalishah, bringing the man of God bread of the firstfruits, twenty loaves of barley, and fresh ears of grain in his sack. And Elisha said, 'Give to the men, that they may eat.' But his servant said, 'How am I to set this before a hundred men?' So he repeated, 'Give them to the men, that they may eat, for thus says Yahve: "They shall eat and have some left."' So he set it before them, and they ate, and had some left, according to the word of Yahve."

It is hard to resist the old suggestion that the Jesus version of the story originated as a profound and beautiful story recited at the eucharistic celebration. The physical multiplication of bread stands for the invisible magnification of spiritual virtue in the bread once consecrated. To haggle over whether it "really happened" is to miss the entire point of what is "really happening" in the eucharist.

Jesus changes water into wine in John 2:1–11, in apparent imitation of the annual miracle of the priests of Dionysus at Eleia. "The worship of Dionysos is one of the principal Elean cults, and they say the god himself visits them at the feast of Thuia. . . . The priests take three empty basins in the presence of the citizens and of any foreigners there may be and deposit them in a building. The priests themselves and anyone else who wants put seals on the doors of the building; the seals can be inspected the next day, and when they go inside they find the basins full of wine (Pausanias *Guide to Greece* 6.26.1–2).[53] This would not be the only Dionysian legacy in the Gospels. John's True Vine discourse (chapter 15) is another. Some ancient writers considered Dionysus and Yahve to be the same deity, and the Sabazius religion of Asia Minor certainly seems to have been built on that premise. 2 Macc. 6:7 tells us that Antiochus Epiphanes forcibly converted many Jews to Dionysus worship, though we may suspect rather that most conversions were voluntary and constituted just the sort of radical Hellenization that the Hasmoneans rebelled against.

As Raymond E. Brown observed, the story has the look of a "preministry" apocryphal tale such as we find in Luke 2:41–52 and the apocryphal Infancy Gospels (see chapter 3, "Childhood and Family"). All such stories, including the one reworked in John 2:1–11, presuppose a young Jesus traveling with his family who know him already to be a wonder-worker. He bears with their stupidity and saves the situation from disasters created by adults. Here, he (originally unaccompanied by any disciples, whom he would not yet have recruited) goes to a neighborhood wedding feast. When the adults' typically poor planning leads to social embarrassment, Jesus' mother immediately looks to him, as Ma Kent might to young Clark, whom she knows is secretly Superboy, to solve the problem by some miraculous trick. He chafes at the trivial request, but Mary knows he cannot refuse her and so tells the master of the feast to do whatever peculiar-sounding thing Jesus may tell him. She's sure he will come up with something. And he does. The party goes on! It is no more a moment from the life of the historical Jesus than is the scene in the Infancy Gospel of Thomas 4:15–16, 6:16–36, where baby Jesus' clothing and bathwater heal the sick.

WE HAVE NEVER SEEN ANYTHING LIKE THIS

Did Jesus perform miracles? We have seen that at the outset early Christians were satisfied that Jesus had done no miracles. Mark 8:11–13 and 1 Cor. 1:22 made it clear that Christian preachers had no miracles to offer to those who sought them as credentials. But we have also seen that a great number of miracle stories (healings, exorcisms, and nature prodigies) were soon attributed to Jesus, many of them rewritten from Old Testament stories or adapted from other Hellenistic heroes and gods. Why such a change? Simply because, as both Mark 8:11–13 and 1 Cor. 1:22 tell us, Christians faced audiences who were hungry for miracles, eager, at least willing, to consider the gospel if it came wrapped in signs and wonders. Paul's enemies criticized him for compromising the purity of the gospel by dropping Torah observance and circumcision to make it more attractive to Gentiles. In the same way, it seems many preachers must have abandoned the earlier appeal to a sheer decision of faith in favor of compelling "proofs." Some might call it pandering, but was not wisdom to be justified, in the final analysis, by her children, the results?

NOTES

1. George A. Wells, "The Historicity of Jesus," in *Jesus in History and Myth*, ed. R. Joseph Hoffmann and Gerald A. Larue (Amherst, N.Y.: Prometheus Books, 1986), p. 32.

2. David Friedrich Strauss, *The Life of Jesus Critically Examined*, trans. George Eliot, Lives of Jesus Series (1835; repr., Philadelphia: Fortress Press, 1972), p. 415.

3. Henry T. Fleddermann (*Mark and Q*, Bibliotheca Ephemeridum Theologicarum Lovaniensium XCCII [Leuven: Leuven University Press, 1995], pp. 130–33) proposes a different way of looking at the passage, making it a Markan abbreviation of the longer Q version (which is not so absolute a denial). His strongest argument, to my way of thinking, is that "this generation" in Mark 8:12 seems an isolated vestige of the Q version, where the point of the word was to contrast Jesus' contemporaries with the superior generations of Jonah and of the Queen of Sheba (Matt. 12:41–42//Luke 11:30–32), who were willing to listen when a prophet or wise man addressed them. On the other hand, Q itself features an abrupt, contextless occurrence of "this generation," in the children in the marketplace pericope (Matt.11:16–19//Luke 7:31–35). And if we adopt the text-critical maxim that the more difficult reading is likely to be the original (since the smoother reading will always make more sense as a harmonization), surely Mark's version must be original. Q's version strikes me as a fumbling attempt to make some new sense of the original denial of miracles by a plain emendation: "except, that is, for the sign of Jonah," this last borrowed from the "men of Ninevah, Queen of the South" pericope with which the Q redactor linked it by means of the fortuitous catchword "generation." It is just like Matthew's softening of the Markan divorce saying, "except for πορνεια" (Matt. 19:9). It is not that Q redacted Mark, but that both independently knew and preserved the same saying, and Q changed it.

4. Gershom Scholem, *Sabbatai Sevi: The Mystical Messiah, 1626–1676*, Bollingen Series 93 (Princeton, N.J.: Princeton University Press, 1973), pp. 252, 265.

5. Norman Perrin, *Rediscovering the Teaching of Jesus* (New York: Harper & Row, 1976), pp. 66–67, incredibly, accepts the text as authentic to Jesus, despite the fact that he himself adduces a parallel midrash from *Midrash Exodus Rabbah* 10.7. Criterion of dissimilarity, anyone?

6. Rudolf Bultmann, *History of the Synoptic Tradition*, trans. John Marsh (New York: Harper & Row, 1972), p. 101.

7. Morton Smith, *Jesus the Magician* (New York: Harper & Row, 1978), pp. 63–64.

8. Similarly, his third-century biographer Philostratus sought to rehabilitate Apollonius of Tyana's prevalent reputation as a wizard in *The Life of Apollonius of Tyana*.

9. Albert Schweitzer, summarizing the view of Hermann Samuel Reimarus, in *The Quest of the Historical Jesus: A Critical Study of Its Progress from Reimarus to Wrede* (New York: Macmillan, 1975), p. 19; see *Reimarus: Fragments*, trans. Ralph S. Fraser, ed., Charles H. Talbert, Lives of Jesus Series (Philadelphia: Fortress Press, 1970), pp. 232–33.

10. Gerd Theissen, *The Miracle Stories of the Early Christian Tradition*, trans. Francis McDonagh (Philadelphia: Fortress Press, 1983), pp. 283–84. Theissen does of course discuss the Asclepius stories, as well as those told of Apollonius and others, but he seems to find qualitative contrasts between the Jesus stories and all others, which I cannot help but attribute to his own apologetical agenda, despite his noble attempts to transcend such concerns.

11. Raphael Patai, *The Hebrew Goddess* (New York: Avon Books, 1978), p. 189.

12. Origen, *Contra Celsum*, trans. Henry Chadwick (New York: Cambridge University Press, 1979), p. 10.

13. Ibid., p. 300.

14. David L. Dungan, trans., in *Sourcebook of Texts for the Comparative Study of the Gospels*, ed. Dungan and David R. Cartlidge, Sources for Biblical Study 1, 4th ed. (Missoula: Scholars Press, 1974), p. 63.

15. Ibid, p. 61.

16. Emma J. Edelstein and Ludwig Edelstein, eds., *Asclepius: Collection and Interpretation of the Testimonies* (Baltimore: Johns Hopkins University Press, 1998), pp. 230.

17. Ibid., pp. 231–32.

18. Ibid., p. 235.

19. Philostratus, *Life of Apollonius of Tyana*, trans. F. C. Conybeare, Loeb Classical Library 16 (Cambridge, Mass.: Harvard University Press, 1912), pp. 363, 365, 367.

20. J. Ramsey Michaels, "Jesus and the Unclean Spirits," in *Demon Possession: A Medical, Historical, Anthropological and Theological Symposium*, ed. John Warwick Montgomery, papers presented at the University of Notre Dame, January 8–11, 1975, under the auspices of the Christian Medical Association (Minneapolis: Bethany Fellowship, 1976), pp. 48–49.

21. Hans Dieter Betz, ed., *The Greek Magical Papyri in Translation, Including the Demotic Spells*, vol. 1: *Texts*, 2d. ed. (Chicago: University of Chicago Press, 1992); John G. Gager, ed., *Curse Tablets and Binding Spells from the Ancient World* (New York: Oxford University Press, 1992); John M. Hull, *Hellenistic Magic and the Synoptic Tradition*, Studies in Biblical Theology, Second Series 28 (Naperville: Alec R. Allenson, 1974); Smith, *Jesus the Magician*.

22. William Whiston, trans., *The Works of Flavius Josephus* (London: Ward, Lock & Co., n.d.), p. 212.

23. Conybeare, trans., vol. 1, pp. 391, 392.

24. Ibid., p. 317.

25. David R. Cartlidge, trans., *Sourcebook of Texts for the Comparative Study of the Gospels*, p. 59.

26. Géza Vermes, *Jesus the Jew: A Historian's Reading of the Gospels* (Glasgow: Collins/Fontana, 1977), p. 209.

27. William Wrede, *The Messianic Secret in Mark's Gospel*, trans. J. C. G. Grieg, Library of Theological Translations (Altrincham: Jones Clarke & Co. Ltd., 1971); see also the recent defense and updating of the theory by Heikki Räisänen, *The "Messianic Secret" in Mark*, trans. Christopher Tuckett, Studies of the New Testament and Its World (Edinburgh: T & T Clark, 1990).

28. John L. Nevius, *Demon Possession* (Grand Rapids: Kregel, 1968), pp. 343–44.

29. Gerd Theissen, *Sociology of Early Palestinian Christianity*, trans. John Bowden (Philadelphia: Fortress Press, 1978), pp. 101–102.

30. Dennis E. Nineham, *The Gospel of St. Mark*, Pelican New Testament Commentaries (Baltimore: Penguin Books, 1963), p. 153.

31. Dennis Ronald MacDonald, *Homeric Epics and the Gospel of Mark* (New Haven: Yale University Press, 2000), pp. 63–76.

32. Edelstein, p. 221.

33. J. Duncan M. Derrett, *The Making of Mark: The Scriptural Bases of the Earliest Gospel* (Shipston-on-Stour, Warwickshire: Peter Drinkwater, 1985), p. 185.

34. Wolfgang Roth, *Hebrew Gospel: Cracking the Code of Mark* (Oak Park: Meyer-Stone Books, 1988), p. 56.

35. Randel Helms, *Gospel Fictions* (Amherst, N.Y.: Prometheus Books, 1989), pp. 69–70.

36. Conybeare, trans., vol. 1, pp. 21, 23.

37. Theissen, *Miracle Stories*, p. 51.

38. Similar stories are told today. In one episode of *Xena Warrior Princess*, Xena brings a large number of casualties from a raided village into the local Asclepium. The priests are swamped, but it hardly matters, because they don't administer any treatment but prayer anyway! Xena comes to realize this when she starts applying what battlefield first aid she knows, and the priests rebuke her for blasphemy! The god will heal them his own way or not at all. She proceeds anyway, saving many and convincing a young priest named Galen to study real medicine. And in *Star Trek IV*, there is a hilarious sequence in which Chekov gets injured during a time-travel visit to 1980s America, and Kirk and McCoy have to rescue him from the Torquemada-like horrors of twentieth-century medicine.

39. George A. Wells, *The Jesus of the Early Christians*, p. 197.

40. Conybeare, trans., vol. 1, pp. 457, 459.

41. Lucius Apuleius, *The Works of Apuleius Comprising The Metamorphosis, or Golden Ass, The God of Socrates, The Florida and his Defence, or A Discourse on Magic. A New Translation* [Anon.] (London: George Bell and Sons, 1910), pp. 401–402.

42. Lucius Apuleius, *The Golden Ass*, trans. William Adlington, ed. Harry C. Schnur (New York: Collier Books, 1962), p. 241.

43. Strauss, *Life of Jesus Critically Examined*, p. 495.

44. Henry J. Cadbury, *The Making of Luke-Acts* (London: SPCK, 1961), p. 264.

45. *Iamblichus' Life of Pythagoras*, trans. Thomas Taylor (1818; repr., Rochester, Vt.: Inner Traditions, 1986), p. 72.

46. Helms, *Gospel Fictions*, pp. 78–79.

47. Cited in George Barton Cutten, *The Psychological Phenomena of Christianity* (New York: Scribner, 1908), p. 39.

48. Sarla Khosla, *The Historical Development of the Buddha Legend* (New Dehli: Intellectual Publishing House, 1989), p. 147.

49. Ibid., p. 148.

50. Edward J. Thomas, *The Life of Buddha as Legend and History*, rev. ed. (London: Rutledge & Kegan Paul, 1975), p. 241.

51. *Narrative Parallels to the New Testament*, ed. Francis Martin, SBL Resources for Biblical Studies 22 (Atlanta: Scholars Press, 1988), p. 151.

52. *Life of Pythagoras*, p. 17.

53. Pausanias, *Guide to Greece*, vol. 2, *Southern Greece*, trans. Peter Levi (Baltimore: Penguin Books, 1971), pp. 363–64.

CHAPTER SIX
MINISTRY
TO THE
OUTCASTS

OUTCAST AT NAZARETH

The story of Jesus' chilly reception in his hometown synagogue (Mark 6:1–6) offers us a fascinating case of traceable growth in the gospel tradition. We begin with what would seem a pre-Markan story of a warm reception in the old neighborhood. It would have read something like this: "He . . . came back to his own country. . . . And on the sabbath he began to teach in the synagogue; and many who heard him were astonished, saying, 'Where did this man get all this?' 'What wisdom is given to him!' 'What mighty works are wrought by his hands!' 'Is not this the carpenter, the son of Mary and Joseph and brother of James and Judas and Simon, and are not his sisters here with us?'" (My guess is that "Joses," short in any case for Joseph, has lost its original place in the list due to later scruples about the virgin birth doctrine.) There is no hint of negativity here. And it is clearly implied that Jesus healed some present: the people are acclaiming what he says and does on *this* occasion, not another.

But Mark must have known of a proverb attributed to Jesus, preserved in Thomas 31, "A prophet is not acceptable in his own country, neither does a physician cure those who know him." If Jesus said it, Mark reasoned, it must reflect his own experience. But then how do we square this data with that in the story of Jesus' happy homecoming? He arbitrarily joins the two units together by mere authorial fiat, adding 6:3c, "And they took offense at him." *What?* After singing, "For He's a Jolly Good Fellow"? He simply reverses the force of the people's acclamation! To this Mark then adds a scene demonstrating their lack of faith and visibly embodying the second half of the proverb after quoting a version of the first half in verse 4: "And he could do no mighty work there, except that he laid his hands on a few sick people and healed them.[1] And he marveled because of their unbelief" (Mark 6:5–6). Sure enough, Jesus cannot heal those who know him, even though the original story implied he had done just that!

Matthew (13:54–58) sees other difficulties, ones of Mark's own creation. Matthew omits Jesus' amazement, because he cannot imagine Jesus could have been taken by surprise. He also chops Mark's statement that Jesus "could not" heal many. Matthew changes that to "did not," as if to have the almighty Jesus punish the crowd for their unbelief rather than being limited by it as in Mark.

Luke (4:16–30) has done major remodeling on the story. First, he supplies the location, hitherto implied, as Nazareth. Second, emulating Thucydides and other Greek historians, he decides he will fill in the tantalizing blank and supply the unrecorded content of the sermon that supposedly roused so much emotion. In the Q reply to John the Baptist's messengers, Jesus had been made to quote Isa. 61:1–2 about the miracles of the age of salvation (Matt. 11:5//Luke 7:22). Luke uses it again here, but he backs up, quoting more of Isaiah: "The Spirit of the Lord is upon me." In this way, Luke connects this scene with that of the descent of the Spirit at the Jordan baptism, which in Luke's chronology (though nobody else's) happened shortly before this scene. Even in Luke its position is anomalous, since Luke himself is aware of previous adventures of Jesus that must have occurred between the baptism and this scene. Jesus has already gained a reputation for healings performed down the road in Capernaum. We must regard this note (verse 23) as either a goof in story continuity or as a paralepsis, the subsequent plugging in of past action we didn't know we had missed.

Luke recognizes the artificiality of Mark's juxtaposition of the crowd's praise with the brusque statement, "And they took offense at him." In verse 22, Luke explicitly says, "They spoke well of him." What, then, turned them hostile? Mark didn't give a clue, so Luke decides that Jesus' not healing them must have been not the *effect* but rather the *cause* of their hostile unbelief! While the crowd still dotes on its local-boy-made-good, Jesus winds up and pitches the apple of discord: "I bet you'll start complaining that I don't do any of the miracles I did in Capernaum, huh?" Why would they do that? Because Jesus is about to make it clear that he will heal no one in Nazareth. He explains by reference to the stories of the Widow of Zarephath (1 Kings 17:17–24) and Naaman the Syrian (2 Kings 5), Gentiles healed by Elijah and Elisha, that he plans, like them, to heal only foreigners! This, as might well be imagined, turns the crowd ugly. While the scene lacks all natural motivation, it does manage to (sort of) connect the dots left by Mark's "clumsy construction."[2]

Luke adds another popular proverb, "Physician, heal yourself," intending it as a request to which the dramatically demonstrated "Neither does a physician cure those who know him" is the answer. "Yourself" here means "your own."

How does Jesus manage to walk effortlessly through the midst of an angry lynchmob? We must take it as the protective providence of the (not only omniscient but also) omnipotent narrator, as in John 8:20, "No one arrested him, because his hour had not yet come." That is as much as to admit that the author just didn't want Jesus' death to happen so soon in the story.

John has made more oblique use of the story (or, as C. H. Dodd would have it, he has made a different mix of the same loose story elements than the Synoptists did). The major elements of the story can be found in John 6:1–59, the episode of the Bread of Life discourse and its aftermath. In John, the action has shifted to the Capernaum synagogue (verse 59), seizing on the mention of Capernaum in Luke's version. Again, as in Luke, here Jesus is made to rebuke the crowd's desire for miracles like those Jesus has previously performed (compare John 6:26–27 with Luke 4:23). Here, too, something abruptly transforms ardent fans (John 6:14) into embittered foes (John 6:41–42, 52, 66), only this time it is the easily misunderstood Bread of Life discourse with its risky remarks on eating human flesh and drinking blood. The crowd exclaims, as it does in the Synoptic versions, "Is this not Jesus, the son of Joseph, whose father and mother we know?" (John 6:42a). But John does something conspicuous by its absence in the Synoptics: he adds other comments (6:42b) that make these words sound like derision rather than praise, thus making Mark's abrupt transition read more smoothly. Now what were words of praise, followed by Mark's comment of disapproval, themselves become words of disapproval already.

John also takes another Markan crowd acclamation ("Where did this man get all this?") and uses it in a different scene in his next chapter: "How is it that this man has learning when he has never studied?" (John 7:15). The comment makes more sense in Mark's context (from whence it must have come) since only his hometown acquaintances would know what Jesus' educational background was like! John, though, has Jerusalemites say it. Similarly, John has taken the proverb about a prophet's lack of honor in his own backyard and used it in yet another alien context, since 4:44, where he places it, is set not in Galilee but in Judea!

What can we surmise about the original story unit with which Mark began, the episode of a happy homecoming for Jesus? My guess is that it originated as a credential list on behalf of the *Desposynoi*, the Heirs of Jesus, who sooner or later claimed blood kinship with the Messiah. The climax, and therefore the punchline of the original story, after all, seems to be the close association of James, Simeon, and Judas with Jesus—and with his wisdom and mighty works! When he is gone, they are the next-best thing. "I will not leave you orphans" (John 14:18). Thus, its function was precisely like that of the sacerdotal credential genealogies that the Zadokite priests brought back with them from the Exile to reinforce their rights to lord it over the people. Again, it is like the spurious genealogies constructed by Matthew and Luke (or their predecessors) to vindicate Jesus' Davidic pedigree. In this case, the setting of the scene in a Galilean synagogue (an anachronism, as we saw in the "Introduction") serves to reinforce the claim of the Heirs of Jesus to respect and support from synagogues, whether in Palestine or in the Hellenistic world of the late first and early second centuries C.E.

MARGINAL MESSIAH

One of the most attractive features of the gospel portrait of Jesus is that of his easy fellowship with the outcasts of his society, which some felt unbecoming to Jesus' position as a religious leader. It enables us to picture Jesus as a man of the people, a Gandhi embracing the *harijans*, a first-century Espresso priest. Some have seen this element as central to Jesus' program. Joachim Jeremias saw Jesus' outreach to those willing to repent at the eleventh hour as so controversial that a great many of his parables were aimed at explaining and defending the policy.[3] More recent scholars[4] have doubted whether Jesus even sought repentance from these outcasts. Rather, they suggest, Jesus identified with the marginal, those viewed askance by the traditionally religious, because Jesus himself was something of a dissident, a beatnik, a Cynic calling the bluff of conventional religion. This portrait of Jesus even shades off into the political revolutionary Jesus, since, if one identifies the outcasts with the downtrodden, Jesus begins to look like Robin Hood or Che Guevara. Others critical of these views suspect that left-leaning scholars, themselves hostile to government, family values, and any sort of traditional patriotism, have just remade Jesus in their own image. I share these suspicions, but it is also possible that they have seen something in the gospel stories that others have missed. It may be that Jesus is shown there as a marginalized figure. And this, in turn, might be the result of ancient marginalized Christians, like modern ones, making Jesus in their own image.

Gerd Theissen draws a fascinating picture of the social identity of those early Christians who found the radical-lifestyle sayings of Jesus valuable and worth preserving. He notes[5] that, given the unsettled climate of the times, the political situation, the economic straits, many people began to gravitate toward the margins of society because there was no place else for them to go. Certain roles were marginal or might even be understood as embodying marginality. Such roles included beggars, demoniacs, monks, hermits, revolutionists, and intinerant prophets. All these types had appropriately marginal ways of dealing with the mainstream and navigating alongside it. Violent conspirators preyed off today's society in the name of another society they hoped would arrive from the future, the only place the Messiah ever really exists. Prophets, the mad, and demoniacs all established a corner where they had a claim for attention and support from the common populace, performing for them and thus earning their alms. One is helpless against insanity and feels conscience-bound at least to accord the mad spare change in compensation for the normal social relations denied them.[6] One feels survivor guilt in the face of the poor, and in the zero-sum mindset of the "limited good,"[7] one might perhaps feel guilty for somehow causing their plight if one did not share it. Giving them alms atones just a bit for the sin of relative prosperity. As for prophets, they draw the circle of holiness about themselves, and one dare not risk it being a hoax, so one might as well give alms, hoping one might share the prophet's reward. To become a prophet or apostle was also a way of dignifying destitution. If one had but a pittance and then renounced it for the sake of the gospel, one had become a hero for a cheap price, a wise investment.

So there is an important sense in which the gospel Jesus, himself portrayed as an itinerant preacher, fits in well with the marginal and the outcast. They had much in common. No wonder he had more to say to them than to settled householders.[8] And, again, it may have gone both ways. Not only may Jesus have found a ready hearing among the marginal; the Jesus figure may enshrine features of marginal individuals who helped paint his portrait. We will be trying to trace the degree and direction of such give and take in this chapter. We will be asking which of the two we know more about: the historical Jesus or the early Christians who found reason to attribute their views to him.

THE USUAL GANG OF SUSPECTS

Just exactly who was Jesus supposed to have fraternized with to the great discomfort of the pious? The Gospels mention certain classes of people, especially tax collectors (or toll collectors) and "sinners" with whom Jesus associated. Who were these people? Tax collectors have usually been pictured as Quislings and scalawags, profiting off their own people's sad state of national occupation by the Romans. The Romans operated a tax-farming system, so that a local collector would owe Rome the estimated percentage of the people's worth, but he could add a surcharge, out of which he would be paid. This arrangement was obviously open to abuse, but not necessarily all tax collectors abused the system. From what few mentions of the tax collectors survive from Jewish and Hellenistic literature of the period, Luise Schottroff and Wolfgang Stegemann[9] have shown that, while some people naturally bemoaned the abuses and condemned those who practiced them, the general scorn expressed for the profession was because of its low-class, low-paying social position. Similar scorn was expressed by the wealthy for other low-rung professions with which they did not soil their hands. Thus, on the whole, the trouble with tax collectors was not that they oppressed the poor, but that they themselves *were* poor. And, with the exception of tradesmen who groused about them the way people do about our own Internal Revenue Service today, the common people would not have despised them. While Pharisees early on drew some lines, refusing to countenance contributions from tax collectors, the more serious measures (for example, of ruling them out as witnesses in trials) came only later, after the time of Jesus. And if a tax collector had used his position to exploit people, there was a protocol for repentance: he had to quit his job and pay restitution to those he had wronged.

Jesus has well-known encounters with two tax collectors, Levi and Zacchaeus. He is briefly described as passing by Levi's tollbooth and summoning him to follow, and Levi does (Mark 2:14). We are not told that Levi was repenting of a life of white-collar crime; he may have decided tax-gathering was not as important in the scheme of things as following Jesus. One wonders if the story, spotlighting as it does a tax-collector recruit, presupposes the rarity of such. We scarcely have time to let this question cross our minds as we read Mark, because he immediately tells us that many tax collectors followed Jesus (Mark 2:15) and clearly implies the rest of them had not abandoned their posts, as the blue-nosed Pharisees still regard them as unfit company for the pious (Mark 2:16). Has Mark just generalized from the single case he knew of? If he did, it enabled him to create the setting for the saying in Mark 2:17, "Those who are well have no need of a physician, but those who are sick. I came to call not the righteous, but sinners." And this saying, really two sayings, may well be secondary. The business about the physician is a Cynic commonplace, whereas the second one reveals itself as a piece of Christian theology by virtue of its retrospective characterization of Jesus' salvific mission. It answers the Christian question, "Why did Jesus 'come,' that is, into the world?" We will come across plenty more of such retrospective minicreeds, all of them to be classified as spurious.[10]

Jesus' second encounter with a tax collector (Luke 19:1–10) may be no more historical, especially as the name "Zacchaeus" is just too good to be true for this character. It is based on the Aramaic *zakki*, "to give alms"! Of course, this was a real name, as was "Nicodemus," but we have to wonder if we are dealing with a real historical figure when the name so closely matches the role of the character as to hint that he is one of Todorov's "narrative-men."[11] Is it a coincidence that Nicodemus (whose name means "ruler of the people") is said in John 3:1 to be "a ruler of the Jews"? Is it a coincidence that Martha, the hostess of Luke 10:38, has a name meaning "Lady of the House"? Is it a coincidence that the tax collector who is about to liquidate his holdings on behalf of the poor is called "Zacchaeus"?

At any rate, we might ask whether Zacchaeus is supposed to be repenting in this cameo scene or not. We usually suppose he is repenting on the spot, moved by the hissing of the crowd and the surprising concern Jesus shows for him. But this is not completely clear. When Zacchaeus says, "Behold, Lord, the half of my goods I give to the poor; and if I have defrauded anyone of anything, I restore it fourfold," is he protesting his innocence against the murmuring of the crowd who regard him as a sinner? Is he describing his *usual practice* of generosity? Is his promise to restore any ill-gotten gains fourfold intended as a challenge to anyone in the crowd to prove him guilty? Is the reaction of the crowd a piece of the anti–tax collector bias described by Schottroff and Stegemann? Perhaps. On the other hand, we might have here a textbook case of a fraudulent tax collector's repentance, complete with restitution, according to Pharisaic requirements. Whether the story is historical, again, is doubtful, all the more in view of the fairy-tale-like manner in which Jesus simply knows his name without being personally acquainted with him.

The Q saying in Matt.11:16–19//Luke 7:31–35 presents Jesus' alleged association with tax collectors and sinners as a smear and a slur equivalent to the notion that he was also a drunk and a glutton, and that John the Baptizer was a demoniac! It is doubtful whether this pericope ought to enter into evidence on behalf of Jesus being in fellowship with the IRS of his day. The same goes for the saying attributed to Jesus in Matt. 11:31, "Amen: I say to you, the tax collectors and the harlots go into the kingdom of God before you." Does this mean these two groups are actually repenting and entering the sphere of salvation? Or does it just mean it will be a cold day in Gehenna before the Pharisees enter heaven? The prospect of tax collectors and prostitutes entering heaven may be equivalent to that of the camel squeezing through the needle's eye (Mark 10:25). Matthew has joined the verse with some Q material that does speak of the repentance of tax collectors and prostitutes (Matt. 21:32//Luke 7:29), but this saying ascribes their repentance to John's preaching, not to Jesus', and it certainly has nothing to say of any chaste company-keeping between either prophet and the ladies of the night.

Speaking of prostitutes, is there any evidence at all that Jesus was especially concerned for their souls' welfare? The whole notion seems to be an extrapolation from the traditional romanticized picture of Mary Magdalene, whom legend makes a reformed prostitute. But the Gospels do not describe her as a prostitute. She is instead a cured demoniac, from whom seven demons were cast out (Luke 8:2; [Mark 16:9]). The number marks the story as legendary, but at least this legend is to be found in the Gospels, unlike the prostitute charge.

There are three stories in which Jesus meets sinful women, but in none of them can he be said to have sought them out. In John, chapter 4, he meets the Samaritan woman who has had five husbands and is cohabiting with a sixth man. She is not said to be a prostitute, though it is quite possible that she stands for Simon Magus's consort Helena, whom he rescued, à la *Taxi Driver*'s Travis Bickle, from a brothel. This implies the story is, as Oscar Cullmann thought, an allegory of the Samaritan mission of Acts, chapter 8, here retrojected into the career of Jesus for a more ironclad pedigree.[12]

In Luke 7:36–50, Jesus is sought out by a repentant sinner who anoints his feet with perfume. Had she been a prostitute? It doesn't say. The story is so confusing and near-incoherent that we cannot be sure we are dealing with history. It is torn apart by narrative contradictions and improbabilities. How did the woman obtain entrance to the Puritanical Pharisee's dwelling? How has he allowed her to continue in this scandalous display ever since Jesus arrived, as Jesus himself is heard to say? How can we account for the absolute rudeness of the Pharisee as a host, since nothing was forcing him to invite Jesus in the first place if he thought he was a deceiver of Israel? And what sense does it make that Jesus says her sins must already have been forgiven—then forgives her? The whole thing seems to be a drastic Lukan reworking of the Markan story of the Bethany anointing (Mark 14:3–9), and the element of the woman being a sinner is one of his gratuitous additions.

Finally, [John 8:1–11], the story of the woman taken in adultery, again, does not deal with a prostitute. Nor does Jesus seek her out; instead she is literally dragged to Jesus. And as to its historicity, the tale comes from a time when early Christians were trying to decide which provisions of the Torah they would retain. Jesus would scarcely have been asked his opinion by a Jewish contemporary on whether the Torah's stipulations ought to be obeyed. "What do you think, Jesus? Will the sun rise tomorrow?"

Who were the "sinners"? No one knows. At least it is hard to identify them in the setting of Jesus. Some have suggested that Jesus consorted with known criminals, like JFK with Sam Giancanna. Others have suggested that the "sinners" were merely the common people who had neither the leisure nor the inclination to take on the burden of Pharisaic piety, which would have been comparable, apparently, to Hasidic Judaism in our day. But whether the derogatory label assigned them by a bunch of fundamentalists would have made the majority of Jews believe themselves to be outcasts is questionable. How many of the targets of Jerry Falwell's critiques either chafe at them or internalize them?

HATE THE SIN AND HATE THE SINNER

One of the most baffling problems of historical Jesus studies, long hidden by residual anti-Semitism, is this: what could the Pharisees have found so vexing in whatever outreach Jesus did have toward sinners? Would they have so despised sinners that they would have urged complete shunning of them by the righteous? They might have. "I look at the faithless with disgust, because they do not keep thy commandments" (Ps. 119:158). And yet who would turn away the repentant?[13] It is significant that rabbinic Judaism venerates holy men who associated with sinners as Jesus is said to have done. Solomon Schechter says, "friendly relations were entertained with sinners in the hope that intercourse with saintly men would engender in them a thought of shame and repentance. Thus, it is said of Aaron the High Priest, who 'did turn many away from iniquity' (Mal. 2:6), when he met a wicked man, he would offer him his greetings. When the wicked man was about to commit a sin, he would say to himself, 'Woe unto me, how can I lift my eyes and see Aaron? I ought to be ashamed before him who gave me greetings.' And he would then desist from sin. (*Aboth of Rabbi Nathan* 24b.) Compare with *Sanhedrin* 37 a, the story of R[abbi] Zera, who entertained certain relations with the outlaws in his neighbourhood for the same purpose."[14] Would Jesus' critics have opposed his successful attempts to reclaim sinners?

It might be suggested that the problem was that he offered the option of repentance without a sufficiently high price tag, without penance. But there is no evidence of this. In fact, the two stories in which Jesus is shown meeting tax collectors, historical or not, show an awareness of what a crooked tax collector would have to do if he repented: leave his job, as Levi does, and repay his victims, like Zacchaeus does. So if Jesus did minister to such people, there is no reason to believe he would have gone any easier on them than the Pharisees did.

Jeremias, as already noted, made much of Jesus' outreach to repentant sinners and his public defense of the same in his parables. Let us take a brief look at some parables attributed to Jesus that seem to deal with the topic. First, a word of warning as to authenticity. It seems to me that virtually all of the parables appearing only in Luke are the work of that evangelist. They are mostly long (comparatively) and detailed, with genuine characters. And they are marked by a minor but significant signature: the soliloquy of a character in a dilemma and his resolution.[15] The Rich Fool asks, "What shall I do? I will . . ." (Luke 12:17–19). The Prodigal Son asks, "What shall I do? I will . . ." (15:17–19). The Dishonest Steward asks, "What shall I do? I will . . ." (16:3–4). The Unjust Judge asks, "What shall I do? I will . . ." (18:4–5). Once he has added it to a Markan parable, that of the Wicked Tenants (Luke 20:13; cf. Mark 12:6 and Matt. 21:37, which lack it).

Several parables (and other sayings) unique to Matthew, proverbially the most Jewish of the Gospels, have such close parallels to rabbinical material that it is tempting to think he has borrowed the material from familiar Jewish sources. The dating of the rabbinic materials is often difficult, but the pattern is so thoroughgoing that one must take seriously the possibility of Matthew's having borrowed from Judaism. The criterion of dissimilarity would never let such parables and sayings slip through the net.

The parable of the Lost Sheep comes from Q, and both evangelists who use it have rewritten it and applied it differently. For Matthew (18:10–14), the parable means that vigilant church leaders should not allow "little ones," or vulnerable church members, to go astray into sin. In view is a sectarian faith community. For Luke the point is rather the validity of Jesus' ministry to sinners. He is not willing to give up on them (or God is not willing to give up on them) any more than a shepherd would take lightly the loss of one of his precious flock. Matthew's version is introduced by this glimpse of heaven: "See that you do not despise one of these little ones; for I tell you that in heaven their angels always behold the face of my Father who is in heaven" (Matt. 18:10), but Luke's vision is a bit different: "Even so, I tell you, there is more joy in heaven over one sinner who repents than over ninety-nine righteous persons who need no repentance" (Luke 15:7). Luke's redaction of this particular piece of Q sounds so much like the words of the Prodigal's father in Luke 15:32 that we are inclined to credit these words to him also. Note as well that Luke introduces the parable with a formula statement: "Now the tax collectors and sinners were all drawing near to hear him. And the Pharisees and scribes murmured, saying, 'This man receives sinners and eats with them'" (Luke 15:1–2), copied from Mark 2:15–16. This makes it appear that Luke 15:7, with its application to sinners who repent, is Lukan, too. Without Luke saying so, it is not quite so clear that this parable is a defense of Jesus' supposed ministry to outcasts.

The Lost Coin (Luke 15:8–10) sounds like a Lukan doublet, created to reinforce the Lukan theme. It appears in no other gospel.

The Prodigal Son, a Lukan masterpiece, is clearly intended as a defense of Jesus' outreach to sinners, as Jeremias says. The older brother, faithful for years, resents the treatment accorded the repentant profligate younger brother. But what are you going to do? It is good that the faithful have been faithful, but what a delightful surprise when the faithless return to the fold! Isn't that good, too? The parable has a close parallel in rabbinic literature. "It is to be compared to the son of a king who was removed from his father for the distance of a hundred days' journey. His friends said to him, 'Return unto your father,' whereupon he rejoined, 'I cannot.' Then his father sent a message to him, 'Travel as much as it is in thy power, and I will come unto you the rest of the way.' And so the Holy One, blessed be he, said, 'Return to me and I will return to you' (Mal. 3:7)" (*Pesikta Rabbati* folios 184b and 185a).[16] The rabbinic version may be the earlier, and it attests to a Jewish concern that no sinner despair of God's mercy. It offers repentance; it does not defend the offering of it, as if it were somehow controversial. Whom was Luke's version aimed at?

The parable of the Workers in the Vineyard (Matt. 20:1–16) repudiates the notion that lifelong religious piety puts one closer to God than a late-coming sinner is as soon as he repents. If all are saved by the grace of God, what does it matter? He doesn't owe salvation to anybody, least of all those who believe they have a claim on it. Does this fine parable go back to Jesus? It has a very close parallel in rabbinic literature, too. Here is Jeremias's summary of it, from the Jerusalem Talmud, *Berakoth* 2.3c. "The situation was like that of a king who had hired a great number of labourers. Two hours after the work began, the king inspected the labourers. He saw that one of them surpassed the others in industry and skill. He took him by the hand and walked up and down with him till the evening. When the labourers came to receive their wages, each of them received the same amount as all the others. Then they murmured and said: 'We have worked the whole day, and this man only two hours, yet you have paid him the whole day's wages.' The king replied, 'I have not wronged you; this labourer has done more in two hours than you have done during the whole day.'"[17] The point is to explain that "only the good die young." Rabbi Zera used the parable to explain the tragic early death of the brilliant young Rabbi Bun bar Hijja about 325 C.E., but Jeremias thinks it might be much earlier, and that Jesus had known it and based his parable of the Workers in the Vineyard upon it. It seems to me more likely that Matthew has borrowed it from rabbinic lore, as he seems (in uniquely Matthean material) to have done several times elsewhere. The originality of the rabbinic version is signaled by the more appropriate rationale for the king's seeming inequity. This is a story, keep in mind, and Matthew's version ends with an arbitrary shocker, unanticipated by the plot. The workers are just stuck, and there is no Labor Board for them to appeal to. Tough luck. The rabbinic version has a climactic explanation that is a true puzzle solution: it doubles back along the path of the action, putting the end in a new light. The king did pay fairly: merit pay, quality, not quantity. So, again, the criterion of dissimilarity denies it to Jesus, and we are also left with the mystery: just whom is this parable trying to convince? Who opposed the repentance of sinners? Who saw their own prerogatives threatened by latecomers?

Christian scholars have, unfortunately and naively, perpetuated the Christian vilification of Jews as merciless legalists, simply by taking gospel texts as history. That made all these passages much easier to understand. It is not uncommon to read how Jesus' preaching of love and forgiveness was itself enough to infuriate the Jews, goading them to judicial murder. But these are the horned Jews of the Oberammergau Passion Play, not the Jews of history, as far as our sources tell us. In some of the conflict stories, where Jesus is made to triumph over the shame-faced Pharisees, we get the feeling the Pharisees have simply been made to look bad as foils for Jesus. But the texts presupposing that an offer of repentance would have been controversial and in need of extensive apologetics seem to require something more than this. We have to think there was an opponent lurking off stage, that these barbs *were* actually directed against *some*one. If Pharisees do not fit the picture, who does? I suggest that the true scenario underlying the gospel preoccupation with the controversial mission to sinners is that glimpsed in Galatians and in Acts, chapters 10–11 and 15: the debate over the Gentile Mission. We have already seen how the stories of healings at a distance, as well as the Great Commission sayings, must have originated in post-Jesus debates over the Gentile Mission, to make Jesus address the question in absentia and thus settle the debate.

I am suggesting that all the business about eating with sinners had to do with the kind of unpleasantness witnessed in Antioch in Galatians, chapter 2. Peter, Paul, and Barnabas, all good Jews, have welcomed Gentile converts to Christianity. They have sat down to eat with them in public fellowship in apparent disregard for kosher scruples. They figure that their common faith overrules old distinctions. But then conservative emissaries of James the Just, head of the Jerusalem church, arrive. Peter and Barnabas fear James's reaction if news of their ecumenical smorgasbord gets back to him, so they begin withdrawing from the common table, eating by themselves with a kosher menu. It is a subterfuge right out of *I Love Lucy*, and it backfires. Apparently, James's men were satisfied, but Paul was infuriated at what seemed to him cowardly hypocrisy. In Acts 11, when Peter has returned from a successful mission to preach to the Gentile Cornelius, his apostolic colleagues in Jerusalem call him on the carpet: was he out of his mind to visit Gentiles—*and eat with them* (Acts 11:3)? Why was the Gentile Mission so controversial? In the first place, it seemed to demand ritual compromise on the part of Jews who might preach to Gentiles (Luke 10:8,

"Whenever you enter a town and they receive you, eat what is set before you"—
this to the Seventy, Luke's symbolic anticipation of the Gentile Mission). In the
second place, there was the huge question of whether Gentiles had to become
Jews in order to become Christians. It seemed logical, after all. Jesus was the
Jewish Messiah. Ought not his followers, as a matter of course, continue to
observe that holy Torah for which so many martyrs had given their lives? Or
could they just get baptized and believe in Jesus?

Because of the first question, there were Jewish Christians who opposed the
Gentile Mission: "Go nowhere among the Gentiles, and enter no town of the
Samaritans" (Matt. 10:5). Most likely these conservatives had no thought of
abandoning Gentiles to damnation. They probably expected that in the last days
all the nations would make their way to Jerusalem to learn the Torah, as Isa.
2:2–4 and Mic. 4:1–3 had predicted. There was no need to take the gospel to
them, especially before the time. We can see echoes of their position, historical
analogies with it, in the initial reluctance of Calvinist church authorities in the
nineteenth century to participate in the great Protestant missionary expansion. If
God wanted the heathen to hear the gospel and be saved, they reasoned, he would
see to it himself. We needn't presume to preempt his providence by our blun-
dering efforts. Again, we might think of the early Orthodox and Hasidic opposition to the State of Israel as an audacious and even blasphemous attempt by
human beings to force the fulfillment of prophecy. There could be no real restoration of true Israel till King Messiah arrived. And in the same cautious spirit, no
doubt, some in the early church believed Gentiles had no share in the gospel
while this age endured. They would get their turn soon enough. And besides,
would not Jewish Christian missioners have their hands full with their fellow
Jews till then anyway (Matt. 10:23)?

In a pronouncement story worthy of the ancients, British evangelist Charles
Haddon Spurgeon was once asked by someone who highly valued his theological
opinion, "Dr. Spurgeon, do you believe in infant baptism?" to which he replied,
"*Believe* in it? Why, man, I've *seen* it!" In the same way, it soon became a moot
point whether one believed in the theoretical propriety of the mission to Gentiles
or not. Those who did pursued it, and very soon there was a legion of Gentile
Christians to deal with. It seemed that the appeal of Christianity was great among
the so-called God-fearers, the devout among the Gentiles, who had embraced
Jewish ethical monotheism and even attended synagogue but balked at submitting
to circumcision and all the rest of the laws, which to them seemed an alien cultural inheritance. There they were, whether they "should" have been or not.

So the question became what to do with them. On what basis could they be
admitted to the household of faith? On equal terms with Jews? And if so, would
that mean they had to sign on for all six hundred thirteen commandments? Or could
they just renounce pagan immorality and all gods but Jesus and his Father? It
seems as if Matthew adopted the former solution (Matt. 5:19, 28:19–20), while
Paul accepted (or even pioneered) the latter. This alternative involved cutting loose

the ceremonial regulations of Judaism as mere cultural mores. Yet a way had to be found to jettison them without denying that they had first been mandated by God himself. The solution was to say that the Torah had merely pointed to Christ, and that, with his coming, he had done away with it in some sense, at least in the sense that Gentiles need not worry about it. The Law should no longer function as a fence separating Jews and Gentiles, since Gentiles need not obey it. But then they never had! God had never held them responsible for more than Noah's terse commandments (Gen. 9:4–6, Acts 15:19–20). Didn't Paul's idea really entail Jewish (Jewish-Christian) abandonment of the Torah, too? The Torah cannot have ceased dividing Jew from Gentile unless they both came to have the same stance toward it. And if Paul says Gentiles need not keep it, he must imply that Jews don't need to either. We do not know whether Paul intended or would have accepted this implication, but we know some so understood him (Acts 21:21).

Again, it is not as if the more conservative Jewish Christians abandoned the enthusiastic new Gentile believers to hell. The alternative to accepting them as equal members of the true Israel was recognizing them as Christian God–fearers, a second tier of salvation, rather like the Vatican II view of Protestants: genuine Christians, yet not beneficiaries of the true church. Or perhaps they might be compared to Solomon Stoddard's "halfway covenant" among the Puritans.

Have we come very far away from the Gospels? No, because now we are in a better position to see what the real controversy was. The intended audience for texts like the Prodigal Son and the Workers in the Vineyard would have been the earliest group of Jewish-Christian conservatives. It would have been people like Peter's opponents in Acts 11 and whoever wrote Matt. 10:5 who must be persuaded to give up their cherished insistence on priority. We can't easily picture Jews who would begrudge fellow Jews an opportunity to repent. But we know there were Jewish Christians who wanted to keep Gentiles in their "proper" place until the end-time scenario. There were a lot more Gentiles than Jews, and perhaps the Jewish Christians foresaw what would happen by the second century: Jews would be a minority within the church, at the mercy of the neophyte Gentile Christians.

Again, the Gentile Mission scenario supplies just what we found missing in the literal picture presented in the Gospels. Since it was hard to imagine repentance per se being controversial, it seemed there had to be some secondary sticking point. But what could it have been? No requirement of sufficient penance for repenting Jewish sinners? We found no reason to believe that. The Gospels even demonstrated converted tax collectors doing precisely what the Pharisees demanded they do. Was there something besides repentance per se at issue? It comes neatly into focus once we look at the early church instead of Judaism in Jesus' day. The "extra" issue was on what terms converting Gentile "sinners" (Gal. 2:15) might be accepted. The Pharisees who mysteriously carp at Jesus for welcoming sinners are really the opponents of Paul who charged him with making things too easy for Gentile converts by dispensing with the Torah, "pleasing men" by offering cheap grace (Gal. 1:10).

Benjamin W. Bacon[18] and Jack T. Sanders[19] pegged correctly, to my way of thinking, the Gentile Mission debate as the true home of the saying attributed to Jesus, "Beware of the leaven of the Pharisees" (Luke 12:1; cf. Mark 8:15, which adds "and the leaven of Herod"; Matt. 16:6, which adds "and Sadducees"). The "leaven," or insidious influence, in view must be that of "false brethren secretly brought in, who slipped in to spy out our freedom which we have in Jesus Christ, that they might bring us into bondage" (Gal. 2:4). Who were these moles? "Some believers who belonged to the party of the Pharisees rose up and said, 'It is necessary to circumcise them, and to charge them to keep the laws of Moses'" (Acts 15:5). Bacon insists that the leaven saying is authentic to Jesus, but he cannot imagine what the original point of it might have been. He admits the saying's only traceable use was its application to the Gentile Mission issue. It seems to me he has made the case for the Gentile Mission debate as the original *Sitz-im-Leben* and thus for the secondary character of the saying.

SECTARIANISM AND SELF-RIGHTEOUSNESS

A second group of parables located in the conflict between Jesus and his opponents centers around accusations that they are complacent in their own imagined righteousness and therefore remain aloof to the preaching of Jesus, unlike the poor sinners who know their spiritual plight and seek to escape it. Those texts discussed in the previous section argue, "They're repenting; don't stand in their way." These next turn the guns on the opponents themselves: "Come to think of it, why aren't *you* jumping on the bandwagon? What's the matter with you, anyway?" Insofar as this is really the issue in the passages we will consider next, it implies the social dynamics of a sectarian movement, a new revivalistic version of an old faith community or a new offshoot from it: Methodism spinning off from the Church of England, the Pentecostals from the Holiness Churches, Hasidic from Rabbinic Judaism. Those attracted and transformed by the new movement look back at the unmoved members of the established church group and infer that they must have needed the new emphasis/experience, too, but that they resisted God's will by staying put in the old ways. The Montanists surely felt this way about their Catholic coreligionists. One can easily imagine the enthusiastic disciples of John the Baptist (nowhere better pictured, I am sure, than in the Martin Scorsese/Paul Schrader film, *The Last Temptation of Christ*) so viewed other Jews. The logic seems to be: "I can be sure of salvation only if the promise is for all. If it were for only some, how could I be sure I was one of them? And if it *is* for all, then all must *need* it, including you. So my confidence in my own salvation rests on my regarding you as a hypocrite stewing in your own pretended righteousness." Does this social and psychological condition underlie any of the following gospel passages?

Matt. 21:28–32, the parable of the Two Brothers, regards those who did not repent at the preaching of the Baptizer (or, by implication, Jesus) as hypocrites. As it stands, it is a Matthean creation, as shown by the phrases "did the will of his father" and "go into the kingdom of God," which echo the uniquely Matthean formula in Matt. 7:21, "Not every one who says to me, 'Lord, Lord,' shall *enter the kingdom* of heaven, but he who *does the will of my Father* who is in heaven." Matthew is no doubt aiming this parable at the leadership of formative Judaism in his own day. For them, on the other hand, no doubt the issue regarding the Jesus sect of Matthew was much like that faced today by Orthodox Jews considering the status of the followers of Menachem Mendel Schneerson: can they still be considered faithful Jews? Or has their exaggerated messianism placed them beyond the pale of Judaism?

Luke 7:41–43 constitute a miniature parable (the Two Debtors) tucked into the heavily redacted Lukan version of the anointing. Luke has made the original into another lesson of the superior regard God has for repentant sinners over the lifelong righteous. As John Drury surmises,[20] the parable was no doubt written by Luke himself for this context, even though his various other additions to the story contradict it. The parable itself betrays significant Lukan special vocabulary, and it fits his characteristic theme of the rejoicing of, or over, sinners who repent. This one does not come out of debates over Gentile "sinners" being converted to Christianity, as some texts discussed in the previous section do. It is simply a narrative embellishment helping to portray Jesus, as Luke wanted to do, as a champion of repentant sinners against those who (for what reason he leaves unclear, having no doubt forgotten the original point of such texts in the Gentile Mission debate) would begrudge them their repentance.

Pretty much the same lesson is inculcated in another Lukan creation, the parable of the Publican and the Sinner (Luke 18:9–14). Given the fact that Luke has organized his gospel's central section around the Book of Deuteronomy,[21] so as to provide a kind of "Deutero-Deuteronomy" for his readers (recalling Matthew's new Christian Pentateuch, comprising his five great discourses), the sequential position of the parable matches that of Deut. 26:13–15, the prescribed prayer for the annual rendering of agricultural tithes: "Then you shall say before Yahve your God, 'I have removed the sacred portion out of my house, and moreover I have given it to the Levite, the sojourner, the fatherless, and the widow, according to all the provisions of your commandment which you have commanded me; I have not transgressed any of your commandments, neither have I forgotten them; I have not eaten of the tithe while I was mourning, or removed any of it while I was unclean, or sacrificed any of it to the dead; I have obeyed the voice of Yahve my God, I have done according to all that you have commanded me. Look down from your holy habitation, from heaven, and bless your people Israel and the ground which you have given us, as you swore to our fathers, a land flowing with milk and honey."

There is nothing particularly self-righteous or chest-thumping about this confession of obedience. The point is exactly the same as the temple entrance liturgies of Psalms 15 and 24, which list the moral requirements of any and all who would seek Yahve there, a kind of "security system" to weed out the hypocrites excoriated by Isaiah (1:12–17): "If you haven't kept these, then don't bother showing up." Doesn't Luke see this? He levels a cruel spoof at the prayer, as if it were the self-worship of a pious windbag. One wonders if there is another agenda here, namely, if Luke is sweeping away the piety of Jews at the time of the Jewish War with Rome: "this people . . . will fall by the edge of the sword, and be led captive among all nations; and Jerusalem will be trodden down by the Gentiles, until the epoch of the Gentiles is concluded" (Luke 21:23c–24). In full view of the Deuteronomic context, that is, Luke is saying that the (imagined) faithlessness of Jews led to God's rescinding the promise he had made to the patriarchs to provide the land flowing with milk and honey. Since the Deuteronomic confession presupposes Israel's obedience as a condition of holding the promised land, the proud Pharisee, by aping the ancient confession, was "asking for it," and so did his entire generation, or so Luke reasons.

The parable of the Great Supper appears in Q (Matt. 22:1–10//Luke 14:15–24) and in the Gospel of Thomas (64), whose version seems to be simpler and perhaps more original in form. But a still earlier version appears in the Jerusalem Talmud (*Sanhedrin* 6.23c. paragraph j, *Hagigah* 2.77d).

> Two pious men lived together in Ashkelon, devoting themselves to the study of the Law. One of them died and no honour was paid to him at his funeral. Bar Ma'jan, a tax collector, died and the whole town honoured his funeral. The remaining pious man was deeply disturbed and cried out that the wicked in Israel did not get their deserts. But his dead companion appeared to him in a dream and told him not to despise the ways of God in Israel. He himself had committed one evil deed and hence had suffered dishonour at his funeral, whereas Bar Ma'jan had committed one good deed and for that had been honoured at his. What evil deed had the pious man committed? On one occasion he had put on his phylacteries in the wrong order. What good deed had the tax collector committed? Once he had given a breakfast for the leading men of the town and they had not come. So he gave orders that the poor were to be invited to eat it, that it should not go to waste. After some days the pious man saw his dead companion walking in the garden of paradise beside fountains of water; and he saw Bar Ma'jan the tax collector lying on the bank of a river, he was striving to reach the water and he could not.[22]

Of course, this version supplies what is conspicuous by its absence in the fragmentary gospel versions: the motive of the invitees for begging off with bogus excuses. The behavior is not at all strange if they realized they were being used by a social climber to lend him undeserved respectability. Jeremias imagines that Jesus must have heard the story and adapted it for his own purposes, using it not only in the parable of the Great Supper but also as the basis for Lazarus and the Rich Man (Luke 16:19–31). But I think it more likely that the Q redactor and Luke are the ones who have helped themselves to the story (or to what was left of it by the time it reached them). One reason for this is the rabbinic setting of the story, which it cannot easily do without. The profession of the tax collector has to be balanced out by a noble profession, an educated sage. Another is the fragmentary character of the tale: the Gospels preserve only a torso. And it is only the *lack of the original rationale* that makes the story available as a story of people rejecting the call of God. Such fragmentariness implies a long period of transmission or the use of a fragmentary written source. At any rate, the attribution of the story to Jesus would be ruled out by the criterion of dissimilarity.

FRIEND OF SINNERS?

Given the increasing importance of the Christian doctrine of Jesus redeeming sinners on the cross, it is not surprising for the theme to have been historicized and read back into the public ministry period before his crucifixion, as if he had sought out sinners in their lairs and persuaded them to repent and be saved, as if he were already doing Christian evangelism. It appears, then, that what was first a piece of soteriology became a piece of biography, or hagiography, much as the detail of Jesus being a "carpenter," metaphorical for his being a Scripture exegete, became, in the eyes of later believers, the datum of his working in a rustic carpenter shop. We have to assume something like this occurred in the present case, because there simply is no real evidence for such an element in the life of Jesus. Some of the relevant sayings seem to have been misconstrued. Post-canonical legend has silently served as mortar to brick other passages together in precisely this arrangement, such as the notion of Mary Magdalene as a harlot. We have found it difficult to locate in the ostensible time of Jesus any available opponents who would have taken the extraordinary approach of refusing to allow sinners to repent. Instead, we have found a natural context for such debates in the early church's struggle over the propriety and terms of the Gentile Mission. So once again, our gospel picture of Jesus seems to be revealed as a tissue of pious fictions created by early Christians for their own needs.

NOTES

1. "Lord, I am affected by a bald patch." Graham Chapman et al., *Life of Brian (of Nazareth)* (New York: Ace Books, 1979), p. 109.

2. John C. Meagher, *Clumsy Construction in Mark's Gospel: A Critique of Form and Redaktiongeschichte*, Toronto Studies in Theology III (New York: Edwin Mellen Press, 1979).

3. Joachim Jeremias, *The Parables of Jesus*, trans. S. H. Hooke, 2d. rev. ed. (New York: Scribner, 1972), pp. 124 ff.

4. E. P. Sanders, *Jesus and Judaism* (Philadelphia: Fortress Press, 1985), pp. 210, 255.

5. Gerd Theissen, *Sociology of Early Palestinian Christianity*, trans. John Bowden (Philadelphia: Fortress Press, 1978), pp. 34–36.

6. As Thomas S. Szasz says, we just can't stand having them around. *The Myth of Mental Illness: Foundations of a Theory of Personal Conduct*, rev. ed. (New York: Harper & Row Perennial Library, 1974), p. 38–39, 267.

7. Bruce J. Malina, *The New Testament World: Insights from Cultural Anthropology* (Atlanta: John Knox Press, 1981), pp. 75–79.

8. Cf. Stevan L. Davies, *The Revolt of the Widows: The Social World of the Apocryphal Acts* (Carbondale: Southern Illinois University Press, 1980), p. 36: "There is a tension here, a conflict between the asocial ideal embodied in the apostle himself and the Christian end the apostle functions to attain. The Christian social structure that emerges at least partially because of the activities of apostles will have to be one which [simply by virtue of *being* a community] to some extent rejects the asocial virtues of the apostles and, therefore, the apostles themselves."

9. Luise Schottroff and Wolfgang Stegemann, *Jesus and the Hope of the Poor*, trans. Matthew J. O'Connell (Maryknoll: Orbis Books, 1986), pp. 6–13.

10. Rudolf Bultmann, *History of the Synoptic Tradition*, trans. John Marsh (New York: Harper & Row, 1972), pp. 155–56.

11. Tevetan Todorov, *The Poetics of Prose*, trans. Richard Howard (Ithaca, N.Y.: Cornell University Press, 1992), pp. 66–79.

12. Oscar Cullmann, *The Johannine Circle*, trans. John Bowden (Philadelphia: Westminster Press, 1976), p. 48.

13. Sanders, *Jesus and Judaism*, pp. 272–73.

14. Solomon Schechter, *Some Aspects of Rabbinic Theology* (New York: Macmillan, 1910), p. 321.

15. John Drury, *The Parables in the Gospels: History and Allegory* (New York: Crossroad, 1989), p. 115.

16. Schechter, *Some Aspects of Rabbinic Theology*, p. 327; another version appears in *Deuteronomy Rabbah* 2.24 and is quoted by Perrin, *Rediscovering the Teaching of Jesus*, p. 91, and despite this, Perrin considers the parable of the Prodigal Son authentic! What happened to the criterion of dissimilarity?

17. Jeremias, *Parables of Jesus*, p. 138.

18. Benjamin W. Bacon, *Studies in Matthew* (New York: Henry Holt, 1930), p. 517.

19. Jack T. Sanders, *The Jews in Luke-Acts* (Philadelphia: Fortress Press, 1987), p. 316.

20. Drury, *Parables in the Gospels*, p. 130.

21. C. F. Evans, "The Central Section of St. Luke's Gospel," in *Studies in the Gospels: Essays in Memory of R. H. Lightfoot*, ed. D. E. Nineham (Oxford: Basil Blackwell, 1955), pp. 37–53.

22. Norman Perrin, *Rediscovering the Teaching of Jesus* (New York: Harper & Row, 1976), pp. 111–12.

CHAPTER SEVEN
THE TWELVE DISCIPLES

DID I NOT CHOOSE YOU, THE TWELVE?

What we know for sure is that among the competing leadership groups of the early Christian movement was a body known as the Twelve (1 Cor. 15:5), later identified by Luke (quite possibly as an innovation) as the Twelve Apostles. This last looks like a conflation of the original Twelve with a different though possibly overlapping honorific, the apostles. The latter was a more inclusive group of pioneer missionaries. The list of resurrection appearances in 1 Cor. 15:3–11 appears to have originated as a list of credentials for the various apostles in the broader sense, a wider group that included names such as Barnabas (Acts 14:4, 14), Andronicus, and Junia (Rom. 16:7). If one claimed apostolic authority, it seems, one had to be able to claim one had been vouchsafed an apparition of the Risen One (1 Cor. 9:1). The Twelve made such a claim collectively (presumably, that is, they claimed to have seen as a group, not individually, the Risen Christ), if we can judge from 1 Cor. 15:5, "he appeared to Cephas, then to the Twelve." The Sunday school notion that the Twelve fanned out across the known world spreading Christianity comes from the second and later centuries when various churches vied with one another in importance by claiming to have been founded by this or that apostle. (The naming of gospels after various apostolic figures partakes of the same tendency.) Originally, the Twelve seem to have been the custodians of the messianic community in Palestine, as were another group, already mentioned, the Heirs, or relatives of Jesus. In Acts, we see Peter patrolling Palestine, not the wider Mediterranean. The charter of the Twelve (Q: Matt. 19:28//Luke 22:28–30), to which we shall return, envisions the Twelve governing the twelve tribes of Israel, not the Gentiles. The world mission of the Twelve is a piece of catholicizing revisionism, designed to assimilate the Twelve to Paul, originally the one and only Apostle to the Gentiles.

It is hardly a surprise that the leadership council of a sectarian movement that viewed itself as the new or the true Israel would constitute itself with twelve members symbolizing the old tribal confederacy. The Qumran sect did the same thing. Each cell had a leadership group of twelve. "In the formal congregation of the community there shall be twelve laymen and three priests schooled to perfection in all that has been revealed of the entire Law. Their duty shall be to set the standard for the practice of truth, righteousness, and justice" (*Manual of Discipline* 8:1 ff.) [1]

As we have seen in chapter 3, there was a pre-Markan etiological story that ascribed the choosing of the Twelve to Jesus' relatives' suggestion that he was overworked and needed to share the burdens of leadership. This story was based upon the story of Jethro suggesting the same thing to Moses in Exod. 18, after which Moses ordains the seventy elders. As a midrashic rewriting of the Moses story, the Christian version is wholly fictive. And it turns out that there is no better reason to believe that the group of the Twelve was established by the historical Jesus, though it is understandable that such a pedigree would be sought, especially given the ongoing factional strife. If all apostles claimed equally to have seen the Risen Christ, it might redouble a group's clout if they claimed to have been chosen by Jesus even before his death and resurrection, and that is most likely what happened with the Twelve, why their constitution as a group was retrojected into the time of a historical Jesus, as so much else was.[2]

Walter Schmithals argues forcefully that Jesus did not select an elite corps of twelve already in his lifetime.[3] He believes the Twelve were so constituted by a shared resurrection vision. Schmithals points out that almost all mentions of "the Twelve" occur in narrative sections of the Gospels, not quoted sayings of Jesus, implying the number was just read back into the tradition by later narrators familiar with it. Conversely, the references to the Twelve on the lips of Jesus are scarce and mostly doubtful. To wit: in Mark 14:20, Jesus says his betrayer is "one of the Twelve," but neither Matthew nor Luke, who follow Mark, have the phrase, though each quotes or paraphrases the surrounding Markan material. Does this mean their copies of Mark, obviously much earlier than ours, lacked the phrase? In John 6:70, Jesus asks ironically, "Did I not choose you, the Twelve, and one of you is a devil?" But John's text, as we have seen, is often his own doing, and in this case, John is obviously just reminding the reader that

Jesus was not taken by surprise by Judas's betrayal. And this is purely theological apologetics, not historical information.

Matt. 19:28//Luke 22:28–30 ("You will sit on [Matthew: twelve] thrones, judging the twelve tribes of Israel") circulated in Q with no context, and Matthew and Luke have chosen very different, equally arbitrary, contexts for it. Originally, this saying must have been addressed, as a prophecy of the Risen Jesus, to any and all Christians who remain steadfast. This is just the way it appears, as a Christian prophetic oracle, in Rev. 2:26–27, "He who conquers and who perseveres in my ways until the end, I will give him power over the nations, and he shall rule them with a rod of iron, as when earthen pots are broken in pieces, even as I myself have received power from my Father." Or it may have been adapted from other Christian writers: "Do you not know that the saints will judge the world? . . . Do you not know that we are to judge angels?" (1 Cor. 6:2–3). "If we endure, we shall also reign with him" (2 Tim. 2:12a). Eventually, it made its way to the mouth of the earthly Jesus, and in contexts where only the Twelve could be heirs to the promise. But for Matthew, context is not good enough: he adds the qualifier "twelve" to the thrones, strictly limiting the number who can participate. This would have been another reference by Jesus to the twelve disciples, but redaction criticism removes it from consideration.

No doubt the major objection to the retrojection hypothesis of Schmithals is the betrayal of Judas Iscariot, one of the Twelve. How can he have betrayed Jesus to his captors and been one of the Twelve if this group were formed only after the resurrection (appearances)? The answer to this question, while not simple, is not too hard to find. We shall wait till the chapter on Judas's betrayal for the full story, but for the moment we may note that there is good reason to question the original and integral position of the character in the passion narrative (for example, why does the arresting party need an insider to point out which man is Jesus, when they are arresting him, in effect, for being too famous? ["Which one of you guys is Elvis?"]). Originally, there may have been no single betrayer, only God who "delivered him up [same in Greek as 'betrayed him, handed him over'] for us all" (Rom. 8:32). By the time the story was told with a human traitor character, the name Judas may have been chosen from the list of disciples so the character could stand for the Jewish people. This implies the story would have arisen in a quarter of the church in which there was no living memory of the Twelve and thus no sense of disgracing someone hitherto venerated as a saint or hero. Or it may be that, as some have suggested, an apostle named Judas (perhaps Judas Thomas) became a heretic in the eyes of the others, and they referred to his espousal of minority doctrines as a "betrayal of the Lord." Later on, this libel became garbled into a historical betrayal of Jesus of Nazareth into the hands of his enemies. At any rate, 1 Cor. 15:5 has a resurrection appearance to the Twelve, while Matt. 28:16, [Mark 16:14], and Luke 24:33 have Jesus appear to the eleven, Judas being offstage. But of course this is what we would expect since the Gospels have assimilated the Judas subplot, while the epistles have not. In any event, Judas poses no real stumbling block for Schmithals's theory. There is no secure, or even very likely, link between a historical Jesus and the circle of the Twelve.

NAMES ON A LIST

We have seen that the Twelve as an authority group, while prominent in the gospel stories, may not have had much connection with the Christian communities best known to us from the New Testament, which fall in one or another camp of Hellenistic or Pauline Christianity. Even Matthew, a Jewish Christian to be sure, was trilingual and depended upon Mark's gospel, which contains a sustained Marcion-like (or actual Marcionite?) polemic against the Twelve as unworthy custodians of the Jesus tradition. Matthew's veneration for Peter is well known, but as Arlo J. Nau has demonstrated, even the Matthean community must have been divided in its loyalty to the Petrine name and cause. And insofar as the Matthean church (in Antioch?) could be called pro-Petrine, this may reflect simply the weighty value of the name in interchurch disputes over the relative authority of their bishops. There need have been little real connection with the actual teaching of Simon Peter decades before. So any historical memory of the Twelve must have been a part of some circles of Christianity largely unknown to us. This is the only way to explain the remarkable paucity of information in the New Testament about them. It is astonishing to realize, for example, that the canonical lists of the Twelve (Mark 3:16–19, Matt. 10:2–4, Luke 6:14–16, John 21:2, Acts 1:13) do not agree in detail, nor do manuscripts of single gospels! If the Twelve were as important as church rhetoric would suggest, how is it possible that such uncertainty should exist even upon the point of who they were? Can we imagine early American histories in which the lists of presidents did not agree?

Luke includes a "Judas of James" who is probably the same as John's "Judas not Iscariot" (John 14:22), but Mark and Matthew both lack this name and have instead the name "Thaddaeus," for which some manuscripts of Matthew have instead "Lebbaeus." In the apocryphal correspondence between Jesus and Abgar, king of Edessa, Addai (Thaddaeus) seems to be one of the seventy, a wider circle, not one of the Twelve. Did he become so popular in Christian legends (or actual missionary activity) that he supplanted Judas of James? Or, as Eisenman suggests,[4] is it possible that Thaddaeus is the same as Judas Thomas (see below), a contracted version of the two names?

Lebbaeus would seem to be another form of the name "Levi." If so, its presence in Matthew (again, in a few manuscripts) may reflect the fact that Matthew the evangelist has omitted the name of Levi from the calling story he took over from Mark 2:14. Mark had a converted tax collector named Levi, who however did not make the final cut for the Twelve, as well as a disciple named Matthew who did. The evangelist Matthew (9:9) has combined both characters, giving us the composite character "Matthew the tax collector apostle." So perhaps some scribe decided to restore Levi where he thought he belonged, among the Twelve and under his own name.

John does not give a complete list, but he seems to consider a character named Nathaniel to be one of the Twelve. In Sunday school, one hears Nathaniel equated with Bartholomew, and, though harmonizing guesswork, it might be the case.

The most important character among the Twelve is of course Simon Peter. The Greek gospels use the Greek name "Simon," but Acts 15:14 and 2 Pet. 1:1 tell us the Aramaic original would have been Simeon, like the Old Testament patriarch. "Petros" is an Aramaic name, apparently meaning "firstborn," but the pun in Matt. 16:18 implies we are rather to think of it as a Greek name signifying "the rock." Is this the original meaning, or has Matthew mistaken it for a Greek name? Peter is usually, and quite naturally, taken as the Greek equivalent for Cephas, Aramaic for "the rock." Cephas is a mighty apostle mentioned in 1 Cor. 1:12, 9:5, 15:5, as one of the factional figureheads and in Gal. 1:18; 2:9, 11, 14, interchangeably with Peter (2:7). But, as some have suspected, it may be that Cephas and Peter were originally not the same character. The Apostolic Church Order, the Epistle of the Apostles, and Clement of Alexandria (*Outlines* 5, cited in Eusebius *Ecclesiastical History* 1.12.2), all considered Cephas and Peter different apostles. And as Hermann Detering has suggested, it may even be that Simon and Peter were not at first the same character! A double name for a single character ought always to raise a scholarly eyebrow. When we read of Narayana Vishnu, we find he is a conflation of two earlier deities. Likewise, Vasudeva Krishna. Likewise Yahve El Elyon (Gen. 14:22). Detering ventures that "Simon Peter" is a monument of the catholicizing tendency discovered by F. C. Baur at work in such books as Acts, 1 Peter, and 2 Peter. The name attempts to harmonize Peter, pontiff of Jewish Christianity, with Simon Magus, whom Detering, following Baur, makes the alias of Paul.[5]

Needless to say, the Gospels treat Simon as the disciple's given name, Peter/Cephas as an epithet assigned him by Jesus. Oddly, the Gospels cannot agree when Jesus bestowed the name on him. Mark seems to imagine Jesus christening him Peter when he chooses him for the Twelve (Mark 3:14). Mark calls him simply "Simon" up to that point and, with a single exception, either Simon Peter or just Peter afterward. Matthew seems to have Jesus rename him upon his confession of Jesus' divine sonship (16:18). John has Jesus call him Peter as soon as he meets him (1:42). This in itself seems a little strange. It sounds like a flurry of attempts to account for the double name to cover up some original explanation—like the one Detering proposes.[6]

The same honorific had also been conferred on Father Abraham: "The matter is to be compared to a king who was desiring to build; but when he was digging for the purpose of laying the foundations, he found only swamps and mire. At last he hit on a rock, when he said, 'Here I will build.' So, too, when

God was about to create the world, he foresaw the sinful generation of Enosh (when man began to profane the name of the Lord), and the wicked generations of the deluge (which said unto God, 'Depart from us'), and he said, 'How shall I create the world whilst these generations are certain to provoke me (by their crimes and sins)?' But when he perceived that Abraham would one day arise, he said, 'Behold, I have found the *petra* on which to build and base the world'" (*Yalkut, Numbers* 766).[7] Again, it is no surprise to see this passage closely paralleling Matthew (16:18), whose special material is decidedly Jewish and probably derivative from that source. And, in accordance with the Abraham parallel, we should realize that to name Peter "the Rock" implies a degree of venerability impossible so early in the career of either Peter or Jesus. We are dealing with a gross anachronism.

We are hardly done with Peter yet, not nearly. For the present, we must note one more name or epithet granted him in Matt. 16:18. Jesus blesses him as "Simon Barjona," which is traditionally taken to mean "Simon son of Jonah." But according to John 21:15–17, his father's name was Jonathan, and Jonah does not seem to have been a short form of Jonathan. It is not hard to imagine the two names becoming confused, but another intriguing possibility suggests itself. As Robert Eisler, followed by Oscar Cullmann,[8] contends, the reference here is not to a proper name, but to the Akkadian/Aramaic loan-word *barjona* or *baryona*, meaning something like "terrorist"! As we will see, the notion of there having been militants and revolutionaries among the followers of Jesus is not far-fetched. Jesus himself may have been viewed as a radical against Rome, or perhaps the Twelve were a later group thriving in the revolutionary period preceding the fall of Jerusalem in 70 C.E.

The other Simon among the Twelve is variously called Simon the Zealot (Luke 6:15) and Simon the Cananaean (Mark 3:18), which are Greek and Aramaic for the same thing. We have simply taken over the Greek word as our "zealous one" or "jealous one." (Despite appearance, "Cananaean" has nothing to do with "Canaanite.") Is this the same character as "Simon Barjona," merely taking up two spaces in the list? Or has Matt. 16:18 confused the two Simons, having Jesus bless the wrong one? Or were there two Simons (admittedly a very common name) with revolutionary connections? Or does "Zealot" just mean this Simon was a religious enthusiast, a pious ascetic, a fanatic (cf. Acts 21:20)? It only gets more confusing when we notice that the Epistle of the Apostles substitutes "Judas the Zealot" for Simon. Some early Old Latin manuscripts of Matt. 10:3 also substitute "Judas the Zealot" for Lebbaeus, himself a stand-in for Judas not Iscariot.

James and John, sons of Zebedee the fisherman (Mark 1:19), are dubbed "Boanerges," an epithet Mark thinks means "Sons of Thunder" or perhaps "Sons of Rage." But that would seem to require one half of the word to be Aramaic (*bar*, son of), the other Greek (οργης, rage). Perhaps the best guess is that of John M. Allegro: *Boanerges* represents an old Sumerian term, *Geshpuanur* (just switching the prefix to a suffix), "upholder of the vault of heaven," which means the same as the title of one of the *Dioscuri*, Castor and Pollux (Polydeuces). When we remind ourselves that James and John are a pair of brothers, and that a James and John were venerated in the early church, along with Peter, as the Pillars, it is hard to evade the force of Allegro's suggestion.[9] We might think also of Rabbi Yosa, disciple of Rabbi Yohanan. "A weaver appeared before R. Yohanan. He said to him, 'I saw in my dream that the heaven fell, and one of your disciples was holding it up.'" Then all the disciples passed before him and he identified Yosa (*Y. Ketuboth* 12.3.7).[10]

These titles seem to hold enormous, nearly forgotten significance. James and John seem to be pictured as human equivalents of Boaz and Jachin, the twin pillars of Solomon's temple. "Peter," the rock, as Hanson suggests, may preserve a reference to the cosmic foundation stone on which the temple was supposed to have been built. The imagery might suggest that these men served as the focus of God's dwelling on earth, perhaps in the absence of the temple after the Roman destruction. ("I am the Mystic Fane which the Hand of Omnipotence hath reared" *Qayyumu'l-asma'* 94).[11] In this event, of course, we would have another case of anachronism, later figures being read back into the first third of the first century. Be that as it may, the designation of these three as the Pillars cannot but remind us of the mystical esteem in which the holy family of the prophet Muhammad are held in Shi'ite Islam. The prophet, plus his adopted son/cousin Ali; Ali's wife, Fatima; and their two sons Hussain and Hassan are believed to be of the very essence of God and the veritable cause of creation. They are known as the Pillars of Islam. The Twelve Imams descended from Ali share these distinctions. All are the Pillars, the bulwarks of Islam.[12] The term 'Pillars" must have cosmic, revelatory significance, as it is a universal symbol of the *axis mundi*, the world axis connecting heaven and earth, like Jacob's Ladder (Gen. 28:12). The same image is used of Jesus himself in John 1:51. The Jerusalem Pillars of the New Testament must have had a similar significance. One of them, James the Just, was thought to be a member of Jesus' family (cf. Mark 6:3, Gal. 1:19), just as the Shi'ite Pillars are said to be related to Muhammad. And of James, the Gospel of Thomas tells us that he, too, was the cause of creation (12). We ought to see the Pillars as analogous to the highest dervish of the Ghulat Shi'ite sect of the Shabak, called the *qutb*, the pole or axis. He is the embodiment of divine wisdom and master of the teachings of the order.[13]

Thomas (Greek: Didymus, "twin") was the Hebrew name for the constellation Gemini, but it was not used as an ordinary proper name. In any case, it must have been an epithet, not a primary name. He would have been known as So-and-So the Twin. Tradition, preserved in The Acts of Thomas, The Gospel of Thomas, The Book of Thomas the Contender, and some manuscripts of John, call him Judas Thomas. But whose twin was he? Well, Jesus had a brother named Judas (Mark 6:3), didn't he? You don't suppose . . . ? In the early church, especially in Syria, many considered Judas Thomas the twin brother of Jesus, perhaps his physical likeness, perhaps his spiritual twin. It is hard to tell which is intended, but it seems as if the former is used as a symbol for the latter. That is, Thomas is upheld as the example of one who has so thoroughly imbibed the spirit and teaching of Jesus Christ that he has become another like him! In the Gospel of Thomas, Jesus blesses Thomas for his wisdom: "I am not your master, because you have drunk, you have become drunk from the bubbling spring I have measured out" (saying 13). "Whoever drinks from my mouth shall become as I am, and I myself shall become he, and the hidden things shall be revealed to him" (saying 108). In one idiom or another, this was the high hope cherished by Ebionite, Gnostic, and Arian Christians. Emerging orthodoxy turned from it shuddering! "Thomas" thus became an allegorical figure, like Christian in John Bunyan's *Pilgrim's Progress* (or, possibly, the Beloved Disciple in John's gospel). Early Christian legend had him preach Christianity in India, but this may be no more than an inference later deduced from the spread of Syriac Thomas literature (the Acts, Book, Gospel, already mentioned, plus the Apocalypse of Thomas) there.

Andrew (Andreas) is Simon Peter's brother and, like him, a fisherman. According to John, he had been a disciple of John the Baptist and heeded the latter's urgings to abandon him and follow Jesus instead. He went and recruited Peter. This all must be dismissed as imaginary since it depends on the late Johannine fiction of John the Baptist publicly endorsing Jesus.

Philip has a bit of a role in John's gospel, where he is made something resembling a subordinate revealer figure. The evangelist himself is the Paracletos next to the Risen Christ (John 13:23), through whom Jesus communicates to all others (repeating Jesus' own role as the unique interpreter of his Father, 1:18). Even so, the Greeks must seek Jesus through Philip ("Lord, we would see Jesus," John 12:21), as Philip in turn seeks a vision of the Father via Jesus ("Lord, show us the Father," John 14:8). As in the Gospel of Philip, the disciple is thus some sort of revealer. This all may reflect Philip's mission to convert the Samaritans to the gospel in Acts 8:4–13. But this Philip is denominated as one of the Seven Hellenists in Acts 6:5. The two were often confused in postcanonical literature, and who's to say this has not already occurred within the canon, too?

Bartholomew (bar-Ptolemy) is another surname, a patronymic, so it is not unreasonable to make it the surname of Nathaniel, but that does not make the identification any less a guess. Obviously, the name entered Jewish culture during the time when Judea belonged to the Ptolemaic Empire, before being ceded to the Seleucid Empire. The Ptolemies had the Jewish scriptures translated into Greek for a wider audience; the Seleucids made it a capital crime to study the same scriptures! A Jewish baby named "Bartholomew" was a wistful look back to the good old days.

We will return to the enigmatic figure of Judas later, but in the meantime, let us observe that his epithet "Iscariot" might mean, with about equal plausibility, three very different things. First, and traditionally, it has been taken to denote

"Judas of Kerioth." Kerioth was the name of a number of villages in Judea, which would make him the only non-Galilean in the group, if not even an Edomite (like Herod!), which is why he is given red hair in Nikos Kazantzakis's *The Last Temptation of Christ* (book and film), the Edomites being notorious redheads. John's gospel must have understood Iscariot this way, since John refers to Judas as the son of Simon Iscariot (13:26). Second, many understand Iscariot as meaning "the Sicarius," making Judas a member of the assassin squad of the revolutionary Zealots. They carried the *sicarius*, or short sword, hidden in their robes from whence they would pluck it to stab their intended victim and then mix in with the shouting crowd. This would place Judas alongside Simon the Zealot and Simon Barjona as militant nationalists. I prefer the third option, the surmise of Bertil Gärtner[14] and others, whereby Iscariot represents the Hebrew *Ishqarya*, "man of falsehood, betrayer." This means, obviously, that Judas would have been called "Judas Iscariot" during his lifetime no more than Jesus would have been called "Jesus Christ." This does not mean, however, that sufficient water has not passed under the bridge by the time of the Gospels that Iscariot could be mistaken for a surname. See Mark 3:19, "Judas Iscariot, who betrayed him." Mark no longer recognized it as a redundancy.

ACTS OF THE DISCIPLES

The disciples of Jesus figure, first, in a set of stories apparently intended to function, despite or even because of their brevity, as recruitment paradigms. They are all rewrites of the story of Elijah calling Elisha to become his disciple and successor: "So he departed from there, and found Elisha the son of Shaphat, who was plowing, with twelve yoke of oxen before him, and he was with the twelfth. Elijah passed by him and cast his mantle upon him. And he left the oxen, and ran after Elijah, and said, 'Let me kiss my father and my mother, and then I will follow you.' And he said to him, 'Go back again; for what have I done to you? ["Sure, go ahead! After all, I'm not kidnapping you!"]' And he returned from following him, and took the yoke of oxen, and slew them, and boiled their flesh with the yoke of oxen, and gave it to the people, and they ate. Then he arose and went after Elijah, and served him" (1 Kings 19:19–21).

Peter and Andrew, James and John are said to be summoned to discipleship in the same dramatic and mysterious manner: "And passing along by the Sea of Galilee, he saw Simon and Andrew the brother of Simon casting a net in the sea, for they were fishermen. And Jesus said to them, 'Follow me, and I will make you become fishers of men!' And immediately they left their nets and followed him. And going on a little farther, he saw James the son of Zebedee and John his brother, who were in their boat mending the nets. And immediately he called them; and they left their father Zebedee in the boat with the hired servants, and followed him" (Mark 1:16–20).

The scene is repeated with Levi, who follows another profession, though not for long: "And as he passed on, he saw Levi the son of Alphaeus sitting at the tax office, and he said to him, 'Follow me.' And he rose and followed him" (Mark 2:14). Nor is Philip immune to the lure of discipleship: "The next day Jesus decided to go to Galilee. And he found Philip and said to him, 'Follow me'" (John 1:43). All these stories give the impression that Destiny has come to call on these average-seeming people, and they recognize its voice. Realizing their accustomed lives cannot hope to compare with the adventure they are invited to share, they snap the clinging cobwebs binding them to their worldly existences and go. In so few words, these anecdotes possess a great power that is only lessened if one posits that Jesus already knew these men and that they had already given his offer long and hard thought, which is merely to rationalize the ancient text. Such things have happened, as in the summer of 1976, when the UFO cultists Bo and Peep (leaders of what would later be called Heaven's Gate) offered hotel ballroom seminars, announcing their mission on earth and inviting people to join them. Many did, leaving jobs and family behind on the spot. So it could have happened. But the clear dependence of the gospel calling stories on the 1 Kings prototype makes it appear that it didn't.

These stories of the disciples are told simply to embolden other recruits and have the same function as other discipleship paradigm stories that happen not to feature a named disciple. Q provides two of them: Matt. 8:19–22//Luke 9:57–60, "As they were going along the road, a man said to him, 'I will follow you wherever you go.' And Jesus said to him, 'Foxes have holes, and birds of the air have nests; but the Son of man has nowhere to lay his head.' To another he said, 'Follow me.' But he said, 'Lord, let me first go and bury my father.' But he said to him, 'Let the dead bury their own dead; but as for you, go and proclaim the kingdom of God.'" Luke adds a third, even more obviously based on Elisha's call: "Another said, 'I will follow you, Lord; but let me first say farewell to those at my home.' Jesus said to him, 'No one who puts his hand to the plow and looks back is fit for the kingdom of God'" (Luke 9:61–62). The Rich Young Ruler (Mark 10:17–22) is a longer, more detailed version of the same thing. The same point is made again in the Lukan parables of the builder and the king, neither of whom was prudent enough to assess his resources before beginning his project (Luke 14:28–33). What we have here is no doubt the stock-in-trade of the itinerant charismatics, the brethren of 3 John and Matthew 25, the apostles and prophets of the *Didache*. Some might heed the call, but the real point was to boast that the itinerants themselves had heeded it and were due the alms of the communities that heard them.

A couple of calling stories provide miracles as the enticement for disciples to follow Jesus. Luke rationalizes the abrupt departure of the four fishermen to follow Jesus by inserting an old Pythagoras miracle (see chapter 5, "The Miracles"), the wondrous catch of fish (Luke 5:1–11), a story that appears as a resurrection narrative in the Johannine Appendix (chapter 21), perhaps because John's gospel already contained an alternate version of the calling of the same disciples in chapter 1. John also has Nathaniel convinced to join Jesus by hearing that Jesus had seen him in a vision from afar (1:45–51). Miracle or no, this story must be discounted as history because of the anachronism, Nathaniel's prejudice toward Nazareth, a village whose only known disrepute among Jews arose decades later precisely on account of Jesus' association with it!

SMEAR CAMPAIGNS

There was as little strictly historical curiosity in the early church about the Apostles as there was about Jesus. Only whereas Jesus is the subject of edifying fictions, the fiction featuring the Apostles is more often of a distinctly unedifying nature, being more in the nature of "negative campaigning" such as we see in modern politics. Apologists have always taken the frequent unflattering depictions of the Apostles as marks of the historical faithfulness of the stories. It seems not unreasonable to suggest that a story, for example, in which Peter is shown as a coward and a liar can scarcely be sanitized propaganda on behalf of Peter! True enough, but they had overlooked something important, namely, the live possibility that such derogatory stories were circulated by the ecclesiastical rivals and theological opponents of those apostles (or of their heirs). There would have been more than one competing propaganda line. Paul tells us that envious colleagues slandered him, invidiously compared him to themselves, and misrepresented his doctrine (2 Cor. 10:7–16, 11:1–6, 12–23 ff.; Gal. 1:18–20. 5:10–11; Phil. 1:15–18). No more does Paul shrink from impugning the motives of his critics, dismissing them as spineless hypocrites and deceitful spies (Gal. 2:4, 12–13; 2 Cor. 11:3, 14; Phil. 1:17–18). It would be no surprise if some of the implied invectives had not managed to find a nesting place in the pages of the Gospels. Indeed, it seems they have.

As we have already mentioned, there were factions among the early Christians who repudiated the Twelve (or at least the brand of Christianity to which their name had subsequently become attached). Marcion (active somewhere between 100 and 150 C.E.) taught that the Twelve were utter failures and had grossly misunderstood Jesus and his teaching, so badly, in fact, that Christ had been forced to wash his hands of these dunderheads and approach a more promising candidate, Paul. The same antipathy toward the disciples of Jesus is clearly to be found in Mark's gospel, as Theodore J. Weeden has shown.[15] The criticism of these men is unrelenting and devastating, with no rehabilitation. Mark misses no opportunity to make the disciples look like dunces. He has them misunderstanding everything (Mark 4:13; 6:52; 8:14–21, 33). In some cases, the misunderstanding motif is a literary device, enabling Jesus to explain some enigma at greater length for the sake of the reader, whose anticipated questions are placed in the mouths of the Twelve. But the same is true of John's depictions of the enemies of Jesus: they constantly make carnally minded rejoinders and ask sarcastic questions, offering Jesus the chance to elaborate his points. We cannot believe that either John or Mark was oblivious of the impression such scenes created of Jesus' interlocutors, in the one case vicious, in the other obtuse.

It is plain that Matthew held the Twelve in higher esteem than Mark did, though Mark remains his principle source. I make Matthew what the church historians called a Nazarene, a Jew who embraced essentially Hellenistic Christianity but also kept the Jewish customs (not unlike Seventh-day Adventists today). His elevated estimate of the Twelve is a matter of ecumenical sensitivity. He knows not what Lebbaeus and the other disciples might have taught, but Matthew writes in the wake of the catholicizing rapprochement between Petrine and Pauline factions. He is a Judaizing Paulinist, like the Galatians. And he does not feel right about treating the Twelve in so ungentlemanly a manner as Mark did. Notice how Matt. 20:20 "corrects" Mark 10:35: where Mark had James and John dare to approach Jesus with the request for a privileged position in the coming age, Matthew posits that Mrs. Zebedee must have been among the Galilean women in Jesus' entourage, and he has her drag her reluctant boys to Jesus and make the request herself, as they groan, "Aw, Mom!" Mark 4:13 showed Jesus exasperated at the thick-headedness of his chosen elite, who seemed to have misplaced the key to understanding the parables. But at the close of Matthew's parables seminar (13:51), he has the disciples assure Jesus that they have understood everything, which verdict Jesus accepts with a blessing. After the wave-walking Jesus climbs into the boat, Mark has them speechless with astonishment (6:51–52); not so Matthew, who has them draw the proper inference and worship their Lord (14:33).

We will see later how Mark himself created the famous scene of Peter's confession at Caesarea Philippi (Mark 8:27–33), at least partly in order to clamp the lid on various Christologies thriving there that he considered heretical. In it Peter divulges that he has penetrated the secret of Jesus' messiahship (so far, like Odysseus, Jesus has been circulating incognito lest his enemies, discovering his true identity, conspire to slay him before he is ready for them).[16] Jesus warns him to keep it under his burnoose and goes on to tell the next step, for which he mistakenly surmises Peter must now be ready: the Son of man must die at the hands of his enemies. Peter rebukes Jesus, such a plan being hardly appropriate for King Messiah! But Peter the rock-headed has misunderstood again, and Jesus denounces him as Satan's surrogate. The story seems to presuppose the primacy accorded Peter in some circles in order to challenge and deflate it. Luke simply cuts the Satan rebuke, while Matthew, as we now read it, has retained Mark's rebuke but pretty much vitiated it with the bestowal on Peter of chancellorship of the Christian community (a gross anachronism, as it features Jesus using the word "church"). Nau is probably correct in suggesting that the first Matthean redactor to adapt Mark had, like Luke, cut the rebuke and then replaced it with the "Blessed are you" unit (Matt. 16:17–19). A subsequent Matthean scribe, not eager to see Peter exalted in so uncritical a way, did not presume to omit the blessing but did try to cut Peter down to size again by restoring Mark's rebuke (and by distributing Peter's chief rabbi status among the whole dodecade college—18:18).[17] Behind all this we have to learn to see the machinations of church-political rhetoric. The question behind how good a portrait of Peter Matthew's gospel should paint is that of the relative authority of the bishops in what was believed to have been Peter's own see, perhaps Antioch as many scholars think.

The most damning anti-Peter story must be that of his denial of Jesus before the high priest's servants (Mark 14:66–72). If there was any sort of pre-Markan passion narrative, we might venture to guess that the story of Peter's denial did not form a part of it. The reason is that it intrudes like a foreign body in the gospel narrative as we now read it. After adjourning the Last Supper, Jesus forewarns the disciples that he will be arrested and that they will all scatter (14:27–28), but that they will meet again subsequently in Galilee. Peter indignantly repudiates this impugning of his loyalty, insisting that no matter what the other capons do, he will not flee! Bracket for the moment the prediction of the denial, verses 30–31a. Then "And they all said the same" in 31b refers back, as it must, to Peter's reaction to the prospect of their scattering in fear. The presence of 30–31a makes them all insist they will not *deny* Jesus, something he has not said they will all do, just Peter. Proceeding to verse 50, we see the prediction fulfilled: "And they all forsook him and fled," with no hint that Peter was any exception. I suggest that Mark has added 30–31a and now verses 54, 66–72, the denial story. As the story would have originally continued, the young man at the tomb reiterates Jesus' promise to meet Peter and the others in Galilee (though we do not hear whether they did meet). This flows pretty smoothly if we do not have Peter's denial to deal with. If we do, why doesn't Mark deal with it? There is no aftermath, positive or negative? Luke and John both seem to have noticed the problem and sought to assimilate Peter's denial into the narrative and to put Peter himself back into Jesus' good graces. Luke 22:31–32 has Jesus forgive Peter in advance and reassimilate him into the group. John 21:15–17 ff. seems to have Jesus offer Peter as many chances to affirm him as he once denied him. (Of course, this is the Johannine Appendix, but it is possible John 13:10 may already be equivalent to Luke 22:31–32.)

The story is thoroughly damning when one considers that it is not simply that Peter, say, passes up an opportunity to witness to his faith one afternoon talking to someone in the fish market. What he is shown doing is, by all standards of the early church, renouncing his faith in Christ and buying himself a one-way ticket to hell. "For it is impossible to restore again to repentance those who have once been enlightened, who have tasted the heavenly gift, and have become partakers of the Holy Spirit, and have tasted the goodness of the word of God and the powers of the age to come, if they then commit apostasy, since they crucify the Son of God on their own account and hold him up to contempt" (Heb. 6:4–6).

"For whoever is ashamed of me and my words in this sinful and adulterous generation, of him will the Son of Man be ashamed, when he comes in the glory of his Father with the holy angels" (Mark 8:38). "For it would have been better for them never to have known the way of righteousness than after knowing it to turn back from the holy commandment delivered unto them" (2 Pet. 2:21). Peter's offense perhaps pales for today's gospel readers because anybody starts looking good next to Judas Iscariot.

Such a story is told for one reason: to blacken the reputation of the disgraceful coward depicted in it. Whether the story had any basis in fact is an entirely different matter. We cannot blithely say that it must have been true or it would not have been preserved, even after the catholicizing rapprochement between the once-feuding Petrine and Pauline sects. As I reconstruct it, the retaining of the story, pointedly in order to qualify Petrine authority (and that of his legacy), was part of the negotiated settlement. Recall how Acts, the great charter of second-century catholic reconciliation, parallels Peter and Paul so that each preaches to Gentiles (Peter in Acts 10, Paul from 9 on), each bests an evil sorcerer (Peter versus Simon Magus in Acts 8, Paul versus Elymas/Etoimas/Bar Jesus in 13:8–11), each heals a congenitally lame man (Peter in 3:1–10, Paul in 14:8–10), each raises the dead (Peter in 9:36–43, Paul in 20:9–12), each heals the sick by means of *mana* (Peter's shadow in 5:15–16, Paul's handkerchiefs in 19:11–12), both impart the Spirit (Peter in 8:17, Paul in 19:6), and both escape miraculously from shackles and prison (Peter in 12:6–10, Paul in 16:25–27). Obviously, the point is to render it impossible for Paulinists to continue to despise a Peter so like their own master and for Petrinists to hate a Paul so like Peter. (Luke or his nativity source paralleled Jesus and John the Baptist with one another for the same reason.) But there was room for the negative as well as the positive. I am persuaded that the story of Peter's apostasy was deemed a counterweight to that of Paul's preconversion persecution of Christians. This last is an equally dubious bit of propaganda based on an earlier Jewish-Christian claim that *as a Law-free Christian* Paul had opposed and "persecuted" the true gospel, the Torah gospel of Peter and James the Just. As the differences between those two factions became retrospectively papered over, the opposition of Torah Christians by Paul was reinterpreted/misunderstood as if he had persecuted Christians period, something he would have had to have done before his own turning to Christianity.[18] If Peter had failed the test of persecution, Paul had been a persecutor, and Christ forgave them both. Such was the compromise of reputations, the mitigation of apostolic authority claims in the early church.

We have seen how James and John appear in a less-than-flattering light, seeking a place of honor for which their very request proves them unfit (Mark 10:35–40). The thrones to the left and right of Jesus are already spoken for, and the important point is that we will not see James and John sitting there in the age to come. Again, we cannot but suspect the story meant to deflate authority claims made on their coattails. The same would probably apply to Luke 9:51–56, where

James and John are itching to play Elijah and call down fire on inhospitable Samaritans, utterly failing to grasp the nature of Jesus' mission. "Ye know not what spirit ye are of; the Son of Man came not to destroy men's lives, but to save them." It sounds quite a bit like Paul's jibe at his theological rivals in 2 Cor. 11:4–5, "For if someone comes and preaches another Jesus than the one we preached, or if you receive a different spirit from the one you received, or if you accept a different gospel from the one you accepted, you submit to it readily enough. I think that I am not in the least inferior to these superapostles." And it is natural to suspect that the Lukan passage is a narrative version of the Pauline one. Imagine, on the other hand, that the story is historical. We must then picture James and John as insane fanatics who believe they can actually summon fire from heaven! It is neither a pretty nor a plausible picture. But most of us simply read it as a story, as we were intended to do.

Apostolic credentials are at stake again in a story that makes John the champion of exclusivism in the name of the Twelve, with Jesus renouncing it in favor of outsiders (like Paul)—Mark 9:38–40, a story clearly rewritten from the aftermath of the anointing of the seventy elders in Num. 11:26–29, "Now two men remained in the camp, one named Eldad, the other named Medad, and the spirit rested upon them; they were among those registered, but they had not gone out to the tent, and so they prophesied in the camp. And a young man ran and told Moses, 'Eldad and Medad are prophesying in the camp.' And Joshua the son of Nun, the servant of Moses, one of his lieutenants, said, 'My lord Moses, forbid them!' But Moses said to him, 'Are you jealous for my sake? Would that all Yahve's people were prophets, so that Yahve would put his spirit upon them!'" It is no coincidence that John is located in a scene (Gal. 2:1–9) where the question of Paul's apostolic legitimacy is being hammered out. Perhaps John was initially in opposition, and this story arose based on the fact. Another tip-off to the post-Jesus character of the story, as Bultmann, following Wellhausen, pointed out,[19] is that the freelance exorcist is not criticized for not following Jesus, but rather for not following "us," a group of early Christians.

SEDIMENTARY ROCK

Peter is, it goes without saying, the most important of the Twelve, as a literary character if not also a historical one. It quickly becomes apparent as one reads the Gospels that Peter is really the single name and face of the Twelve collectively. Peter simply *is* the Twelve. We catch up with the logical implication of this tendency in those medieval legends of Jesus and Peter, where it is finally just the two of them wandering the dusty roads together.[20]

Here we might draw an analogy with one of the greatest pulp fiction characters, Doc Savage, based on the real-life adventurer Colonel Richard Henry Savage. Doc Savage was the hero of some 180 pulp magazines (*Doc Savage,*

Street and Smith Publications, Inc., March 1933 through summer 1949). In all of them, he had an "amazing crew" of five assistants, each a colorful second or third banana with his own specialization: Renny the engineer, Long Tom the electrical inventor, Ham the lawyer, Johnny the archaeologist, and Monk the rough-and-tumble chemist, crudely spoken, loyal, courageous, and resourceful. He and Ham, a dapper Epicurean, always sparred in a friendly way. As the long series of stories progressed, more and more of Doc's lieutenants were found to be superfluous. What could any of them do that Doc couldn't do as easily himself? More and more of the stories began to feature just Ham and Monk alongside Doc. By the time Doc Savage made it onto radio, Monk was the only sidekick left. In the same way, Peter begins as one of twelve disciples but quickly absorbs the rest of them. He hogs the whole of the role he first shared with the rest: *the disciple*. And that role is essentially that of Doctor Watson, assistant and chronicler of Sherlock Holmes. His main service is not to Holmes, who plainly has not the slightest need of anyone's help, but rather to the reader. He asks what the reader wants to know: "I say, Holmes! But how did you know little Sally was really the Shropshire Slasher?" Thus, we are treated to what Holmes would have kept to himself, a chain of ratiocination lending credence to Paul de Man's dictum that a logical argument is really just another kind of fictive plot.

First, let us observe how Peter's role has expanded with the growth of the gospel tradition. In Mark 7:17, it is the disciples in general who ask Jesus to explain his astonishing remarks about kosher laws. But in Matthew, it is Peter who asks on behalf of the rest of them (Matt. 15:15). In Matthew and Mark, Jesus sends two unnamed disciples to get the Upper Room ready for the Last Supper, but in Luke 22:8 we hear that he sent Peter and John, anticipating their apostolic team-ups in Acts (3:1, 3; 4:13, 19; 8:14). In all three Synoptics, we read that some one of the disciples strikes the servant of the high priest in the Garden of Gethsemane, but in John's gospel, the sword-wielder has become none other than Peter (18:10). In Mark 7:45–51, it is only Jesus who walks on the water, but Matthew adds a whole new episode in which Peter, too, strolls on the waves. Originally, Q (retained in Luke 17:4) has Jesus volunteer his comment about the need to forgive one's brother seventy times seven. No one says anything to solicit it. But in Matt. 18:21 ff., Peter first asks how many times he must forgive.

Even in most of the stories that feature Peter in their earliest known versions, Peter seems to function in the same way. He is either the collective voice of the disciples (Mark 10:28–30, "We have left everything to follow you." Mark 11:12–14, 20–22, "Master, look! The fig tree which you cursed has withered!"), or he is the straight man for Jesus, a foil whose questions or misunderstandings give Jesus the opportunity to explain himself at greater length for the reader's benefit. Was the historical Peter (if there was one) really such a dullard? We have no real data to tell us so. This impression is simply the by-product of his being shown, for didactic reasons, as baffled and corrected time and again (though, as we have seen, Mark had his own reasons for fostering such an image of Peter).

Peter's role in the Gospels (which, by the way, has entirely changed in Acts, and not because the Holy Spirit transformed him, but because he is now Jesus' successor and the star of the show) is entirely analogous to that of the Buddha's favorite disciple, Ananda, a bumbler. Ananda, in Buddhist writings, often appears as the Buddha's interlocutor, asking questions the reader might want to ask during a discourse. He may even be sharply rebuked for rash misunderstandings (the relative harshness being an index of how serious the issue is). Ananda's question or comment may furnish the occasion for some pronouncement by the Buddha. For example, Ananda asks his master concerning the fate of certain monks, now departed. The Buddha tells him, then supplies the "Mirror of Doctrine" formula by the use of which anyone can gauge the soundness of his own spiritual state: "Unwavering faith in the Buddha, the Dharma, and the Sangha." (The last two are the doctrine and the monastic community of Buddhism.) As the disciples gather round the Buddha's deathbed, Ananda asks him not to depart before answering a few key questions, prompting the reply, "Be ye lamps unto your own selves."

Ananda's stubborn lack of faith serves to highlight the Buddha's miracles, as when the Buddha asks him to fetch bathwater from a stream ford. Ananda is reluctant because the water must be filthy from the boat traffic. Finally, he obeys and is startled to find the water miraculously clean and pure! Similarly, his spiritual dullness causes him to botch opportunities, as when the Buddha hints as to how, through magical rites undergone in the past, he is able to extend his earthly sojourn by a whole cosmic cycle if only anyone would ask him. Like Percival at the hall of the Fisher King, Ananda fails to catch on at first, and when he finally does, it is too late. Think, too, of the strange hint in Mark 14:37 ff. that, had Peter been able to keep vigil with Jesus, he might somehow have prevented his arrest.

Ananda's well-intentioned suggestions backfire because he thinks he knows better than the Buddha, as when he prevails on the Buddha, against the latter's better judgment, to allow women to join the Sangha as nuns. The Buddha warns that now the true doctrine will pass from the earth after a mere five hundred years instead of the full millennium it would have lasted otherwise. In the same way, Peter in the Gospels makes pious but stupid suggestions, corrected by Jesus. "Sure, my master pays the temple tax! Why wouldn't he?" (Matt. 17:24–27). "Aren't I being generous to forgive Andrew seven times?" (Matt. 18:21–22). "Lord, it is good for us to be here! What say we build three shrines, one for you, and one each for Moses and Elijah?" (Mark 9:5).

WHEN SHALL WE THREE MEET AGAIN?

There are three (or four) gospel scenes in which the focus on the disciples narrows to the inner circle of three: Peter, James, and John. They are three of the first four recruited, and the fourth, Andrew, joins the other three for one of the relevant scenes. Peter, James, and John are initiated into the inner adytum with Jesus at the awakening of Jairus's daughter (Mark 5:37), the Transfiguration (Mark 9:2), the Olivet Discourse (Mark 13:3, adding Andrew), and the Garden of Gethsemane (Mark 14:33). What are they doing there? Why are the others excluded? "No particular reason," answers conventional scholarship, to whose eyes the Gnostic bands of the early Christian spectrum remain invisible. But if we recognize these scenes as the starting point of the second- and third-century Gnostic trajectory that made of these (and select other disciples) mystagogic revealers of esoteric truths, we can make some sense of them. All four scenes have the three (or four) invited to witness what others cannot know. And it must be that they are considered by Jesus (or by Mark, or his source) to be the advanced elite, the πνευματικοι among the Twelve, the remaining eight or nine lagging behind as the mere ψυχικοι, unworthy of the βαθμοι Χριστου.[21]

First, Jesus takes them in tow, along with Mr. and Mrs. Jairus, into the sick room where he will revive the young maid (comatose or dead). No one must know of the feat, even though the house is ringed by wailing mourners. The secrecy motif, as Wrede knew, must be artificial, since how can Jesus have expected the parents to carry on the pretense that their daughter was dead? Erect a false grave, tell everyone that Jesus failed, keep the girl locked away in a shuttered room? The point is that Mark, who has added the secrecy motif, has also added the element of the inner circle of disciples. They are privy to the secret; were the other nine allowed to believe the girl stayed dead? Mark no doubt neglected to think it out that far.

Second, the Transfiguration is probably the clearest scene in meaning, especially in view of the Hellenistic-Buddhist flavor of it. Only the spiritually attuned can behold the *Sambogkya* (divine) body of the Buddha beneath the illusion of his *Nirmankya* (earthly) body, recognizing, for example, the tuft of hair between the eyes, the elongated ear lobes, the topknot of hair, and the gigantic height. Just so, Jesus takes with him only his most advanced disciples who will be either able or worthy to see him as he really is, in his divine form. When he warns them to divulge nothing of what they have seen, we must suppose this includes, again, the other nine. We think inevitably (or we should) of Thomas 12, where Jesus has vouchsafed privileged gnosis to Thomas, who has proven himself worthy. The other eleven would like to be let in on the secret, but Thomas warns them it would shatter their ears as blasphemy, and they would stone him to death as a deceiver of Israel.

Third, Jesus muses how the stones of the Herodian temple, so glorious a tourist attraction now, will shortly lie as a field of ruins. Eight are incurious, but Peter, Andrew, James, and John are eager to learn more of this secret information Jesus has to dispense. He has given only a hint of greater knowledge, but he is waiting for someone to ask, thereby demonstrating their worthiness to know. So they approach him privately (13:3). This issues in the Olivet Discourse, the Synoptic Apocalypse, which belongs to a genre inherently gnostic ("Let the reader understand," Mark 13:14; cf. Rev. 13:18, "This takes wisdom: let him who has understanding reckon the number of the Beast"). It is secret knowledge of the future, as was that imparted to Daniel: "But you, Daniel, shut up the words and seal the book, until the time of the end" (Dan. 12:4). The sign of the fig tree is for them alone: the gnosis will give them an advantage when the time comes. The discourse has been modified in the wake of (non-)events: now the Son himself lacks the needful key, and as much knowledge as he has is open to everyone ("What I say to you I say to all," Mark 13:37). This is because the forewarning of the end proved of no avail, and there was no longer any need for secrecy.

Fourth, the retreat with Jesus into the garden just before his arrest is for the three closest disciples only (Mark 14:33), and there is some hint that a faithful vigil might avert disaster. The heaviness of sleep overtakes them, just as it does in Luke at the Transfiguration (Luke 9:32), possibly denoting the impingement of the supernatural in both cases. We might wonder if Mark intended the presence of Peter, James, and John to explain how anyone knew what Jesus had said in prayer to his Father. But this is ruled out by the fact that they slept through it.

Though only traces remain, we can recognize a pattern in which the disciples Peter, James, and John are portrayed as special guardians of private revelation, sources of secret knowledge allegedly from Jesus after the resurrection (Mark 9:9). Here the parallel to the Pillars of Jerusalem is complete, and we cannot help thinking that Peter, James, and John in the Gospels represent the retrojection into the time of Jesus of the later Triumvirate. It hardly matters whether the two Jameses were the same, or whether the two were confused or conflated. Keeping the distinctions straight might not have been especially useful.

MISSING LINKS

The doctrine of the apostolic succession of bishops, visible already in Acts 20:28, "all the flock, in which the Holy Spirit has made you επισκοποι" (*episcopoi*, i.e., supervisors, overseers, bishops), was part of the authority structure of emerging catholic orthodoxy. It sought to trace the teachings (and teaching authority) of the second-century bishops back to Christ himself on the basis of the fiction that Jesus had taught the essentials of the creed to the Twelve, who, in their missionary journeys through the known world (itself an apocryphal notion), had appointed and trained bishops to govern the churches in their stead. By contrast, it was said, Marcion, Valentinus, Cerinthus, and the rest were just making it up as they went along. The notion of the Twelve Apostles functions in a similar way for today's apologists and conservative scholars, as a historical bridge back to a historical Christ. All right, he may not have taught them precisely everything that became normative Christianity, and they may not have started churches outside of Palestine, but the fact there were such persons at all seemed to provide a bridge to which a farther shore must connect. There must have been a historical

Jesus on the far side. The fact of the disciples/apostles seemed to allow us to "shake the hand that shook the hand." But I believe Walter Schmithals has blown up that bridge. He has shown that it is more likely that some group of Jewish-Christian leaders, patterning itself on the twelve patriarchs of Israel (like the Qumran councils), subsequently claimed (or someone later claimed on its behalf) it had originated as Jesus' own hand-picked apprentices. Furthermore, the impressive cosmic imagery associated with the three Pillars implies there is both much more and much less than meets the eye in our gospel accounts, since the secondary link with Jesus tends to obscure an original, quite different, conception of these figures and the nature of their authority.

NOTES

1. *Dead Sea Scriptures in English Translation*, trans. Theodor H. Gaster (Garden City, N.Y.: Doubleday/Anchor, 1957), p. 55.

2. Arthur Drews, *The Christ Myth*, trans. C. Leslie Burns, Classics in the Study of Religion (Amherst, N.Y.: Prometheus Books, 1998), pp. 271–72.

3. Walter Schmithals, *The Office of Apostle in the Early Church*, trans. John E. Steely (New York: Abingdon Press, 1969), pp. 68–70.

4. Robert Eisenman, *James the Brother of Jesus: The Key to Unlocking the Secrets of Early Christianity and the Dead Sea Scrolls* (New York: Viking Penguin, 1997), pp. 932–38.

5. E-mail communication dated April 26, 2000, from Detering to the present writer.

6. In just the same way, the original character of the Levite priesthood as the hierophants of Nehushtan or Leviathan, the Serpent God, Yahve's grandfather and Elyon's father, has been covered up by three alternate accounts of their origin: a tribe descended from Jacob, a professional class of oracle mongers from various tribes (Judg. 17:7), and a group of zealous Mosaic enforcers who win membership in the group by instant, ruthless execution of idolaters in the camp (Exod. 32:25–29).

7. Quoted in Solomon Schechter, *Some Aspects of Rabbinic Judaism* (New York: Macmillan, 1910), p. 59.

8. Robert Eisler, *The Messiah Jesus and John the Baptist* (New York: Dial Press, 1931), p. 253; Oscar Cullmann, *Peter: Disciple-Apostle-Martyr: A Historical and Theological Study*, trans. Floyd V. Filson (Philadelphia: Westminster, 1953), pp. 21–22; Cullmann, *Jesus and the Revolutionaries*, trans. Gareth Putnam (New York: Harper & Row, 1970), p. 9.

9. John M. Allegro, *The Sacred Mushroom and the Cross: A Study of the Nature and Origins of Christianity within the Fertility Cults of the Ancient East* (New York: Bantam, 1971), pp. 100–102; cf. Anthony Tyrrell Hanson, "The Foundation of Truth: I Timothy 3:15," chap. 1 in *Studies in the Pastoral Epistles* (London: SPCK, 1968), pp. 5–20.

10. Jacob Neusner, *Why No Gospels in Rabbinic Judaism?* Brown Judaic Studies 135 (Atlanta: Scholars Press, 1988), p. 22.

11. *Selections from the Writings of the Bab*, trans. Habib Taherzadeh (Haifa: Baha'i World Centre, 1976), p. 74.

12. Matti Moosa, *Extremist Shi'ites: The Ghulat Sects*, Contemporary Issues in the Middle East (Syracuse: Syracuse University Press, 1988), p. 81, 87, 101.

13. Ibid., p. 89.

14. Bertil Gärtner, *Iscariot*, trans. Victor I. Gruhn, Facet Books, Biblical Series (Philadelphia: Fortress Press, 1971).

15. Theodore J. Weeden, *Mark: Traditions in Conflict* (Philadelphia: Fortress Press, 1971).

16. Dennis Ronald MacDonald, *The Homeric Epics and the Gospel of Mark* (New Haven: Yale University Press, 2000), pp. 44–54.

17. Arlo J. Nau, *Peter in Matthew: Discipleship, Diplomacy, and Dispraise*, Good News Studies 36 (Collegeville, Minn.: Liturgical Press, 1992), pp. 109–12.

18. Robert M. Price, "The Legend of Paul's Conversion," *Journal for the Critical Study of Religion* 3, no. 1 (fall/winter 1998): 7–22.

19. Bultmann, *History of the Synoptic Tradition*, p. 25.

20. A. S. Rappoport, "Hospitality Rewarded," *Medieval Legends of Christ* (London: Ivor Nicholson and Watson, 1934), pp. 144–45; "Christ and the Old Soldier," pp. 148–50; "The Lord and the Blacksmith," pp. 154–55; "The Master-Smith," pp. 155–59; "Jesus and the Bear," pp. 168–69.

21. "Deep things of Christ," secrets of the illuminati, as in 1 Cor. 2:10 and Rev. 2:24. The *psuchikoi* are the average believers, while the *pneumatikoi* are the Gnostic "spiritual ones." If you had to look up this endnote, you're not one of them!

CHAPTER EIGHT
THE HINAYANA GOSPEL

YOU TAKE THE HIGH ROAD AND I'LL TAKE THE LOW ROAD

Generations of gospel readers have puzzled over both a set of severe passages in which Jesus commands would-be disciples to give up all possessions and another that assumes they have not and will not. The fact of a contradiction between groups of gospel sayings should not by now surprise us, but the challenge is to explain where such a contradiction came from. And it seems that is entirely possible, and without contrivance, once we invoke a simple analogy from another religion. Buddhism, long before Christianity, had developed a two-track system of salvation. Christianity, I believe, whether spontaneously or by some current of influence no longer readily traceable, developed the same sort of double form, already by the time of the New Testament. Such a suggestion is not at all odd; it just recovers traditional Catholic exegesis whereby Jesus stipulated "counsels of perfection" in addition to the gospel for the masses.

The Buddhist religion began, as far as we know, in the sixth century B.C.E. in northern India. It was a monastic, elitist movement in that it prescribed a way of salvation so rigorous that it was thought beyond the ability of anyone to attain it while living an ordinary life in the mundane world. The everyday world was considered *maya*, a kind of illusion, a tissue of false values and assumptions, where the impermanent was habitually mistaken for the permanent and where, as a result, human beings were engaged in an endless chase for a satisfaction that can never be found. Not in this world, at least. One could heed the Buddhist *dharma* (doctrine, gospel), however, and find a way beyond this vale of tears and frustration. One could, already in this life, penetrate to that state of mind called *Nirvana*, where pain and desire, the cause of pain, are alike forever extinguished. Having done so, one could depart this life without regrets, that is to say, without craving the world one left behind, without wishing for another chance to do it better. Because if one did leave with that in mind, one would indeed reenter the world, again and again, for another round of the same frustration. This potentially endless cycle of suffering and reincarnation (which many Christian Gnostics also believed in) was called *Samsara*. The escape from it was by the simple (in principle) but difficult (in practice) means of meditation. One looked within and followed the Eightfold Path, a program, much like traditional Yoga, by which one shut out worldly distraction, stilled all desire, and attempted to see past the illusion of a stable ego-identity. The one who successfully trod the Eightfold Path was known as an *arhat* and would be venerated as a sage by others hard at work on their own sainthood. An arhat was necessarily a monk or a nun, because, Buddhists felt, mundane concerns would prove too much of a distraction from the quest. What of the laity? They could not hope for Nirvana, but if they played their karmic cards right, they could still go to one of the heavens. Nirvana was the cessation of individual existence; no good or bad karma might henceforth be generated. Heaven was a godlike existence, blissful but inferior to the ultimate Liberation of Nirvana. Heaven might be attained by the pious layman who scrupled to keep basic Buddhist morality (no intoxicants, no harm to living creatures, no lying, no stealing, no adultery) and by having faith in the Buddha and supporting the monks. The monks would make daily rounds among the huts of the laity and receive whatever food they doled out. Such charity was a valuable source of good karma for the average Buddhist. In one's next life, who knows, one might don the saffron robe and seek Nirvana, too, but for now, the low road, Plan B, was not so bad.

Some centuries later, apparently in the first century C.E., Buddhism changed. It was largely taken over by a new doctrine and a new approach. The traditional arhat ideal came to be considered too selfish, a fatal irony in a religion professing to believe there was no true selfhood! It was considered too selfish merely to seek one's own entrance to Nirvana, leaving everyone else to fend for themselves. Might there be a way to save others? The ideal of the *bodhisattva* was born.[1] The word means, literally, "enlightenment being" and denotes "Buddha-to-be." It was first used to refer to the various earlier incarnations of the one who would become Prince Siddhartha, Gautama Buddha. But now others saw the possibility and the duty to become bodhisattvas, too. They thought it incumbent upon them not only to tread the path the Buddha marked out, the path to salvation, but also to follow in the Buddha's own footsteps, to become a savior as he did! They knew they were signing on for a great number of incarnations during which they might master the ten stages and the ten perfections appropriate to them. It was a long career dedicated to the salvation of all beings. One did as many good deeds as possible so as to build up far more good karma than one could possibly need for oneself. After abolishing desire, the adept was entitled to lay down the burden of individual existence and enter the Nirvanic state of final bliss. And the arhat would have. But the bodhisattva swore to do what it was believed all past Buddhas had done, namely defer his own final fulfillment for the sake of others. As heavenly beings lingering on the threshold of Nirvana, these selfless ones answered the prayers of the faithful, since this was a fertile source of the good karma they needed to speed them on their quest to saviorhood. And the relationship was symbiotic, since the faithful laity were happy to receive the help! Sometimes a bodhisattva might deign to appear on earth to be present to help, heal, or teach his devotees in the flesh (or the docetic appearance of flesh). The Dalai Lama of Tibet is one of these, the earthly *tulku* (projection) of Avalokitesvara, the great Bodhisattva of Compassion. Devotees of the bodhisattvas might petition them for worldly benefits, for spiritual help unto salvation, or even for assistance along a short path to one's own Buddhahood!

The later type of Buddhism dominated and today holds sway in all North Asia: Korea, China, Mongolia, Japan, Tibet, Bhutan, Sikkim, and Nepal. These Buddhists refer to themselves as *Mahayana* Buddhists, signifying "the greater raft" accommodating the greater number to salvation. South Asian Buddhists, in Vietnam, Burma, Thailand, Laos, Cambodia, and Sri Lanka, call themselves *Theravada*, meaning "the Way of the Elders." But Mahayana Buddhists call them *Hinayana*, meaning "the narrow raft," an elite path only for some. In a sense, this distinction is misleading, since both Buddhisms have always had a provision for the laity. There was always some sort of easier path for those who were not especially heroic. Both admit that only a few go above and beyond the call of conventional religious duty, and that to aid them advances one's own prospects for salvation. Thus, I prefer to use the term "Hinayana" to refer to the minority path of religious heroism, "Mahayana" to refer to the easier way of the masses.

Gerd Theissen, Dieter Georgi, Walter Schmithals, Stevan L. Davies, and others[2] have shown how important in early Christianity were a whole class of itinerant prophets, wandering radicals, called variously "the brethren" (Matt. 25:40; 3 John 5–8), "the saints" (1 Tim. 5:10), or "apostles" (1 Cor. 9:3–7; *Didache* 11:3–13:7). These knights of faith (whose marching orders we find preserved, as if delivered to the direct disciples of Jesus, in Mark 6:7–13; Matt. 10:1–23; Luke 9:1–6, 10:1–12) trod the paths of Palestine and the Mediterranean world, preaching the gospel from village to village, from house to house. They had no family or property, having renounced all such ties to this fallen age in the name of Christ. In this they were similar to the wandering Cynic apostles who said God had sent them into the world to show that an uncomplicated life according to the will of the creator, a life according to nature like the birds and flowers lived, was possible. One remained a slave to the Principalities and Powers, the structures of this age, only so long as one decided to. But one might break all those chains and live free. One might live as an unencumbered child of God, capable of uncompromising obedience to God's will. And further, such freedom from material connections was the only way one could be absolutely free for God. Such similarity to the Cynic mission implies a close kinship and a common descent. We will follow up that thread presently.

What gospel, besides that of the simple life, did the Christian itinerants preach? No doubt they repeated, and expounded on, many of the sayings collected in Q, Luke, and Mark, which will concern us later in this and the next chapters. They pointed to the heavenly Son of man as their invisible patron who watched over them and would repay whatever honor or dishonor their hearers paid them (precisely the point of the Sheep and the Goats scene in Matt. 25:31–46, already referred to): "Whoever in this generation of sinners and adulterers rejects me and my words, him will the Son of man reject when he comes with his angels!" They claimed to embody the light-essence of the Christ and sought out, like Diogenes, the rare individual who also glowed with that supernal inner radiance. In them the itinerant apostles recognized fellow members of that Man of Light: "You are the light of the world!"

They summoned those who had ears to hear to leave all behind and to join them. Others might as well not bother. Keeping the conventional commandments was no doubt good enough for them. But let them not forget the *poverellos* of the gospel, the itinerants themselves. The layman could gain quite as rich a reward in heaven as these had merited: "Amen: I say to you, whoever gives you a cup of water to drink in the name of your being Christ's will by no means lose his reward" (Mark 9:41). "He who receives a prophet because he is a prophet shall receive a prophet's reward, and he who receives a righteous man because he is a righteous man shall receive a righteous man's reward. And whoever gives to one of these little ones even a cup of cold water because he is a disciple, amen: I say to you, he shall not lose his reward" (Matt. 10:41–42). In the same way, if one bet on the wrong horse and welcomed a false apostle, one risked a share in his damnation: 2 John 11, "He who greets him shares his wicked work."

The Central Asian Sufi master Arif Dikkaram "would never accept any kind of present, considering that to accept is a disaster for the recipient. He said: 'The giver of a gift acquires the *baraka* [blessing], merit, which the recipient forfeits. Only a perfected man can have the grace that makes gifts harmless. I do not have that gift.'"[3] Presumably that is why "It is more blessed to give than to receive" (Acts 20:35). The bodhisattvas of the Son of man, too, in this manner traded spiritual value for physical. See also the Druze oral tradition first recorded by Sami Nasib Makarem: "The Emir [Fakhruddin II (ca. 1572–1635 C.E.)] ironically once asked his uncle, 'Why have I been granted all this power and wealth in spite of my ungodliness and impiety?' The sage replied, 'Perhaps in a previous life, once having found someone sleeping in the sun you were kind enough to wake him up and ask him to move into the shade. This kindness to someone deserving is enough for you to experience a life such as you are now living.'"[4] Giving to the wandering preachers and prophets, then, entitled one to share vicariously in their rewards, as if one had oneself renounced all to follow the way of Jesus. It was a kind of "short path" to salvation. Beyond this, of course, the laity were charged to observe the traditional commandments, to live righteously.

One wonders if the commands to turn the other cheek and to give the coat off one's back to anyone who asks were directed originally to the radical one hundred percenters or to everyone. Did they belong to the Hinayana gospel or to the Mahayana gospel? The former, I suspect, as the sayings plainly assume a complete lack of social responsibilities and obligations. Of the radical disciple it was required that he give up all property. By contrast, the Pastorals regard it as a worse sin than unbelief if one should fail to care for one's own household (1 Tim. 5:8). That and Mark 7:9–13's scathing condemnation of those who deprived their aged parents of support by pledging money to the temple instead are quite compatible with the radical sayings so long as one supposes that the "give all" sayings applied to the itinerants, while the rest applied to the householders who supported the itinerants. As all who have tried to obey the radical commandments to give all while hoping to maintain a more or less normal social and family existence have found, it is sheer lunacy because it just does not fit, apples and oranges. Look at Tolstoy's experience. Again, we find the same sort of two-track system in Buddhism, and such seems to be presupposed in the Gospels, where, for instance, Jesus is on good terms with Martha and Mary, who support him but do not give away all their property and follow him on the road (Luke 10:38–42). A similar picture is attested in Matt. 10:14–15, Mark 15:40–41, Acts 16:15, 3 John 5–8, and 2 John 9–11.

LIVING ON THE EDGE

The command to turn the other cheek implies that one has opted out of the prevailing honor-shame system and chosen instead a marginal existence. By the rules of the honor-shame social system, one gains or loses honor according to how one responds to challenges from one's equals/rivals. "Oooh! Are you going to take that!" One must return an equal or better blow, or put-down, or one "loses face," as we still say. That makes turning the other cheek when slapped a perfect example, since to strike the face is to invade directly the zone of honor.[5] To receive a blow and shrug it off forfeits honor among one's fellows, and then one recalls all those Matthean sayings about trading the esteem of one's fellows for that of one's heavenly Father, who sees what is performed in secret (Matt. 6:1–6, 16–18). (Oddly, though the New Testament is well aware of the honor-shame game of one-upsmanship among scholars [John 5:44, "you . . . receive glory from one another and do not seek the glory that comes from the only God"], Jesus is constantly depicted as gaining honor in the eyes of the people by besting scholarly opponents in debate [Mark 2:8–12, 16–17, 18–22, 24–27; 3:1–6; 7:1–23; 10:2–8; 11:27–33; 12:13–27, 35–37]).

Such marginality or "liminality" is also what made holy men valuable as social and economic mediators (which is why someone approaches Jesus asking him to settle a dispute, Luke 12:13; cf. Exod. 18:13–16), as they were known to have renounced any vested interest in the worldly system. It also made them obvious choices when the mob desired a scapegoat, in which case the marginal figure's isolation made him seem sinister, a threat to the prevalent order. The asexuality of the holy man was not thought improper, though any worldly man without a wife might be thought effeminate, at least dishonorable. The wandering apostles sometimes traveled with a chaste female companion (a "sister as wife," 1 Cor. 9:5), an arrangement some thought scandalous only because they did not take the claimed state of holy marginality seriously. But they did understand the concept, or there would have been nothing to sneer about.

The poverty of the holy man was not considered the curse of God as might that of a failed businessman. In fact, this is why some found the life of holy poverty a great boon. Lucian tells us how Proteus Peregrinus was up to his eyeballs in debt on inherited property and cleverly contrived to escape his difficulty by giving it all to the people of his village in grand Cynic style, whereupon he was proclaimed a great philosopher and benefactor of the people (*Passing of Peregrinus* 14–15). One could, by "giving all," trade dishonor in financial terms for great honor in spiritual terms, even in the eyes of fellow mortals, not to mention God, in whose heavenly ledgers one had entered great amounts of heavenly treasure by the same transaction. It was a brilliant way of making virtue of necessity.

Those who had left the social system to live on its borders, Christian radicals and Buddhist arhats alike, had renounced all rank. "You know that those who are supposed to rule over the Gentiles lord it over them, and their great men exercise authority over them. But it shall not be so among you; but whoever would be great among you must be your servant, and whoever would be first among you must be slave of all" (Mark 10:42–44). The Buddhists disregarded caste within their own *sangha*. It was all part of "this world" of Samsara. Thus, Ananda can meet a woman of a different caste at a well and ask her for a drink: "Thus have I heard: at that time the Lord dwelt at Sravasti in the Jetavana, in the park of Anathapindada. Now the elder Ananda dressed early, and taking his bowl and robe entered the great city of Sravasti for alms. After his round, and having finished his meal he approached a certain well. At that time a Matanga (outcast) girl named Prakrti was at the well drawing water. So the elder Ananda said to the Matanga girl, 'give me water, sister, I wish to drink.' At this she replied, 'I am a Matanga girl, reverend Ananda.' 'I do not ask you, sister, about your family or caste, but if you have any water left over, give it me, I wish to drink.' Then she gave Ananda the water" (*Divyavadana* 611).[6] Jesus does the same in John, chapter 4, accosting the Samaritan woman, who is astonished, since "Jews have no dealings with Samaritans" (John 4:9). Buddhists signaled their having dropped out of Samsara by wearing the distinctive garb of the dead—funeral shrouds. Cynic apostles were recognized by their habit of tunic, cloak, staff, and pouch. Christian apostles sacrificed even the cloak, pouch, and staff, and went barefoot as well (see below).

Albert Schweitzer[7] called the extreme-sounding sayings of Jesus part of an "interim ethic" intended only for the brief time anticipated before the Final Judgment. He believed that Jesus taught the soon-coming end of the age and that emergency rules therefore applied. One suddenly had both the opportunity and the necessity to live according to the perfect and rigorous standards of God. Ordinarily, it might be thought regrettable to use force to defend oneself and one's property, but what choice did one have? One had obligations to family and clients, after all. But not any more! Ordinarily, one might admit it would be nice to give to the poor, but if one donated to every beggar, one would soon find oneself impoverished, and one's family members would ask why one had not thought of them first? But no more! Since the time was supposedly short, with no mundane future on the agenda, there was no reason to save money! Soon it would be useless, so why not use it for the only thing it was still good for: feeding those starving right now? In that way one might pave one's way into heaven (Luke 16:9). This framework made good sense of many texts, though it has now fallen out of favor, partly because none of the texts in question explicitly mentions the end of the age as a condition of the recommended behavior. So I am proposing an alternative. Instead of an *interim* ethic, I think we ought to discern in the Gospels a *liminal* ethic. It is an ethic of extremes, as was Schweitzer's paradigm, but the ethic of liminality is predicated upon *social* boundaries, not *temporal* ones. The boundary line in question is not that of the coming end of the age, ticking away as we speak, but rather the border lines of the social map. The hundred percenters had moved to the margins of the social system, both literally (they wandered the roads) and figuratively (ordinary mores did not apply to them). They did so for precisely the same reasons the original Buddhist monks and nuns had: it was impossible to live a pure and perfect life in the midst of the workaday world.

Were not all saved by the same gospel? Not exactly: the Hinayana gospel was for the hundred percenters, the Mahayana gospel for their supporters. All presumably would be saved, would have real estate when the kingdom of God should dawn. But to the elite there is a greater promise: "Amen: I say to you, there is no one who has left house or brothers or sisters or mother or father or children or lands for my sake and for the gospel who will not receive a hundredfold" (Mark 10:29–30a—the rest of the passage appears to have suffered from interpolations, whether in the oral or written transmission). Presumably it was shares in this vast treasury of merit that the itinerants traded for the earthly favors done them by their householder supporters.

We have a cameo of a man poised at the brink of hundred-percent discipleship, offered to the reader to see if the shoe fits. It is Mark 10, the famous story of the rich man, or rich young ruler. A man seeks Jesus out and asks him his prescription for salvation, "What must I do to inherit eternal life?" Socratically coy, Jesus comments that surely it is no mystery. Does the man not know the commandments? The implication is that they ought to be sufficient. "All these I have observed from youth onward" (Mark 10:20). "And Jesus, looking upon him, loved him, and said to him, 'You do lack one thing: go, sell what you own and give to the poor and you will have treasure in heaven; and come, follow me" (Mark 10:21). Sobered, the once-enthusiastic inquirer departs, perhaps daunted, perhaps planning to do as Jesus asked; we never hear more. And that is because the real concern is with the reader or hearer; it is he who will decide how the story comes out, for it is really his own story: the story was passed down as a recruitment story. Like the Marines, Jesus is looking for a few good men. But the alternative is not damnation, only the nonheroic faith of the laity. Jesus is shown as suspecting from the man's zeal that he sensed there was something more: the way of the gospel bodhisattva. Not everyone feels that call, and for them there was the wider raft. (We will examine the terms of the Mahayana gospel in the next chapter.)

It is worth asking, given the mendicant nature of the ministry of the itinerant apostles, just what, or rather, *whom*, they intended when they counseled their hearers to liquidate property and give the proceeds to "the poor." Were they talking about some sort of ancient socialism? Land redistribution? Such is a cornerstone of liberal theological, social gospel exegesis. But is not another alternative much more ready to hand? What is more natural than for "the poor" to be the disciples themselves? Jesus and his men, the literary incarnations of the itinerant ideal, are after all said to have been supported by wealthy women (Luke 8:1–3). Presumably these women model the generosity sought on behalf of the wandering apostles. Jesus would, then, be pictured as asking for the money to go to him and his disciples, and they maintained a common purse to keep it in (John 13:29). It would not have been unusual in the context of ancient philosophers: "The most shocking thing of all, though, is this. Every one of them will talk about lacking nothing and even shout to the housetops that the only rich man is a wise man. But then a minute later he will come up to you to ask for money— and fly into a rage if he doesn't get it. It's as if someone in a king's robes with a diadem and tiara on his head plus all the other marks of a monarch were to stop his inferiors in the street and beg from them. Whenever any of them has occasion to accept money, then there's much talk about, 'Wealth should be shared,' 'Money is a matter of indifference,' 'What's gold or silver? No different from the pebbles on the beach'" (Lucian *The Fisherman* 35).[8]

SINNERS AND CYNICS

In the first Christian centuries, some outsiders had difficulty distinguishing between Christian and Cynic apostles. And so do some modern scholars, for the two are very close indeed, perhaps to the point of veritable identity. F. Gerald Downing[9] has long argued that early Christianity, whether Jesus or his successors, had welcomed the basic insights of popular Cynic-Stoic preaching, well known all over the Empire for hundreds of years. Founded by Antisthenes of Athens, a disciple of Socrates, and by Diogenes of Sinope (the same place Marcion hailed from, centuries later) in the fourth century B.C.E., Cynicism was, as we have anticipated, a way of life modeled upon the rootless freedom of the stray dog (κυνος, hence Cynic). Humans ought to learn from the superior wisdom of animals to live in accordance with nature by reason. Such a course would free us from the entanglements of marriage, finances, government, and all social conventions. All worries would flee, evaporating in the joy of perfect freedom. What few needs one possessed would be met, in the providence of the divine creator, the same way the needs of the birds and flowers are met. And one day, death comes. That, too, is part of nature. Some Cynics were gentle in their preaching, others rude and abusive, like the Zen masters whose antics theirs often resembled. Some Cynics rejected all moral conventions, while others were puritanical. When some criticize him keeping bad company, Jesus dismisses them, saying he is but a doctor visiting the sick ward. When some criticize Diogenes for entering a brothel, he compares himself to the sun, whose light shines into a latrine without being polluted. They lampooned conventional rank and religion. They begged for alms on the grounds that they were only asking for what was as much theirs as yours in the nature of things. They expected persecution and felt bound to love their abusers. They did not demand everyone follow their example, but they said God had sent them into the world as living witnesses that it was possible for humans to live according to God's blueprint.

They traveled the roads of the ancient world, and one could point to the presence of the renowned Cynic Meleager in Gadara (familiar from Mark 5:1, "They came to the other side of the sea, to the country of the Gadarenes") in the first century B.C.E. Cynicism might have, almost must have, been very familiar to Jews in Jesus' day. Already in the Mission Charge, the stipulations for the preaching journeys of the itinerant apostles, there is what appears to be an attempt to distinguish Christian apostles from their Cynic counterparts. According to Mark 6:8–9, the itinerants may take a staff on the road with them, but not a purse or a second tunic. Matt. 10:10 and Luke 9:3, 10:4 deny them even the staff. Why? Because Cynic wanderers were proverbially recognized by their modest costume of a staff, a pouch, and a threadbare cloak. Christians did not want to be confused with their competitors. If we had reason to doubt it, this very nitpicking attempt to contrast the two groups ought to count as proof enough that

Cynicism was a well-known phenomenon in the early Christian milieu, easily possible as an early influence. In fact, the scrupling over the Cynic-like staff and purse ought to be understood as an example of "the anxiety of influence," the attempt to minimize the similarities and maximize the differences between a movement and earlier ones that influenced it.

Though it is not hard to produce numerous examples of Jewish proverbial wisdom that counsel us to trust in God like the rest of his creatures do, the gospel admonitions to renounce family and property and livelihood are paralleled only in Cynicism. They are so close as practically to demand a genetic relationship. There is both internal and external evidence that Cynic teaching was assimilated into Christianity and passed into Christian scripture. The internal evidence is the shape and content of the earliest discernible stratum of the Q document. As Burton L. Mack, John Kloppenborg, Leif Vaage, and others[10] break it down, Q appears to have gone through at least three stages, from least to greatest Christian coloring. In Q3 we meet Jesus the Christian Lord, who will judge the righteous and the wicked, and in whose name miracles are wrought (the stock in trade of the radical itinerants, by the way: 2 Cor. 12:11–12; Mark 6:7, [16:17]; Matt. 7:22, 10:8; Luke 9:10). But in Q1, grouped into seven neat topical sections, there are maxims and proverbs that might have been coined by any Cynic. Those New Testament scholars who recognize the thoroughly Cynic flavor of the Q1 sayings and yet profess to find there also a distinctive voice, that of Jesus, somehow fail to realize that the distinctive "voice" is simply that of Cynicism, as witnessed by the fact that parallels to the Q1 sayings are drawn from *various* Cynics.

What shall we do with the criterion of dissimilarity? Heed it, that's what. We ought, however reluctantly, to bid these sayings good-bye, at least as candidates for authentic sayings of the historical Jesus. Contra Downing, Mack, Crossan, and others who recognize the Cynic character of the Q1 sayings, the issue is not whether Jesus himself was a Cynic or influenced by Cynics. That possibility may disturb some for theological reasons: the Son of God just *knew* what was true; he did not "learn" "views" or "beliefs" from mere mortals! But that is not the issue either. The important question is whether Cynic material has entered into the early Christian mix. If so, where did it come from? Here we might remind ourselves of Bultmann's dictum about the great man quoting. While people may easily misattribute quotes to one they deem a likely source, they are not likely to remember a sage quoting previous great men. They are liable either to attribute a juicy quote to their favorite sage (as when Muslim *hadith* ascribe the Lord's Prayer to Muhammad!) or to skip it and dwell on something their own hero said instead. In the same way, must we reduce the historical Jesus to the status of one more Cynic sage? If all that Cynicism was borrowed and brought into Christianity by Jesus himself, then such a Jesus is minimally original and, in effect, ought himself to be regarded as merely one more voice in the *Gemeinde*, the creative community of the early Christians, which would then overlap the Cynic community. What seems to have happened instead is that, just as the Synoptic evangelists sought to differentiate an almost indistinguishable Cynicism from their own Christianity by haggling over whether to carry a stick and a pouch, so did the Q redactors eventually try to distance themselves from the Cynic origin of their material by attributing it to the name of Jesus. Jesus is then reduced to the same status as the controversial staff!

What external evidence is there for an interpenetration of Cynics and Christians resulting in the production of Christian scripture? It comes from the second-century satirist Lucian of Samosata, who tells us so many important things about the religious environment of the New Testament. In his *Passing of Peregrinus*, Lucian tells his version of the life and career of a well-known itinerant philosopher (mentioned with respect by a number of ancient writers). He tells us Proteus Peregrinus was sometimes a Cynic, at others times a Christian. While within the Christian fold, he came to rank almost as a second Christ and wrote certain treatises still venerated by Christians: "During this period he apprenticed himself to the priests and scribes of the Christians in Palestine and became an expert in that astonishing religion they have. Naturally, in no time at all, he had them looking like babies and had become their prophet, leader, Head of the Synagogue, and whatnot, all by himself. He expounded and commented on their sacred writings and even authored a number himself. They looked up to him as a god, made him their lawgiver, and put his name down as official patron of the sect, or at least vice-patron, second to that man they still worship today, the one who was crucified in Palestine because he brought this new cult into being" (11). But even before his final break with the Christians he took up the dress of a Cynic and was hailed as "the only true follower of Diogenes" (15).[11]

I am suggesting that Q1 came over into Christianity, into Christian scripture, via the additions of the Q redactors, in the same fashion as did Peregrinus's writings, whatever they may have been.

BIG-TICKET DISCIPLESHIP

We turn now to the various individual sayings that mandate voluntary poverty—which sounds like an oxymoron but is not. They are not categorical but hypothetical imperatives, stipulating what one must do *if* one hopes to reach a certain goal. That is clear in the first and most direct: "So therefore, whoever of you does not renounce all that he has cannot be my disciple" (Luke 14:33). This saying, modeled upon the Q saying considered just below, seems to be a Lukan formulation, one of his typical built-in interpretations. Luke tends to introduce what he wants a parable to mean just before (Luke 12:41; 15:1–2; 18:1, 9; 19:11) or at the end of (12:21, 48b; 13:5; 14:11; 15:7, 10; 16:9; 17:10; 18:7–8) the story, so no one will be left in doubt as to the moral. In the present case, he means to sum up the sense of verses 25–33.

A related saying requires one to follow Jesus, carrying one's cross, though it does not actually say Jesus carried one or that he was crucified. The Q version reads: "If anyone comes to me and does not hate his father and mother and wife and children and brothers and sisters, yes, and even his own life, he cannot be my disciple. Whoever does not bear his [Luke: own] cross and come after me cannot be my disciple" (Luke 14:26–27). Matthew has softened the language somewhat: "He who loves father or mother more than me is not worthy of me, and he who loves son or daughter more than me is not worthy of me; and he who does not take up his cross and follow me is not worthy of me" (Matt. 10:37–38). Matthew has added the love of son and daughter in order to tie the double saying in with the quotation from Mic. 7:6 ("for the son treats the father with contempt, the daughter rises up against her mother, the daughter-in-law against her mother-in-law; a man's enemies are the men of his own house") that Q has placed beside the sayings (Matt. 10:35//Luke 12:52), mistakenly thinking it a saying of Jesus. In view in the basic Q saying is, for one thing, the requirement of the itinerant that he abandon family responsibilities, as James and John are said to have done in Mark 1:20, and as Prince Siddhartha did when he sought enlightenment. Mark has altered Q, omitting the family breach, and reshuffling the rest: "If any one would come after me, let him deny himself and take up his cross and follow me" (Mark 8:34). Both Matthew and Mark have paraphrased Q's original "be my disciple" (which Luke retains). Mark's version is, as a result, redundant. Perhaps Matthew and Mark did not want to restrict the meaning of the word "disciple" to the role of the wandering charismatics.

Does the saying mean to refer to the crucifixion of Jesus? If it does, at least we may observe that there is no implied doctrine of the atoning death of Jesus, since the emphasis would be on imitating Jesus, not accepting some sacrifice of his on one's behalf. The question of whether Jesus' own crucifixion is implied here has relevance for the larger issue of the implicit theology of Q. Did the Q fellowship (probably not really a community, in light of their prickly independence) believe in any special death of Jesus? We cannot say, as the evidence is ambiguous. But that is the same as saying we have to read Q as if there was no significance attached to the death, since either way we must admit we are left with no hard evidence for Q belief in the saving (or any!) death of Jesus. That is, we cannot assume they believed something when there is no clear textual basis to say so. Nor can we assume that what one segment of early Christians believed in, all must have believed in.

But I will confess that it does seem to me more than coincidence that Jesus, whom we otherwise associate with crucifixion, is shown here urging people to tread the *Via Dolorosa* in his wake. I suspect it does intend a reference to the cross of Jesus, and then we can be absolutely certain the saying is post-Jesus. What sense would it have made to anyone before Jesus' death? Remember, he is depicted making this announcement to the crowds who cannot have been privy to whatever esoteric teaching about his coming death we might attribute to him. (As we will see, the passion predictions, presented as if esoteric instruction to the disciples in private, are all later editorial devices.)

A Q section (Matt. 6:19–21, 25–33//Luke 12:22–31, 33–34) gathers a number of sayings germane to the calling of the itinerant apostles. Matthew has inserted a couple of similar sayings, while Luke has more freely paraphrased Q. Matt. 6:19–21 is surely closer to the original: "Do not lay up for yourselves treasures on earth, where moth and rust corrupt and thieves break in and steal, but lay up for yourselves treasures in heaven, where neither moth nor rust corrupts and where thieves do not break in and steal. For where your treasure is, there will your heart be also." Luke has flattened Q's poetry into didactic prose: "Sell your possessions and give alms; provide yourselves with purses that do not grow old, with a treasure in the heavens that does not run out, where no thief approaches and no moth destroys. For where your treasure is, there will your heart be also." Whereas Q/Matthew leaves it open as to how one banks heavenly wealth (the doing of good deeds generally?), Luke specifies liquidation of all holdings. For every coin that in the poor box rings, another shekel into one's heavenly account springs. Either way, the saying is pretty explicit: one must not accumulate earthly wealth since one's heart inevitably gravitates in the direction of one's treasure, like a dowsing rod. It cannot be otherwise, so mundane wealth must be renounced. This is the Cynic position vis-à-vis possessions: they will perforce possess their ostensible owner. Let the would-be pious householder comfort himself with the (Stoic) delusion that he can maintain all his property and yet his heart be in heaven with God. It cannot be. Even today the saying is invariably interpreted homiletically as if it said, "Amass treasure on earth; just don't let your heart be there."[12]

Coupled with the previous saying is Matt. 6:25–34//Luke 12:22–31. The birds and wildflowers are called as witnesses for the proposition that God may be trusted to provide for his creatures; thus, the faithful Christian will not be anxious. This much would be compatible with the Mahayana gospel, assuring the Christian householder that he need not worry whether his labors will be enough, or whether he will lose his job. God will take care of him, come what may. But we must suspect it is really aimed at the wandering charismatics because of the detail that the birds and flowers *do not sew garments or plant crops*. Is not the point of comparison that God provides the necessities of life for those of his creatures who do not spend their time securing basic worldly necessities? In this the itinerants are like the birds and flowers. Might Jesus have said this? Indeed he might have, but again, the criterion of dissimilarity weights it on the side of the early church, a product of the itinerant apostles.

Appended to the story of the rich young ruler is a pair of sayings about wealth and its peril: "How hard it will be for those who have riches to enter the kingdom of God." "It is easier for a camel to go through the eye of a needle than for a rich man to enter the kingdom of God" (Mark 10:23b, 25). The first saying, which we must assume to have originally stood by itself, might allow for there being pious wealthy people, warning such hearers to watch their step (cf. 1 Tim. 6:17–19, "As for the rich in this world, charge them not to be haughty, nor to set their hopes on uncertain riches but on God who richly furnishes us with everything to enjoy. They are to do good, to be rich in good deeds, liberal and generous, thus laying up for themselves a good foundation for the future, so that they may take hold of the life which is life indeed"). And one way in which they could increase their chances of salvation would be to give substantially to the needs of the itinerant preachers. The second saying seems to rule out the very possibility of salvation for the rich, bidding them to renounce wealth and take to the road, again, like Prince Siddhartha. Again, Jesus might have said it, but it could as easily be the invention of the itinerants themselves. After all, it is to these, and not to Christian believers in general, that the promise was addressed: "He who hears you hears me" (Luke 10:16a), a warrant to coin an unlimited number of new sayings from the heavenly Christ (subsequently to be ascribed to the historical Jesus). This is one of them.

The uniquely Matthean pair of parallel parables, the Treasure Hidden in the Field and the Pearl of Great Price (Matt. 13:44–46), may have been among the rhetorical arrows in the itinerants' quiver: "The kingdom of heaven is like treasure hidden in a field, which a man found and covered up; then, in his joy he goes and sells all that he has and buys that field. Again, the kingdom of heaven is like a merchant in search of fine pearls, who on finding one pearl of great value, went and sold all that he had and bought it." If the dominant note here is "selling all" for something worth that and more, then we have a picture of the kingdom of heaven as both supremely valuable and supremely costly. It is worth everything, and we must surrender everything we have to gain it. We may not have much, but it will take all we do have. The totality of the sacrifice is what matters, not the amount (also the point of the Widow's Mite story in Mark 12:41–44). Once we try to make this sacrifice into something compatible with retaining one's property, it vanishes in a puff of exegetical smoke. The hundred percenters, however, could have told you what it meant. They had sold everything to buy the satisfaction they now enjoyed.

It is possible that the two parables are pre-Matthean, since a version of each appears in Thomas, sayings 76 (the pearl) and 109 (the treasure), but that does not mean much unless, as most scholars today think, Thomas is independent of Matthew. That, however, is a judgment I cannot share. While it is too large a topic to pursue here, let me just say that, contra Stephen J. Patterson[13] and others, it seems evident to me that Thomas does occasionally preserve earmarks of the redaction of Matthew and Luke, implying that he was working with these gospels. An obvious case would be Thomas's version of the saying about hating relatives and bearing the cross, saying 55, "Whoever does not hate his father and his mother will not be able to be a disciple to me. And whoever does not hate his brothers and his sisters, and does not take up his cross in my way will not be worthy of me." Thomas has harmonized Luke and Matthew. He has Luke/Q's "hatred" of relatives *and* Matthew's addition of son and daughter. Thomas has Luke/Q's "be my disciple" *and* Matthew's "be worthy of me." "Take up his cross in my way" paraphrases "take up his cross and follow me."[14] It appears that Thomas knew the Synoptic gospels by hearing them read or from having once read them, but without a copy ready to hand. His departures from their versions are often loose memory quotations. Even when, as with the parable of the Great Supper (*Thomas* 64), we have something that might appear to be an independent, more authentic version than the canonical versions,[15] I cannot but suspect that we have a memory quotation, streamlining the canonical versions and trimming away the differences instead of harmonizing them. Likewise, Thomas leaves out allegorical interpretations of parables shared with Matthew simply because he has forgotten them or omitted them on purpose. Thomas, of course, does preserve a number of independent sayings as well as apparent creations of his own.

All this leaves us with uniquely Matthean parables that begin to look more and more like Matthean creations. When we compare the Matthean parable collection (Matt. 13) with the Markan original (Mark 4), it becomes apparent that Matthew has added to Mark's parable of the Mustard Seed (Mark 4:30–32//Matt. 13:31–32) the similar Q parable of the Leaven in the Loaves (Matt. 13:33//Luke 13:20–21) but otherwise has created the rest of his own parable chapter out of whole cloth. The parable of the Wheat and the Tares is all his, a pastiche of Mark's parable of the Sower. Likewise, the detailed allegorical interpretation of it was suggested by the secondary interpretation of the parable of the Sower (Mark 4:14–20). Ditto the parable of the Dragnet (parallel to the Wheat and the Tares), the Treasure in the Field, and the Pearl of Great Price. When they show up out of nowhere and bear distinctive marks of Matthean ideas and vocabulary (e.g., "at the close of the age" in verses 40, 49, cf. 24:3, 28:20; angels gathering souls in verses 41, 49; burning the wicked in the furnace with the gnashing of teeth in verses 42, 50, cf. 22:13, 24:51, 25:30 [derived from Q: Matt. 8:12//Luke 13:28]), surely the most economical explanation is that they are Matthean creations.

The Lukan parables of the Rich Fool (12:15–21), the Dishonest Steward (16:1–9), and Lazarus and the Rich Man (16:19–31) seem, as we have seen, to be Luke's own creations (the third adapted from the rabbinic tale of Bar Maj'an the tax collector), so their comments on wealth and its proper use do not go back to Jesus.

The Beatitudes (blessings) appear in Matt. 5:3–12 and Luke 6:20–23. It appears that Q had the basic set of four blessings on the poor, mourners who weep, the hungry, and those persecuted on account of Jesus. Matthew has added blessings on the meek, the merciful, the pure in heart, peacemakers, and those persecuted for the kingdom of heaven's sake (resulting in two blessings for the persecuted). Luke has added no new blessings but has balanced out the blessings with corresponding woes, recalling the lists of blessings and curses in Deut. 27–28, which is probably where he got the idea. Luke curses the rich, the sated, the jovial, and the popular (Luke 6:24–26). It is fashionable to understand the beatitude on the poor as a piece of rabble-rousing or "conscientization" by Jesus, who is then pictured as trying to foment class conflict.[16] Matthew's addition of the words "in spirit" is taken as an apolitical spiritualization, a domestication of the Q version, which, as still in Luke, had simply "poor." It hardly matters, it seems to me, since in any case the beatitude sounds like a piece of pie-in-the-sky cold comfort. Nothing here suggests that Jesus is summoning the proletariat to throw off the chains of its capitalist bosses. Rather, we are to think again of Lazarus and the Rich Man: in the next world, there will be an evening up. (This is especially clear when we compare the Lukan woe on the rich, which does not appear in Q.) But which poor are in view? It may be the poor who did not choose their lot, or it may be the voluntary poor who follow in the way of Jesus, the bodhisattvas of the gospel.

THE SAINTS GO MARCHING IN

We have tried to reconstruct a double-track system in early Christianity parallel to that in Buddhism. There was a straight and narrow path of discipleship for the heroic and a winding, slower road for the rest, though they could avail themselves of the greater merits of the hundred percenters. With the help of their betters, they might get further along the path to heaven than their own good works deserved. They might finally be saved, not by their own bootstraps, but on the coattails of the saints. Again, nothing in this sketch should strike the reader as strange, for it is surely the logic by which early Christianity developed the cult of the saints.[17] And it closely parallels the growth of North Asian Buddhism with its galaxy of Buddhas and bodhisattvas eclipsing Gautama Buddha and dispensing salvation by grace through faith to the laity.

One can still find living, or earthly, bodhisattvas in Asia, and they are what one would have to call wandering charismatics, venerated by the crowds to whom they minister. But most of the bodhisattvas, named, attributes catalogued, distinctive iconographic images fixed, are believed to inhabit the *Sambogkya*, the heavenly realm of the Buddhas and bodhisattvas. It is in such celestial repose that they hear and answer the prayers of mortals. It is also the supramundane realm in which some perform special saving acts, such as Amitabha Buddha's creation of the Pure Land, or Avalokitesvara's sufferings on behalf of the wicked in hellfire. Those considered Buddhas (Gautama, Amitabha, Dipankara, and so on) have already visited earth for the last time, whereas those still considered bodhisattvas have yet to undergo the formality of that last incarnation before achieving the rank of Buddha. There is little or no practical difference, and in fact Avalokitesvara, though a "mere" bodhisattva, is esteemed by his/her devotees to be higher and greater than (and even inclusive of) all other Buddhas and bodhisattvas combined!

In the same way, as history marched on, the role of the itinerant apostles was taken over by martyrs and confessors. They earned their haloes by bearing the cross in the most literal sense, dying at the hands of pagan inquisitors and lynch-mobs. Even in death they played the role of the itinerant apostle. As had their predecessors, they provided a counterweight to the growing settled hierarchy of the church. Living, the charismatics had been wildcards, independent bearers of holiness whose clout as Christ's vicars easily rivaled that of those administrators whose claims rested on dubious credentials of apostolic succession. In other words, average believers could hardly help being more impressed with holy scarecrows who actually wandered the land without possessions and claiming miracles, like the old stories had Jesus doing, than with their local bishop. Martyrdom only served to increase the charismatic clout of the former, albeit posthumously, for their tombs and relics became zones of holiness rivaling the churches (once there *were* churches). People gathered at the tombs of martyrs, where their relics were on display, on the anniversary of their deaths. The sacred dead were believed to be invisibly present in power to heal and answer prayer. In short, they became Christs—as they had been in life! The brethren of the Son of man, that is, more Sons of men. They remained on the margins, literally, since their shrines were just outside the city walls. Their cults served as alternate foci, over against the clergy, of the oval of ecclesiastical life and authority. Eventually, major bishops managed to co-opt the saints' charisma by having their relics transferred from the cities' perimeters into the churches. But the cult of the saints certainly lost none of its power, as all know. It grew to the point where eventually the Protestant Reformers deemed Catholicism polytheistic, with Christ lost in the saintly shuffle. We have here an exact parallel to the cult of the bodhisattva in Mahayana Buddhism. Even the role of the two greatest saints, Jesus the great Atoner and his Mother Mary, have astonishing parallels in Amitabha Buddha, dispenser of saving grace, and Avalokitesvara, Bodhisattva of Compassion (who even became female, the goddess Kwan-Yin, in China). These Christian and Buddhist parallels suggest the unfolding of a shared inner logic. We will try to pursue it further in the next chapter as we consider the Mahayana gospel for the masses in the Gospels.

NOTES

1. Har Dayal, *The Bodhisattva Doctrine in Buddhist Sanskrit Literature* (1932; repr. New York: Samuel Weiser, 1978); Leslie S. Kawamura, ed., *The Bodhisattva Doctrine in Buddhism*, SR Supplements 10, Papers Presented at the Calvary Buddhism Conference, September 18–21, 1978 (Waterloo: Wilfrid Laurier University Press, 1981).

2. Gerd Theissen, "The Wandering Radicals: Light Shed by the Sociology of Literature on the Early Transmission of Jesus Sayings," in *Social Reality and the Early Christians: Theology, Ethics, and the New Testament*, trans. Margaret Kohl (Minneapolis: Fortress Press, 1992), pp. 33–59; Theissen, "Legitimation and Subsistence: An Essay on the Sociology of Early Christian Missionaries," in *The Social Setting of Pauline Christianity: Essays on Corinth*, trans. John H. Schütz (Philadelphia: Fortress Press, 1982), pp. 25–67; Dieter Georgi, *The Opponents of Paul in Second Corinthians*, trans. Harold

Attridge et al. (Philadelphia: Fortress Press, 1986), pp. 27–40, 164–70; Walter Schmithals, *The Office of Apostle in the Early Church*, trans. John E. Steely (New York: Abingdon Press, 1969), pp. 114–230; Schmithals, *Gnosticism in Corinth: An Investigation of the Letters to the Corinthians*, trans. John E. Steely (New York: Abingdon Press, 1971), pp. 279–82; Stevan L. Davies, *The Revolt of the Widows: The Social World of the Apocryphal Acts* (Carbondale: Southern Illinois University Press, 1980), pp. 29–49; Stephen J. Patterson, *The Gospel of Thomas and Jesus* (Sonoma: Polebridge Press, 1993), pp. 158–214.

    3. John G. Bennett, *The Masters of Wisdom* (New York: Samuel Weiser, 1980), p. 176.

    4. Sami Nasib Makarem, *The Druze Faith* (Delmar, N.Y.: Caravan Books, 1974), p. 56.

    5. Bruce J. Malina, *New Testament World: Insights from Cultural Anthropology* (Atlanta: John Knox Press, 1981), pp. 34–39.

    6. In Edward J. Thomas, *The Life of Buddha as Legend and History* (London: Routledge & Kegan Paul, 1975), p. 242. Also in Rudolf Bultmann, *The Gospel of John: A Commentary*, trans. G. R. Beasley-Murray, R. W. N. Hoare, J. K. Riches (Philadelphia: Westminster Press, 1971), p. 179; Jack Kornfield, ed., "The Woman at the Well," *Teachings of the Buddha*, trans. E. Bureuf and Paul Carus, rev. ed. (New York: Barnes & Noble Books, 1999), pp. 105–106.

    7. Albert Schweitzer, *The Quest of the Historical Jesus: A Critical Study of its Progress from Reimarus to Wrede*, trans. W. Montgomery (1906; repr., New York: Macmillan, 1968), pp. 365–66; Schweitzer, *The Mystery of the Kingdom of God: The Secret of Jesus' Messiahship and Passion*, trans. Walter Lowrie (New York: Macmillan, 1954), pp. 53–60; Schweitzer, *The Kingdom of God and Primitive Christianity*, trans. Ulrich Neuenschwander (New York: Seabury Press, 1968), pp. 81–88; Jack T. Sanders, *Ethics in the New Testament: Change and Development* (Philadelphia: Fortress Press, 1975), pp. 1–29.

    8. *Selected Satires of Lucian*, ed. and trans. Lionel Casson (New York: Norton, 1968), p. 352.

    9. F. Gerald Downing, *Cynics and Christian Origins* (Edinburgh: T. & T. Clark, 1992).

    10. Burton L. Mack, *The Lost Gospel: The Book of Q and Christian Origins* (San Francisco: HarperSanFrancisco, 1993), pp. 106–14; John S. Kloppenborg, *The Formation of Q: Trajectories in Ancient Wisdom Collections*, Studies in Antiquity and Christianity (Philadelphia: Fortress Press, 1987); Leif E. Vaage, Appendix One, "The Formative Stratum of Q: Agreement and Disagreement with John S. Kloppenborg, *The Formation of Q*," *Galilean Upstarts: Jesus' First Followers According to Q* (Philadelphia: Trinity Press International, 1994), pp. 107–20; Arland D. Jacobson, "Recent Q Research: Recovering the Compositional History," chap. 3 in *The First Gospel: An Introduction to Q* (Sonoma: Polebridge Press, 1992), pp. 33–60.

    11. Casson, pp. 368, 370.

    12. J. D. Salinger, *Franny and Zooey* (New York: Bantam Books, 1964), p. 148: "As a matter of simple logic, there's no difference at all, that *I* can see, between the man who's greedy for material treasure—or even intellectual treasure—and the man who's greedy for spiritual treasure. As you say, treasure's treasure, goddamn it, and it seems to me that ninety percent of all the world-hating saints in history were just as ac*quisi*tive and unattractive, basically, as the rest of us are."

13. Patterson, *Gospel of Thomas and Jesus*, pp. 44–45.

14. Patterson's suggestion that Thomas matches Q in using *both* "cannot be my disciple" and "is not worthy of me" and that Matthew and Luke have each chosen one phrase and harmonized the other to it strikes me as highly unlikely, just a harmonization of his own that looks good to him only because it gets him out of a tight spot.

15. Joachim Jeremias, *The Parables of Jesus*, trans. S. H. Hooke, 2d. rev. ed. (New York: Scribner, 1972), pp. 68, 70–71, 74, 77, 79, 85, 87–89, 110, 176.

16. Juan Luis Segundo, *The Historical Jesus of the Synoptics*, trans. John Drury, Jesus of Nazareth Yesterday and Today, vol. 2 (Maryknoll: Orbis Books, 1985), pp. 86–91 ff.

17. Peter Brown, *The Cult of the Saints: Its Rise and Function in Latin Christianity*, Haskell Lectures on History of Religions, New Series 2 (Chicago: University of Chicago Press, 1981).

CHAPTER NINE
THE MAHAYANA GOSPEL

MEETINGS WITH UNREMARKABLE MEN

The Gospels contain a great number of sayings ascribed to Jesus (perhaps merely a question of genre convention: had they been collected into the Epistles instead, they would have been attributed to Paul or Peter), which lay down requirements for salvation. Considering the whole range of them, we might feel inclined to follow the ancient scribes who sought to rank them and decide which was the greatest commandment. But it is doubtful whether any single one might be viewed as a distillation of them all. Any such move is a logo-centric cheat, chopping off all but one branch of a spreading tree. Asking, "What is the essence of the Law (or of the gospel, or Christianity)?" is really to ask, "What is your favorite part?" In other words, the Gospels, like the Torah before them, provide a number of commandments or conditions for salvation, any of which may be considered necessary, but none of them sufficient. Is it, then, a question of "salvation by works," the anathema of Protestantism? No, because there is also plenty of talk in the Gospels about forgiveness and divine mercy (though, as we will see, that, too, is conditional). Jesus is heard speaking of both the prophetic, the demands of God, and the priestly, the forgiveness of God. And that is necessary, because these sayings apply not to the perfect, the true imita-

225

tors of Christ, whose gospel we examined in the previous chapter, but to the rank-and-file Christians, the *psuchikoi* (1 Cor. 2:14), the weaker brethren (Rom. 14:1). The trick, of course, is to tell which is which.

You Know the Commandments (I Don't)

We have already seen how Mark 10:17–19 seems to draw a clear line between heroic and conventional morality: when the inquirer asks Jesus for the secret of salvation, he in effect answers that it depends on just how "saved" one wants to *be*! For most, keeping the commandments is enough, and Jesus implicitly recognizes that the inquirer has done so. The man hears a call to higher things that most do not hear and so presses his question. But for most folks, the commandments appear to be enough. For the record, Mark has Jesus enumerate only six commands. "Do not kill. Do not commit adultery. Do not steal. Do not bear false witness. Do not defraud. Honor your father and mother" (Mark 10:28). Absent from what seems intended as a partial list of the Ten Commandments (Exod. 20:1–17) are the specifically cultic or religious commands not to have other gods, not to make images, to keep the sabbath, and one "secular" command, not to covet. It might be that these commands are randomly chosen examples, but the lack of all three cultic commandments indicates a weighting toward the moral, away from the specifically religious, the ritual, pole. It would appear that social behavior is more in view, and that acts are perhaps more important than motives, as the omission of coveting eliminates the only mandate regarding inner dispositions. And the defrauding commandment does not form part of the Decalogue anyway. Did Mark think it did? Matthew (19:19) has corrected him, omitting the defrauding business but replacing it with "Love your neighbor as yourself" from Lev. 19:18. The lack of the cultic commandments and the addition of another secular one imply that the Markan Hexalogue, if not his own invention, derives at any rate from the Gentile church, where the prohibition of images could not be taken seriously, where sabbatarianism was alien, and where even monolatry was questioned or qualified. It is just impossible that a Jewish Jesus would omit what he elsewhere makes the first and greatest commandment, the exclusive worship of the God of Israel (Mark 12:29), or that he should not be able to keep straight which commandments were in the Decalogue.

But it may well be that Mark 10:28's set of Six Commandments was the very formula of righteousness required by the wandering apostles of their householder supporters. Interestingly, they are analogous to the Tetralogue, or Four Commandments, ascribed to James the Just for the Gentiles in Acts 15:29: abstain from food previously offered as an idolatrous sacrifice, from consuming blood, from eating the meat of animals killed by strangulation, and from certain degrees of consanguineous marriage. These commandments are vestiges of the Jewish code, all cultic in character, the diametrical opposite of the Markan Hexalogue.

Luke 18:18–23 repeats the story of Mark 10:17–22, making the rich man a "ruler" and omitting the apocryphal "do not defraud" commandment. But Luke 10:25–28 offers a wholesale rewrite of this Markan passage, combining it with Mark 12:28–34, omitting entirely the original comparison of the Mahayana and Hinayana paths. Now it is a simple prescription of the way of the layman: "And behold, a lawyer stood up to put him to the test, saying, 'Teacher, what shall I do to inherit eternal life?' He said to him, 'What is written in the law? What is your reading?' And he answered, 'You shall love the Lord your God with all your heart, and with all your soul, and with all your strength, and with all your mind; and your neighbor as yourself.' And he said to him, 'You have answered right; do this, and you will live [eternally].'"

THE BABY AND THE BATHWATER

John 3:1–21 represents yet another rewrite of Mark 10's story of the rich young man. This time the ruler (as in Luke 18:18) is given a name: Nicodemus. John has omitted the ruler's original question, "What must I do to inherit eternal life?" Why? To answer this, we need to look briefly at Matthew's redaction of Mark's original. Mark had the man address Jesus with the polite honorific, "Good teacher," prompting Jesus to recoil in pious humility, "Why do you call me good? No one is good but God alone!" Matthew did not like this. He felt it unbecoming that Jesus should thus proclaim himself a sinner! So he changes the inquirer's words, shifting the "good" from Jesus to the man's question about salvation: "Teacher, what *good thing* must I do to inherit eternal life?" This obviates the need for Jesus to decline the man's praise. Instead, he says, "Why do you *ask me about what is* good?" (Matt. 19:17). John saw the same problem. He who has Jesus challenge his opponents, "Which of you can prove I have sinned? Well?" (John 8:46), is not about to have Jesus disclaim being good! So whereas Matthew reworded both the inquirer's salutation and his question, John has reworded the address ("Rabbi, we know that you are a teacher come from God; for no one can do these signs that you do, unless God is with him," verse 2) but omitted his question completely! And yet it is the original question John has Jesus (now abruptly) answer: "Amen, amen: I say to you, unless one is born again/from above, he cannot see the kingdom of God." That is, he cannot inherit eternal life. The ruler is nonplused: "How can a man be born when he is old? Is he to enter his mother's womb and be born a second time?" But he isn't on the same wavelength, as Jesus goes on to explain: "Amen, amen: I say to you, unless one is born of water and the Spirit, one cannot enter the kingdom of God" (3:4–5). Jesus goes on to explain that he didn't mean so much born *again* as born *from above*, from the Spirit which, like the unbounded wind, streams through the sky in untraceable courses. And for this rebirth, one must pass through the water of baptism.

Here is a dialogue that never took place: the whole thing depends upon Jesus and Nicodemus speaking Greek! For the misunderstanding of the latter stems from the ambiguity of the Greek word ανωθεν, which can mean either "again" or "from above." The pun does not exist in Aramaic or Hebrew, and we cannot very well imagine these two Palestinian Jewish scribes discoursing in Greek. The pun originated in the mind of the evangelist, but he was drawing the notion of baptismal regeneration from Mark, even if not from the rich young man story. Mark 10:15, just up the page from the story of the rich young man, caught John's eye, so he replaced Jesus' original reply about the commandments with it: "Amen: I say to you, whoever does not receive the kingdom of God like a child shall not enter it." Long ago Oscar Cullmann[1] pointed out that this saying, and the pronouncement story that it caps, originated as a piece of liturgy for infant baptism. It is recognizable as such by the occurrence of the stage direction "do not prevent them," which we find in one form and another associated with baptism in Acts 8:36 ("What is there to *prevent* my being baptized?"); 10:47 ("Can anyone *forbid* water for baptizing these people who have received the Holy Spirit just as we have?"); and 22:16 ("And now, why do you *wait*? Rise and be baptized, and wash away your sins, calling on his name"), and see Lucius Apuleius, *The Golden Ass*, chapter 48: "Why dost thou *stand idle and delay*? Behold the day which thou didst desire with prayer, when as thou shalt receive at my hands the order of most secret and holy religion, according to the divine command of this goddess of many names."[2] John recognized the text as baptismal in character, and that is why the rebirth Jesus prescribes includes water. Only John is thinking of adult ("believer's") baptism ("when he is old," John 3:4), not children's, as in Mark.

So in John, things have taken a decidedly sacramental turn. Instead of obeying the commandments, it is water baptism that entitles one to eternal life in the kingdom of God. John no doubt expected the baptized to live righteously as well, as the whole of his gospel shows, but it is important that baptism is given such a privileged position. It marks the turning of a sociological corner in the life of a sect, one that occurred equally in Christianity and in Buddhism. As Protestant philosopher Max Scheler[3] explained it, a sectarian movement begins enthusiastically embracing a prophet's call to high standards of morality and piety. To survive, the sect must have its relative few members united in intense revivalistic fervor. They view their founder as one who leads by example and points the way. It is up to the disciple to follow him. But after the movement enters its second generation, and the founder is gone, its members tend to relax. Their values slip back toward the mainstream and intensity relaxes. Standards fall to levels of mediocrity, and all this is rationalized by the elevation of the founder to the status of a divine savior.[4] He does not put before us an example to follow, because we are sinners/mortals. His achievement was superhuman. He did what he did because he was a god. And in fact he did it *for us*, not to show us how to do it, but rather so we could be excused for *not* doing it! In fact it would be sheer effrontery to think oneself capable of emulating the savior. Instead, he will be satisfied with token efforts. Here is the shift from sect to church. Here is the passage from Theravada to Mahayana, from the religion *of* Jesus to the religion *about* Jesus. And from our point of view, it represents the passage of early Christianity into a kind of moral pessimism (or laziness, as Feuerbach would have it). Whether the saying applies to Jesus or the itinerant apostles for whom he so often stands in the Gospels, it typifies the shift: "'What must we do to be doing the work of God?' 'This is the work of God, that you believe in him whom he has sent'" (John 6:28–29). And baptism was the making official of that faith. The accent is less on righteous living, more on religious allegiance. One is riding the bodhisattva's coattails. Needless to say, Mark 10:15, like John 3:3, 5, belongs to the early church, and not even to the earliest stage of the early church. It cannot originate with Jesus.

Matt. 18:3 is a moralizing rewrite of the saying in Mark 10:15: "Amen: I say to you, unless you turn and become as little children, you will never enter the kingdom of heaven." The next verse, "Whoever humbles himself like this child, he is the greatest in the kingdom of heaven," is a rewrite of Mark 9:35–36a, "'If anyone would be first, he must be last of all and servant of all.' And he took a child and put him in the midst of them." In fact, all Matthew has done in 18:3 is to insert Mark 10:15 into the story of Mark 9:33–37. It does not represent an independent, nonsacramental version of the same saying.

NOT SO FAST

To listen to the Gospel of Thomas (saying 27), one would certainly have to add fasting and sabbath observance to the list: "Unless you fast from the world, you will not find the kingdom. Unless you keep the sabbath as sabbath, you will not see the Father." Fasting "from the world" is an ascetic emphasis typical of Thomas's implied monasticism. See also saying 56, "Whoever has found the world has found a corpse, and whoever has found a corpse, of him the world is not worthy." Thomas also speaks of the unregenerate state as one in which "you ate dead things" (11). To fast from the world is to see the world as spoiled meat and to abstain from eating it. It would not be surprising if saying 27 represents Thomas's redaction of an earlier saying that spoke simply of traditional fasting and sabbath-keeping. But could such a saying go back to Jesus himself? Not likely; to whom would he have had occasion to say it? It presupposes an audience who had renounced both traditional Jewish practices and who thus needed the exhortation to resume them. Who would this have been? We know Philo dealt with radically Hellenized Jews in Alexandria who, like him, allegorized the Torah, but who, unlike him, henceforth felt no obligation to keep the Torah commandments, including even circumcision. But would Jesus have dealt with anyone like this? The only Galileans who look anything like this are Jesus and his disciples! Mark 2:18 contrasts the disciples of Jesus with the sects of the

Pharisees and John the Baptist, who do fast and are scandalized that Jesus and his merry band do not.

Why don't they? The original answer appears to be Mark 2:21–22, "No one sews a piece of unshrunk cloth on an old garment; if he does, the patch tears away from it, the new from the old, and a worse tear is made. And no one puts new wine into old wineskins; if he does, the wine will burst the skins, and the wine is lost, and so are the skins; but new wine is for fresh skins." The contrast is one of old and new, of form and content. The saying assumes that a new spiritual reality has arrived that cannot be confined or expressed in terms of the old. Hence to maintain the old forms would suffocate the new reality, so new ones must be sought. The proper *Sitz-im-Leben* of this saying, its context of origination, is the Gentile Mission, where Paul and others experimented with what missions theorists now call "indigenization," allowing the new converts from alien cultures to adapt their new faith in new ways. Such experiments always dismay traditionalists, who naturally fear something essential may be lost, while bad things may be gained in a process of illicit syncretism. Likewise, it is Gentiles, faced with the daunting prospect of keeping the hundreds of Torah commandments, who see the Law as a burden from which Christ frees them, not Jews, for whom the Torah constitutes the water for the fish. Mark 2:21–22 speaks of indigenization and casting off Jewish customs perceived as needlessly binding. And of course this means the verses are no sayings of Jesus. As Bultmann knew, this much at least should have been obvious from the simple fact that the conduct in question in the frame-story is that of the disciples, why *they* do not fast, signaling the origin of the passage in the early church, not the career of Jesus.

But someone has interpolated still another view of fasting into the midst of the pericope, neutralizing the point made by the patches and wineskins similitudes. Verses 19–20 seek to reinstate fasting, specifically Friday fasting, and to make Jesus legitimize the practice in advance: "Can the wedding guests fast while the bridegroom is with them? As long as they have the bridegroom with them they cannot fast. The days will come when the bridegroom is taken away from them, and then they will fast in that day." So Jesus and his disciples did not fast, but just wait: once Jesus is out of the picture, they will take up the old custom again. Does it make any sense at all for Jesus to say such a thing to his critics, who can have no idea what he is talking about? The reader understands because he already knows what happened to Jesus. It is plainly anachronistic.

Matt. 6:16 simply assumes that Christians fast; they just don't do it as their hypocritical rivals do, to demonstrate their piety to all and sundry, as, say, when people have ashes smeared on their foreheads on Ash Wednesday. In passing, we ought to note that the whole triptych on almsgiving, prayer, and fasting (Matt. 6:1–6, 16–18) originated with Matthew. These three pious practices were the cardinal marks of Pharisaism, Matthew's Javneh-era rivals. The verses return again and again to the Matthean signature phrase "your heavenly Father." And of course the references to people rising to pray in the synagogues marks the whole thing as too late for Jesus.

Thomas 14 has some choice comments on the same three pious practices: "If you fast, you will beget sin for yourselves. If you pray, you will be damned. And if you give alms, you will do evil to your spirits. And if you go into any land and wander in the regions, if they receive you, eat what they set before you, attend to the sick among them. For what goes into your mouth will not defile you, but rather what comes out of your mouth, that is what will defile you." Here in one fell swoop, Jesus, or rather Thomas, dispenses with fasting, prayer, almsgiving, and kosher laws! One may ask whether perhaps originally the first half of the saying came from a version of anti-Pharisee denunciations like those found in the vitriolic Matthew, chapter 23, condemning them for the hypocrisy of their pious observances, done merely for audience consumption. That being the case, such actions, far from accumulating heavenly merit, will only backfire. Perhaps Thomas has blundered by making the disciples the audience for what was originally a denunciation of Jesus' enemies. Or perhaps the saying comes from a group of Gnostic elitists who, like Shankara or the Druzes, felt they had progressed to so high a level of enlightenment that all traditional forms of religion would only perpetuate spiritual retardation.

So where are we? Did Jesus teach that fasting was necessary for salvation? Or that it would damn the soul? Did he teach that fasting, though once quite legitimate, had been rendered irreparably passé? Did he say that there was but a temporary moratorium on fasting? Did he assume his disciples do fast? All these views are ascribed to him in Mark, Matthew, and Thomas, more than one in some gospels. In such a clamor, there is no way to recognize the authentic voice of Jesus, if there was one. Maybe he said nothing about fasting at all, or if he did, maybe it was not recorded. The various sayings reek of Hellenizing, Judaizing, Gnosticizing. All appear tendentious, none historical. But by the same token, there is no real reason to doubt that all these views were promulgated by various early apostles who prophesied their opinions in the name of the Son of man, speaking to different audiences. They would all be variations, wide variations to be sure, on a theme in the Mahayana gospel for the laity.

THE WAY OF DAMNATION

We can get a better idea of the gospel requirements of salvation if we venture to view the matter in "the mirror of man's damnation."[5] Positive requirements, stipulations of what must be done, tell only part of the story. What deeds must one avoid lest one tumble off the knife-edge bridge into Gehenna's magma pits?

Clearly the biggest-ticket item on the hamartological list must be blasphemy. The issue has grown confused in the transmission of the gospel sayings. Here is the Q version of the warning against blasphemy (Matt. 12:32//Luke 12:10):

"Everyone who speaks a word against the son of man will be forgiven, but he who blasphemes against the Holy Spirit will not be forgiven." (Matthew has added, "either in this age or in the age to come.") Once one understands the biblical/Hebrew idiom "son of man" as meaning simply "human being" (as in Ps. 8:4, "What is man that you are mindful of him, or the son of man that you care for him?"), the Q saying makes eminent sense: Everyone who speaks a word against a fellow human being will be forgiven, but he who blasphemes against God will not be forgiven. "Blaspheming" just means "slandering, badmouthing," though, ironically, the word's use vis-à-vis God has sanctified it, so that it is no longer used of offense against humans. Q employs the euphemism "Holy Spirit" precisely to distance the name of God from the very term blasphemy. But there is nothing here of the later distinction between God and the Holy Spirit. (If there were, it would imply the Holy Spirit is not God, as the distinction would be between the Holy Spirit and "God," not "the Father.") The point of the original saying is clear, then: blasphemy is the sole sin that will stand in the way of a universal amnesty to be offered by God some time in the future.

Mark consulted Q and, writing in Greek, hoped to avoid any confusion occasioned by the "son of man" idiom, which would make no sense in Greek. So he pluralized the term to something more readily recognizable as meaning "mankind" and shifts it further down the sentence so that it applies to the human sinners who are to be forgiven their blasphemies. His version: "Amen: I say to you, all sins will be forgiven the sons of men, and whatever blasphemies they utter; but whoever blasphemes against the Holy Spirit never has forgiveness, but is guilty of an eternal sin" (Mark 3:28).

Matthew rewrote Mark, interlarding Q material with it, so he found both versions of this (and other) sayings and harmonized them. He begins by paraphrasing Mark's version: "Therefore I tell you, every sin and blasphemy will be forgiven men, but the blasphemy against the Spirit will not be forgiven" (Matt. 12:31). Then he continues with Q: "And whoever says a word against the son of man will be forgiven; but whoever speaks against the Holy Spirit will not be forgiven, either in this age or in the age to come." This last phrase is his paraphrase of Mark's "but is guilty of an eternal sin." Does he understand what "son of man" meant? Probably so, since where Mark has Jesus say "The son of man has authority on earth to forgive sins" (Mark 2:10), Matthew repeats it and then makes the crowd interpret it: "they glorified God who had given such authority to men" (Matt. 9:8). There is nothing here about Jesus the Son of man. That will come later, once someone mistakes a Hebrew idiom for a messianic title (and we will deal with that development in a later chapter). It may be that eventual misunderstanding of "Son of man" as a Christological title that led to the gratuitous ascription of the saying to Jesus.

MILLSTONE NECKTIE

One becomes hell's kindling also by causing someone else to sin: "Whoever causes one of these little ones who believe in me to sin, it would be better for him if a great millstone were suspended from his neck and he were thrown into the sea" (Mark 9:42). Here the Risen Lord Jesus speaks to his gathered church. It is a post-Jesus saying, at least the phrase "who believe in me." But even the rest of it smacks too strongly of the early church not to belong there: "And so by your knowledge the weak man is destroyed, the brother for whom Christ died. Thus, sinning against your brethren and wounding their conscience when it is weak, you sin against Christ. Therefore, if food is the cause of my brother's falling, I will never eat meat, lest I cause my brother to fall" (1 Cor. 8:11–13; cf. Rom. 14).

"Judge not that you be not judged. For with the judgment you render you yourself will be judged" (Q: Matt. 7:1//Luke 6:37a). If this saying has in mind the judgment of God, it implies that the unmerciful will be damned, just as in Matthew's parable of the Unmerciful Servant. Most read the saying that way, taking the passive, as Joachim Jeremias proposed, as the so-called "divine passive," avoiding the active voice so as to leave the name of God tacit. But there is no special reason to think so. It is perhaps more natural to understand the saying as meaning, "Judge not, since others will not be inclined to show you mercy you have not shown." This is especially true in view of the continuation: "for the measure you give is the measure you will get" (Matt. 7:2).

WIRETAP TRANSCRIPT

Finally, one may find one's way to Hades by the simple expedient of loose lips. "I tell you, on the day of judgment men will render account of every careless word they speak; for by your words you will be justified, and by your words you will be condemned" (Matt. 12:36–37). "Whatever you have said in the dark shall be heard in the light, and whatever you have whispered in private rooms shall be proclaimed upon the housetops" (Luke 12:3). The uniquely Matthean saying just quoted is explicit in locating the condemnation at judgment day, implying that the gossip and the tale-bearer will be damned for his or her indiscretion. But Luke's saying (from Q) leaves open the possibility that, again, it is other people who will find out what you have said, imagining you could keep it secret. That is, of course, what always happens! Matthew has transformed the Q saying into a command of Jesus to proclaim publicly what he has told them privately (Matt. 10:27). This last, though it changes the subject of the saying, is important for us. It should be recognized as parallel to John 16:12–15, implying the production of many post-Jesus sayings to be ascribed to his name, as if they had hitherto been secret. "Why haven't we heard this before?" "Because Jesus told us to keep it under wraps for the time being." That's the ticket.

Among that class of prophetic fabrications, we must number sayings such as Matt. 10:32//Luke 12:8–9: "Whoever acknowledges me before men, I will also acknowledge before [Luke: the angels of] God [Matthew: my Father in heaven]; but whoever denies me before men, I will also deny before God [Matthew: my Father in heaven]." Here it is a question of creedal confession of Jesus, something inappropriate to the time of Jesus but intelligible in the time afterward, when Christianity became a controversial sect. Another would be the apocryphal Mark 16:16, "He who believes and is baptized will be saved, but he who does not believe will be damned" (part of the spurious Longer Ending of Mark, added later by scribes). Here Jesus is invoked on behalf of the Gentile Mission, a much later development.

THE HANDS-OFF POLICY

Mark 9:43–48 warns of besetting sins, habitual sins that must lead to damnation unless repented of. "If your hand causes you to sin, chop it off; it is better for you to enter [eternal] life maimed than with two hands to go to Gehenna, to the unquenchable fire. And if your foot causes you to sin, chop it off; it is better for you to hobble into [eternal] life than with two good feet to be thrown into Gehenna. And if your eye causes you to sin, pluck it out; it is better for you to grope half blind into the kingdom of God than with eyes wide open to be thrown into Gehenna, where their worm does not die, and the fire is not quenched." Thomas has what appears to be the same saying paraphrased: "When you make an eye in the place of an eye and a hand in the place of a hand and a foot in the place of a foot, then shall you enter the kingdom" (saying 22b). But Thomas's version is positive: one can attain salvation once certain bad habits are replaced with good ones. Mark is negative: if these sins are not expunged, there will be hell to pay.

Is there any clue as to what specific offenses are in view? According to Aramaic-speaker George M. Lamsa,[6] the metaphors used here, to cut off the hand and foot and to pluck out the eye, bespeak theft, intrusion (trespassing, perhaps adultery), and the lustful gaze. One might warn a likely thief, "Cut off your hand from my lawn mower!" One might, shotgun in hand, warn the interloper, "Son, I'll give you till three to cut off your foot from my garage!" One might warn a Brumalia party flirt, "Cast away your eye from my wife, you lush!" It is hard to imagine any context in which literal self-mutilation along these lines would have been practiced.

At any rate, Jesus warns sinners to get the required soul surgery now, before it is too late. He has no anesthesia to dispense except the realization that one quick yank now will save one an eternal toothache later. Better to enter eternal life maimed than to find oneself perfectly intact—burning in hell!

Notice that this saying envisions no resurrection at the end of the age. It assumes a new age of salvation will arrive, and if one passes on into it, one will take along any physical deformities. Here is someone who, like the Thessalonians, assumed those alive at the time would be lucky enough to see the Millennium, while the dead were just left holding the bag (1 Thess. 4:13–18). Again, here is one who imagined that flesh and blood was capable of inheriting eternal life (contra 1 Cor. 15:50).

Mark 9:8, "where their worm does not die and the fire is not quenched," comes directly from Isa. 66:24, but whose voice are we listening to in the preceding verses? It might be Jesus, but then again, it might be anybody. Then as now, there were plenty of fire-and-brimstone preachers. And, since the climax of the pericope is a quotation of Isaiah, implying the whole thing is something of a sermonic commentary on it, we must deny it to Jesus. Again, who remembers the great man quoting someone else?

CAN A MAN PETITION THE LORD IN PRAYER?

Kierkegaard called prayer the breathing of the soul, with possibility the air it breathes. What do the Gospels say? They depict Jesus as a man of prayer and as a teacher of prayer. Actually, as the basic premise of form criticism tells us, even the picture of Jesus the praying man has to be a didactic device: it, too, is teaching, some of it about prayer, some about Jesus.

First, what of the prayer life of Jesus himself? Do we have any data on the personal habits of piety of the historical Jesus? Let us review the evidence. Mark 1:35 says that Jesus used to withdraw from his healing and teaching activity to pray. We might psychologize the text, as is the wont of many, and suggest that in such hours of divine communion Jesus sought refreshment, to recharge his energy, to gain guidance from his heavenly Father. But we need not bother. The statement is Markan narrative, one of his famous iterative generalizations, and we have no way to know what if anything he based it on. It may simply have been his guess as to what would be a fitting lead-in to a traditional pericope that began with the prompt of the disciples, "Everyone is looking for you." Or the whole pericope, functioning as it does to move the story along to its next phase, may well be Markan. In neither case do we have any real evidence for Jesus' prayer habits.

Q (Matt. 11:25–26//Luke 10:21) gives us a look at a spontaneous "prayer" of Jesus, rejoicing at God's strange wisdom in hiding the truth of his gospel from the sophisticated and educated and revealing it instead to the simple and child-like. The sentiment is typical of know-nothing sectarianism that characteristically belittles education ("Oh, so you're studying at theological cemetery?"), since the educated invariably have no use for sectarianism! They know things are never as simple as sectarian preaching makes them. So virtue is made of necessity, and this sort of sour grapes is the result. Why don't the wise accept what we know is the truth? Either God or Satan must have blinded them to it. Serves them right for being so stuck up! We find the same sort of thing in 1 Cor. 1:26–29, where Paul reminds the Corinthians how few of them had any credentials for worldly wisdom, fortunately in view of the fact that God had designed the plan of salvation to elude the wise and intelligent. In view of this similarity, we have to reject the Q saying as likely enough a church product, putting the sentiments of 1 Cor. 1:26–29 into the mouth of Jesus. And it fits 1 Corinthians better, since there we are definitely dealing with the life of a young sect, whereas in Jesus' day, his followers would not yet have been so perceived. Jesus is pictured as more of a revival preacher to Jews in general, not a sect leader like Joseph Smith. Finally, even if authentic, the Q utterance is more in the nature of an apostrophe than a real prayer, like, "O Death, where is thy sting?"

Mark 6:46 has Jesus send his disciples in a boat across the Sea of Galilee, while he remains behind to pray. But this is just a plot device, accounting for Jesus' temporary separation from the Twelve. Nothing is said of arrangements for a period spent apart, as in Mark 6:7. Nor is there any arrangement for meeting up again, because the author, unlike the disciples, knows Jesus will shortly catch up with them by walking on the waves. The praying is no more historical than the walking on water.

The most intimate glimpse of Jesus at prayer is Mark 14:32–36, where Jesus agonizes in Gethsemane. But this is obviously the wholesale fabrication of Mark himself. How does he know what Jesus said on that occasion? He has gone to some trouble to eliminate any possible witnesses from the scene! Jesus first leaves eight disciples behind, taking with him the inner circle of James, John, and Peter. But then he leaves them far enough behind that he discovers them sleeping only once he rises from prayer to return to them. And, asleep, they were in no position to know what he may have said. So how did Mark know? He "knew" because he made it up. He is the omniscient narrator (which is also how he always knows what Jesus and other characters are thinking).

John's version of the Gethsemane prayer is the so-called High Priestly Prayer of John, chapter 17. The Johannine idiom and theology is thick enough to cut with a knife. It cannot go back to Jesus, though it is interesting to speculate that it might represent a farewell prayer by the unnamed leader of the Johannine community who has recently died (21:23–24), he who had claimed, like his contemporary Montanus, to be the living Paracletos.

Luke has created a picture of what some have called "the praying Christ" from the fuzzy fabric of piety, inserting the element of Jesus deep in prayer at several points where his sources lacked it. Luke's Jesus prays after his baptism, just before the Spirit-dove descends (3:21), before making the choice of the Twelve (6:12), before eliciting Peter's confession of faith (9:18), before the Transfiguration (9:29), and before issuing the Lord's Prayer (11:1). He has prayed for Peter's apostolic reinstatement (22:32) and prays from the cross, yielding his spirit to God (23:46). In every one of these cases, the praying is

Luke's addition to his source. Presumably he means to make Jesus an example to the faithful.

Surely the most glaringly artificial prayer ascribed to Jesus is his stage-whisper to God in John 11:41b–42, "Father, I thank you for hearing me. Of course, I knew that you always hear me, but I have said this for the benefit of those standing here, so they may believe that you sent me."

What does Jesus teach on the subject of prayer? It fits the possible origin of the sayings among the wandering prophets and charismatics that the prayer doctrine ascribed to Jesus is of a bold and optimistic nature, something recognized by today's Pentecostals, who take the sayings at face value and expect miracles. They may not get them, but they certainly appear to be following the lead of verses like Mark 9:23 ("All things are possible for one who believes") and Mark 11:22–24 ("Have faith in God. Amen: I say to you, whoever says to this mountain, 'Be taken up and cast into the sea,' and does not doubt in his heart, but believes that what he says will come to pass, it will be done for him. Therefore I tell you, whatever you ask in prayer, believe that you will receive it, and you will").

There is presupposed in such sayings an almost Zen-like sense that expectation governs reality, or the perception of reality, which is the same thing, and that if one could for a moment put on the shelf one's sense of normalcy, of what is and is not "possible," one might loose the moorings of consensus "reality," and anything would become possible.[7] One can expect the mountain to move only if one strips away every sense of proportion and probability. This is, of course, the recipe for fanaticism in case anyone should achieve it. We can tell well enough that it will not work because occasionally we do see some people who have managed to attain the escape velocity needed to penetrate the suffocating atmosphere of normal expectation: some people will genuinely believe they can fly and will take what we might call a Kierkegaardian leap off the madhouse roof. They always crash.

But does the saying mean to encourage such madness? There is a major clue that it does not. Note the hyperbolic character of "mountain-moving faith" in 1 Cor. 13:2: "If I have all faith, so as to remove mountains, but have not love, I am nothing." I do not say "metaphorical," for that is to try to evade the difficulty. I say "hyperbolic," that is, an exaggeration for effect, implying a degree of faith no one actually has (cf. "Even if I had all the money in the world." Or Mark 8:36, "For what profit would a man have made if he had gained the whole world but paid his own life for it?"). Coiled within what appear to be charters of the boldest faith is a backpedaling clause, an advance acknowledgment that it is not going to work. No one is going to have to redraw the topological survey maps of Galilee anytime soon for the sake of missing mountains. Luke 17:5–6, a Lukan paraphrase of Mark 11:22–24, strikes a surprising note of pessimism: "The apostles said to the Lord, 'Increase our faith!' And the Lord said, 'If you had faith as a grain of mustard seed, you could say to this sycamine tree, "Be uprooted and planted in the sea!" and it would obey you.'" The point is surely that, since such a thing is plainly never going to happen, you can see how little faith any one will ever have. It is like the rhetorical question of Luke 18:8, "When the Son of Man comes, will he find faith on earth?" The same double bind has caught the father of the deaf-mute epileptic in Mark 9:24, "I believe; help my unbelief!" (How striking that the single most poignant and insightful New Testament statement about faith is made not by the Messiah or an apostle or prophet, but just by . . . some guy!)

On the one hand, we can understand this fly in the ointment of confident prayer as the mark of rueful experience, a cautionary note so that, after the fact, the disappointed suppliant will be able to fall back onto the implied excuse for the failure of his prayer. 1 John 5:14 has a different device: "And this is the confidence we have in him, that if we ask anything according to his will, he hears us." Yes, one can be pretty confident that God will do what he was going to do anyway! Modern piety has yet another excuse at the ready: "God will answer your prayer, but he may answer 'no.'" But it is safe to say that no one renounces prayer for the little reason that it seldom gets the requested results, any more than anyone renounces reading the horoscope. Seemingly, all that is required is the momentary feeling of assurance.[8]

On the other hand, there may be something deeper going on. Elaine Pagels[9] argues that Saint Augustine contributed a similar double bind to Western Christianity by means of his doctrine of Original Sin. Whereas previous theologians took seriously the potency of baptism to regenerate sinners and to enable them to live sanctified lives, Augustine argued that even the baptismal gift of the Spirit did not significantly improve one's moral quality and, for this reason, Christians would be like straying sheep without the bishops and the church (not to mention the Roman Empire) to keep them safely in line: "Thy rod and thy staff, they comfort me." Specifically, lay Christians were to believe both that sex was inherently sinful and that the church absolved them of this necessary evil. Only the celibate could be perfect, and that left most folks out. Of course, we are back to the two-track system, one path for the Hinayana elite, the other for the Mahayana masses. The double bind, whether it is a question of perfect chastity or of perfect faith to move mountains, preserves the distinction between the spiritual elite, the gospel bodhisattvas, and their mass of cowed but grateful supporters. "We are taking the high road, the hard path, so you won't have to. But if you support us, it will be as if you had. God will transfer our merit to your account." This is very close to an atonement doctrine. The fourteenth-century heirs of the itinerant apostles, the Flagellants, made it an atonement doctrine pure and simple: they lashed and crucified themselves so as to bear the sins of plague-ravaged Europe.

Did the wandering apostles claim for themselves the power to move mountains? It is worth noting that 1 Cor. 13:1–3 depicts the claimed abilities and deeds of the charismatic apostles. They impressed their audiences with their revelations of mysteries and gnosis (cf. 1 Cor. 2:10–16). They had given away all they possessed. One of the most famous wandering Christian apostles, Proteus Peregrinus, gave over his body to be burnt, so that he might gain the glory of a martyr's crown (to adopt both readings of 1 Cor. 13:3—and, depending upon the date of this portion of 1 Corinthians, this is not improbably an actual reference to Peregrinus). Perhaps they claimed to be able to do these feats, boasting of their own power and implicitly denigrating and discouraging the congregation members, who must not learn to think of themselves as the apostles' equals lest they no longer feel the need for their ministry.

THE MONKEY'S PAW

And notice that the "faith" being discussed in all these prayer passages is a charismatic endowment, an active power of which one may possess and exercise more or less. "Having gifts that differ according to the grace given us: if prophecy, in proportion to our faith" (Rom. 12:6). Hence the language of having a little or a lot of it, and it being so rare that a single seed's worth would have cosmos-shaking results. The focus is on one's own will-force, not on God's ability, for if it were the latter, it ought to be a much simpler matter: Can the all-powerful God do what you ask, or can't he? Obviously he can. What else does faith need to know? How can there be a little or a lot of faith? Do you believe God can do it, or don't you? Your options are belief or atheism. But then this does not work, and since God cannot have failed, the blame must lie elsewhere, and you're the only remaining candidate. Ironically, it is only by denying that you have (enough) faith that you can retain your faith in God (whom one would have thought to have failed the test of answered prayer).

Why not say that God knows better than we do, and that he may withhold a requested blessing because he knows it might turn out like "The Monkey's Paw," and backfire? Not a bad idea, but it seems to be disallowed by Q (Matt. 7:9–11//Luke 11:11–13), where we read that God, like any earthly father, will not withhold any good thing from anyone who asks, implying that we can surmise well enough what is good for us and thus be quite confident we will get it. Q is no less optimistic at Matt. 7:7–8//Luke 11:9–10, where we are told it is as simple as knocking on a door and expecting someone to answer. Luke 11:5–8, 18:1–8 are a pair of Lukan creations aimed at dealing with the problem of unanswered prayer. They urge the supplicant not to give up, to keep pressing his request until God feels compelled to break his Deistic silence and grease the squeaky wheel. Luke 11:5–8, the parable of the Importunate Friend, is inserted right before the Q passage on asking, seeking, and knocking so as to head off the objection of the disappointed seeker: you gave up too quickly! The parable of the Unjust Judge (Luke 18:1–8)[10] makes the same point. Luke has similarly redacted the Q passage about God the giver of good things to those who ask (Matt. 7:9–11//Luke 11:11–13), omitting "good things" and inserting "the Holy Spirit" instead. Whereas one can tell whether specific good things requested did or did not arrive, the arrival of the Holy Spirit is presumably less easy to verify. If these texts were not all patently Lukan creations and secondary backpedaling in character, they would be ruled out as secondary simply by comparison with the Matthean advice not to chew the Almighty's ear: "And when you pray, do not say *batta* like the heathens do; for they imagine they will be heard for their prolixity. Do not be like them, for your Father knows what you need before you ask him" (Matt. 6:7–8). This saying, taking aim as it does against the tongues-speaking of the crazy-seeming Gentile Christians (1 Cor. 14:23), is Matthew's creation. But it witnesses to his ignorance of any teaching of Jesus to the effect that persistence in prayer pays off. For Matthew, it remains true that God will answer prayers; indeed he must.

The case is analogous to that of magic and religion: what was the advantage of religion over magic? Magic too often failed. You said the formula right, did the rain dance right, and still nothing happened. Magic was the belief in hidden natural laws that could be manipulated if one knew the technology of voice and gesture. Religion posits instead that all phenomena are controlled by personal wills like ours, those of the gods or ancestors or demons. We cannot control them, but we can petition them. It might not work; they might answer "no" for their own inscrutable reasons. If, as James Frazer said, religion replaced magic once magic's shortcomings were seen, how did it seem to be superior? It did not get more reliable results. No, but religion enabled you to save face. It could explain (sort of) the results if the desired blessing did not come. There was never any guarantee that it would. Magic had made a guarantee: it had to work, but it didn't work. Prayer might not work either, but you knew that going in. Thus, no uneasy feeling that you were barking up the wrong tree. Better to believe that, even if you and the shaman couldn't control nature, the gods could. You might not prefer the particular results you were getting, but you had the security of feeling that at least somebody was in charge.

In the same way, an almighty deity must answer prayer. There is no chance he might not be able to do it. If the prayer has not been answered, there must be another variable: your faith. And that meant miracles were wrought by your power (of faith), not by God. This is consistent with the assurance of Jesus to those he healed, "Your faith has made you well" (Mark 5:34). But the same story, that of the bleeding woman, makes it quite clear that it was Jesus' own supernatural power that healed her: "Jesus, perceiving in himself that power had gone out of him . . ." (verse 30). I should say that this passage perfectly illustrates, by means of this paradox, the sort of faith inculcated by our wandering apostles in their claimed power to work miracles. It is only faith that heals, if one is endowed with great amounts of it. The ailing woman illustrates the nature of that faith, but Jesus stands for the charismatic who alone is liable to have it. Yes, faith makes well, but you are not likely to have it. The man of God has it, and that is why you need him. Believe in his faith. It is vicarious faith.

LORD OF PRAYERS

Perhaps the most important gospel teaching concerning prayer is the Lord's Prayer (Q: Matt. 6:9–15//Luke 11:2–4). There is nothing especially remarkable about it. The criterion of dissimilarity is fatal for it. Consider the parallel prayers bequeathed us by contemporary Judaism. The *Qaddish* reads,

> Exalted and hallowed be his great name
> in the world which he created according to his will.
> May he rule his kingdom
> In your lifetime and in your days
> and in the lifetime of the whole house of Israel, speedily and soon.
> And to this, say: Amen.

Or this ancient evening prayer:

> Lead me not into the power of transgression,
> And bring me not into the power of sin,
> And not into the power of iniquity,
> And not into the power of temptation,
> And not into the power of anything shameful.

What we have is an ancient Christian prayer that, by its content, may as well have been simply borrowed from Jewish liturgy. It might have been written by anyone, but there is about as much reason to accept the ascription to Jesus as there is to accept the Twelve Apostles as the authors of the Apostles Creed. That said, let us look briefly at the prayer in both its versions and try to boil it down to an earlier, common text. Here we follow the majority of scholars in thinking that Matthew has padded out the prayer with bits of traditional Jewish liturgy and piety, while keeping the wording of the pre-Matthean petitions close to their original wording. (This fits Matthew's general tendency to expand his material more than Luke does, for example, the Beatitudes, the Sermon on the Mount, the Olivet Discourse.) Luke, on the other hand, seems not to have added any petitions (with one important exception), but to have reworded the petitions to some extent. And yet this is not beyond dispute, since Luke elsewhere shows the tendency to flatten out the poetry inherited from either Mark or Q. So conceivably he may have trimmed away such poetic parallelism from the Q version as struck him as superfluous. On the face of it, it would seem more likely for someone to add to the prayer than to cut any of it, given the sacred character of it (whether or not attributed to Jesus). If the prayer were gradually expanded with poetic and explanatory additions, this would certainly fit the normal process of liturgical evolution in which texts can be observed to grow in just this way, as for instance the eucharistic words of institution from gospel to gospel, and as the Lord's

Prayer itself has done from manuscript to manuscript in the process of copying. First, Matthew's additions.

"Our Father" fits Matthew's tendency to be extra reverent with the divine name. Jewish usage had long since judged the Tetragrammaton (YHWH) too sacred for common use, and the same sensitivity began to attach itself to the less sacrosanct "God" (Elohim). Thus, Matthew prefers circumlocutions and paraphrases (except when the Pharisees use them—Matt. 23:16–22). Thus, he usually (though not always, even in his own coinages) changes "kingdom of God" in Mark and Q to "kingdom of heaven," a common idiom of rabbinic piety.

"Who is in heaven" is a Mattheanism. "My/your Father in heaven" is a favorite Matthean phrase, lacking in Luke's version of the prayer. Matthew has often added "in heaven" to his source material.

"May your will be done on earth as it is in heaven." Matthew explains what it means for the kingdom of God to "come" in the Q petition he has glossed. Of course God reigns over the universe as king, but he has allowed the forces of evil to hold sway on earth in the present age, for whatever reason, and soon he will call a halt to this demonic occupation. Then he will reign de facto and not just de jure. The apocalyptic worldview thus mirrors, and no accident, the condition of Israel occupied for centuries by foreign powers. But God's will shall be done once he reigns unopposed. The same hope ignites Shi'ite passions today. Matthew has also added the phrase "May your will be done," or "Thy will be done," to Jesus' prayer in Gethsemane (26:42). In fact, "be done" appears often in Matthew but is rare elsewhere.

"But deliver us from the Evil One" is either a poetic expansion to provide an antithetical parallel to Q's "Lead us not into temptation" or another explanatory gloss to explain that the preceding phrase does not mean God would tempt you; rather it would be the devil, whom Matthew also calls the Evil One in Matt. 13:38. Now on to Luke's rewordings of the Q petitions.

"Give us *each* day our daily bread" modifies Q's "Give us *this* day our daily bread." Luke has added the same motif to the cross-bearing saying, "Whoever does not take up his cross daily . . ." (Luke 9:23).

He has changed Q's "Forgive us our debts" to "Forgive us our sins," which is the point anyway in Aramaic usage: "debts" one owes to God are sins. Luke has left Q's original unchanged in the following line, "as we forgive those indebted to us." But Luke has changed this last to "*everyone* indebted to us," reflecting his tendency elsewhere to add "each one," "everyone," and so on. Also, whereas Matthew retains Q's "as we have forgiven," Luke changes it to "for we forgive," meaning we are now entitled to receive God's forgiveness. It is like the Psalmists' protestations of innocence in the course of their petitions for help (e.g., Ps. 26).

According to some early manuscripts, as well as Marcion's Ur-Lukas, Luke's version had, instead of "May your kingdom come," "May your Spirit come upon us and sanctify us." If this is what Luke originally had, someone very early substituted the more familiar version. This reopens the question of whether Matthew has after all added "May your will be done on earth as it is in heaven." It suddenly looks as if "May your Spirit come upon us and sanctify us," with its parallel members, is a Lukan substitution for an earlier version that had two members—just like Matthew's version. So Q would have after all contained Matthew's version, Luke would have substituted his Spirit-version, and a harmonizing copyist would have restored the Q original, albeit in truncated form, just "May your kingdom come," as we presently read in most copies of Luke.

Did Luke change Q, adding a petition for the Spirit? Yes, he probably did. He does the same thing, after all, in Luke 11:13. Where Matthew, following Q, envisioned the Father giving "good things" to any who ask, for Luke it is the Holy Spirit he will dispense. And in Acts, chapter 1, when the disciples ask about the coming of the kingdom, Luke's Jesus answers with the coming of the Spirit (verses 6 and 8). This would leave the Q original as follows:

Father,
May your name be hallowed.
May your kingdom come;
May your will be done
On earth
As it is in heaven.
Give us today our daily bread.
And forgive us our debts
As we have forgiven those indebted to us.
And lead us not into temptation.

To this, in most manuscripts, has been added the Doxology: "For yours is the kingdom and the power and the glory for ever and ever. Amen." It must have been based on the wordy 1 Chron. 29:11, "Yours, O Yahve, is the greatness and the power and the glory and the victory and the majesty, for all that is in the heavens and in the earth is yours; yours is the kingdom, O Yahve, and you are exalted as head over all." It is first found attached to the Lord's Prayer in the *Didache* (late first–early second century) in this form: "For yours is the power and the glory for ever. Amen." Thereafter it shows up in various forms in the manuscripts of the Gospels.

FORGIVENESS AS A GIVEN

An important gospel teaching that pops up in the Lord's Prayer is that, if one hopes to be forgiven by God, one must be prepared to forgive others. God will not forgive the unforgiving. The same idea is found in Matt. 6:14–15//Mark 11:25–26 and in the Matthean parable of the Unmerciful Servant (18:23–35).

This one has in common with another Matthean creation, the Sheep and Goats scene in Matt. 25:31–46, a peculiar self-subversion paradox. As Matthew 25 urges upon the reader the very course of action for which the wicked goats were damned to hellfire, a cynical willingness to help the Son of man had they only known it was he, so does Matt. 18:23–35 demand heartfelt forgiveness, something one might think necessarily a matter of spontaneous free will,[11] under threat of eternal torture! "And in his anger his lord delivered him to the torturers till he should pay all his debt. So will my heavenly Father do to every one of you, if you do not forgive your brother from your heart." Yes, sir!

If we can at least hazard a guess as to what quarter of early Christianity the Lord's Prayer came from, we have not far to look. The petition for today's bread is most poignant if we envision as its *Sitz-im-Leben* the situation of the itinerant apostles. "Take no gold, nor silver, nor copper in your belts, no bag for your journey, nor two tunics, nor sandals, nor a staff; for the laborer deserves his food. And whatever village or town you enter, find out who is worthy in it and stay with him until you depart" (Matt. 10:9–11). "Do not be anxious about your life, what you shall eat or what you shall drink, nor about your body, what you shall wear. . . . Therefore, do not be anxious, saying, 'What shall we eat?' 'What shall we drink?' 'What shall we wear?' . . . Your heavenly Father knows that you need them all. But seek first his kingdom and his righteousness, and all these things shall be supplied you" (Matt. 6:25, 31, 32b–33). How interesting that the Lord's Prayer first "seeks" (asks for) the kingdom of God, then for his righteousness ("May your will be done"), and then for bread from God's providential hand. I say it is a creation of the itinerant prophets and apostles, bequeathed to their supporters.

THE MEDIOCRE ROBE

Of course, central to the Mahayana gospel for the masses was the obligation to support the wandering brethren. Matt. 25:41–45 promises salvation to those who have taken pains to meet the needs of the itinerants and equally damnation to those who had better things to do. The "least of these my brethren" are by no means to be identified with the poor and downtrodden generally (as traditional social gospel exegesis would have it), but rather those who are persecuted and jailed for their preaching as Paul so often was in Acts, those who are hungry and naked because their hearers shun their responsibility to be the channels of God's providential care like Diotrephes in 3 John, those who do not deem the worker deserving of his wages. It is the nations whom Matthew expects to be judged, because it is to the nations that he has the Risen Christ dispatching the brethren (28:19). Note that nothing is said of whether the nations have otherwise done righteously. They stand or fall according to whether they have been generous and attentive to the wandering brethren! Not even allegiance to Jesus is the criterion on Judgment Day, only whether one has contributed to the wandering apostles.

It is the rank and file, the householders, who are exhorted in Matt. 5:42//Luke 6:30, "Give to him who begs from you, and do not refuse him who would borrow from you." Such words are pointless when spoken to someone who has already renounced all his property! And the beggars must be the wandering brethren themselves. We may also be sure it is their voice we are hearing in Mark 14:7, "You always have the poor with you, and whenever you want you can do good to them; but you will not always have me."

In this shift from good works and keeping the commandments to attending to the itinerant prophets, the latter replacing the former as the focus of duty, we can see a significant evolutionary step toward faith in Jesus Christ as a vicarious savior. It is this very shift of focus that will make possible the rise of Jesus-centered faith. For people to be able to tap the itinerants' treasury of merit by exchanging for it concrete gifts (or "loans," given the anticipated return on Judgment Day) looks forward to a stage in which one's prayers to their successors, the saints, are themselves contributions of honor rendered by clients to their unseen patrons, brokers of God's grace. The increased store of honor thus accumulated by the patron, in heaven as on earth, is simply another name for the treasury of merit itself. It is worth asking whether Calvin, historically speaking, had things reversed: "Then in looking for patrons, everyone follows his own fancy. One selects Mary, another Michael, another Peter. Christ they very seldom honour with a place in the list. Indeed there is scarcely one in a hundred who would not be amazed, as at some new prodigy, were he to hear Christ named as an intercessor. Therefore, passing Christ by, they all trust to the patronage of saints."[12] May it rather be that Christ or Jesus was one name among many ("each one of you says, 'I am of Paul,' or 'I am of Apollos,' or 'I am of Cephas,' or 'I am of Christ,'" 1 Cor. 1:12), who gradually emerged from the crowd of saints to assume dominance? Or perhaps he was an idealization of the itinerant apostles themselves, as Avalokitesvara was, having never existed as a historical figure to begin with.

Notes

1. Oscar Cullmann, Appendix: "Traces of an Ancient Baptismal Formula in the New Testament," *Baptism in the New Testament*, Studies in Biblical Theology 1 (London: SCM Press, 1950), pp. 71–80.

2. Apuleius, *The Golden Ass*, trans. William Adlington, rev. Harry C. Schnur (New York: Collier Books, 1972), p. 276.

3. Max Scheler, *Problems of a Sociology of Knowledge*, trans. Manfred S. Frings, International Library of Sociology (London: Routledge & Kegan Paul, 1980), pp. 84–85; see also Adolf Holl's discussion of Scheler's point in *Jesus in Bad Company*, trans. Simon King (New York: Avon/Discus, 1974), pp. 47–49.

4. Thomas J. J. Altizer, *The Gospel of Christian Atheism* (Philadelphia: Westminster Press, 1966), pp. 31–40, 45–46; Altizer, *Mircea Eliade and the Dialectic of the Sacred*

(Philadelphia: Westminster Press, 1963), pp. 83–92, sees the same movement at work in the growth of theism generally: the definition of "man as sinner" and "God as transcendent" measures a mutual alienation between the human and the divine. Altizer is influenced here by Feuerbach, who similarly saw the creation of God as a stratagem by human beings to avoid living up to the standard of their own innate greatness.

5. Christopher Woodforde, "The Mirror of Man's Damnation," in *A Pad in the Straw* (London: J. M. Dent & Sons, 1952), pp. 24–35.

6. George M. Lamsa, *Gospel Light: Comments from the Aramaic and Unchanged Eastern Customs on the Teachings of Jesus*, rev. ed. (Philadelphia: A. J. Holman, 1939), pp. 35–37.

7. Joseph Chilton Pearce, "Don Juan and Jesus," chap. 9 in *The Crack in the Cosmic Egg: Challenging Constructs of Mind and Reality* (New York: Pocket Books, 1973), pp. 162–89.

8. Gustav Jahoda, "Superstition and Uncertainty," chap. 8 in *The Psychology of Superstition* (Baltimore: Penguin/Pelican Books, 1970), pp. 127–37.

9. Elaine Pagels, "The Politics of Paradise," chap. 5 in *Adam, Eve, and the Serpent* (New York: Random House, 1988), pp. 98–126.

10. Or at least the Lukan redaction of it—see Robert M. Price, *The Widow Traditions in Luke-Acts: A Feminist-Critical Scrutiny*, SBL Dissertation Series 155 (Atlanta: Scholars Press, 1997), pp. 191–201.

11. See Paul Watzlowick's discussion of this, the "Be Spontaneous" Paradox, in his *How Real Is Real? Confusion, Disinformation, Communication: An Anecdotal Introduction to Communications Theory* (New York: Random House/Vintage Books, 1977), pp. 19–21.

12. John Calvin, "The Necessity of Reforming the Church," in *Calvin: Theological Treatises*, trans. and ed. J. K. Reid, Library of Christian Classics, Ichthus Edition (Philadelphia: Westminster Press, 1954), p. 194.

CHAPTER TEN
JESUS AND JUDAISM

JESUS AND THE TORAH

In the present ecumenical climate, in which, thankfully, Jews and Christians are working to overcome their long hostility, there is a tendency among Christian and Jewish scholars alike to maximize the connection between the two faiths (something amenable to the Christian apologetical agenda, since this trend minimizes possible influences on early Christianity from Hellenistic Mystery Religions or Gnosticism). An important part of this interfaith program is to make Jesus as conventional a Jew as possible. In my opinion, such a move is more of a construction of Christology than a sketch of the historical Jesus. That is, it is an attempt to come up with a Christian "Jesus Christ" that will prove more useful for ecumenical dialogue. The a priori character of the whole endeavor is evident from the way such scholars simply assume that the gospel stories and sayings must be interpreted in Jewish categories even when there are as good or better paradigms available to make sense of the sayings, for example, Cynic or Gnostic. As long as there is a Jewish parallel available, even when forced, these scholars will automatically prefer it. This is theological reasoning, not historical criticism.

What *is* historical criticism is to recognize that the early Christians were wont to do the same sort of thing! The result is that various gospels have fashioned images of Jesus that accord with the particular evangelist's own understanding of the relationship of Christianity to the Torah. This, of course, is the factor that makes it so difficult to determine what, if anything, Jesus may actually have taught on the matter. We will briefly catalogue various possible frameworks in which to understand the relevant gospel materials, both the range of early Christian positions and the spectrum of Jewish attitudes. And, remember, according to the criterion of dissimilarity, the more Jesus' actions and teachings seem to conform to any of these positions, the less likely the material is authentic, or the more likely it is that Jesus was a considerably less interesting figure than generally thought, one more proponent of common views. That is the heavy price to pay for disregarding the criterion of dissimilarity.

THE EARLY CHURCH

On one end of the Christian spectrum, there were what Epiphanius of Salamis in the fourth century C.E. called "Jesseans" and "Nazoreans," Jewish baptizing sects overlapping the Essenes. These would never have used the term "Christians" of themselves. They would have been pious Jews who revered saints including Jesus, John the Baptist, James the Just, and perhaps Dositheus and Simon Magus. It is possible that internecine strife eventually broke these groups up into rival sects, with the Dead Sea Scrolls sect rallying to the memory of James the Just, the Righteous Teacher; the Mandaeans venerating John the Baptist; Simonians and Dositheans advocating the Gnostic teachings of their champions—and others revering Jesus the Nazorean. Since "Nazorean" meant "keeper" of the Torah (or possibly, of the secrets), we may picture this group as pious Torah observers, whatever mystical interpretations they, like later Kabbalists, may have put upon it.

Such believers detested the name of Paul, the Apostle to the Gentiles, because he dared say the Law was unnecessary for Gentile converts to the faith. Pagans could, in other words, become Christians without having to become Jews first. Paul saw Torah-observance (for which he uses circumcision as shorthand) as a false stumbling block placed in the way of pagans who might otherwise be eager to accept Jesus Christ and turn from idolatry and vain philosophy. Things like sabbatarianism, circumcision, and dietary laws had served to preserve the identity of the Jewish people, but Paul wanted to break down the old wall that separated Jews from Gentiles. To abolish requirements like circumcision would do this, admitting Gentiles into the household of faith along with Jews. The question that suggests itself is whether the wall would not remain after all, as long as Jews continued to keep the Torah when Gentile believers did not. Scholars cannot agree on whether Paul taught Jewish believers in Jesus that they could slough off the commandments, too. Either he did, or Jews inferred that he did (Acts 21:20–21), and he became the object of violent hatred among Torah Christians. They probably understood the danger of pulling down the wall between Jews and Gentiles. There were two ways to do it: either Judaize Gentiles, or assimilate Jews into the Hellenistic culture. One can see why they preferred the former to the latter alternative. It is difficult to identify the actual constituency of "Paulinism" in the early church. The first known Paulinists were the second-century Marcionites and Gnostics. They may have been the original Paulinists if the Pauline Epistles are, as the Dutch Radical School of W. C. van Manen and others, following Bruno Bauer, suggested, all late first– and early second–century products.

There appear also to have been a number of Christians, Jews as well as Gentiles by birth, who first embraced something like the Pauline point of view and then Judaized or accepted Torah observance on top of faith in Christ and baptism. Galatians seeks to win back a group of ex-Paulinists who were Judaizing. In our day, an analogy might be the growing number of African Americans who, like Malcolm X, first converted to the Nation of Islam (the faith of Elijah Muhammad and Louis Farrakhan) and subsequently realized that it was not quite the "real thing" when compared to historic Sunni Islam and then joined the latter. These would be the Nazarenes of whom Justin Martyr and Jerome inform us, Jews who embraced incipient Catholic Christianity but also kept the Torah. My guess is that we ought to locate the community of Matthew's gospel in this band of the spectrum. Justin tells us that, while some Nazarenes were content to grant Gentile Christians the right not to keep the Torah, others thought they must. The latter is plainly Matthew's view (Matt. 5:17–19, 28:20).

Ebionites (the Poor)[1] seem to have been direct descendants of the Jerusalem church. They revered James the Just and Peter and understood Jesus to have been the latest reincarnation of the True Prophet, a quasi-gnostic revealer who had appeared in the world first as Adam and many times thereafter as Enoch, Noah, Moses, and others. This type of Christology eventually gave rise also to Manicheanism and Islam,[2] and it provided the graft point for Sethian and Melchizedekian Gnostics to enter the Christian fold. The Ebionites were firmly committed to the Torah, but they had a revisionist understanding of it, cherishing a secret revelation from Jesus to the effect that the Torah contained numerous "false pericopes" interpolated by Satan's agents, the scribes and priests who thereby inserted their disgusting practices of animal sacrifice (among other things) into the text (cf. Jer. 7:21–22; 8:8). Valentinian Gnostics made the same claim, attributing various portions of the scriptures to angels and to Satan. Marcionites went the whole way and wrote off the Scripture (the Old Testament) as the product of the creator God, but not of the Father of Jesus, whom they deemed an entirely different deity first revealed by Jesus.

JEWISH SECTS

The most conspicuous Jewish party in the Gospels are the Pharisees, Jesus' main opponents. They would later claim their name meant *Perushim*, "pure ones," which certainly made good sense since they were a hasidic sect who, though laymen, sought to live every day within the strict standards of ritual purity required scripturally only of priests while on duty. They knew they were in this way going beyond the letter of the Torah, but they wanted to be as holy as possible. As E. P. Sanders has shown, there is no evidence that Pharisees despised or condemned as apostate those Jews who did not adhere to such strict standards.[3] People did, however, generally admire them and tended to accept the interpretations of the Torah offered by the scribes who led the sect. There were some six thousand Pharisees in Palestine in New Testament times, out of a total Jewish population of about five hundred thousand. And this was the largest of the sects. Most Jews belonged to none, so the Jewish sects were not quite analogous to Christian or Jewish denominations in our day. You could just be a faithful Jew, and most were.

"Pharisee" probably originally denoted "Parsee," or Persian Zoroastrian, and must have been a term of reproach cast at them by their enemies,[4] especially Sadducees who thought the Pharisees had gone off the deep end, adopting all manner of new-fangled heresies from Zoroastrianism, encountered in a major way during the Exile, under the Persian Empire. These doctrinal innovations included the notion of Satan as the evil archenemy of God (reinterpreting Satan along the lines of Ahriman, the antigod of Zoroastrianism), a vast angelology, the notion of an end-time deliverer who would raise the dead (the Saoshyant), the periodization of history in a predetermined apocalyptic timetable, and a pronounced ethical dualism of Light versus Darkness. None of these elements appears in pre-Exilic portions of the Old Testament, but they suddenly appear after the Exile, borrowed in all probability from Zoroastrianism. It would not have been hard to understand Ahura Mazda as another name of Yahve. Besides these new doctrines, Pharisees also practiced fasting, prayer, and almsgiving.

As to the Law, we have already seen how the Pharisees took upon themselves the yoke of round-the-clock ritual purity. Apparently by the same logic, they laid the groundwork for the rabbinic practice of "erecting a hedge about the Torah." This meant unpacking the literal commandments so as to stipulate exactly what counted as obedience and disobedience. For instance, the Torah forbids work on the sabbath day (Exod. 20:8–11). But did that mean one could not expend effort in recreation? Could you do some home carpentry for which no one paid you? Or was any unnecessary effort ruled out? Eventually, all possible acts were classified and ruled upon. It was a serious matter to keep the word of God. One had to try to get it right. Also, the hedge around the Torah implied creating a buffer of "safety net" rules that should prevent one from coming within breaking distance of the scriptural commandments. For example, the commandment not to take the name of Yahve in vain—what did it mean? As near as we can tell from Old Testament examples of people "taking the name of Yahve," it probably meant not to commit breach of contract (sealed in Yahve's name) or perjury (having sworn your testimony will be as true "as Yahve lives"). Did it also include magical conjuration? We don't know, and no one was too sure in New Testament times either. So the scribes thought it best to play it safe: let's not speak the name at all, with the sole exception of the High Priest, who uttered the sacred name once a year, on the Day of Atonement, inside the Inner Sanctum of the temple. They knew good and well that their ancestors had felt free to speak the name in various circumstances, and that the commandment could not have intended such strictness as they practiced. But the idea was to keep the commandment sacrosanct: if no one ever uses the divine name at all, there is precious little chance of anyone abusing it even by accident. The point is exactly the same in fundamentalist churches that forbid their members going to the movies. They don't think seeing *The Sound of Music* would be sinful in any way, but if one is free to decide for oneself which movies to go see, one may err, or yield to temptation, and go see *Debbie Does Dallas*.

The Sadducees were the elders of the temple, the aristocracy of Judaism. Most of the High Priests were of their number. Most scholars think their name denotes "Zadokites," the priesthood of David. The Dead Sea Scrolls sectarians referred to themselves as "Sons of Zadok." But it seems more likely that "Sadducees" is simply a version of the Greek word "Syndikoi," syndics, members of a board or syndicate.[5] The Sadducees were "the elders of the people," councilmen. We are told that they rejected the traditions (and the Zoroastrian doctrines) of the Pharisees, and even that they held only the Pentateuch (Genesis through Deuteronomy) as fully authoritative. They are also said not to have believed in life after death (certainly not taught in the Pentateuch) or angels and spirits (Acts 23:8)—perhaps they did not understand the "messengers" of God (which we are accustomed to translating "angels") in passages like Genesis 19 as referring to disincarnate spirits. It is unclear. The rabbis reviled the memory of the Sadducees (they disappeared along with the temple) as Greek-influenced rationalists and hedonists, calling them "Epicureans," just as the Sadducees had called the rabbis' own forbears "Parsees." The charge of hedonism meant to dismiss their lack of belief in an afterlife as fear of a final judgment that their sins would have given them reason to fear. That of rationalism was to discount their rejection of the Pharisees' doctrines, assuming they were divinely revealed, so that only rationalistic skeptics, not fellow biblicists, would reject them.

If the Dead Sea Scrolls are any evidence, the Essenes (described for us in Philo *Every Good Man Is Free* and *Apology for the Jews*; Josephus *Jewish War* Book II and *Jewish Antiquities* Book 18; and Pliny the Elder *Natural History* Book 5) were far more strict than the Pharisees. Rather than "merely" living like on-duty priests twenty-four hours a day, they deemed their communal monastic life the only true temple service, having written off the Jerusalem sanctuary as corrupted by hypocritical priests and erroneous rituals (especially the wrong calendar, the lunar rather than their own Enochian solar calendar). Some were celibate so as to devote their full attention to religion. They were vegetarians, presumably as a matter of fencing in the Torah, since in this way they could avoid any chance of eating meat improperly butchered. They were great believers in astrology and predestination. Light/dark dualism was very important to their outlook, as was a special *gnosis* of the angels and their secret names. They were in general pacifists, or better, quietists, awaiting the final War of the Sons of Light against the Sons of Darkness, when they would take up the sword of *jihad*. They were baptized daily to rid themselves of ritual impurity. Their canon of scripture was very wide. Copies of all Old Testament books (plus Hebrew Sirach, minus Esther) have been found at Qumran, along with whole or partial copies of books including 1 Enoch, Testaments of the Twelve Patriarchs, the Book of Jubilees, the Genesis Apocryphon, and others.

Samaritans[6] were the people of the old Kingdom of Israel, possibly mixed long since with other Semitic peoples, colonists from elsewhere in the Assyrian Empire. Their version of Hebrew religion evolved along a different path. It centered on their temple (destroyed by the Maccabees) on Mount Gerizim, where they believed one day the eschatological prophet like Moses would appear to reveal the lost temple vessels. As to the Torah, our concern here, they held only the Hexateuch (Genesis through Joshua) as canonical, dismissing the rest, understandably in view of its Judean (Southern) bias. They had no expectation of a Davidic Messiah or of the restoration of a Davidic monarchy. In this they were analogous to Anabaptist churches, pioneers of the separation of church and state, who regard the official patronage of the church by Constantine in the fourth century as a kind of Fall of the church. The Samaritans believed Hebrew history had gone off track with the establishment of the monarchy.

Géza Vermes[7] has called attention to still another group of Jews with whom Jesus may possibly have been connected, this time not a sect, but a particular class of legendary holy men, the Galilean hasidim. These were charismatic pietists and rainmakers, continuators of the line of ancient Israelite seers and fortune-tellers. Hanina ben Dosa (some of whose miracle stories we have already examined) is perhaps the most important of these figures. He flourished about 70 C.E., but a close second is Honi the Circle-Drawer (first century B.C.E.), and his grandson Hanan. (Honi would draw a circle around himself and inform God he would not move from it till God sent rain, and God, indulgent with his favorite, would accede to his petulance.) Some of the surviving legends, again, as we have seen, depict Hanina ben Dosa as known to the demons by name. They had to defer to him on account of his great holiness. In one story, a heavenly voice declares him "my son Hanina." Hanan, apparently representing the practice of these hasids, called God *Abba* (though the evidence, of necessity, is pretty fragmentary: there is not an awful lot of evidence *period*). It is obvious that similar stories were told of Jesus, which might mean he was another of these Galilean holy men, or that he has simply attracted to himself some of their typical legends as he did from Asclepius, Apollonius, Osiris, and others. This much was already implicit in our brief references to Hanina's miracles in our chapter on that subject. What interests us now, however, is that the pattern of the Galilean hasid entails a certain posture vis-à-vis the Torah. These men were notorious in their disregard for the niceties of the Law and thereby earned themselves the wrath of the conventionally orthodox. Though it may seem a light thing to us, Hanina aroused suspicion by the simple fact of walking alone by night. He owned goats, which the Mishnah forbade. He once carried the unclean carcass of a dead snake (the one who died from biting him). Another hasid was similarly lax, and Rabbi Joshua ben Hananiah found him to be ignorant of the very existence of one of the biblical laws of ritual uncleanness.[8] Another sneered at the Mishnaic prohibition against using liquids kept in an uncovered jar overnight. These notices provide dots to be connected to form the stereotype of a "loose cannon" holy man. As Jacob Neusner has shown,[9] a holy man is spotlighted in the rabbinic accounts only when he is used as a lesson of dangerous nonconformity. The idea is to admit the holiness of the individual, not to blacken his reputation as a heretic, and yet to make the point that safety is found within the mainstream and the majority opinion/practice of the sages. The views of the sages as a group are preserved anonymously because they are believed to agree with revelation, which has no human author. Neusner sees Jesus, or at least the Christian picture of Jesus as a charismatic outsider at odds with orthodoxy, as a signpost that the early Christian community had decided it would not go the way of emerging Mishnaic Judaism, would disregard majority rabbinic opinion in favor of a new halachah pioneered in the name of one of these charismatic holy men. Neusner's view comports well with the existence of a historical Jesus and his conformity to the type of the Galilean hasid.

But the case is not quite closed, because we must ask whether the Christian option of nonconformity stems from the nonconformist piety of Jesus himself (as Vermes would have it) or whether such a portrait of Jesus is not rather a function (a literary embodiment) of such heterodoxy. Whether a historical Jesus championed nonconformity to the Torah or parts thereof, he may yet have been adopted and refashioned in the image of those (like the wandering apostles) who occupied such a stance vis-à-vis the mainstream. Perhaps Gentile "Godfearers" who maintained a relationship of friendly rivalry and debate with the synagogue (Christians, some converts from Judaism, continued to attend synagogues for centuries)[10] used the figure and name of Jesus in their controversy stories written to embody their point of view. As Neusner reminds us, all we can really be sure of in such stories of holy heretics is that opinions fathered onto them are in debate, not whether their narrative instantiations genuinely represent history.

THE LAW OF CHRIST

Jesus is depicted in the Gospels in several contradictory ways when it comes to the matter of legal observance. Matthew's gospel presents Jesus not merely as a new Moses but virtually as a new Torah. As "Moses" and "Torah" had become practically synonymous, so would "Jesus" and "Gospel" become interchangeable, and for Matthew, Jesus is the new Torah. Matthew organizes the teachings he attributes to Jesus into five major blocs: The Sermon on the Mount (chapters 5–7), the Mission Charge (10), the Parables (13), the Manual of Discipline/Community Rule (18), and the Diatribe against the Pharisees/Olivet Discourse (23–25). The fact that he has squeezed the last two, rather different, topics together only underlines his urgency to get all the material into five sections, each of which ends with a similar statement: *"And when Jesus finished* these sayings, the crowds were astonished at his teaching" (7:28). *"And when Jesus had finished* instructing his twelve disciples, he went on from there to teach and preach in their cities" (11:1). *"And when Jesus had finished* these parables, he went away from there" (13:53). *"Now when Jesus had finished* these sayings, he went away from Galilee . . ." (19:1). *"When Jesus had finished* all these sayings, he said to his disciples . . ." (26:1). And yet this new Torah is in no way intended to replace the traditional one. It belongs to a curious genre of contemporary documents that provide a sort of "new edition" of the old Torah. Other examples are the Book of Jubilees and the Qumran Manual of Discipline. Thus, Matthew can have Jesus speak as if nothing at all has changed: "Do not think that I have come to abolish the Scriptures;[11] I have come not to abolish them but to fulfill them. For amen: I say to you, *till heaven and earth pass away, not a yodh, not a vowel point will pass from the Law until all is accomplished.* So whoever relaxes one of the least [important] of these commandments and teaches others [to do] so, shall be called least in the kingdom of heaven; but he who does them and teaches them shall be called great in the kingdom of heaven" (Matt. 5:17–19). Of all this, only the italicized portion is from Q, paralleled by Luke 16:17, "But it is easier for heaven and earth to pass away than for one dot of the Law to become [null and] void."

The Q saying thus isolated is already strange if we take it as a saying of Jesus, for it is a polemical proposition against someone who posits the Torah is obsolete. Who would Jesus have been talking to? Reform Jews? But the saying fits perfectly into the context of the Gentile Mission and the Pauline debate over the Torah, and that is where we have to leave the saying. The same goes for Matthew's homiletical expansion of the Q saying, just so no one misses the implication: no one is to go around, like Paul, teaching that Jesus came to abolish scripture so that some commandments are no longer binding. The *Sitz-im-Leben* (context in life) of this saying, too, is clearly that of early Christian debate, trying to invoke Jesus to rule on an issue he had never actually addressed, since, if he had, no debate would have subsequently arisen on the point.

It has struck many readers (and ought to have struck more) how strange it seems to have Jesus in one verse swear to the perpetuity of the Torah and then declare several portions outmoded! So great appears the contrast between the Torah commandments and the gospel alternatives that scholars have learned to call this passage (Matt. 5:21–48) the Matthean Antitheses, Matthean, because it seems the evangelist himself is responsible for pairing each old command with each new one.

The transition to the set of Antitheses from the programmatic statement that Jesus does not do away with the Law is Matt. 5:20, "For I tell you, unless your righteousness exceeds that of the scribes and Pharisees, you will never enter the kingdom of heaven." And then we pass into the sequence of contrasts, all framed with the formula, "You have heard it was said to the ancients . . . but I say to you. . . ." Sometimes Matthew fills in these blanks with earlier gospel material (from Q or Mark), but the unit as a whole is certainly his own, marked by his distinctive themes and vocabulary, for example, his special vendetta against the Pharisees. This simple observation is nonetheless worth noting since some scholars have used the Antitheses as imagined evidence that Jesus must have deemed himself greater than Moses, even divine, since he possessed what would otherwise be the awful effrontery to overturn the Torah. As we will see, though, not only do the Antitheses not go back to Jesus, but even if they did, their point is not at all to subvert the Torah.

In rapid-fire succession, we read that anger and insults are just as damning as murder itself (verses 21–22); that lusting for another man's[12] wife, even if the lust is not consummated, is just as immoral (or unfaithful) as the act of adultery (verses 27–28); that having so equivocal a reputation that a vow would be required of you is as bad as breaking a vow (verses 33–37). These are the first, second, and fourth Antitheses. They share a certain logic, that of building the fence around the Torah, keeping one's distance from the commandments, recognizing them as the final, not the initial, barriers to sin. If one can cut off the motive that leads to sin, one will not have to worry about breaking the commandment itself. This focus on inner motive rather than external action is what Adolf Harnack called the "higher righteousness"[13] of Jesus, higher than that of contemporary Judaism, which Matthew also thought, as these provisions constitute the righteousness that exceeds that of the scribes and Pharisees (Matt. 5:20). But in fact it does not. It appears, if we may trace backward the ethical trajectory of rabbinism into its direct ancestor Pharisaism, that the same moral distinction was traditional there, too. It was the distinction between mere *goodness* (the minimum requirement of obedience, out of the fear of God) and of superior *holiness* (the will to go the whole way, to approximate as closely as possible the whole will of God, out of love for God). The old rabbis even give three of the same examples: murder, adultery, and oaths. Western moderns are inclined to dismiss the "hedge around the Torah" approach as casuistic legalism, preferring this nobler-sounding ethic of motive, but it is a mistake to see any difference between them. There certainly was none in Jewish eyes.[14] After all, what is the origin of the impulse to erect a protective fence around the commandments if not a perfect (inner) zeal to honor and obey them? What else could have led anyone to join the Pharisee sect and adopt its "above and beyond the call of duty" approach to holiness, living all the day in a state of on-duty priestly purity—especially since they were not priests? It is unfortunate that the heat of sectarian rivalry has caused Matthew (and the Gospels generally) to vilify a group based on the will to perfect holiness as if it were a hypocrites' club specializing in hair-splitting legalism and the charade of externalism.

Another piece of rabbinic logic underlies the other three Matthean Antitheses, namely the willingness to forego what is permitted one by the Torah, since some commandments stipulated only the minimal requirements of goodness, knowing that most would never attain true holiness.[15] Hence some things, while legitimate, are not God's true will. For this reason, that the divorce commandment was accommodated to the hardness of the human heart,[16] Jesus counsels a higher path than divorce, especially in view of the fact that a divorced woman had no choice but to seek another husband to protect and provide for her, and this will make her, in a technical sense, an adulteress since the bond to her original husband still exists in the mind of God (Matt. 5:31–32). This one, by the way, comes from Mark 10:2–12, though he has softened Mark's more radical statement that divorce is always tantamount to adultery by adding a qualifier, μη επι πορνεια, "except for indecency," retrieved from Deut. 24:1.

By the same token, Matt. 5:38–39 has Jesus advise foregoing one's due access to the *lex talionis*, the law of retaliation, "an eye for an eye, a tooth for a tooth." It is not personal revenge-taking Jesus forbids but proper legal recourse: just swallow the offense and move on. You have the right to courtroom justice, but it would be better, nobler, not to avail yourself of it. In the same way, Matt. 5:43–44 counters a rabbinic inference from the ancient commandment to love one's neighbor (Lev. 19:18), that one might legitimately hate one's enemy (probably Gentiles are in view). No, as Q had it (Luke 6:27), the follower of Jesus must love his enemies. It is not, strictly speaking, that one does not have the right to hate them; it would be better to love them, since even God loves his enemies and treats them well.

To catch the difference between abrogating the law and protecting it from violation by making less likely the acts it forbids, think of the very different implications of abrogating the law of retaliation or of divorce and choosing to forego the privileges allowed by them. You may choose not to press charges and give a crook a break, but you wouldn't necessarily want to rescind the law against stealing. You might advise people to try and make yet another attempt at saving a failing marriage, but you wouldn't want to make it impossible for an abused woman to escape her lout of a husband by divorcing him.

Another important collection of relevant texts is the group of sabbath controversies. Two questions to ask here are, first, are they authentic? Second, is Jesus shown breaking, violating, overthrowing the sabbath commandment? Our exegesis must not be swayed by theological preference. Lutherans sometimes see Jesus overthrowing the Law, influenced, one might guess, by the Lutheran dichotomy between law and grace. Ecumenical theologians like to see Jesus as a pious, observant Jew. Another warning: we must bear in mind that it is by no means enough to point to the accusations of Jesus' enemies in the stories, who charge him with breaking the sabbath law. The point will be the nature of his response: is Jesus shown defending his breach of the Law (or of overthrowing the Torah in general)? Or is he rather shown defending his actions as faithful to the commandment, albeit by a different interpretation from that held by his opponents?

The first is Mark 2:23–28, where a group of Pharisees with nothing better to do on the sabbath spy on Jesus allowing his men to glean grain and then pop up behind the corn row to cite Scripture in condemnation. What seems to be the trouble, officer? It is not that they are helping themselves to grain someone else has grown. No, the Torah had centuries ago stipulated that the farmer must leave some grain at the edge of the field unharvested for the poor to collect, or "glean" (Lev. 19:9–10). Jesus and his disciples are mendicants, thus eligible. But must they glean *on the sabbath*? Jesus defends his hungry disciples with a citation of 1 Sam. 21:1–6, "Have you never read what David did, when he was in need and was hungry, he and those who were with him? How he entered the house of God when Abiathar was high priest, and ate the Bread of the Presence, which it is not lawful for any but the priests to eat, and also gave it to those who were with him?" Morna D. Hooker[17] considers the possibility that the argument hinges upon Jesus, as the Davidic Messiah, having the same privileges as King David himself. If that were so, we should certainly have an anachronism here, since even had Mark pictured Jesus thus flushing the messianic secret down the toilet, he would still be replacing a smaller controversy with a larger one. How could Jesus expect to win an argument about a point of sabbath observance by asserting grandiose messianic prerogatives? No, the point of comparison must be the poverty of both groups of men, his and David's, and their hunger, and the latter superseding the ordinary rules of holiness. Is his point cogent? It is hard to imagine any but Christian readers finding this reasoning persuasive. David's men do not in fact profane the Holy Bread; the priest allows them to have it only because they have taken care to maintain ritual cleanness by pregame celibacy and keeping a set of kosher dishes in their field packs. There is also the little problem of Abiathar, for he was not the High Priest in question: that was rather Ahimelech. Finally, Mark appends another saying: "The sabbath was made for man, not man for the sabbath," and then a paraphrase of the same: "Therefore the son of man is lord over the sabbath." The former is a rabbinic commonplace. We find the saying "The sabbath is delivered unto you; you are not delivered unto it" ascribed to several ancient rabbis. It is hard to picture a controversy over it, as we see in Mark. The weakest point in Jesus' rejoinder is simply this: what was stopping the disciples from gleaning enough grain the day before to tide them over (as the ancients had been commanded to do with the manna on the sabbath, Exod. 16:5)? The Pharisees forbade no one to meet emergency needs on the sabbath. Abba Tachno is said to have set aside the sabbath rules to help a leper in distress (*Midrash Ecclesiastes* 9.7 [41B]). Isn't Jesus really presented as arguing for mere *convenience* superseding the sabbath? If so, we have no sabbath rule at all.

Thus, the passage swarms with difficulties. The scriptural argument seems ineffectual. (Perhaps this is why Matthew supplemented Mark with two more scriptural arguments, 12:5–7). The reference to Abiathar is an error. The position of the Pharisees (at least as implied by early rabbinism, and we have no other evidence) is attributed to Jesus instead, who is made to argue with those who would have agreed with him. The failure to distinguish necessity from convenience smacks more of Gentile antipathy toward the prospect of adopting cultural mores alien to them. All these factors mark the saying as a product of the Gentile church that had only a vague acquaintance with Scripture or with Jewish thought. But it would be enough to rule the saying out as inauthentic that it makes Jesus defend the practice, not of himself, but of his disciples, that is, of the church. Otherwise, why not frame the debate in terms of why Jesus himself does what he does? For what it is worth, the saying seems to come from someone (like the superficially Judaizing Gentiles of Galatians; cf. Gal. 5:3) who felt obliged to keep the sabbath in some sense (like Seventh-day Adventists today) and thought he had mounted an argument in favor of extenuating circumstances for minimizing perceived sabbatarian legalism.

Mark 3:1–5 has Jesus, in a synagogue in Galilee, healing a man's withered hand on the sabbath. He defends his actions to the Pharisees, "Is it lawful on the sabbath to do good or to do harm, to save life or to kill?" Again, the tradition is both confused and unreliable, showing a lack of knowledge of first-century Judaism. First, there is no evidence for synagogues in Galilee. Second, the healing is so much like that of the king's withered hand in 1 Kings 13:1–6 that we must certainly consider it more probable that Mark has copied it. Third, the position here attributed to the Pharisees is unknown to us in any of our evidence, whereas we do have rabbinic passages that specifically allow healing by word (i.e., incantation, faith healing) on the sabbath, forbidding only the professional practice of physicians for money on the sabbath. Fourth, the words of Jesus ("or to *kill*?") do not reflect the situation seen by the characters in the scene but rather anticipate the conclusion, the secret collusion of scribes and Herodian agents to eliminate Jesus.

We have seen already that Luke's healing stories of the dropsical man (14:1–6) and the woman with the bent spine (13:10–17) are secondary creations by Luke himself, the former a vehicle for the Q saying that appears in Luke 14:5, the latter a vehicle for a paraphrase of the Q saying. Both presuppose that anyone, including Pharisees, would do a simple kindness to a farm animal on the sabbath, so why not do a good deed (of healing) for a human being on the sabbath? The whole argument depends on being able to assume that Pharisees, too, would free an animal from a ditch on the sabbath, but, as Neusner points out, our evidence shows the Pharisees would by no means have agreed.[18] Eliezer ben Hyrkanus and Joshua (Javneh rabbis) deny that one may remove the trapped animal on Passover, much less the sabbath, unless one intends to slaughter it for the feast; otherwise one must feed it where it is until the holy day is past. "Eliezer says that if an animal and its offspring fall into the pit on the festival, one raises the first on condition of slaughtering it and does slaughter it, and feeds the second in its place, so that it will not die. Joshua says one does not actually slaughter the first, and then raises the second to slaughter that one. So he is able to remove both from the pit" (*Tosefta* Y. T. 3:3). The Dead Sea Scrolls community also refused to lift the trapped animal out on the sabbath: "No man shall assist a beast to give birth on the sabbath day. And if it should fall into a cistern or a pit, he shall not lift it out on the sabbath" (*Damascus Covenant* 11).[19] Again, as far as we can tell, the gospel writers just do not seem to have known Jewish practice.

But even if all had agreed the poor animal might have been rescued, the synagogue superintendent in chapter 13 would still have the better of the argument: "There are six days on which work ought to be done; come on those days and be healed, and not on the sabbath." Is one more day going to make any difference? No one's life is at stake. Assuming that people like the woman with the spinal condition could have had recourse to Jesus on some other day of the week, Jesus' rejoinder seems very lame because the vast difference between the woman and the animal is that between livestock, who lack the freedom to choose whether to fast on the sabbath or to stay in the ditch, and humans, who can and should take the trouble to keep the sabbath. But we need hardly blame it on Jesus, since the location in an anachronistic synagogue and its misrepresentation of the Pharisee opinion on faith healing on the sabbath both mark the saying as too late for Jesus.

A fascinating pericope that appears only in a single manuscript (Codex Bezae) of Luke, following 4:4, reads: "On the same day, seeing a man carrying wood on the sabbath, he called out to him, 'Man, blessed are you if you know what you are doing. But if you do not know what you are doing, cursed are you, and a transgressor of the law.'" The only historical *Sitz-im-Leben* we know of where this would make any sense is that on display in Romans, chapter 14, where on the one hand the observance of holy days is a pious act if one understands it so, while on the other, rejoicing in one's liberation from the shackles of sabbatarian legalism is equally pious. Accordingly, if the man carrying the wood understood his act as compatible with piety, fine; Jesus salutes him. But if, like Rabbi Zwi Chaim Yisroel, he "regarded God's covenant with Abraham as 'just so much chin music,'"[20] Jesus says he is in big trouble. Given the stress on "knowing what he is doing," we should perhaps even think of the Gnostic libertines of 1 Corinthians, chapter 8, who believe they can partake of idol sacrifice banquets without qualm, knowing that the pagan rite is just a sham anyway. For the man of knowledge (the "Gnostic"), all things are lawful.

If this were not enough to remove the passage from the context of Jesus as usually imagined, there is also the manifest fact that the episode is an exact antithetical parallel to Num. 15:32–36, "While the people of Israel were in the wilderness, they found a man gathering sticks on the sabbath day. And those who found him gathering sticks brought him to Moses and Aaron, and to all the congregation. They put him in custody, because it had not been made plain what should be done to him. And Yahve said to Moses, 'The man shall be put to death; all the congregation shall stone him with stones outside the camp.' All the congregation brought him outside the camp, and stoned him to death with stones, as Yahve commanded Moses." Someone in the early church is here trying to counter a provision of the old Law with one from the new. But whether Jesus taught anything one way or the other on sabbath observance, we cannot tell. Nor can we simply assume, by default, that, being a Jew, he must have been a pious sabbatarian.

Is any position on purity laws attributed to Jesus? Yes, indeed. In Mark 7:5 the Pharisees and scribes demand to know why Jesus' disciples eat without ritually washing their hands. (This was purely a matter of ceremonial purity, not hygiene.) "Why do your disciples not conduct themselves in accordance with the tradition of the elders, but eat with hands defiled?" We do not hear any direct answer. The challenge is just a springboard for a general Markan attack on scribal tradition. Once again, the fact that it is the practice of the disciples and not of Jesus himself that comes into question is a dead giveaway that the story originated amid the deliberations of the early Christians. Not only that, but in verses 3–4, where Mark explains to his obviously Gentile readers the quaint customs of the Jews (as if he were writing a travelogue about some remote tribe), he gets it wrong: "For the Pharisees, and for that matter, all the Jews, do not eat unless they wash their hands, observing the traditions of the elders; and when they come from the market place, they do not eat unless they purify themselves; and there are many other traditions which they observe, the washing of cups and pots and vessels of bronze and beds." Mark has observed the purity behaviors of Diaspora Jews and gratuitously assumed Palestinian Jews observed the same rules. Though they did of course have purity laws, the ones Mark mentions were necessitated by the fact that Diaspora Jews, unlike their counterparts in the Holy Land, lived among a pagan majority that threatened to contaminate the purity of their own subculture by simple proximity. Even the reference to Pharisees and scribes having come to Galilee from Jerusalem betrays anachronism, preserving in garbled form the fact that Pharisees and scribes took refuge in Galilee only after the fall of Jerusalem in 70 C.E.

Having introduced the note about scribal tradition, Mark follows it up with more material of his own creation, "Isaiah prophesied well of you hypocrites, as it is written, 'This people honors me with their lips, but their heart is far from me; they worship me in vain, teaching for their doctrines man-made precepts.' You spurn the commandment of God, and cling to the tradition of men." This cannot be authentic either, since the whole argument is predicated on a prooftext from Isaiah in the Greek Septuagint: "teaching for their doctrines the precepts of men," while the original Hebrew has, "their fear of me is a commandment learned by rote," which does not fit Mark's point. Mark knew the Septuagint and quotes it as naively as we might quote the King James Version simply as "the Bible." But for Jesus and the Jerusalem scribes, "the Bible" would have been some version of the Hebrew Tanakh.

Mark next paraphrases the previous sentence as a kind of redactional seam to apply the principle of the Septuagint Isaiah quote to another specific issue:

"And he said to them, 'You have a fine way of rejecting the commandment of God, in order to keep your tradition. For Moses said, "Honor your father and mother," and "He who speaks evil of father or mother, let him die the death." But you say, "If a man tells his father or his mother, 'What you would have gained from me is *Corban*, that is, an offering [to the temple],' then you no longer permit him to do anything for his father or mother, thus nullifying the word of God through your tradition which you hand on. And many such things you do"'" (verses 9–13). There is no feel of real dialogue here, just pedantic expository prose, especially the generalizing conclusion. It sounds like a Markan treatise, which is exactly what it is.

It is interesting to compare this tirade with the Matthean Antitheses, in that both juxtapose a biblical commandment to a more recent one: "You have heard it was said [by God through Moses], *You shall not kill*, but I say to you, *Whoever is angry with his brother is no better than a murderer*." "Moses said, *Honor your father and mother*, but you say, *Don't bother*." In both cases it is a question of whose midrash on the written commandments is to be accepted: Christian or (ostensibly) rabbinic?

The abuse Jesus is here made to attack certainly existed, but as it happens, we know about it not because contemporary rabbis advocated it, as Mark/Jesus implies. Rather, all who mention it attack it. The maverick Javneh rabbi Eleazer ben Hyrkanus held that honoring one's parents was sufficient cause to break a vow. His views are often rejected as reasonable but heterodox. But we find the same sentiment ascribed to others. Rabbi Obadiah of Bertinova said, "When a man, by a vow, deprives his father of his property, the sages open a way for him" to get out of it. Similarly, Rabbi Gershom said, "When he vows things required by his father and mother, the sages open a way for him."

Has Mark again vilified the Jews out of ignorance of their opinions? Maybe, though it is possible some held the view attacked by Jesus, Eleazer, Obadiah, and Gershom, but that they were so soundly trounced in debate that their views did not survive in the Mishnah. And yet, no evidence is no evidence. On the other hand, insofar as Mark has attributed to Jesus a halakhic opinion common to scribal opinion, the criterion of dissimilarity rules it out anyway. There is no reason that the opinion, which seems to have made the rounds of attribution to various rabbis whether or not each actually said it, could not as easily have been ascribed to Jesus because it sounded good to Christians.

Mark moves on to the kosher laws (verses 14–23). Here we have left behind acts of tradition and supererogation, like hand-ablutions. We have graduated as well from cases of unintended ramifications like Corban. Now we are talking about the very statutes of Torah, which are righteous altogether, which purify the soul, which are more to be desired than honey and the honeycomb. Only the apostate from Israel denies them. Will Jesus? At the center of this sequence is what sounds like a traditional saying, found also in Thomas 15c, "What goes into *your mouth* will not defile you, but what comes out of *your mouth*, that will defile you." This version of the saying is a piece of Hellenistic rationalism, disdaining food purity laws in favor of moralism: a man's evil words contaminate him if anything does. Mark's secondary interpretation of this "parable" or riddle moves in this direction, pedantically stipulating all manner of evil thoughts and deeds (verses 21–23). But another comment (verses 18–19) takes a different approach. It speaks not, as Thomas does, of what goes into and out of "a man's mouth," but into and (implicitly) out of "a man." That is, what comes out may exit via a different orifice than it entered. "Do you not see that whatever goes into a man from outside cannot defile him, since it enters not his heart but his stomach, and on into the toilet?" The implication seems to be that it is the food, whether technically kosher or not, that defiles since it goes into and *comes out* of a man, ending in the commode, where it has become defiling feces. If all kosher food is so destined, how kosher can it be? This sort of sarcastic lampoon sounds much like Cynicism and may have originated there. In any case, the denial, common to all three version, that what enters a man cannot defile him, would seem to render kosher laws superfluous.

And yet there is an element of ambiguity. Mark goes on to add a conclusion, not even bothering to put it into the mouth of Jesus, "Thus he declared all foods clean." Why? Didn't he think the preceding material was already clear enough in its implications? Perhaps he did not. After all, all the Torah-zealot Matthew did when he copied this portion of Mark was to omit Mark's comment, apparently feeling that was enough to remove the sleight to the Torah. Apparently, Matthew did not think the rest of the material he took from Mark was by itself anti-Torah. But how could he not? We may have a parallel in a story about Matthew's contemporary Johannon ben Zakkai. One day an idolater asked him if the ritual of the red heifer really purified uncleanness incurred by contact with the dead. Wasn't this just magic? Johannon agreed that it was, but then, he asked, why should the Gentile ridicule it when the Gentiles followed their own superstitions? Abashed, the pagan departed. But the rabbi's disciple was shocked and asked his master if he really believed what he had just said. He replied, "By your life! It is not the dead that defiles nor the water that purifies! The Holy One, blessed be he, merely says, 'I have laid out a statute. I have issued a decree. You are not allowed to transgress my decree'" (*Numbers Rabbah* 19.8). It is conceivable that Jesus' remarks in Mark 7 imply the same thing. But it seems to me unlikely, since without an explanation such as that given by Johannon ben Zakkai we should never have guessed such thinking left room for the continued observance of the purity laws. And in Mark there is no such explanation. (From his standpoint, Matthew should have made it clearer that he disagreed with Mark's judgment, but we can tell that he did by the simple expedient of seeing that he omitted the closing comment.)

So Mark presents Jesus as abrogating kosher laws, while Matthew thinks he did not. Is there any other evidence? Acts, chapters 10–11, paint a clear picture of Jesus' disciples still keeping kosher decades later. It takes a direct revelation from the Holy Spirit to make Peter change his mind, and it takes his relating of the same vision to his colleagues in Jerusalem to get them to change their minds. How is it possible that if Jesus really had said any of the things Mark has him say in Mark 7 that Christians could be found many years later shocked at the very suggestion of eating "unclean" food? "God forbid, Lord! For I have never eaten anything that is common or unclean" (Acts 10:14). It is not that the Acts story must be historically true. It is just that Luke would never have written such a fiction, if that is all it is, if Christians had always known Jesus had settled the issue for them back in Galilee. Rather, we must assume that the Mark 7 material is another contribution, like Acts 10–11, to the post-Jesus debate over whether Christians (especially missionaries) might eat nonkosher food.[21]

Some have seen in Mark 5:24b–34 evidence that Jesus disregarded purity laws by being willing to touch the hemorrhaging woman. This is absurd and would be even if the story were authentic (see our discussion of it in chapter 7 on miracles). After all, Jesus does not initiate contact with the woman, but he does venture to touch the leper in Mark 1:41. If we, because of our study of the Bible and the Mishnah, discern a ritual purity issue here, that does not mean that Mark did. In fact, his apparent obliviousness of the whole issue, which he does not mention, might imply his ignorance of Jewish custom, and as a result the inauthenticity of the stories, as in Thomas, where the evangelist appears to think nothing of the gross incongruity of a Samaritan carrying a lamb to Jerusalem for Passover (60). Besides this, it is to misunderstand the nature of the purity laws to imagine that a faithful Jew would feel himself forbidden by them to touch a sick person to help him. If that were the case, there would have been no midwives, no butchers, no undertakers, no physicians. Any number of daily obligations might cause one to become "unclean" till the sun went down or till one could manage the proper ablution. It wasn't that big a deal.[22] Think of Luke's parable of the Good Samaritan, where it is perhaps the ritual purity of the priest and the Levite, on their way to Jerusalem for the temple service, that prevents them from stopping to help the bloodied victim of robbers. Obviously the parable holds these sacrosanct hypocrites up to scorn, assuming that any reader will take for granted that purity laws must always yield to human need. Would it have been revolutionary, or a disdain for purity laws, that would have moved Jesus to heal the leper or the bleeding woman? Nonsense.

Jesus assails the Pharisees in a Q saying (Matt. 23:23//Luke 11:42) for their skewed perspective that enables them to major in minors. "Woe to you, scribes and Pharisees, hypocrites! For you tithe mint and dill and cumin, and have neglected the weightier matters of the law: justice, mercy, and faithfulness. These you ought to have done, without neglecting the others." I have quoted Matthew's version. Luke's has some minor differences, but Codex Bezae omits from Luke the phrase "without neglecting the others," which has the ring of an afterthought anyway. I think Codex Bezae has preserved the original text of Luke here. If so, then we must choose between the Matthean and Lukan versions to get back to the

Q original. And there, too, the choice is clear. Matthew has no problem with scribal halakhah in general: "The scribes and Pharisees occupy Moses' seat;[23] so practice and observe whatever they tell you, but not what they do; for they preach and do not practice" (Matt. 23:2–3). I suspect he did not like Q's apparent disdain for minutiae like tithing herbs just in case the farmer had not tithed them as he should have, so he added the pedantic "not that there's anything wrong with that!"

Did Jesus attempt to reduce the whole Torah to a single commandment or pair of commandments, a reduction to essentials? He is asked by a scribe in Mark 12:28–34: which is the greatest (most important) commandment of the six hundred thirteen in the Torah? Matt. 22:35 and Luke 10:25 make this a trick question, but it is entirely legitimate in a Jewish context. It was certainly no heresy to rank the commandments. Jesus nominates two. Number one is the Shema from Deuteronomy, "Hear, O Israel! Yahve your God is one, and you shall love Yahve your God with all your heart, soul, mind, and strength." The second, almost as important and nonnegotiable, is Lev. 19:18, "You shall love your neighbor as yourself." Some are eager to make this statement equivalent to Gal. 5:14, "For the whole law is fulfilled in the commandment, 'You shall love your neighbor as yourself.'" Given the context of Galatians as a whole, the point would have to be that one need not bother with the whole raft of commandments so long as one conducted oneself in love. But there is no reason to read Jesus that way in Mark 12:28–34. Rather, one should compare the passage to the story of Hillel: once an impudent Gentile accosted Rabbi Hillel and told him he would be quite willing to convert to Judaism if the good rabbi could just teach him the whole law while standing on one foot. Hillel readily agreed, saying, "What is hateful to you, do not do to your neighbor. This is the whole law. The rest is commentary; go and learn it." The notion of "plenary inspiration" invites the abuse of leveling the whole text, as if it were all of the same quality and value. Judaism escaped this trap by ranking the laws, even by reducing them to many implications of a single principle. But it never saw this as an excuse no longer to keep them. So the opinion attributed to Jesus in Mark 12:28–34 may well be that of the historical Jesus, but the criterion of dissimilarity cannot tell us so, for to accept the saying would again make Jesus simply one more name on a list of people who assented to the notion. And this he may have been, but we cannot be sure of that, either, since we have to reckon with the likelihood that, as in the Mishnah, the same opinion may be variously attributed to many names, none necessarily authentically.

Did Jesus approve or practice sacrifice in the temple? Here we face two opposed texts. The Gospel of the Ebionites has Jesus come out swinging against the practice: "I have come to destroy sacrifices; and if you do not cease sacrificing, the wrath [of God] will not cease from you." As much as we might prefer Jesus to have held such sentiments, given our distaste for bloody sacrifice, this saying cannot be authentic because of the retrospective theology of it: "I came to. . . ." And it is tendentious, that is, it fits just too well the dogmatic viewpoint of the Ebionites, tailormade, and thus unavailable by virtue of the criterion of dissimilarity. The opposite text has the same problem: "If you are offering your gift at the altar, and there remember that your brother has something against you, leave your gift there before the altar and go; first be reconciled to your brother, and then come and offer your gift" (Matt. 5:23–24). This uniquely Matthean text should really have been included in his fourth bloc of teaching, his manual of discipline for the Christian community.

A similar text is that of the temple tax, or two-drachma tax (Matt. 17:24–27). Both do not assert, but simply assume in passing, that (Matthean) Christians patronize the Jerusalem temple. This need not bode well for a pre-70 C.E. date, much less for authenticity. The sayings could easily stem from after 70 C.E. by analogy with the Mishnah in which the rabbis debate fine points of the temple service in order to prepare, as the drafters of the Priestly Code of the Pentateuch did, for the day when a new temple should be built.[24] All such discussions are phrased as if the temple were still standing. But the "leave your gift" saying is of a piece with traditional Judaism such as we read in Isaiah, chapter 1, and Entrance Psalms such as 15 and 24, where the wicked and unrepentant are told not to bother showing up. The criterion of dissimilarity tells us we have no reason to accept it.

The taxation story has problems of its own. While this one does mention the practice of Jesus himself, not just that of his disciples, it is hard to escape the impression that the same point, winking to the reader that it is really Christian practice in question, is being made when we read "Give it to them for me *and for yourself*" (verse 27). Besides this, there is the peculiar ecclesiology implied in the parable, where the Jewish Christians occupy the position traditionally predicated of all Jews, that of sons of God, while the rest of Jewry now takes the subordinate place traditional for the Gentiles, as mere slaves. The same contrast between Christian and non-Christian Jews is drawn in John 8:31–36 ff. Both come from a time long after that of Jesus, a later period in which stark lines of separation and sectarian rivalry have been drawn. This presupposes considerable historical development and is thus anachronistic for Jesus.

Obviously, the story of the Cleansing of the Temple is relevant to this topic, but at present suffice it to say that the actions of Jesus in shutting down the sacrifices for some hours have been interpreted in opposite ways (a moratorium on sacrifice until the people repent to Jesus' satisfaction, or a protest against the sacrificial system in favor of prayer, period) and is equivocal.

Once again, we are left without adequate evidence for what Jesus may have thought or taught about issues of Judaism and the Torah. Early Christians of various tribes made and remade Jesus to accord with their views on these as other issues. Ecumenical theologians continue the same process today. Their efforts are understandable, commendable in motive, but in the long run, as methodologically unsound as the analogous scholarly conceits of Afrocentrism.

Notes

1. Hans-Joachim Schoeps, *Jewish Christianity: Factional Disputes in the Early Church*, trans. Douglas R. A. Hare (Philadelphia: Fortress Press, 1969), pp. 38–98.

2. Tor Andrae, *Muhammad: the Man and his Faith*, trans. Theophil Menzel (New York: Harper & Row Torchbooks, 1960), pp. 98–108.

3. E. P. Sanders, *Jesus and Judaism* (Philadelphia: Fortress Press, 1987), pp. 180–81.

4. T. W. Manson, *The Servant Messiah: A Study of the Public Ministry of Jesus* (Cambridge: Cambridge University Press, 1953), pp. 18–19. For other perspectives on the Pharisee sect, see W. D. Davies, *Introduction to Pharisaism*, Facet Books, Biblical Series 16 (Philadelphia: Fortress Press, 1967); Ellis Rivkin, *A Hidden Revolution: The Pharisees' Search for the Kingdom Within* (Nashville: Abingdon Press, 1978); Jacob Neusner, *The Pharisees: Rabbinic Perspectives* (New York: Ktav, 1973); Hyam Maccoby, *The Mythmaker: Paul and the Invention of Christianity* (London: Weidenfeld and Nicolson, 1986); Sanders, *Jesus and Judaism*, pp. 187–99.

5. Manson, *The Servant Messiah*, pp. 15–16.

6. R. J. Coggins, *Samaritans and Jews: The Origins of Samaritanism Reconsidered*, Growing Points in Theology (Atlanta: John Knox Press, 1975); James Alan Montgomery, *The Samaritans: The Earliest Jewish Sect: Their History, Theology and Literature* (1907; repr., New York: Ktav, 1968); John MacDonald, *The Theology of the Samaritans*, New Testament Library (London: SCM Press, 1964).

7. Géza Vermes, "Jesus and Charismatic Judaism," chap. 3 in *Jesus the Jew: A Historian's Readings of the Gospels* (Glasgow: Collins/Fontana, 1977), pp. 58–82.

8. "Once, while he was on his way to synagogue to celebrate the sacred Jewish holiday commemorating God's reneging on every promise, a woman stopped him and asked the following question: 'Rabbi, why are we not allowed to eat pork?' 'We're *not*?' the Rev said incredulously. 'Uh-oh.'" Woody Allen, "Hassidic Tales, with a Guide to Their Interpretation by the Noted Scholar," in *Getting Even* (New York: Vintage Books, 1978), pp. 50–51.

9. Jacob Neusner, *Why No Gospels in Rabbinic Judaism?* Brown Judaic Studies 135 (Atlanta: Scholars Press, 1988), pp. 70, 72; Neusner, *In Search of Talmudic Biography: The Problem of the Attributed Saying*, Brown Judaic Studies 70 (Chico: Scholars Press, 1984), pp. 26–127, 133–35.

10. Rodney Stark, *The Rise of Christianity: A Sociologist Reconsiders History* (Princeton: Princeton University Press, 1996), pp. 65–71.

11. Literally, "the Law and the Prophets."

12. I do not mean to use sexist language. Rather, the point is that, like the Torah itself, the Sermon on the Mount is pictured as directed at men, though Matthew does occasionally show women present to hear Jesus teach; 14:21, 15:38.

13. Adolf von Harnack, *What Is Christianity?* trans. Thomas Bailey Saunders (New York: Harper & Row Torchbooks, 1957), pp. 70–74.

14. Schechter, *Some Aspects of Rabbinic Judaism*, pp. 210–15.

15. Already a Jewish principle: ibid., p. 210.

16. Ibid., p. 210.

17. Morna D. Hooker, *The Son of Man in Mark: A Study of the Background of the*

Term "Son of Man" and Its Use in St Mark's Gospel (Montreal: McGill University Press, 1967), pp. 97–102.

18. Neusner, *In Search of Talmudic Biography*, p. 114.

19. Géza Vermes, trans., *Dead Sea Scrolls in English* (Baltimore: Penguin Books, 1975), p. 113.

20. Allen, *Getting Even*, p. 51.

21. It is amazing to me that Perrin, *Rediscovering the Teaching of Jesus*, p. 150, could regard Mark 7:15 as authentic, since it fits so well into the situation of the Gentile church, for example, Rom. 14:17, "For the kingdom of God is not food or drink, but righteousness, peace, and joy in the Holy Spirit."

22. Sanders, *Jesus and Judaism*, p. 183.

23. In view here is the seat of Moses, a cathedrum occupied by the rabbi in a synagogue able to afford such an ornate throne. But we have no evidence of them in the first century C.E. J. Andrew Overman, *Matthew's Gospel and Formative Judaism: The Social World of the Matthean Community* (Minneapolis: Fortress Press, 1990), p. 145.

24. Neusner, *In Search of Talmudic Biography*, pp. 81, 95.

CHAPTER ELEVEN

THE ANOINTED ONE

JESUS AS THE CHRIST

Whatever else Jesus is or was, Christian tradition has made him, paramountly, "the Christ," the Messiah or Anointed One. Did Jesus claim such dignity for himself? What would such a claim have meant? In what kind of context would it have been made? For we cannot be too sure too quickly that we already know what the epithet means. Here we will first survey the probable evolution of the concept "Messiah," then ask how Jesus came to be hailed as Messiah. This will entail a side-trip into both the contemporary Mystery Religions in which "messiah" had an entirely different connotation, as well as the eschatological (end of the age) preaching attributed to Jesus in the Gospels. Nor can we escape examining the gospel passages in which Jesus seems to claim the title/office of Messiah.

SACRED KINGSHIP

The Messiah idea exists for one purpose: to reinforce the divine right of kings. It comes from the "royal ideology" of the Davidic monarchy. Sigmund Mowinkel's *He That Cometh: The Messiah Concept in the Old Testament and Later Judaism*[1] is the classic treatment. As all Bible students know, the very institution of the monarchy was simply lifted from the nations surrounding Israel, replacing an earlier, much looser tribal confederation (1 Sam. 8:4–5). It should come as no surprise then, that the accoutrements of the institution were borrowed, too, lock, stock, and barrel (which is what the warnings against monarchy in 1 Sam. 8:10–18 and Deut. 17:14–20 were concerned with). Among these was an ideology exalting the king's authority to that of a god on earth. The propaganda value of this is obvious: what would Richard Nixon not have given for such an aura of, or legitimation for, absolute power?

This is why the king of Judah could actually be addressed as God (Ps. 45:6–7, a royal wedding song) or as the earthly son of God (Ps. 2:7, a birth oracle or coronation song—see below) just like the Egyptian Pharaohs, whose names denoted their divine parentage: Thutmose (Son of Thoth), Ramses (Son of Ra). When each new king was crowned, he came into possession of his divine status or nature, and hopes were expressed for a reign of perfect righteousness, universal justice and amnesty to prisoners, even peace among animals. Court prophets would deliver stereotyped oracles predicting all these great boons and blessings to issue forth from the new monarch's reign. It appears that the same sort of glad tidings were issued at the birth of each new royal heir, and it is hard to tell the difference between such birth oracles and the related coronation oracles. We find the same pattern attested for the sacred kings of ancient Iran. And we ought to note that all Judean kings were "Messiahs," anointed with oil as a symbol of consecration to their office. This, too, we find in Psalm 2.

Now we are in a position to recognize that several passages that were reinterpreted by New Testament writers as predictions of a Messiah were first intended as birth or enthronement oracles, or as coronation anthems. The "Messiah" and "son" of Yahve in Psalm 2 is every new king of Judah, as the song was ritually performed by both the king and a Levitical singer each time a new king came to the throne. Psalm 110 makes pro forma predictions for military victories by the new sovereign and secures for him the hereditary prerogatives of the old Melchizedek priesthood (taken over by David when he annexed Jebusite [Jeru-]Salem and made it his capital). It (110:3) also makes him, like the king of Babylon (Isa. 14:12), the son of the Semitic dawn goddess Shahar (translated incorrectly as a common noun, "dawn," in most Bibles).

Isa. 9:2–7 is either a coronation oracle or a birth oracle, uttered as a matter of course, again, like a chaplain's prayer to open the session of Congress, by a court prophet in honor of a newborn heir to the throne, depending on whether "unto us a child is born, unto us a son is given" (verse 6) refers to the literal birth or the adoption as Yahve's "son" on the day of coronation ("this day I have begotten thee," Ps. 2:7). The epithets bestowed on the king in Isa. 9:6, "Wonderful Counselor, Mighty God, Everlasting Father [cf. 1 Kings 1:31, "May my lord King David live forever!"], Prince of Peace," are the divine titles of Pharaoh and have been borrowed directly from Egyptian court rhetoric.

Isa. 61:1–4 is apparently yet another piece of inauguration liturgy, much like the inaugural oath sworn by the president of the United States, hand on Bible, pledging universal justice and amnesty to prisoners (which may or may not actually have been granted).

Isa. 7:14 may perhaps have been a similar birth oracle, casting the newly conceived or newborn royal heir in the role of the son of the virgin goddess Anath (equivalent to Shahar as in Psalm 110). It has been reapplied by the writer/redactor of Isaiah 7 as a reference to one of Isaiah's own sons, whom he used to name for his prophecies so as to remind people of his words once they came to pass (as if he had named his son Mark, for "Mark my words!"), as he also does in Isa. 8:1–4, similar in other important details to 7:14 as well.

It now becomes easy to recognize two other pieces of supposed "messianic prophecy" as birth/coronation oracles of this type, and thus as ornamental court rhetoric, not as genuine predictive prophecies at all, or at least not predictions of distant events. The first of these is Jer. 33:14–18, where the "righteous branch" seems certainly to be Zedekiah ("Yahve is Righteous"), the Judean king carried off into exile, whose ignominious fate thus belied the early hopes expressed on his behalf. If this optimistic appraisal of Zedekiah seems little to comport with Jeremiah's dim view of this king expressed elsewhere in the book (contrast also 33:18 with 7:22 and 8:8), it may come as no surprise to find that these verses (33:14–18) do not appear in the Septuagint version of Jeremiah and thus may be later interpolations.

Another likely birth/coronation oracle is Isa. 11:1–10, referring to the projected glories of a newborn or newly crowned king. Still another is Mic. 5:2–4, which speaks of a new ruler with ancient origins, "from of old," namely from Bethlehem, the town of David. While early Christians took this verse to mean the Messiah would be born literally in Bethlehem, it may well be a piece of metonymy, using David's hometown to stand for his name. "From Bethlehem" probably intends no more than "from David's dynasty."

Zech. 9:9 is in all likelihood a piece of the same royal liturgy, this time an "entrance liturgy" (cf. Psalms 24, 46, 48, 118) as the prince rides to the palace to be inaugurated. He rides a donkey, a peacetime mount, rather than a war stallion, so as to anticipate the glorious peace that should mark his reign. There is no future reference, though later scribes will interpret it that way.

THE COMING MESSIAH

The hope of a future "Messiah," a new king, appeared first in ancient Judah (not Israel, for which we lack evidence, given the Judean bias of the compilers of the Bible), after the destruction of the Davidic monarchy by the Babylonian conquerors in 586 B.C.E. Jeremiah made this crisis understandable by announcing that the conquest was the result of God punishing his people for their failure to live up to King Josiah's Deuteronomic Covenant. The people continued to worship the Baals and reneged on their pledges to free their slaves. Such disobedience would cost them their independence. While most Jews remained in their homeland, their aristocrats and priests were deported to Babylon. King Zedekiah lived under house arrest in the Babylonian court. For centuries Jews, whether under foreign rule in their own land or among the Diaspora, longed for the return of national sovereignty. Since, unlike the north (the Kingdom of Israel), their monarchy was restricted to Davidic rulers, a return to national sovereignty meant a return to Davidic rule. 2 Sam. 2:11–16, repeated in Jer. 33:14–18 and Ps. 89:19–37, served as the dynastic charter for the house of David.

In the cold dawn of the Babylonian conquest, the hope for a restored dynasty of David began to express itself in the reinterpretation of the birth/coronation oracles, as if to make them into prophecies of the restoration of the monarchy. This was simple, for all one needed to do was to interpret "shoot" or "stock" of Jesse in the oracles as meaning "stump." Originally, each new monarch was hailed as the latest sprout from David's family tree. But once one took the word to mean "stump" instead of "trunk," the idea was that Yahve had taken an ax to the trunk of the Davidic monarchy, but that eventually he would relent and allow a tender shoot of new life to emerge from the old, apparently dead stump of the royal family tree: a new Davidic heir.

Are there any prophecies from the Exilic or post-Exilic period that explicitly predict the coming of a Messiah, that is, the restoration of the monarchy? Genuine messianic prophecies are few and far between. Ezek. 34:22–24, 37:24 has in view the return of the leaders of Judah from the Babylonian exile, and in this context it envisions a restoration of the Davidic monarchy. Ezekiel uses the name of "David" himself to stand for the restored monarchy.

By my reckoning, there remains a pair of messianic texts in the Old Testament, though these, again, are a kind of enthronement oracle, royal propaganda. They are Hag. 2:20–23 and Zechariah, chapters 4 and 6:9–13a, which are post-Exilic and presuppose civil war in the Persian Empire, which these prophets supposed would lead to the fall of Persia and the restoration of Jewish sovereignty. Haggai and Zechariah were great champions of Zerubbabel, a Davidic descendant appointed governor of Judea by the Persian overlords. He had seen to the rebuilding of the temple, and for this Haggai and Zechariah decided he must be the anointed, the Messiah. Haggai and Zechariah, then, do not so much predict the future coming of some Davidic successor; they are already unstoppering the anointing oil! They have a candidate in mind! Sadly, they were a bit premature. (And this casts an interesting light on the incorporation of the generic birth/coronation oracle at Zech. 9:9 about the royal entry into Jerusalem: it is already a quotation of older material in Zechariah, and Zechariah has applied it to his favorite, Zerubbabel, just as Matthew and John will apply it to Jesus).

It is crucial to note that in all these cases, what we read of is an expectation, a promise, of the resumption of Judean independence under the Davidic dynasty.

What we do not read of is the coming of one immortal, divine man who will reign forever. This element will eventually appear in later Judaism, for example, in 4 Ezra 7:28–29, where we read that the Messiah will reign for four centuries.

THE SUFFERING SERVANT

We might as well consider Isa. 52:13–15, 53:1–12 here. Nothing in the text suggests any connection with the hope of a coming Messiah, and it seems to have had nothing to do with birth or coronation oracles, but it does represent an aspect of the royal ideology of the ancient Judean god-king, again, derived from the adjacent civilizations. This time, as Helmer Ringgren shows at considerable length,[2] we are dealing with a fossil of the ancient New Year's Festival, which, like its prototype in Babylon, renewed the heavenly mandate of the monarchy by having the king undergo, in ritual drama, the fate of the ancient gods whose kingship he represented on earth.

Psalms 74 and 89 preserve substantial fragments of the myth of Yahve's primordial combat with the dragons Leviathan, Behemoth, Rahab, and Tiamat, as well as the ensuing creation of the world and ascension of the young warrior god to kingship among his brethren, the sons of El Elyon. (See also Deut. 32:6–9 ff.; Dan. 7:1–7, 9–10, 13–14.) Like his analogues in Babylon and Canaan, the king of Judah must have annually renewed his divine right to rule by ritually reenacting this combat. It is to such continued ritual use that we owe the preservation of such mythemes in the biblical canon at all.

In the same way, the kings of Babylon, Iran, and others, as part of the same ritual, would reenact the death and resurrection of a god (Tammuz, Baal, etc.), a drama in which the king ritually assumed the burden of the fertility of the land and the sins of his people. Sometimes this entailed a mock death, sometimes the actual death of a hapless surrogate chosen by lot, sometimes a mere ritual humiliation, as when the Babylonian high priest publicly removed the king's crown, tweaked his ears, and slapped his face. Protesting his innocence, the king would don his robe and crown again and rise to full power once more, redeeming his people in a ritual atonement in which he himself had played the role of scapegoat. Isa. 52:13–15, 53:1–12 seems to reflect the Hebrew version of the same liturgy, which gave way after the Exile (with no king on the throne anymore) to the familiar Yom Kippur ritual. Another surviving vestige of the worship of Tammuz and his divine consort Ishtar Shalmith ("the Shulamite") is the Song of Songs. Remember that Ezekiel attests explicitly the worship of Tammuz in Jerusalem in Ezek. 8:14.

Even the later "redeemed redeemer" theology of the Gnostics seems to stem from this aspect of the royal ideology. Ancient Babylonian myth depicts Marduk being devoured by Kingu, then escaping and destroying him. Canaanite myth has Baal being devoured by Mot, then raised by Anath, then triumphing. Centuries later Manichean myths have the Primal Man of Light devoured by the Darkness

Dragon and then being rescued. The older royal ideology has been abstracted into the story of a Gnostic redeemer, reflecting the role of the Gnostic initiate. This was possible because the dying-and-rising god had already been anciently interpreted as symbolic of (or inclusive of) the whole human race.[3] So, as in all the Mystery Religions, the initiate took on the role of the savior, reversing the historical order of the evolution of the ritual, whereby the savior was himself the mythic projection of the one undergoing the rite, whether that was originally the king or, as later, the common initiate into the Mysteries.

But what is the function of the text in its present context: the announcement of glad tidings of the impending return of the Exilic community of aristocrats and priests to the Holy Land? The old text has been updated, reapplied to a new situation. As Morna D. Hooker[4] argues, the text as we now read it functions as part of an apologetic for the returning exiles who sought to enhance their position in the eyes of their contemporaries who had remained in the homeland all this time and had ascribed the deportation of their leaders to the leaders' sinfulness, not their own. The so-called Servant Song of Isa. 52–53 attempts to turn the tables by insisting that it was the innocent minority (or righteous remnant) who was taken away to punishment, not because of its own sins but in the place of those who (the priests said) actually did the sinning, the reprobate masses who remained behind! Thus did the priests think to theologize the privilege accorded them by their royal Persian patrons. We are not surprised to learn in Ezra and Nehemiah of severe tensions between the newly returned leaders, with their arrogant "take-charge" attitude, and the people of the land who had never left.

So Isa. 52–53 in its present context represents a secondary reinterpretation whereby the returning exiles are the Suffering Servant of Yahve, once mistakenly blamed for their own punishment when, from their own viewpoint, they were taking it on behalf of the very upstarts who contemned them as sinners. It is they who, having suffered on behalf of sinners, will be exalted to the glory due them (in their own estimation, anyway). The Suffering Servant is not the Messiah. It is a parallel development, though, in that the Servant represents another theological projection of a pre-Exilic institution to the far side of the Exile. Instead of a projection of the kingship (the Messiah), the Servant represents an ideal projection of the priestly hierarchy.

Thus, many of the texts commonly taken to be messianic predictions were not originally predictions at all. Rather, they formed part of the royal ideology of Judah. Once the monarchy was cut off by the Babylonian conquest, sacred kingship was transferred from present experience to future expectation. Thus the texts, originally having present reference, came to be reinterpreted as futurist predictions of a restored king to come. When Christians acclaimed Jesus as Messiah, the old texts came along, and with them came the associations of the old royal ideology. Thus Jesus the divine king. Meanwhile, official Judaism, coming ever closer to strict monotheism, had stripped the kingly role of all divine trappings, lest the coming messiah appear to be a second god.

THE KINGDOM OF GOD

Bultmann and others have made the striking suggestion that while Jesus did not regard himself as the Messiah of Israel, he had predicted the advent of such a one, and that after his death, his disciples' visions of him convinced them that Jesus had been the Messiah, or had now been exalted to that rank (Acts 2:36, Rom. 1:4). More strictly, as of his resurrection, he had been appointed to the office (Acts 3:20–21) and would fulfill it at his second coming (that is, his second coming as Jesus, his first coming as the Messiah).[5] He would shortly make a victorious return to the earth in messianic glory and judgment. As time passed and Jesus did not return, his messiahship was retrojected into his earthly ministry, beginning at the baptism. At this stage of things, his sonship was conferred at the baptism, as in Mark.[6] Later still, as witnessed by Matthew and Luke, the sonship/messiahship was pushed back even further to his nativity.[7] This reconstruction[8] makes a good deal of sense. Moreover, it has received new plausibility in recent years in the wake of the death of the Lubavitcher Rebbe, Menachem Mendel Schneerson.

Rabbi Schneerson was a charismatic rabbi who taught Torah to packed meeting houses in Brooklyn. He preached the soon coming of the Messiah and urged Jews to repent so as to hasten the day. Many or most Lubavitcher Hasidim suspected that their beloved Rebbe was himself the Messiah. His untimely death did nothing to dislodge their hope. They concluded that he was the Messiah and would shortly rise from the dead in appropriate glory to inaugurate the Messianic era. These events certainly lend a sense of historical verisimilitude to Bultmann's theory. But the parallel depends on the judgment that Jesus was, as Bultmann thought, following Schweitzer, a preacher of the end of the age, an eschatological prophet. Had Rabbi Schneerson not avidly fomented expectation of the Messiah, no one would have accorded him that office. And if Jesus was not an eschatological preacher, why would anyone have thought to connect him with such hopes, to the point of making him the star of the show? Many of today's gospel scholars, including most of the Fellows of the Jesus Seminar, do not think Jesus taught the soon-coming end. What did Jesus have to say about the coming kingdom of God, the era of judgment and salvation, of immortality and universal peace?

The problem is twofold: first, a number of eschatological statements attributed to Jesus are probably inauthentic; second, many are not clearly dealing with the end of the age, though it is possible to take them that way. As to the first, we have already seen that texts unique to Luke are usually, as we can show on other grounds, his own invention. This would omit from our consideration here all those passages (e.g., Luke 6:20–26, 14:11, 13:30, 16:19–31) in which Jesus is shown anticipating a great reversal of fortunes, the mighty being cast down, the rich impoverished, and so forth.

Matt. 8:11–12//Luke 13:28–29 ("You will weep and gnash your teeth when you see Abraham, Isaac, and Jacob and all the prophets in the kingdom of God and yourselves thrown out! And men will come from east and west, and from north and south, and sit at table in the kingdom of God") cannot be authentic for the plain reason that the text presupposes and celebrates the Gentile Mission, the replacement of Jews by Gentiles in God's favor as the ones who heed the Christian evangel. The same goes for Matt. 12:41–42//Luke 11:30–32, where we find the (conspicuously Gentile) Ninevites and Sabeans lionized for their repentence at the expense of stiff-necked (non-Christian) Jewry. Anachronistic.

We have already seen that the parables unique to Matthew are most likely his own creations, and that eliminates several of the judgment scenes ascribed to Jesus, namely, the parables of the Wheat and Weeds (Matt. 13:24–30, 36–43), of the Dragnet (Matt. 13:47–48), the Unmerciful Servant (Matt. 18:23–35), and the Guest Without a Wedding Garment (Matt. 22:2, 11–14). The last of these is an interesting case, because it seems parallel to, if not derivative of, the parable of Rabbi Johannon ben Zakkai (first/second century C.E.): "A king issued an invitation to a banquet without specifying the hour. The wise attired themselves, while the foolish went on with their work. Suddenly the summons came, and those who were not dressed in clean clothes were not admitted to the banquet" (b. Shab. 153a, Jeremias's paraphrase).[9] Of course, the clean clothes are repentence; the banquet is the heavenly board.

The so-called parables of growth, the Mustard Seed (Mark 4:30–32) and the Leavened Loaves (Matt. 13:33//Luke 13:21), contrast the small, virtually microscopic, beginnings of the gospel, that is, of Christianity, with its fantastic, all-embracing reach when mature, having spread throughout the known world (Col. 1:23). As James Breech points out, these parables are triumphalistic glances backward after the fact. They cannot go back to Jesus.[10] Other anachronistic parables concerning the end of the age would include those dealing with the delay of the Parousia, the second coming of Christ. In these parables we encounter what is highly improbable: Jesus *predicting* an *unanticipated* delay! (Or, as Dale Gribble says in an episode of *King of the Hill*, "This change in plans wasn't in the original plan!") One is the Q parable of the Householder's Return (Matt. 24:45–51//Luke 12:42–46). It appears to be a rewrite of an earlier version that Mark has preserved, preferring it to the Q version, Mark 13:33–37. In Mark's version, the stress is on the *uncertainty* of the hour of the master's return, whereas in Q, the reason for vigilance is that the master's return has been *delayed long past the hour originally stipulated*! Similarly, the Matthean parable of Wise and Foolish Virgins (25:1–13) is entirely predicated on the element of delay. Jeremias tries to rescue this one, arguing that the delay motif is not arbitrary but fits naturally into ancient wedding feast customs.[11] Point granted, but this in no way mitigates the plain focus of the parable on the delay motif, something that surely implies the delay of the Parousia. Jeremias has only shown that the parable took no liberties with genuine wedding customs to set up the comparison of situations.

The single largest chunk of eschatology in the Gospels is the Olivet Discourse (Mark 13, Matthew 24, Luke 21). Matthew and Luke have very heavily edited the Markan original, adding, subtracting, paraphrasing, and thereby illustrating the danger feared by John the Revelator in Rev. 22:18–19, "I warn every one who hears the words of the prophecy of this scroll: if any one adds to them, God will add to him the plagues described in this scroll, and if any one takes away from the words of the scroll of this prophecy, God will take away his share in the tree of life, and in the holy city which are described in this scroll." As Timothee Colani argued long ago, Mark 13 existed before it came into Mark's hands. It must have circulated as a separate leaflet and was probably the same as the "revelation" Eusebius (*Ecclesiastical History* 3.5) says alerted the Jerusalem Christians to flee the doomed city before the Roman siege locked down. Note that it presents itself as a *written document*: "Let the reader understand" (13:14; cf. Rev. 13:18, "Let him who has wisdom count the number of the Beast"). The whole thing, though purporting to come from Jesus, is merely a cento of Old Testament texts (Mark 13:7 comes from Dan. 2:28; Mark 13:8 from Isa. 19:2 and/or 2 Chr. 15:6; Mark 13:12 from Mic. 7:6; Mark 13:14 from Dan. 9:27, 12:11, Gen. 19:17; Mark 13:19 from Dan. 12:1; Mark 13:22 from Deut. 13:2; Mark 13:24 from Isa. 13:10; Mark 13:25 from Isa. 34:4; Mark 13:26 from Dan. 7:13; Mark 13:27 from Zech. 2:10, Deut. 30:4).[12] So would Jesus have advised his contemporaries to count down the signs of the coming of the end (Mark 13:28–30)? Not if this is the evidence for it. And, interestingly, Luke counters the whole idea (despite keeping most of Mark 13!) in Luke 17:20–21, "Being asked by the Pharisees when the kingdom of God was coming, he answered them, 'The kingdom of God is not coming by observation; neither will they say, "Lo, here it is!" or "Over there!" for, behold, the kingdom of God is within you.'" This tossing of a wet blanket over eager eschatological hopes is part of Luke's agenda. Compare the Pharisees' question here with that of the disciples in Acts 1:6–8 and the hopes of the mob in Luke 19:11–15, all Lukan. Thomas liked this saying and elaborated on it in three new versions, equally vivid (sayings 3, 51, 113). He, too, was a debunker of apocalyptic fanaticism. Which side would Jesus have taken in this debate? We can never know, since, precisely as on the fasting question, both sides put words in his mouth.

There are other kingdom of God/heaven sayings where the apocalyptic reference is not clear, where the phrase could just as well denote going to heaven after death, understanding heaven as an invisible location above our own. "Entering the kingdom of God/heaven" in such sayings need mean no more than "going to heaven" (e.g., Matt. 5:3, 10, 19, 20; 6:33; 7:21; 8:11; 13:24, 44, 45, 47; 18:1, 3, 4; 19:12–14, 23–24; 21:31; 23:13; 26:29; Mark 9:47; 12:34; Luke 9:62; 14:15; John 3:3, 5; 14:22; cf. 1 Cor. 6:9, 15:50; Gal. 5:21; 2 Thes. 1:5; 2 Pet. 1:11). In other passages, it seems to denote the sphere of God's sovereignty and our obedience to him (Matt. 12:28; 13:52; 16:19; 21:43; Luke 10:9, 11; cf. Acts 1:3, 8:12, 19:8; Rom. 14:17; 1 Cor. 4:20) and in others some inner reality (Luke 17:21).

There are, to be sure, passages about the kingdom "coming" (Matt. 6:10; Mark 1:15, 9:1, 15:43; Luke 21:31, 22:18), and these must be admitted to be classically apocalyptic in character. We have already guessed that Matt. 6:1 preserves the hopes of the hand-to-mouth wandering apostles. In Mark 1:15, Jesus preaches that the alotted time according to God's dispensational plan of the ages is up, and the kingdom of God is close at hand. But this is not even put forth as a saying of Jesus; it is Mark's editorial narrative. Mark 9:1, "There are some standing here who will not taste death before they see the kingdom of God coming with power," seems to be a rewritten version of some earlier saying, such as Mark 13:30 (cf. Mark 14:62), in which the entire generation should not taste death till the eschaton. Mark 9:1, like John 21:21–23, is a backpedaling rewrite of some such universal promise in light of its failure (2 Pet. 3:3–4). For obvious reasons, we do not have the original to analyze. Mark 15:43 is not even purportedly a saying of Jesus. Luke 21:31 is a Lukan rewrite of Mark 13:29, part of the spurious Olivet Discourse. Luke 22:18 similarly adds the element of the kingdom's "coming" where the Markan original (14:25) did not have it.

SON OF MAN

Perhaps the most explicit eschatological/apocalyptic sayings ascribed to Jesus are those in which he predicts the coming of the Son of man. Unfortunately, this term is even more ambiguous than the phrase "the kingdom of God." Though, as we have seen, "son of man" is just poetry for "man, human being" (e.g., Ps. 8:4; Ezek. 2:1, 3:1, 4:1, etc.), it begins to take on messianic associations in Dan. 7:13, where the author has taken over an old piece of creation mythology according to which Yahve, a young warrior (cf. Exod. 15:3) defeats the great sea monsters (Dan. 7:3; cf. Ps. 74:13–14) and comes forward to assume sovereignty at the hand of his divine Father, El Elyon (Dan. 7:9, 13–14; cf. Deut. 32:8–9, Ps. 89:5–14), just as Marduk took over for Ea after defeating Apsu and Tiamat, as Indra took over from Varuna after whelming Vritra, as Baal assumed coregency with his father El after defeating Mot, and as Zeus defeated and succeeded his monstrous father, Kronos. Just as this mythic contest had long ago been demythologized into an allegory of God's defeat of Egypt ("Rahab") at the Exodus (Isa. 51:90), so Daniel makes it an allegory of the coming defeat of the Seleucids at the hands of the Hasmoneans (Dan. 7:19–27). In the myth, the "one like a son of man" was Yahve himself, distinguished in form from the beasts of the pit whom he vanquished. To Daniel, he may have been a symbol for victorious Judea. But for later rabbis, the "one like a son of man" came to be a trope for King Messiah who should come. As Maurice Casey, Géza Vermes, and Norman Perrin have shown,[13] forever after in Jewish literature, "the son of man" functions, not as a title for Messiah, but as a kind of shorthand reference to him by way of his symbolic representation (as they thought) in Daniel 7. "Who is this 'son of man'?" (John 12:34). He is the Messiah, whoever that turns out to be. In 1 Enoch, references to the Messiah, the transfigured Enoch himself, are to "this son of man," "that son of man," "the son of man who is born unto righteousness." But it is not a title.

Whence derive the "son of man" references in the Gospels? Again, most are not apocalyptic in nature. "Son of man" was a familiar Aramaic self-reference exactly equivalent to our "a man" or "a guy." "A man's got to have something to live for," by which I mean to say that I myself must have something to live for. "You really know how to hurt a guy," namely, me! A number of gospel sayings seem to have no more than this in mind by the use of "son of man." Mark 2:10, "the son of man has authority on earth to forgive sins" argues that human beings can forgive sins on earth as God does in heaven. And thus, Jesus defends his own granting of absolution. Mark 2:28, "The son of man is lord even of the sabbath" is just a poetic paraphrase of "the sabbath was made for man, not man for the sabbath." Jesus in this way defends his own practice (or rather that of his disciples). Mark 8:31, "The son of man must suffer many things" is classical usage, as one especially seeks to distance oneself from impending misfortune, as if to say, "God forbid." The same applies to Mark 9:12, "How is it written of the son of man that he must suffer many things and be treated with contempt?" Ditto Mark 9:31 and 10:33. Mark 10:45 (as the Lukan version makes clear—Luke 22:27) has nothing to do with some sophisticated "suffering Son of Man" Christology (as many would have it).[14] It simply means that Jesus came to serve, not to be served, and the keynote of humility accounts for the circumlocution "the son of man," as if to say, "this humble servant," still a familiar idiom. (The saying does not go back to Jesus in any case, since it looks back over his career in a theologically interpretive way.)

Mark 14:21 ("The son of man goes as is written of him, but woe to the one by whom the son of man is betrayed!") is a proverb with no original connection to Jesus or indeed to any specific individual at all. It just means that a man goes to destruction (or any other pitfall) as is written for him in God's book of destiny (Ps. 139:16, "in your book were written, every one of them, the days that were formed for me, when as yet there was none of them"), but this in no way mitigates the guilt of one's enemy. The saying is another version of Mark 9:42 or Matt. 18:7, "Woe to the world for temptations to sin! For it is necessary that temptations come, but woe to the man by whom the temptation comes!"

Matt. 8:20//Luke 9:58 ("Foxes have holes, birds of the air have nests, but the son of man has no place to rest his head") is a Cynic-style saying justifying the speaker's wandering lifestyle. Usually, Cynics said we ought to emulate the animals, but this one distinguishes mankind from the other animals, but simply as another species with different habits, which it is equally natural for us to follow—as itinerants! The hadith of Muhammad report a somewhat similar saying of the Prophet: "The son of man has no more right than that he should have a house wherein he may live, and a piece of cloth whereby he may hide his nakedness, and a chip of bread, and water." There is obviously no question of the Son of man as a title here.

We have already seen how the saying about "speaking a word against the son of man" (Matt. 12:32//Luke 12:10) simply means vilifying fellow mortals as against the spiritual peril of blaspheming the divine Spirit.

And of course there is a group of "son of man" sayings that use the term as direct allusions to Daniel 7, like those in 1 Enoch. They speak of the end-time coming of the Messiah. These include Matt. 10:23; 13:41; 19:28; 25:13, 31; Mark 8:38; 13:26; 14:62; Luke 12:40; 17:24; 18:8. Norman Perrin[15] has shown how all these sayings are the product of an early Christian midrashic tradition in which Dan. 7:13 ("behold, with the clouds of heaven there came one like a son of man") was combined on the one hand with Ps. 110:1 ("The Lord says unto my lord: 'Sit at my right hand, till I make your enemies your footstool'") and on the other with Zech. 12:10a ("when they shall look upon him whom they have pierced, they shall mourn for him, as one mourns for an only child, and weep bitterly over him, as one weeps over a first-born son"). The first was made to refer to the enthronement of the crucified ("pierced") Jesus upon his resurrection (Acts 2:34–35, "For David did not ascend into the heavens; but he himself says, 'The Lord said unto my lord, "Sit at my right hand, till I make your enemies a stool for your feet."' Let all the house of Israel know assuredly that God has made him both Lord and Christ, this Jesus whom you crucified"). The second was applied to his future coming in judgment, leaving his heavenly throne to appear in the sky for the final assize: "Behold, he is *coming with the clouds*, and every eye *shall see him, every one who pierced him*; and all the tribes of the earth will *wail on account of him*" (Rev. 1:7). Matt. 24:30, "Then the sign of the *son of man* will appear in heaven, and all the tribes of the earth *will mourn*, and *they will see* the *son of man coming on the clouds of heaven* with power and great glory." Jesus warns those who are about to have him "pierced" that their roles will soon be reversed: "You *will see* the *son of man sitting at the right hand* of power and *coming with the clouds*" (Mark 14:62). Indeed, from these two sets of midrashic connections came all the gospel sayings about the coming of the Son of man. Not one of them is a genuine piece of dialogue or self-proclamation. All alike are spliced, crafted, fashioned products of the scribal imagination. Think again of the voice from heaven at Jesus' baptism: would God be quoting Scripture? The real thing posing as an imitation?

So it would seem there is precious little evidence that Jesus was, like Menachem Schneerson, a preacher of the soon-coming end of the world. And that endangers the prospect of his having been acclaimed as Messiah upon his death and subsequent apparitions. Such an identification seems highly arbitrary if he had not been building up anticipation of the coming of the Messiah among his followers.

WHAT DID JESUS CLAIM?

But why should we forage among implications and hints of whether Jesus believed the end was at hand; do not the Gospels depict him as setting himself forth as the Messiah? By implication, they do. But it remains an astonishing fact that, even if one were to judge authentic every single saying of Jesus in every one of the Gospels, one would still lack such an explicit statement by Jesus as "I am the Messiah" or "I am the Christ."

Two passages come pretty close, however. One is John 4:25–26: "The woman said to him, 'I know that Messiah is coming . . . ; when he comes, he will show us all things.' Jesus said to her, 'I who speak to you am he.'" But this passage has three problems: first, it is found in John, who makes no attempt whatsoever to segregate what Jesus may have said on earth from what he is saying prophetically through the Paracletos. Second, the passage cannot be authentic because it is based squarely on a misunderstanding of Samaritanism, as if the Samaritans shared the Jewish belief in the coming Davidic monarch. Actually, Samaritans, whose ancestors had long before decisively rejected any and all connection with the house of David (1 Kings 12:16, "What portion have we in David? We have no inheritance in the son of Jesse. To your tents, O Israel! Look now to your own house, David!"), expected the Taheb ("Restorer"), the Prophet like Moses (Deut. 18:15), perhaps even the return of Joshua himself. The coming of the Messiah was simply not an article of Samaritan faith. And third, it is not absolutely clear that Jesus' reply should be translated, "I who speak to you am he." One could translate, "I am he who is speaking to you now." The point would be to cut off the woman's attempted deferral of the matter to the future when the answer man would come. *The Messiah may indeed come one day, but I am speaking to you now.* The passage taken this way would be parallel to both John 11:24–26, "Martha said to him, 'I know that he will rise again in the resurrection at the last day.' Jesus said to her, 'I am the resurrection and the life; he who believes in me, though he were dead, yet shall he live, and he who lives and believes in me shall never die,'" and Thomas 52, "His disciples say to him, 'Twenty-four prophets spoke in Israel, and they all spoke of you.' He says to them, 'You have ignored the living one who is in front of you and prated about the dead.'"

The other text is Mark 14:62. When the high priest asks Jesus if he is indeed the Christ, he replies, "I am." Or does he? Matt. 26:64 has Jesus answer, "You have said [so]." Luke 22:67 has "If I tell you, you will not believe; and if I ask you, you will not answer," borrowed from the John the Baptist debate in Luke 20:1–6, where Jesus refuses to answer their question since they will not answer his. It seems odd that both evangelists should alike blur the clear affirmation of Jesus before the Sanhedrin. But what if the copies of Mark they read (far older than ours) had a less univocal answer than the one we now read? Sure enough, there are a couple of surviving manuscripts of Mark 14:62 that have Jesus answer, "You say." I should regard this to be the Markan original, which Matthew barely rephrased, and which Luke heavily rewrote, though maintaining the equivocation. Some scribe later thought to improve Mark's version.

Before going further, let us remind ourselves of the attested stages of Christological belief in the New Testament writings. We have seen how Acts 2:36, 3:20–21 and Rom. 1:4 preserve clear marks of an adoptionist doctrine that understood Jesus to have become the Christ upon his resurrection (as does every New Testament citation of Psalm 110). But that such a Christology arose at all is absolutely inexplicable if Jesus had claimed before his crucifixion to be the Messiah. This means all passages that have him do so cannot possibly be historical, but must instead represent later statements of faith put into his mouth by the evangelists. We will see, however, that even without the counterweight of the adoptionistic texts, the few statements in the Synoptic gospels where Jesus is seen claiming to be Messiah teem with insurmountable problems of their own. The situation will be seen to parallel precisely that of the miracle stories, where we had an early statement ascribed to Jesus that he would do no miracles, which could not but undermine the credibility of any miracle tales balanced against it.

The central text we have to deal with is Mark 8:27–30. "And Jesus went on with his disciples to the villages of Caesarea Philippi; and on the way he asked his disciples, 'Who do men say that I am?' And they told him, 'John the Baptist; and others say, Elijah; and others, one of the prophets.' And he asked them, 'But who do you say that I am?' Peter answered, 'You are the Christ.' And he charged them to tell no one about him [or, about *it*]." What a powerful and fascinating story! And not the least intriguing is that the crowds could even be capable of a prolonged misimpression that, all this time, it was John the Baptist they were seeing and hearing! A great untold tale lurks here. My guess is that the story means to dispense with "false" Christologies held by "heretics" in the Caesarea Philippi area in Mark's day. The scene itself, as Gerd Theissen has demonstrated,[16] is Mark's own creation and represents no earlier tradition. Mark has reworked the scene from his earlier scene in 6:14b–15: "Some said, 'John the Baptizer has been raised from the dead; that is why these powers are at work in him.' But others said, 'It is Elijah.' And others said, 'It is a prophet like one of the prophets of old.'" Mark has simply abbreviated his own earlier text to use it again in chapter 8. Notice that 6:14–15 elucidates the mentions of John and "one of the prophets" in 8:28; if we had only the latter text we would be left asking, "How can they have confused him with John? Hadn't John already been executed?" And "Did they mean he was one of the ancient prophets returned? Jeremiah, maybe?" But, having read Mark 6:14–15, we know they meant a *resurrected* John and a prophet *like* the ancient ones. But the decisive factor is grammatical. In Mark 6:14b, the acclamations appear as direct speech, thus in the nominative case, and introduced by ὅτι. In 8:28 they have become indirect speech ("They say that you are") and thus should be in the accusative case. But only the first two acclamations are in the accusative; the third is still nominative. And though οτι cannot introduce the accusative, it is still there in the first two acclamations! Mark only partially adjusted the grammar as he rewrote it.

It is interesting to see what the subsequent evangelists have done with Mark's story. Luke has treated it with restraint, omitting the geographical location, of no interest to him. And he has Peter confess, "You are the Christ *of God*" (Luke 9:20). Matthew has Peter say, "You are the Christ, the *son of the living God*" (Matt. 16:16). Perhaps he is sensitive to the parallel some will see with pagan demigods: Jesus is the son of the God of Israel, not of the false ("dead") gods of the surrounding heathen. At any rate, John has already had various characters confess their faith in Jesus in exalted terms (John 1:29, 34, 41, 49; 4:42), and when he gets to Peter, his confession is anticlimactic: "You are the Holy One of God" (John 6:69), strangely, the very same acclamation offered by the Capernaum demoniac in Mark 1:24. Thomas 13 has a different set of options. "Jesus says to his disciples, 'Make a comparison to me, and tell me who I resemble.' Simon Peter says to him, 'You are like a righteous angel.' Matthew says to him, 'You are like a philosophical man of comprehension.' Thomas says to him, 'Teacher, my mouth will not at all be capable of saying who you are like.'" To which Jesus replies that he is no longer Thomas's master and has nothing left to teach him, judging by the spiritual insight of his reply. Here the contrast is no longer between those on the outside and those of the inner circle, but rather between the *psuchikoi* and the *pneumatikoi* among the disciples (and in the church of Thomas's day). None of this goes back to Jesus.

There is also a small group of sayings in which Jesus is made to refer to the Christ in the third person. Mark 9:41, "Whoever gives you a cup of water to drink in the name of your being Christ's, amen: I say to you, he shall not lose his recompense." This is a howling anachronism if Luke is correct that the disciples were first dubbed "Christians" in Antioch in the time of the Apostles (Acts 11:26).

Matt. 23:10 is again grossly anachronistic. It is a piece of Matthean sectarian polemic, criticizing the supposed pomposity of the leaders of formative Judaism in Galilee or Syria for sporting the title "Rabbi," "my master, my teacher," which Jewish sources make clear was only beginning to become common at the end of the first century C.E.[17] And at any rate, it is patently the voice of Matthew, not Jesus, that we are hearing in the third person use of "the Christ," which obviously, in context, suggests a reference to Jesus by a Christian, something we might expect to hear in a Pauline epistle.

Mark 12:35 ("How can the scribes say the Christ is the son of David?") is revealed by its form to be an excerpt from a collection of apologetical rejoinders to common Jewish criticisms of Christian faith. Another is Mark 9:11, "Why do the scribes say Elijah must come first?" It attests an earlier stage of Christology in which Jesus was admittedly not an heir to the throne of David. The strategy of those who advocated his messiahship was to deny, as the partisans of the Hasmonean kings must have, that the Messiah had to be Davidic. Later on, Christians gave it up and began to posit that Jesus was after all descended from David and fabricated genealogies to prove it.

What about Palm Sunday? Was Jesus offering himself to Israel as her Messiah at his entry to Jerusalem? Not according to the earliest version. To *make* it into a messianic entry, Matthew, Luke, and John have all had to reword the acclamations of the crowd as Mark had them. Mark 11:19: "Blessed is the kingdom of our father David that is coming! Hosanna!" Matt. 21:9: "Hosanna to the son of David!" Luke 19:38: "Blessed be the king who comes in the name of the Lord!" John 12:13: "Blessed is he who comes in the name of the Lord, even the king of Israel!"

SON OF GOD

Jesus is frequently called the Son of God in the Gospels. Already in Psalm 2, this title belongs to every king of Judah while he reigns. It was synonymous with Messiah, or anointed one. Did Jesus call himself God's son? Did he accept the honorific from others? Again, dismissing John's gospel as a piece of dramatized theology pure and simple (which is no criticism!), we have three main pieces of evidence to consider. The first is a Q passage (Matt. 11:27//Luke 10:22), often called "the Johannine Thunderbolt" erupting into the placid Synoptic sky. We might rather call it a scrap of Johannine Christology sewn like a patch into the fabric of the Synoptics, whose Christologies are usually more modest. "All things have been delivered to me by my Father; and no one knows the Son except the Father, and no one knows the Father except the Son and anyone to whom the Son deigns to reveal him." If we may adapt to this saying C. H. Dodd's suggestion about John 5:19–20a (that it should be boiled down to a "parable of the Apprenticed Son"),[18] we might theorize that this passage has been grossly over-interpreted, as if it intended Trinitarian language, when it may be no more than a parabolic statement: no one really knows a father like his son does, since the latter is a chip off the old block. What would be the implied comparison? Perhaps the point was the missionary task of Israel to witness to the nations of God, since only Israel relates to God as children to a father, while the nations can be no more than slaves to God—unless they rise to embrace the faith of Israel, too. That is certainly possible.

But let us assume that the text is meant as a piece of Christology. As such it is parallel to John 1:18, "No man has ever seen God; the only begotten son, he who rests in the bosom of the Father, has made him known" (and to Akhenaten's *Hymn to the Sun*, "O Aten, no man knoweth thee save for thy son Akhenaten!/ Him hast thou initiated into thy designs and thy power"). It is impossible for the ministry of the historical Jesus, as it presupposes the resurrection and exaltation, like Matt. 28:18, "All authority in heaven and on earth has been given to me."

See also Eph. 1:20–23 and Phil. 2:6–11. One must also mark the clearly Marcionite character of the saying, which is urgent to deny that previous prophets and seers had known God after all (the true God, anyway!). So much for Abraham and Moses, so-called friends of God who knew him face to face! This is probably a stray piece of such a Gnostic revelation discourse as those that pepper the pages of John's gospel and the Mandaean writings.

Second, the parable of the Wicked Tenants (Mark 12:1–9) is a transparent allegory of salvation history as viewed by Christians: God has sent his stubborn people prophet after prophet, despite their track record of rejection and martyrdom. Finally, in one last effort to persuade them to render him his due honor as their creator and redeemer, God sent his son, but he fared worse than the rest, being cast out of the city (to Golgotha) and killed, prompting God to wash his hands of the people and to deal with the Gentiles instead. There is a bit of confusion over whether the wicked sharecroppers are supposed to stand for stubborn Israel as a nation or for the corrupt temple elders (Mark 12:12). In the former case, the new tenants must be the Gentile Christians, as Matthew makes explicit (21:44, "the kingdom of God will be taken away from you and given to *a nation* producing the fruits of it"). In the latter case, presumably the new tenants are the conquering Romans.

Either way, the story is an anachronism looking back on the career of Jesus. Jeremias tries to make the "son/servants" element an integral part of the political/economic color of the parable, not of the theological meaning, and so to secure it for the historical Jesus. Thus, Jesus wasn't necessarily thinking of himself as a son distinct from the prophets in some Christological sense. No, Jeremias says, the story requires the appearance of an heir so the tenants can mistakenly infer his father is dead and assume that, if they kill the heir, they will inherit the land by squatter's rights.[19] But this does nothing to mitigate the problem: it only explains why the sharecropper business was an attractive basis for a parable about the murder of the Son of God! If that is not the point, why is the arrival of the son even in the story? Why does not the absentee landlord simply send in men to kill the wicked tenants and replace them (as in Matthew's version of the Great Supper, Matt. 22:6–7, "the rest seized his servants, treated them shamefully, and killed them. The king was angry, and he sent his troops and destroyed those murderers and burned their city")? We don't need to get as far as the son's murder unless we want the parable to describe the murder of God's son.

Plus, there is the matter of the parable's sympathies. Is it really likely that Jesus, a popular Palestinian preacher, would have symbolized God as a rapacious absentee landlord and made the poor sharecroppers the villains? At any rate, if this parable went back to Jesus himself, we would indeed have a statement, only minimally veiled, that he deemed himself the Son of God. But we don't.

The third major bit of evidence urged upon us for Jesus' awareness of his divine sonship is his prayer in Gethsemane (Mark 14:36, "*Abba*, Father, all things are possible for you"). *Abba*, an Aramaic word meaning "Father," as of course Mark himself tells us, has been the occasion of a flood of homiletical sentimentalizing. Joachim Jeremias,[20] himself a devout Lutheran pietist, claimed that contemporary Jewish prayer language featured nothing so informal as this, that *Abba* really meant something on the order of "Daddy" or "Papa," and that Jesus was therefore on the most intimate terms with the Godhead—and that he initiated Christian believers into the same saccharine fellowship, since Paul and the early church had inherited the word (Rom. 8:15, Gal. 4:6). But, as Raymond E. Brown pointed out,[21] *Abba* had indeed begun as the familiar language of the household, but by New Testament times it had become the common word for father, denoting no special degree of tender intimacy. After all, Mark and Paul both translate it simply as "father." In any case, Jeremias had the direction of borrowing reversed. Certainly the *Abba* address passed from Aramaic-speaking Christians to Greek-speaking ones like Paul and Mark, and thence into the mouth of Mark's Jesus. Remember, no one was there to hear what Jesus had said in prayer. Mark created the scene out of whole cloth. Again, this is no evidence for what the historical Jesus may have thought of himself.

But does not Jesus refer habitually to God as "my Father," implying a singular relationship? There are no such statements in Mark, one in Q (the Johannine Thunderbolt), two in Lukan redaction (22:29, added to Q as preserved in Matt. 19:28, 24:49), *fifteen* in Matthew, and *thirty-two* in John. I think it is pretty obvious what is going on here.

ANOTHER ANOINTING

How on earth did a wandering teacher come to be identified as the Messiah of Israel, David's latter-day successor, when there is no evidence of his claiming to be such, and when nothing he is depicted as doing has the least resemblance to military action? Just as striking is the fact that, in Paul's letters, Jesus is often called Christ, virtually synonymously, as if it were just another name. There is not a single place in the epistles where "Christos" is necessarily or even likely an allusion to the heir to the throne of Israel and Judah. For Paul, Jesus is no more traditionally Jewish a Messiah than he is in the Koran. All this makes one wonder whether the identification of Jesus as the anointed king of David's line is secondary, occasioned by the fact Jesus was already called "Jesus the Anointed," though with a very different meaning in mind. That is what I want to suggest. In short: like Osiris, Jesus was originally described as being anointed with the ointment of resurrection. Jesus Christ denoted originally "Jesus the Risen One." The background and imagery are those of the Mystery Religions. Early on, heterodox Jews embraced this savior, so similar to their own familiar Tammuz and Baal, but the next generation eventually felt the need to "Judaize" Jesus and thus reinterpreted "Messiah" in connection with the anointing of the king.

Dying and rising gods were nothing new to Jews. Ezekiel (8:14) had bemoaned the Jerusalem women's public ritual laments for Tammuz, a Babylonian deity who had died and descended to Sheol, where his divine consort Ishtar sought him out and took his place for half the year. The story of their love stronger than the grave had once been hymned in what we know as the Song of Solomon. The "Shulamite" in that poem was Ishtar Shalmith, her lover and brother Tammuz. The names were omitted somewhere along the line as a compromise with emerging Jewish monotheism. The Canaanite god Baal (a cognate double of Yahve himself) died in battle, devoured by the death monster Mot, but Anath discovered the bloody ground where he was consumed (a "field of blood") and there lamented him before plunging into the netherworld to save him, whereupon he joined his father El on the throne. As any Bible reader knows, Baal was worshiped alongside Yahve in Israel, to the consternation of prophets like Elijah and Jeremiah, for centuries. The Egyptian Osiris died and rose from the dead, too. He was assassinated by his brother Set (god of the desert as Osiris was of the grain) and dismembered. Osiris's sisters/wives Isis and Nephthys went in search of the body, lamenting the god's death. Once Isis had reassembled the members, she anointed him with oil, and he came back to life, remaining on earth long enough to beget on her his own reincarnation Horus, who would in later years take revenge on Set.

Aeneas, too, was anointed unto immortality. "When his body was purified, his mother anointed it with a divine perfume, touched his lips with a mixture of sweet nectar and ambrosia, and made him a god whom the Roman people welcomed with a temple and altars, giving him the name Indiges" (Ovid *Metamorphoses* Book 14).[22]

The story of Osiris appears three times in the Bible. Joseph the patriarch had already been Osiris. It is no coincidence that the story of Joseph is set in Egypt, of all places. He is betrayed by his brothers, as Osiris was by his brother Set. Joseph's brothers envy his illustrious future as ruler, shown forth in his dreams. Set envies Osiris's present rule. Osiris is actually dismembered, while Joseph is falsely said to have been torn limb from limb. Joseph is first dropped into a pit and then, once brought to Egypt, he is imprisoned in a cell, from which he is finally liberated. Both sequences parallel Osiris's enclosure in the casket and his release. Just as Osiris assumes the rulership of Amente, the netherworld, judging the arriving souls, so does Joseph rise to power in the "netherworld" he has entered, Egypt. He becomes vizier to Pharaoh. He marries Asenath, daughter of a priest of On, itself a short version of the name Osiris. With Joseph "down" in Egypt, young Benjamin, born to Jacob in Joseph's absence, takes his place as Jacob's favorite son, just as Horus, born posthumously to Osiris, takes Osiris's place in the world of the living. Finally, Joseph becomes the savior of the whole world by stockpiling grain, thus redeeming the world from drought and famine. This is a job for Osiris, the savior and god of grain! By his resurrection he ensures the grain will renew itself and not perish forever as it would have had Set, the desert god, gone unchallenged.

The second biblical version of Osiris, as Randel Helms[23] has shown, is Lazarus in John, chapter 11. Bethany, where the sisters Mary and Martha and their brother Lazarus live, is a Hebraicized version of "House/City of Annu/On," Heliopolis, the city of Osiris. Martha and Mary are Nephthys and Isis, mourning their brother. Lazarus (from Aramaic "Eleazar") represents "El-Osiris." As in Egyptian funerary texts that bid Osiris to come out, not to decompose, Lazarus is told to come out, and he doesn't reek as everyone naturally assumes he must.

Jesus, of course, is the third Osiris of the Bible. Just as Osiris's devotees celebrated a eucharist of bread and beer, symbolizing his body and blood (he is after all the grain god), Jesus declares the wine to be his blood, the bread his body (Mark 14:22–24). Unless dogmatic bias be allowed to prevail, it cannot but be obvious that the Lord's Supper of Christianity stems from the same circle of associations, and that the connection with the Exodus and the Passover is a subsequent and arbitrary attempt to Judaize the rite.

And, like Lazarus, Jesus is raised from the dead at Bethany. For that is the original significance of the anointing scene of Mark 14:3–11, "And while he was at Bethany in the house of Simon the leper, as he sat at table, a woman came with an alabaster jar of pure nard, very costly, and she broke the jar and poured it over his head. But there were some who said to themselves indignantly, 'Why was the ointment thus wasted? For this ointment might have been sold for more than three hundred denarii, and given to the poor.' And they reproached her. But Jesus said, 'Let her alone! Why do you trouble her? She has done a beautiful thing to me. For you always have the poor with you, and whenever you want, you can do them a good deed, but you will not always have me. She has done what she could; she has anointed my body beforehand for burying. And, amen: I say to you, wherever the gospel is preached in the whole world, what she has done will be told in memory of her.'" The story has been reworked, though only slightly, to fit the new place (before the crucifixion) Mark has assigned it. We have already suggested that "You always have the poor with you and you can do them a good deed whenever you want, but you will not always have me" represents the "holy arrogance" (Jerome) of the itinerant brethren of the Son of man. Probably John's version, "Let her keep it for the day of my burial" (John 12:7) is closer to the original, which would have read, "She has kept it for the day of my burial."

Originally, the anointing woman must have been Mary Magdalene, who came to Jesus' tomb with her sisters Mary of James and Salome and "brought spices, so that they might go and anoint him" (Mark 16:1b). They are Isis and Nephthys, and their roles were played yearly by female ritual mourners, to whom we owe the empty tomb story, as well as the anointing story. Originally, the unnamed bystanders complained about wasting the ointment on the dead body, especially as it was two or three days late to do anything for the corpse. "Why waste it on the dead when it might have been of greater use to the living?" Their pious carping functioned originally as the skepticism stage of the typical miracle story, and the miracle it all led up to in this story was the resurrection of Jesus as a result of the sacred anointing. Remember that Ps. 110:3, a coronation psalm, was early applied to the resurrection of Jesus in the New Testament. Usually the part cited is the opening, "The Lord said to my lord, 'Sit at my right hand till I make your enemies a stool for your feet.'" Heb. 7:21 quotes Ps. 110:4, "The Lord has sworn and will not change his mind: you are a priest forever." I suggest that early Christians saw the anointing for resurrection in verse 3b, "From the womb of Shahar the dew of your youth [i.e., your rejuvention, rebirth, resurrection] will come to you." Shahar, Hebrew goddess of the dawn, was more or less equivalent to Isis. Because of this anointing, Jesus was known as Jesus Christ, Jesus the Anointed One, signifying Jesus the Resurrected One. It had not a thing to do with Jewish messianism, except insofar as it kept alive the ancient themes of the dying and rising god that had once been integral to the royal ideology of the divine king.

NOTES

1. Sigmund Mowinkel, *He That Cometh: The Messiah Concept in the Old Testament and Later Judaism*, trans. G. W. Anderson (New York: Abingdon Press, 1954).

2. Helmer Ringgren, "The So-Called Servant Psalms," chap. 4 in *The Messiah in the Old Testament*, Studies in Biblical Theology 18 (London: SCM Press, 1956), pp. 54–64.

3. Geo Widengren, *Mesopotamian Elements in Manicheanism and Mandeanism* (Uppsala: A.-B. Lundeqvista Bokhandeln, 1946).

4. Morna D. Hooker, "The Servant Passages: Their Meaning and Background," chap. 2 in *Jesus and the Servant: The Influence of the Servant Concept of Deutero-Isaiah in the New Testament* (London: SPCK, 1959), pp. 25–52.

5. John A. T. Robinson, "The Most Primitive Christology of All?" *Twelve New Testament Studies*, Studies in Biblical Theology 34 (London: SCM Press, 1962), pp. 139–53.

6. William Wrede, *The Messianic Secret*, trans. J. C. G. Greig, Library of Theological Translations (Altrincham: James Clarke, 1971), pp. 215–19.

7. Raymond E. Brown, *The Birth of the Messiah: A Commentary on the Infancy Narratives in Matthew and Luke* (Garden City: Doubleday Anchor, 1977), pp. 312–14.

8. Reginald H. Fuller, *The Foundations of New Testament Christology* (New York: Scribner, 1965), offers a detailed discussion and exposition of this paradigm.

9. Joachim Jeremias, *The Parables of Jesus*, trans. S. H. Hooke. (New York: Scribner, 1972), p. 188.

10. James Breech, *The Silence of Jesus: The Authentic Voice of the Historical Man* (Philadelphia: Fortress Press, 1983), p. 73.

11. Jeremias, *Parables*, pp. 171–74.

12. John Bowman, *The Gospel of Mark: The New Christian Jewish Passover Haggadah*, Studia Post-Biblica 8 (Leiden: E. J. Brill, 1965), pp. 241–42; Dale Miller and Patricia Miller, *The Gospel of Mark as Midrash on Earlier Jewish and New Testament Literature*, Studies in the Bible and Early Christianity 21 (Lewiston, N.Y.: Edwin Mellen Press, n.d.), pp. 300–301.

13. Maurice Casey, *The Son of Man: The Interpretation and Influence of Daniel 7*

(London: SPCK, 1979), pp. 137–39; Géza Vermes, "Jesus the Son of Man," chap. 7 in *Jesus the Jew: A Historian's Reading of the Gospels* (Glasgow: Fontana/Collins, 1977), pp. 160–86; Norman Perrin, *Rediscovering the Teaching of Jesus* (New York: Harper & Row, 1976), pp. 164–72.

14. Rudolf Otto, "The Son of Man as the Suffering Servant of God," chap. 11 of book 2 in *The Kingdom of God and the Son of Man: A Study in the History of Religion*, trans. Floyd V. Filson and Bertram Lee-Woolf, rev. ed. (Boston: Starr King Press, 1943), pp. 249–55; Hugh J. Schonfield, "The Suffering Just One and the Son of Man," chap. 3 of part 2 in *The Passover Plot: New Light on the History of Jesus* (New York: Bernard Geis/Random House, 1965), pp. 215–27; Joachim Jeremias, "Can Jesus Have Referred the Servant Passages of Deutero-Isaiah to Himself?" chap. 3 of part 4 in *The Servant of God*, ed. Walther Zimmerli and Joachim Jeremias, Studies in Biblical Theology 20, rev. ed. (Naperville, Ill.: Alec R. Allenson, 1952), pp. 99–106.

15. Norman Perrin, "Mark 14:62: The End Product of a Christian Pesher Tradition?" chap. 2 in *A Modern Pilgrimage in New Testament Christology* (Philadelphia: Fortress Press, 1974), pp. 10–22.

16. Gerd Theissen, *The Miracle Stories of the Early Christian Tradition*, trans. Francis McDonagh (Philadelphia: Fortress Press, 1983), p. 171.

17. J. Andrew Overman, *Matthew's Gospel and Formative Judaism: The Social World of the Matthean Community* (Minneapolis: Augsburg Fortress, 1990), pp. 44–45.

18. C. H. Dodd, *Historical Tradition in the Fourth Gospel* (New York: Cambridge University Press, 1963), p. 386; Archibald M. Hunter, *According to John: The New Look at the Fourth Gospel* (Philadelphia: Westminster Press, 1968), pp. 80–81.

19. Jeremias, *Parables*, pp. 70–73.

20. Joachim Jeremias, "Abba," chap. 1 in *The Central Message of the New Testament* (New York: Scribner, 1965), pp. 9–30. This is just devotionalism reading itself into the text.

21. Raymond E. Brown, "The Pater Noster as an Eschatological Prayer," chap. 12 in *New Testament Essays* (Garden City: Doubleday Image, 1968), p. 284.

22. Ovid, *Metamorphoses*, trans. Mary M. Innes (Baltimore: Penguin Books, 1955), p. 327.

23. Randel Helms, *Gospel Fictions* (Amherst, N.Y.: Prometheus Books, 1989), pp. 98–100.

CHAPTER TWELVE
JERUSALEM

PASSION AND ACTION

As we leave the teaching ascribed to Jesus and return to the narrative of the Gospels, we find Jesus headed for the denouement in Jerusalem. "Let us go also" (John 11:16). We will find that this stirring narrative is a clever combination of old Scripture passages brought to life and historical reports of later days garbled and reapplied to Jesus. There are very few pieces we will not be able to account for in this way, very little reason to believe we are dealing with a historical account at all, much less an accurate one. In this chapter and the next, we will cover what is traditionally called the Passion narrative, "passion" meaning suffering.

A FACE IN THE CROWD

On what we call Palm Sunday, did Jesus offer himself to Israel as her Messiah? Was it a Triumphal Entry into the capital, or did Jesus enter as one more pilgrim? Let us begin with Mark and try to find out the original meaning of this story. In Mark 11:1–10, Jesus gives two disciples instructions to enter the city ahead of him. They will, he says, readily spot a donkey tied to a doorknob along the street. They are to untie it and bring it back. If anyone should notice them, say, the owner, they are to say, "The Lord has need of it," and he will let them go with no further questions. All happens as he has said, including someone stopping them to ask what they are doing. And, as foretold, he is satisfied with their answer. It is possible to take the story as implying Jesus has already arranged things with a contact in Jerusalem, who is just making sure the right people, and not common thieves, are taking his donkey. But it seems more likely Mark means us to see Jesus' gift of prescience at work. After all, how would he have pre-arranged things, except by the expedient of sending disciples, as he is doing here? This seems to be the first any of them has heard of it. This is the only arranging he does. And the note that they found the beast just as he had said would be superfluous if the whole thing were prearranged, nothing worthy of remark. This much of the story, like the similar sequence where he sends the disciples to arrange for the Passover (Mark 14:13–16), is probably based on 1 Sam. 9:5–14, where Saul and his companion are likewise looking for donkeys and enter a city in their quest, where they hope to meet the seer Samuel to ask him the whereabouts of the missing livestock. The note that no one had ever ridden the donkey before reflects 1 Sam. 6:7, or the underlying custom, namely, that only something virginally new must be used for sacred transport, just as the Philistines put the Ark of the Covenant on a brand new cart drawn by cows that had never before been yoked.

Having borrowed the donkey, the disciples contrive a makeshift saddle, heaping their cloaks on the animal for Jesus to sit on. Others pave the dirt road with their cloaks and leafy branches to give him the red carpet treatment. The crowd (of disciples?) cries out (repeatedly), "Hosanna! ["O save!"] Blessed be he who comes in the name of the Lord! Blessed be the kingdom of our father David that is coming! Hosanna in the highest!" There is a double entendre here. Mark preserves the messianic secret motif. He and the reader know that this man riding on a donkey (as many did that day) was himself the Messiah the crowd fervently expected to come some Passover soon, bringing with him the resumption of the Davidic monarchy. But the crowd spoke more truly than it knew. All the people meant was to bless Jesus as a visiting pilgrim, coming "in the name of the Lord," that is, for the holy festival. For Mark, Jesus is coming in the name of the Lord as the Messiah, but he cannot mean to say that the crowds know this. Nor does he have them say it outright.

Things are rather different in subsequent gospels, Luke for example. In Luke 19:28–38, the crowd no longer cheers for the coming kingdom of David, but for Jesus himself as the Davidic king: "Blessed is the king who comes in the name of the Lord!" This fuses together Mark's two acclamations in a strategic way: Luke has cast the messianic secret aside. He already had Jesus announce himself as the fulfillment of Isaiah's prophecy back in Luke 4:21. Matthew, too, makes the crowd hail Jesus as the Messiah, though in different words, implying that he and Luke independently changed Mark. Matthew's disciples shout, "Hosanna to the son of David! Blessed be he who comes in the name of the Lord!" Interestingly, Matthew implies Jesus is unknown in the city (verses 10–11). Matthew sees the whole scene as the fulfillment of prophecy (Zech. 9:9), which he quotes in verse 5. Matthew has the peculiar habit of doubling characters, as he does when he gives the Gadarene demoniac a playmate (8:28) and clones two new blind men from Bar-Timaeus (9:27), but these are nothing to the grotesque extravagance of Matt. 21:2–3, 7, where Jesus is said to have ridden two animals at once—rodeo style?[1] Flesh and blood have not revealed it to him, much less historical memory, but rather slavish scriptural literalism. Zechariah describes Jerusalem's king as riding on "a donkey, and on a colt, the foal of a donkey." The point of this was similar to having Jesus ride a donkey no one had ridden before, the finest mount, only here it is stressed that the creature is purebred, a donkey, not a mule. Zechariah's oracle employed the familiar device of synthetic parallelism, making "a donkey" equivalent to "a colt, the foal of a donkey." Only the best for the king! How on earth could Matthew not have understood this, especially when he himself actually employs the same technique in his own creations? But, however artless, Matthew is not stupid. We know from the rabbis that, while they, too, recognized poetic parallelism and used it in their own compositions, they felt obliged to treat biblical poetry as if it were prose, so as to squeeze all (supposedly) available information from it. This is exactly what Matthew has done, albeit with ludicrous results.

John 12:12–19 is very much like Matthew, and perhaps based on Matthew's text. He, too, quotes Zech. 9:9 as a prediction fulfilled by the Triumphal Entry— only he admits that it occurred to no one at the time. It was a product of theological afterthought, a fact that tends to undermine the whole notion that Jesus was wittingly putting himself forward as the Messiah that day. But that is what John has him doing anyway! He, too, has changed the acclamation of the crowd, this time to: "Blessed be he who comes in the name of the Lord, even the king of Israel!" We may hope John intended this last phrase as a parenthetical explanation, like 4:25, 9:7, 19:13, 20:16, rather than part of what the crowd shouted. But even in that case, he thinks the crowd meant to hail Jesus as the Messiah.

It seems pretty clear that Mark, who originated the story, did not intend, indeed, in light of his messianic secret theme, could not have intended, to have Jesus acclaimed as the Messiah entering Jerusalem. The later gospel writers have not been able to resist repainting the scene, making explicit the originally unspoken Christological significance all Christians subsequently saw in the events. If events they were! For now we must suggest that, as the arrangement of the donkey was rewritten from 1 Samuel, the entry itself was composed on the basis of Psalm 118, an ancient entrance liturgy. Note that no evangelist presents "Blessed be he who comes in the name of the Lord" (Ps. 118:26) as a quote. You are not necessarily supposed to know that Psalm 118 is in the background here. Two details suggest the fictive (midrashic) character of the whole scene. First, the Psalm 118 entrance liturgy was historically used not at Passover, but rather at the autumnal feast of Tabernacles (as indeed the wording suggests, as Tabernacles was the yearly Enthronement Festival, and much of Psalm 118 presupposes the role of the king in the celebration). There is some reason to suppose it had come to be used at all three annual festivals in Jesus' day, but no one knows. This means it is unlikely that the crowd would be chanting these words at Passover (though possible). Second, the mention of spreading palm fronds in the Gospels is a reapplied detail from Ps. 118:27b, "Bind the festal procession, up to the horns of the altar." Mark does not depict anyone doing precisely this. Instead, they line the road with the branches, and yet the mention of branches cannot be a coincidence. He simply got the idea of having branches from the psalm. Thus, Psalm 118 provided raw material for the story, but the story is not a historical report of people making ritual use of Psalm 118.

THE FIG TREE LEARNS ITS LESSON

Mark's Triumphal Entry story fizzles into an anticlimax: it is already late in the day, so Jesus just takes a look at everything and leaves the city again, to return tomorrow. Matthew's climax is artistically better: Jesus at once enters the temple and begins turning over the tables. But Mark's version allows him to accommodate the two-part story of the fig tree (11:12–14, 20–21 ff.), which he makes symbolic of the temple and its fate.

Mark quite properly found the fig tree story something of an embarrassment as it originally stood. It is clearly a piece of apocrypha such as we find larding the Infancy Gospels, aimed at demonstrating the raw power of Jesus as a demigod walking the earth. He is hungry and looks for figs on a fig tree, which disappoints him. How dare a mere tree frustrate the very Son of the Most High? The palms of Egypt knew their master and stooped to feed him and his blessed mother: "Then the child Jesus, reposing with a joyful countenance in the lap of his mother, said to the palm, 'O tree, bend your branches and refresh my mother with your fruit.' And immediately at these words the palm bent its top down to the very feet of Mary; and they gathered from it fruit with which they all refreshed themselves" (*Infancy Gospel of Matthew* 20).[2] So Jesus blasts the tree: if it will not feed him, it will never feed anyone again! And at once it withers from the roots up. *That'll* teach it! The story seems to have grown from the seed of Ps. 37:35–36, "I have seen a wicked man overbearing, and towering like a cedar of Lebanon. Again I passed by, and, lo, he was no more."

Mark may have added to the end of the story various sayings about faith, prayer, and forgiveness (verses 22–26) to make it into a lesson of faith, though the connection is painfully artificial. It is an attempt to make a bad text look good. But Mark may have found the sayings already attached to the story, since he makes his own attempt to redeem the story, by making it symbolic of the judgment on the temple. He got the idea from the phrase he found in the Little Apocalypse, Mark 13:28, "From the fig tree learn its lesson."

He has also tried to improve the story by adding an explanation for the barrenness of the tree: "it was not the season for figs," but this only makes it worse! Wouldn't Jesus have known that? And then why not have Jesus miraculously cause the fig tree to sprout figs, as Tim Rice had Jesus do to satisfy the hunger of his disciples in a scene omitted from the final version of *Jesus Christ Superstar*?[3] All things are possible for an omnipotent author, after all. But my guess is that somewhere in the background lurks a local etiological legend about a blasted fig tree, cut from the same cloth as that of Lot's wife as the origin of a woman-shaped, wind-eroded column of rock salt (Gen. 19:26).

Luke for his part made the story into a couple of parables (Luke 17:6, 13:6–9), a wise move. While Mark had Jesus use a tree as an object lesson for a saying about causing a mountain to be thrown into the sea, Luke combines the two, so that a tree is thrown into the sea!

HELTER SKELTER

There is either much more or much less to the story of the Cleansing of the Temple than meets the eye. As it stands the story is filled with improbabilities. Jesus turns over the tables of moneychangers and livestock sellers. For the convenience of the pilgrims, the temple staff had pre-approved sacrificial animals on hand to buy so one need not drag one's own scrawny lamb down from the hill country, only to have it inspected and refused once you got there. They exchanged Roman coins (stamped with "idolatrous" images of Caesar) for Jewish and Phoenician coins that could be used in the sacred precincts to buy the animals. Jesus puts a stop to this. He disallows anyone to bring temple vessels through the area. He sits down to teach the crowd of worshipers, and he says, "Is it not written, 'My house shall be called a house of prayer for all the nations'? But you have made it a den of robbers." The chief priests and scribes seem to overhear this, as if they are simply lingering at the fringe of the crowd. They see that the crowd heeds his every word, and they resolve then and there to have him killed. The scene is very much like that in Mark 3:6, where the Pharisees, publicly embarrassed, make a discrete exit and start to plot Jesus' downfall. But this mild reaction is unthinkable in the situation of chapter 11.

We are in the habit of envisioning this scene as if Jesus had burst into a church basement and disrupted a rummage sale. And that is no accident. Mark seems to have had virtually no idea of the true scale of the temple, which in fact occupied more than thirty-five acres, equal to thirty-four football fields![4] The story as Mark tells it simply cannot have happened. For Jesus to have been able to turn over "the" (not *some* of the) tables would have required a huge number of fellow conspirators. And for him then to refuse to allow anyone to bring sacrificial vessels through the temple clearly demands that he had occupied the whole space, and that with armed men. And since there were armed guards posted in the temple for just such occasions (not to mention twice as many Roman troops as usual camped right down the street in the Antonia Fortress for the Passover season), he could never have done this without a pitched battle. Forget about fearing the wrath of the people, lest there be a tumult! There would have been no chance of avoiding one. *This was* the tumult!

S. G. F. Brandon[5] held that Jesus did lead such a raid on the temple; it is to be identified with the "insurrection" in connection with which Barabbas killed someone (Mark 15:7). Brandon says Mark has whittled it down in order to paper over the revolutionary origins of the Christian movement, so as to avert Roman suspicion and persecution in his own day. Jesus was executed as king of the Jews because he had set himself up as one. This is not out of the question, but as Burton L. Mack[6] argues, the Markan text may be too shallow soil for the historian to find a historical root beneath it. For one thing, the "teaching" of Jesus amounts to no more than two quotes (one unacknowledged), from Isa. 56:7 and Jer. 7:11. As always, we must credit the scriptural citations to Mark who is, so to speak, foraging building blocks from an old structure to build a new one. Besides this, what else constitutes the scene? Not much. The element of the crowd's amazement is typical Markan acclamation, starting back in the Capernaum synagogue (1:27). And the plotting of Jesus' enemies, as we have already seen, is more of the same, modeled upon Mark 3:6. Mack rightly declares the whole thing a Markan fiction.

But we are entitled to ask where Mark may have derived the idea for his fiction, and there is an obvious answer. Mark 13:5, 21–22 shows an uneasy awareness that Christians might have had trouble keeping their Messiahs straight during the siege of Jerusalem, some thinking perhaps that various anti-Roman rebels and would-be kings were the Messiah instead of Jesus, or perhaps counted *as* the return of Jesus, as the Baptist had served as the return of Elijah. As it happens, several features of the Passion narrative bear an uncanny resemblance to the stories of some of those rival Messiahs. There was even a Triumphal Entry of Simon bar-Gioras, a rebel against Roman occupation who had been fighting against another rebel band, the Zealots, and their allies from Idumea (Edom). The Zealots, under their leader John of Gischala, occupied Jerusalem. Their Idumean allies broke with them and, fighting their former compatriots, drove them back into the temple compound. Then the Idumeans conspired with the priests to appeal to Simon, outside the city walls, to come in and deal with the Zealots. "In order to overthrow John, they voted to admit Simon, and olive branch in hand to bring in a second tyrant to be their master. The resolution was carried out, and they sent the high priest, Matthias, to implore Simon to enter, the man they so greatly feared! The invitation was supported by those citizens who were trying to escape the Zealots and were anxious about their homes and property. He in his lordly way expressed his willingness to be their master, and entered with the air of one who intended to sweep the Zealots out of the city, acclaimed by the citizens as deliverer and protector" (Josephus *The Jewish War*, 5, 9, 11).[7] The temple, then, had become a den of "robbers" (as revolutionists were called), and the messiah Simon cleansed the temple of their infection. Sound familiar?

THE LAST (SUPPER) SHALL BE FIRST

We have already seen that both the errand of the two disciples to fetch the donkey for the Triumphal Entry and the mission of two disciples to find the room for the Last Supper have been based on 1 Sam. 9:5–14, where Saul enters a city looking for his donkeys and meets women carrying water jars.[8] Here the disciples are to look for a man carrying one and to ask him the way to the room where they will gather for the Passover seder. Again, the point seems to be Jesus' prophetic clairvoyance and the miraculous providence of God—or what is the point of telling the story?

In Mark and Matthew, the only mention of it being Passover is in this introductory episode. Once we get into the scene of the supper, there is absolutely nothing to mark it as a Passover meal, and we may suspect that the connection is not original to the tradition. Some have suggested that the story of the disciples seeking the man with the water jar once stood on its own as an example of how God will provide for his own. Mark may have inserted it before the Last Supper story, making the supper a seder by means of the juxtaposition. It is in Luke's retelling that we have Jesus at table actually say it is a Passover meal: "I have earnestly desired to eat *this Passover* with you." In John's gospel, the meal cannot possibly be a seder, since John explicitly says the Last Supper took place before the Passover (13:1, 29).

Annie Jaubert proposed a way of harmonizing John and the Synoptics, positing that John preserves a tradition of Jesus celebrating Passover according to the Enochian solar calendar of the Essenes, a day before all other Jews.[9] It could be so, but the fact remains that the account of the supper itself makes no reference to the accouterments of the Passover, and that, most damning of all, John himself, the one who locates it a day early, does not describe it as a Passover feast.

It seems far more likely that the Passover connection is a later attempt to supply a more recognizably Jewish pedigree to a rite that had a very different origin, namely, among the Mystery Religions, the marks of which it still plainly bears. For it is just unthinkable that a sacramental meal in which one symbolically consumes human flesh and blood could have originated in any form of Judaism we know anything about. On the other hand, when we hear the words of a savior bequeathing to his devotees bread as his body and wine as his blood, we know we are in the presence of some Frazerian Corn King like Tammuz, Osiris, or Dionysus, whose impending death means the death of vegetation and whose coming resurrection marks the return of it.

The central concern of the supper scene is ritual, to establish the liturgical Words of Institution. Of this section we have no fewer than six canonical versions: 1 Cor. 11:23–26, Mark 14:22–25, Matt. 26:26–29, Luke 22:15–19a (Codex Bezae), Luke 22:12–20, and John 6:48–57 ff. The different versions stem, at least partly, from liturgical modifications of the Words of Institution as used in each church community represented by each New Testament writer. There are also cases of redactional modification. Again, both processes may be traced in the manuscript tradition of each gospel, where evolving differences no doubt reflect adjustment to the particular copyist's church's usage or his own proclivities. Sometimes scribes also tended to harmonize one gospel version with another. That is, a scribe might recall the form of the Words of Institution from one gospel and automatically reproduce them when he came to the next gospel, failing to notice the difference in wording. Some scribes decided they had best make the Gospels agree, combining details from various versions on purpose.

Mark 14:22–25 reads, "And as they were eating, he took bread, and blessed, and broke it, and gave it to them, and said, 'Take; this is my body.' And he took a cup, and when he had given thanks he gave it to them, and they all drank of it. And he said to them, 'This is my blood of the [new?] covenant, which is poured out for many. Amen: I say to you, I shall not drink of the fruit of the vine until that day when I drink it new in the kingdom of God.'" Most scholars, following Schweitzer and Jeremias,[10] hold Mark's version as closest to the original. Does Matthew's version make sense as a modification of it? "Now as they were eating, Jesus took bread, and blessed, and broke it, and gave it to the disciples and said, 'Take, *eat*; this is my body.' And he took a cup, and after he had given thanks he gave it to them, saying, *'Drink of it, all of you*; for this is my blood of the [new?] covenant, which is poured out for many *for the forgiveness of sins*. I tell you I shall not drink again of *this* fruit of the vine until that day when I drink it new *with you* in *my Father's* kingdom" (Matt. 26:26–29). Matthew has added the clause explaining to what effect the blood of Jesus will be poured out. It is salvific. He adds Mark's (only implicit) command to "eat" and reshuffles Mark's words "and they all drank of it," making it into an imperative, "Drink of it, all of you," which results in two parallel ritual commands. Matthew has incidentally heightened the Christology, characterizing God as Jesus' Father. He also anchors the vow of abstinence more firmly into the narrative context by specifying that Jesus will one day partake of wine *with the same men* in some future paradise. So Matthew seems, on the one hand, to be sharpening the liturgical focus of the text, so people will know just what to do on signal at the eucharist and, on the other, to avoid any implication that the vow of abstinence is of any wider application than to Jesus himself.

With Luke, we have to make a choice between two different forms of the text. The Western Text (Codex Bezae) has a longer version than other manuscripts. The additional text is indicated here in italics: "And when the hour came, he sat at table, and the apostles with him. And he said to them, 'I have earnestly desired to eat this Passover with you before I suffer; for I tell you I shall not eat it [some manuscripts: "never eat it again"] until it is fulfilled in the kingdom of God.' And he took a cup, and when he had given thanks he said, 'Take this and divide it among yourselves; for I tell you that from now on I shall not drink of the fruit of the vine until the kingdom of God comes.' And he took bread, and when he had given thanks he broke it and gave it to them, saying, 'This is my body *which is given for you. Do this in remembrance of me.' And likewise the cup after supper, saying, 'This cup which is poured out for you is the new covenant in my blood'"* (Luke 22:14–20). Luke has thus doubled the vow of abstinence, adding to it a moratorium on observing Passover till the kingdom should dawn. This echoes Matthew's agenda of historicizing the vow of abstinence so that it applies only to Jesus: now the cup of wine is reinterpreted as referring to the cups of wine at the seder, not wine generally. (Matthew may mean the same thing by changing Mark's "the fruit of the vine" to "*this* fruit of the vine.") The parallel remains between the presentation of the wine and that of the bread, but it is incomplete. Like Matthew, Luke has replaced Mark's indicative, "They all drank of it," with a command, "Divide it among yourselves," but unlike Matthew he has avoided the simple word "drink." And of course there is no command at all vis-à-vis the bread, which now comes first. One gets the distinct impression that Luke does not mean this scene to provide a script for a liturgy. The avoidance of "drink" implies as much, as does the erasure of the rest of the Markan text on the bread. That Luke must have stopped here is evident from the fact of his having inserted the vow of abstinence at the beginning, knowing he would not have Mark's ending from which to hang it. Codex Bezae (with some other manuscripts) adds to the text, trying to harmonize it with Mark, adding a note on the salvific significance of the body (derived perhaps from 1 Cor. 11:24) and restoring that about the wine, in the process adding a second cup. So Codex Bezae has the Lukan Last Supper as the script for the eucharist after all.

The reluctance of scholars like Jeremias to part with the Bezan padding has retarded the realization that Luke meant to negate the ransom soteriology of Mark, as skimpy as it was. Luke chopped Mark's "blood of the covenant, poured out for many." In addition, Luke rewrote Mark 10:45 ("For the son of man also came not to be served but to serve, and to give his life a ransom for many") as "For which is the greater, one who sits at table, or one who serves? Is it not the one who sits at table? But I am among you as one who serves" (Luke 22:27). Notice Luke has transferred the saying to the Last Supper and has omitted the nontitular use of "son of man." But most striking, his version lacks Mark's reference to giving his life as a ransom. Some have thought Luke preferred a hypothetical earlier version of the saying, lacking the ransom element, in which case we might dismiss the ransom as a later embellishment, perhaps added by Mark himself. But this is less likely (because more complex) than Luke having cut Mark.

What, precisely, was the "blood ransom" theology that so disturbed Luke? Hard to say, but the closest we can come to it would probably be the Jewish doctrine of the atoning merit of martyrdom. We find it among both Hellenized Jews and their more traditionalist Palestinian counterparts. In 2 Maccabees, seven brothers are being hideously tortured to death for refusing to take a bite of ham, metonymy for apostasy from the Jewish covenant. "I, like my brothers, give up body and life for the laws of our fathers, appealing to God to show mercy soon to our nation . . . and through me and my brothers to bring to an end the wrath of the Almighty which has justly fallen on our whole nation" (2 Macc. 7:37–38). In 4 Macc. 6:28–29, Eleazer, an elder of the people, is also brutalized in a stomach-turning display. He prays, "Be merciful to your people, and let our punishment suffice for them. Make my blood their purification, and take my life in exchange for theirs." Eventually the faithfulness of the martyrs pays off when the tyrant Antiochus is brought down. The martyrs had "become, as it were, a ransom for the sin of our nation. And through the blood of those devout ones and their death as an expiation, divine Providence preserved Israel that previously had been afflicted" (4 Macc. 17:21b–22). The suffering and/or death of the righteous was traditionally regarded as atoning for the sins of the people as a whole. In times of suffering and persecution, more than one rabbi exclaimed, "Behold, I am the atonement of Israel" (*Mekhilta* 2a; *Mishnah Negaim* 2:1).[11] Thus, for Jesus to plan "to give his life a ransom for many" would be to attribute to his suffering an atoning value, to alleviate his people's suffering under Roman occupation. The notion is so thoroughly Jewish that it is natural to attribute the saying to early Hellenistic Jewish Christians, not necessarily to Jesus.

Similarly, what about the business of Jesus' blood inaugurating a covenant and being shed for many? The "blood of the covenant" must refer back to Exod. 24:8, "And Moses took the blood and threw it upon the people, and said, 'Behold, the blood of the covenant which Yahve has made with you in accordance with all these words.'" It almost doesn't matter whether Matthew and Mark originally wrote "new" before "covenant" as some manuscripts have, because the point is pretty much the same either way: Jesus, in his coming death, will be doing the same thing Moses did, only with his own blood. He will be establishing a new covenant, with himself as the sacrifice to seal it. Even the phrase "for many" fits this framework of symbolism, since Jesus' blood is to be poured out even as that of the oxen was poured out into a basin and sprinkled upon (representatives of) Israel by Moses. We must not hasten to read into this single clause whole doctrines and theories of salvation that are not spelled out here. Matthew, with his five-book Torah of Jesus' teaching, and Luke, with his "Deutero-Deuteronomy" in his Central Section, both catch the hint quite well, making explicit what is implicit in Mark, beginning with Mark 1:22, 27, "he taught them as one having authority, and not as the scribes. . . . 'A new teaching!'" The new covenant is a new set of commands. This is something of a new dispensation, especially as regards the Gentiles, but it does not exactly come under the heading of a new plan of salvation. Compare the theological prototype Jer. 31:31–34, where the new covenant is a matter of renewed faithfulness to the old laws.

The next version to consider is not, as might be expected, that of the fourth gospel, but rather that of 1 Cor. 11:23–26, "For I received from the Lord what I in turn delivered to you, that the Lord Jesus, on the night he was delivered up, took bread, and when he had given thanks, he broke it, and said, 'This is my body *which is [broken?] for you. Do this in remembrance of me.*' In the same way also the cup, after supper, saying, 'This cup is the new covenant in my blood. *Do this, as often as you drink it, in remembrance of me.*' For as often as you eat this bread and drink the cup, you proclaim the Lord's death until he comes." This version also appears to be descended from Mark's original. The differences can be explained quite easily as redactional alterations. For instance, where does 1 Corinthians get the phrase it appends to the saying about the body, that it is "for," or "broken for," you? It looks as if someone has clipped the modification of the blood having been "poured out for you," omitted the "poured" for obvious reasons, and transferred it to the body saying. Then a copyist, deciding that "which is for you" sounded too abrupt, filled out the phrase with "broken," as we read in some manuscripts. 1 Corinthians very definitely intends the material as a ritual script, having added two "Do this in remembrance of me" commands. Also, most likely, the word "new" modifies "covenant" in some manuscripts of Mark and Matthew because scribes picked it up from here in 1 Corinthians and added it to these gospels.

Such a piece of seeming gospel narrative is out of place in a Pauline epistle. What is it doing here? Some have argued that the pericope has been interpolated, which certainly seems to make sense given the seeming dependence upon Mark. And this is all the more likely because of the writer's claim to have received this material directly from the Risen Lord as a revelation. That he should have received a revelation in narrative form is itself a little odd. We might think of the numerous "revealed histories" of the Koran, but these, too, are suspect as genuine (i.e., spontaneous) revelations and instead appear to be labored compositions later ascribed to direct delivery by Gabriel's inspiration to Muhammad. Even at that, however, the fact that the form of the Words of Institution is secondary in general, and specifically derivative from Mark, makes the claim implausible. It appears to be an attempt by Paulinists to claim autonomous independent possession of the eucharistic material, to deny their dependence on other quarters of Christianity for it, much in the vein of Gal. 1:11–12.[12] Just as Paul had insisted he derived his gospel from no man but directly from Jesus Christ, so is he depicted here as having received the [Markan] Last Supper material directly from Christ.

The furthest removed from the Markan tradition is John's version, which is not even presented as part of the Last Supper. Its place there is taken by the apparent institution of "washing the feet of the saints" (John 13:1–17, 1 Tim. 5:10), itself quite possibly suggested by John's reading of Luke 22:27, where Jesus is a servant at the table. For John the Last Supper is not a Passover seder, but he moves his version of the Words of Institution over to a different Passover setting as part of a synagogue sermon or debate in Capernaum (John 6:59). "I am the living bread which came down from heaven; if anyone eats of this bread he will live forever; and the bread which I shall give for the life of the world is my flesh. . . . Amen, amen: I say to you, unless you eat the flesh of the Son of man and drink his blood, you have no life in you; he who eats my flesh and drinks my blood has eternal life, and I will raise him up at the last day. He who eats my flesh and drinks my blood abides in me, and I in him" (John 6:51–56). Roman Catholic exegetes are no doubt correct that these words are meant to refer to the eucharist. And Bultmann[13] is no doubt correct that John the evangelist did not write them. They have been added to the gospel in exactly the same way and for the same reason that Codex Bezae added more material to Luke's version of the Words of Institution: to restore an implicit sacramentalism an earlier writer had omitted. And in the words of the Ecclesiastical Redactor of John we have pretty much already arrived at Ignatius's view of the eucharist as the "medicine of immortality" (Ignatian Ephesians 20:2).

Of our six versions of the Last Supper eucharistic words, Matthew, Codex Bezae, and 1 Corinthians seem to view the Words of Institution as a liturgical formula, while Mark, Luke, and the Ecclesiastical Redactor of John do not. These last may well have used something similar in their own liturgy, but when it came to the gospel narrative, they apparently did not feel the need to make Jesus explicitly initiate and authorize the liturgy. And yet, as Loisy recognized, the whole thing must have begun as, or been directly derived from, a liturgical text. For Jesus, clearly the celebrant, to offer the elements of bread and wine, and to present each with an interpretive word, "This is . . . This is . . ." clearly bespeaks liturgy.[14] We must suppose Mark derived the Words of Institution from his own church's liturgy (descended, originally, as I have argued, from a Mystery rite like that of Osiris). Thus, the depiction of the Last Supper began as an etiological legend, an ideal prototype for all the Lord's Suppers to come, though as in all such cases, the order is just the reverse: the practice begat the story.

We have alluded more than once to the *vow of abstinence*: "Amen: I tell you, I shall not drink again of the fruit of the vine until that day when I drink it new in the kingdom of God" (Mark 14:25). Schweitzer concluded that this was the original Last Supper saying of Jesus and that the Words of Institution represent a subsequent addition. Mark and Matthew, Schweitzer thought, inherited the complex from tradition. But all Jesus had actually said was that he would drink no wine before the eschatological denouement transpired, so quickly did he expect it. But, I would suggest, there is no reason to ascribe even this much to Jesus. It, too, is a piece of liturgy, or there is no reason not to view it so. It sounds to me like the text of a vow to be taken by teetotaling ascetic Christians, who were legion in the early church. It was such Christians as these who famously practiced the eucharist with bread and water (as some North African churches did into the third century) or bread and salt (the Ebionites). In fact, it would make sense if such vows were taken publicly by the newly baptized at their first eucharist. That may be what it is doing here at all: it is a vestige of an alternative eucharist. And read this way, it implies nothing about the soon-coming end of the world. It only means that the one taking the oath will never drink wine in this life. It is this vow that Matthew and Luke have decided must apply only to Jesus in his unique circumstances. That is no accident; remember, Matthew wants his Words of Institution used as a liturgical script, which means he expects communicants to be drinking wine. Luke does not mean to write a communion rubric, but he elsewhere shows himself opposed to teetotalism (Luke 5:39; 1 Tim. 4:3–5, 5:23).[15]

On the way from the supper to the Garden of Gethsemane, Jesus delivers the latest in a series of Passion predictions (Mark 14:26–30). This time he predicts the disciples will abandon him and flee—this very night! All these predictions (Mark 8:31; 9:9b, 31–32; 10:33–34) are historically spurious literary devices, "scenes from the next episode," exact summaries of just what Mark will relate once we get to it. They serve to reassure the reader that the coming events, while seeming disastrous, are in fact preordained by the will of God, and that Jesus walks into them with eyes wide open so that scripture may be fulfilled. The passages are perfect disclosures of what Derrida[16] calls the "simultaneity" of the text: it is all there as a structured unit from the moment the reader starts reading, and each section is therefore like a hologram, each part containing anticipations, traces, of all the other parts. That the predictions are aimed solely at the reader, not at the characters in the story to whom they are ostensibly spoken, is evident from the fact that they go right over the heads of those characters.[17] Mark intends to have them surprised at the later developments, but how can they be if they have been told plainly about them several times in advance? He sees the problem and makes incredible excuses such as that the disciples do not know what "rising from the dead" means, 9:10 (despite the fact Mark has had them inform Jesus that people think he is John the Baptist raised from the dead!), or that they just plain didn't understand it (10:32) and were afraid to ask. Luke slightly improved on this by having God himself prevent the disciples from understanding: "But they did not understand this saying, and it was concealed from them, that they should not perceive it, and they were afraid to ask him about it" (Luke 9:45), just as the identity of the Risen Jesus was concealed from the two Emmaus disciples (Luke 24:16, "Their eyes were kept from recognizing him").

In fact, one Passion prediction in particular seems to have a ritual basis similar to the vow of abstinence just considered. In Mark 10:35–45, James and John approach Jesus with outrageous brazenness, asking him to reserve the seats of greatest honor for them when he takes power. "You do not realize what you are asking. *Are you able to drink the cup that I drink? Or to be baptized with the baptism I am baptized with?*" Looking at one another, the brothers buck up and reply, "*We are able.*" "And Jesus said to them, '*The cup that I drink you will drink, and with the baptism I am baptized with you will be baptized.*'" But in fact those choice seats have already been reserved for someone else—perhaps the thieves on the crosses to either side of Jesus? The italicized portions, I am sure, represent a formulaic liturgical exchange between early Christian initiates and their initiator (a bishop?) on the occasion of baptism, which would be followed by one's first communion. In the antiphonal script, the initiator takes the role of Jesus, or even simply speaks for himself as someone who is already entitled to take communion by virtue of baptism. Eventually, the text was placed in the present narrative context as a bit of polemic against the authority of James and John (or, more to the point, of their ostensible successors). As historicized liturgy, though, it has no claim to historical authenticity.

GARDEN OF FEAR

The Garden of Gethsemane on the Mount of Olives, a frequent place of rest and retreat, is the place Jesus knows he will meet Judas and his fate in incongruous surroundings. He could escape but instead walks right into the trap. For it must be so. He is compelled by prophecy and the will of God. He has evaded danger before, but now the designated hour has come, or so it now reads in the Gospels. What are the roots of this episode? It has probably been inspired by the story of King David's flight after his son Absalom has usurped his throne (2 Sam. 15:24–31, 16:1–14).[18] Consider the parallels: David, the anointed king, has been rejected by the people, just as Jesus, the Davidic Messiah, has been (or soon will be). David makes for the Mount of Olives, as does Jesus, both accompanied by retainers. David tells three[19] of his men to turn back to the city, while Jesus leaves eight behind, takes three with him, but then tells them to stay put while he goes a bit further. David is weeping at the fate that has befallen him, just as Jesus is sorrowful unto death. After David leaves Olivet, he is accosted and insulted by Shimei, a partisan of Saul rejoicing in David's downfall. He curses David. David's man Abishai is indignant and asks permission to behead the man, but David forbids it, saying Shimei is doing no more than God, who brought David low, has assigned him to do. So they continue on their way, Shimei mocking and pelting them with rocks. Mark seems to have reworked this sequence, turning Shimei into "Shimeon" Peter, the "rock," who does not exactly mock but does deny Jesus, or will in the next scene. Mark has made the zealous Abishai into the disciple (whom John will specify as Peter, but the Synoptics leave anonymous) who tries to cleave the skull of one of the arresting party, missing and slicing only his ear. Jesus tells him to stop, as David told Abishai. Jesus, like David, insists that they follow the path ordained by God, however humiliating it may seem at the present. And just as David said God must have bidden Shimei to curse him, so does Jesus predict the denials of Peter as inevitable.

In the sequence of the prayer and the arrest in Gethsemane, Matthew and Luke generally follow Mark, but each with greater and greater liberties as they go along. Luke becomes so different at certain points that many have posited a special Lukan Passion narrative that he subsequently harmonized with Mark. It almost makes no difference. It would just be a question of whether Luke has made up his additional material or borrowed it from oral tradition or a written source. John seems to know Mark and Luke, but as usual he has gone his own way, not troubling to follow any source very closely.

In Matthew and Luke, Jesus takes the inner circle of Peter, James, and John with him, though he then leaves them behind. Luke omits the business about the three and their soporific temptations, but Mark seems to imply that their presence was quite important. His Jesus prays to be spared the cross, then returns to the three disciples, only to find them sawing wood. He rebukes them and tries it again, returning to find them asleep again. He tries it a third time and, to his manifest disgust, sees they could not manage to stay awake. And now it is too late. It is hard to escape the impression that Jesus thinks, had they remained steadfast and vigilant in prayer, they might have spared him the ordeal. His prayer for deliverance might have been answered. Did he need their petitions added to his own? Or does he just mean they might have kept watch and alerted him at the first sign of trouble—so he could have escaped? This is not the only sign we will see of a kind of countersignature in the text according to which Jesus tries and finally succeeds in cheating death on the cross. It may represent an earlier version that Mark has overwritten.

We have already seen that the agonized prayer of Jesus, however poignant and plausible, cannot be authentic for the simple reason that no one could have been there to hear it. As for the content, we ought to mark two echoes of Classical antiquity. For one, the "cup" of death is surely meant to recall the heroic death of Socrates, his cup of hemlock. The other is the petition, "Let this cup pass from me," a technical piece of toastmaster rhetoric whereby one modestly sought (or pretended to seek) to decline a proffered honor, suggesting it go to someone more worthy.[20] Here we might wonder if, again, we do not after all detect some echo of an underlying version of the story in which Jesus is not going to die on the cross, but perhaps someone else will take the honor instead, as many early Christians believed for some centuries (and as Muslims believe today).

Luke embellishes the scene. His Jesus prays but once, and there is no trio of sleeping disciples, but Luke has Jesus sweating bullets (tears like drops of blood, Luke 22:44) and brings down an angel from heaven to strengthen him in some way (Luke 22:43). Some manuscripts omit these verses, but they must have been present in the copy of Luke John read, for he refutes them, together with the request to be spared the cross, in John 12:27–29, "'Now my soul is troubled. And what shall I say? "Father, save me from this hour"? Ha! It is for this purpose I have come to this hour! Father, glorify your name!' Then a voice came from heaven, 'I have glorified it, and I will glorify it again.' The crowd standing by heard it and said that it had thundered. Others said, 'An angel has spoken to him.'" So Jesus did feel some apprehension, John admits, but pray to escape the decisive hour? Not likely! And did he need an angel's help? No again; only the spiritually obtuse, like Luke, thought so!

JUDAS, PRIEST

Then disciple number twelve arrives on the scene with an entourage of his own, an armed band of goons on loan from the temple authorities. He has earlier conspired with the chief priests and elders to put Jesus in their power. Why was this thought necessary? Remember, had the temple cleansing actually transpired, we would be witnessing none of this, for Jesus cannot have survived the melee that must have ensued. But suppose he had managed to slip out and go into hiding? In such a case, Judas's help would indeed have come in handy, but this is not what the Gospels say. That would be to defend a story none of them tells. In any case, why was Judas's assistance necessary? Mark has Judas provide an advance signal to the arresting officer: "The one I shall kiss is the man" (14:44). So they needed him to identify Jesus. But this makes Judas not only the twelfth disciple but also the fifth wheel! Jesus is in trouble because he is so popular that the authorities fear an uprising! How can anyone not have known who he was? Medieval Muslim commentators[21] spotted the problem and imaginatively proposed that all the disciples were suddenly miraculously transformed into exact likenesses of Jesus! Thus, the point would have been, "Will the real Jesus please stand up?" Judas's task would have been to distinguish the real one. It seems that Mark is looking for something for Judas to do, trying to justify his presence in the narrative.

But Mark has given Judas's betrayal as little motivation as he has utility. Why on earth would one of the twelve disciples chosen by Jesus to share his presence and his mission suddenly turn him over to his enemies? What a story! But it is one we do not hear. Mark simply has Judas one day approach the Sanhedrin and offer them his help (Mark 14:10–11), whereupon they agree to compensate him for his trouble. It is Matthew, sensing the artificiality of this, who makes Judas sell Jesus out for a few extra bucks (Matt. 26:15). In his version, Judas goes to the lair of Jesus' foes and asks how much they would be willing to pay! In both Matthew and Mark, the meeting of Judas with the elders and priests occurs just after the anointing of Jesus at Bethany, allowing for the possibility that (as per John) Judas had been one of the bystanders who carped about the waste of the expensive ointment. Perhaps Jesus' seeming narcissism ("You do not always have me") was the last straw. But Mark does not tell us this, and he could have easily enough, simply by naming Judas as the complainer.

Luke answered the question of Judas's motivation differently: he decided such a despicable and altogether arbitrary act must be the result of nothing less than possession by Satan (Luke 22:3), so we must picture Judas, eyes glowing sulphurously, voice with a slight echo, appearing suddenly in the shadows at the high priest's mansion. "How'd *he* get in here? What do you want?" John liked both Luke's and Matthew's guesses as to Judas's motivation, so he makes Judas both a petty crook (John 12:6) and a Satan-possessed monster (13:27). And here is an interesting detail. For Mark and Matthew, it is Satan's goal to have Jesus avoid the cross, for when Peter suggests Jesus give it a miss, Jesus calls him Satan (Mark 8:31–33, Matt. 16:21–23). For them, Judas is not Satan's tool. He has his own motive (or no motive) for what he does. But for Luke and John, Satan's design is to put Jesus on the cross and so he hijacks Judas to bring this about. And, consistently, neither Luke nor John has Peter suggest Jesus skip the cross. Luke cuts out the rebuke of Peter where Mark and Matthew had it (after Peter's confession, Luke 9:22), and in his version of the same incident, John has Jesus call Judas, not Peter, "a devil" (John 6:70–71).

Where did this character come from? Recent scholars including Frank Kermode and Hyam Maccoby[22] have suggested that the character of Judas Iscariot (Judas the False One) is one, as I would say, one of Todorov's "narrative-men," an actantial incarnation, or a character who consists of nothing more than his function in the story. A narrative-man[23] is simply a story-function that bears a human name. "Judas Iscariot" would be a political cartoon figure representing the imagined Jewish betrayal (rejection) of Jesus Christ. The Wandering Jew is another, illustrating the wandering, suffering, and weariness of Jews after the destruction of Jerusalem, supposedly in punishment of their rejecting Jesus.[24] At first there was no one human betrayer of Jesus in the story. Jesus needn't have been sold into the hands of his enemies. 1 Cor. 11:23 speaks of the supper "on the night he was 'betrayed,'" but that word παραδιδομαι can mean, as it does in Romans 4:25, 8:32, "delivered up," as God is said to have delivered up Jesus to the cross for our salvation. It might as easily mean that in 1 Cor. 11:23, and it most likely does. But in time someone took this to mean some man had betrayed him, and the symbolic Judas Iscariot/Jewish Betrayer character was waiting in the wings. It only remained for someone to close the circle by suggesting that (as in Nikos Kazantzakis's *The Last Temptation of Christ*) Judas performed a priestly and heroic act by delivering Jesus up for sacrifice so he could accomplish his sacred purpose, and the Cainite Gnostics are in fact said to have believed this: "the Archons knew that if Christ were given over to the cross, their weak power would be drained. Judas, knowing this, bent every effort to betray him, thereby accomplishing a good work for our salvation. We ought to admire and praise him, because through him the salvation of the cross was prepared for us and the revelation of things above occasioned by it" (Epiphanius of Salamis *Panarion* or *Medicine Chest* 38.3.4–5).[25]

Luke and Matthew each supply what he deems a dramatically fitting word from Jesus to Judas: "Friend, why are you here?" (though I prefer the RSV marginal translation, "Friend, do what you came for," Matt. 26:50. "Judas, would you betray a man [literally, "the son of man"] with a kiss?" Luke 22:48).

As Abishai nearly does, one of the disciples whips out a sword and unleashes a poorly aimed blow that misses its target, succeeding only in clipping a man's ear off. The man is a servant of the high priest, and John alone names him Malchus. John and Luke specify that he lost his right ear. John also names the sword wielder: Peter. This is in accord with both the general tendency of later documents to fill in narrative detail, including names of anonymous characters (in the late Gospel of Nicodemus, we learn that the thieves crucified with Jesus were named Demas and Gestas, for example), and the specific tendency of the Gospels to make Peter the embodiment of the disciples in general.

At this first appearance of violence, Matthew, Luke, and John have Jesus intervene to nip it in the bud. Matthew and John have Jesus order his impulsive disciple to sheathe his sword, while Luke preempts further blows by performing a miracle, picking up the severed ear and reattaching it to the servant's head! Mark (14:48) moves immediately to Jesus' ironic words to the crowd who apparently regard him as some sort of desperado to whom only an armed mob will be equal. This is too abrupt: was there no reaction to the first blow being struck by one of Jesus' men? It appears as if Mark did know that something came next but omitted it. As E. A. Abbott saw, there must have been some text or tale of the arrest in which, at this point, Jesus said, "Let it be restored to its place!" Mark did not know what to make of it and so omitted it. Matthew and John correctly surmised that "it" referred to the disciple's weapon: "Put your sword back into its place" (Matt. 26:52a). "Put your sword into its sheath" (John 18:11a). But Luke imagined that "it" must be the severed ear! Hence, "And he touched his ear and healed him" (Luke 22:51b).[26]

Jesus reminds his followers (actually, the reader) that he is not being taken against his will. Despite appearances, the Father's will is being done. "Do you think that I cannot appeal to my Father, and he will at once put more than twelve legions of angels at my disposal? But how then should the scriptures be fulfilled, which say that it must be this way?" (Matt. 26:53–54). John narratizes the same theological reassurance to the reader, and in spectacular form: "Then Jesus, knowing all that was to befall him, came forward and said to them, 'Whom do you seek?' They answered him, 'Jesus of Nazareth.' Jesus said, 'I am he.' . . . When he said to them, 'I am he,' they reared back and fell to the ground. Again he asked them, 'Whom do you seek?' And they said, 'Jesus of Nazareth.' Jesus answered, 'I told you that I am he; so if you seek me, let these men go'" (John 18:4–8). The artificiality of this episode is clear from the lack of any aftermath from Jesus' devastating word. We must imagine the soldiers climbing to their feet, dusting themselves off, and obtusely saying, "Now, where were we?" as if nothing that important had happened! And of course nothing did! It is just a parenthetical comment by John that is exactly the same in intent as Matthew's saying about Jesus having thousands of rescuing angels at his disposal had he wanted to use them. In fact, what we are seeing is another version of Elijah receiving a party of fifty Samaritan guards sent to apprehend him. Elijah calls down fire on their heads, then incinerates a second group likewise, and finally agrees to go with the third, now that he has made it sufficiently clear that he is going of his own volition (2 Kings 1:9–15).

A singular feature of Mark's gospel omitted by the rest is the bizarre detail of the young man who is nearly captured by the soldiers but escapes by the skin of his teeth, leaving his linen sheet in a soldier's hand and fleeing naked (Mark 14:51). Who is this? Why is this brief bit in the story at all? In all probability this is a barely narrative attempt to assert that the prophecy of Amos 2:16 was fulfilled: "In that day the strong man shall flee away naked." The phrase "in that day" would have suggested to an early Christian scribe the fateful hour that had come at last, "the day when the bridegroom is taken away from them."

Before moving on to the next scene, the trials of Jesus before the Sanhedrin and Pontius Pilate, let us look briefly at the rest of Judas's saga, after his fifteen minutes of fame. There must have been some vague oral tradition attached to Judas, associating him in some way with a place called *Akeldama*, the Field of Blood. My guess is that this meant merely that Judas was responsible for the death of Jesus, the Field of Blood being a metonym for this, based on the bloody field where the soon-to-be-resurrected Baal died. At any rate, Matthew and Luke each strove mightily to make sense of it. Matt. 27:3–10 tries to explain and fill out this story with the aid of Old Testament proof texts. He has taken the Syriac text of Zech. 11:12–13 ("Then I said to them, 'If it seems right to you, give me my wages, but if not, keep them.' And they weighed out as my wages thirty shekels of silver. Then Yahve said to me, 'Cast it into *the treasury*'—the lordly price at which I was paid off by them. So I took the thirty shekels of silver and cast them into *the treasury* in the house of Yahve") and on the basis of it, he has Judas think better of his act and return the bounty money to the priests, who spurn it, whereupon he throws it into the temple treasury. What happened to the money then? Matthew takes the Hebrew text of the same passage, which has one difference. Instead of "cast it into the treasury," the Hebrew has "cast it to *the potter*." On the basis of this, he has the priests supply some off-the-cuff halakhah: 'Hmmm . . . it is not lawful to put it into the treasury, seeing it is blood money.' So they took counsel, and bought with them [the thirty pieces of silver] the potter's field, to bury indigent strangers in" (Matt. 27:6b–7). And this, Matthew informs us, happened so that prophecy might be fulfilled. Whose prophecy? As familiar as he was with both Syriac and Hebrew versions of Zechariah, he goes on to attribute the text to Jeremiah! And Judas goes on to hang himself, unable to live with what he has done. Matthew has borrowed the hanging from 2 Sam. 17:23, where Ahithophel, a traitor to David and ally of Absalom, hangs himself.

Luke (in Acts 1:18–19) has Judas himself use the blood money to buy the field, and there he dies in a particularly gruesome manner, swelling up and exploding! Thus, it was forever after called the Field of Blood. The usual translation, "*falling headlong*, he burst open in the middle," attempts to harmonize Luke's version with Matthew's, as if Judas had hanged himself with a length of old, rotting kite string that snapped under his weight, and the impact of the fall caused the body to split open. Not only is this far-fetched on the face of it, but it will not even work as a harmonization, since the priests buy the field in Matthew, and Judas buys it in Acts. And Matthew says nothing about Judas dying *in* the Field of Blood. For Matthew, it is called that simply because blood money (bounty money) paid for the property. And while Matthew borrowed the manner of Judas's death (unknown, because it never happened, Judas being a symbolic character), Luke took it from Ps. 109:18 (Greek Septuagint). He has Peter quote verse 8 with reference to Judas in Acts 1:20. And for Judas's death, Luke is tacitly drawing upon Ps. 109:18, "Yes, he put on cursing as a garment, and it is come as water into his bowels, and as oil into his bones."[27] Thus, Judas "swell[ed] up and burst in the middle, and all his bowels gushed out" (Acts 1:18).

TRIALS AND TRIBULATIONS

As Erich Auerbach pointed out,[28] there are really two trials going on side by side in our next sequence. Jesus and Peter are both in the dock; only Peter seems not to recognize it. As Jesus is hustled into the house of the high priest, Peter, who has mustered sufficient courage to follow Jesus at a safe distance, slips into the courtyard and waits for the inevitable outcome. He turns out to be more notorious than he expected and dislikes the attention that is suddenly fixed on him. It is as if, writing off Jesus for dead, people are already beginning to look to Peter as his successor—only he doesn't want the job. Jesus had predicted that Peter's role in the preordained drama was that of coward. Now the spotlight falls on him, and he is up to the part!

Matt. 26:34, Luke 22:34, and John 13:38 all have Jesus say Peter will thrice deny him before the cock crows next sunrise. Mark's version is a bit more complicated: Peter's three repudiations will span two rooster crows. Either way, the result is a masterpiece of suspense, painted in swift, broad strokes. Peter, warming himself at the fire along with the returned arresting party and the household servants, is galvanized with fear as, one by one, they begin to recognize him. First a maid (Mark 14:66–68, Matt. 26:69–70, Luke 22:56, John 18:17–18) asks him if he were not apprehended along with the Galilean prisoner. *No, lady, you're seeing things!* Mark has the same woman press the question (14:69–70), while Matthew has a second maid (26:71–72) take up the questioning. Luke and John make it "someone" (John 18:25) or "someone else" (Luke 22:56). Am I right? Wasn't he one of that gang? *You're crazy, I tell you!* (At this point, in some copies of Mark, the cock crows *for the first time*.) By this time, the whole crowd has joined in. Mark 14:73–74 and Matt. 26:73–74 call them "the bystanders," while for Luke it is "still another" (22:59–60). John has the third questioner a relative of poor injured Malchus. His interest in Peter, who in John was the one who sliced off Malchus's ear, is potentially very ominous! Sure you're one of them! You even talk like them! *Look, pal, I don't even know who you're talking about! May God strike me dead if I'm lying! Okay?* As Peter finishes his blue streak of denials, and the crowd begins to lose interest in him, the rooster crows (for Mark, a second time). And, having saved his worthless yellow hide, Peter is overcome with self-loathing and weeps.

We have already observed that this distasteful incident probably originated as propaganda from the circles of Paul's (or James's) supporters, as a smear against Peter's apostolic character, really at the authority of his self-proclaimed successors. It has about the same chance of being historically true as the reports that Jesus was a lush and that John the Baptist was a demoniac.

Meanwhile, inside, the previous efforts of the priests to stack the deck against Jesus have come to naught. The idiots they had bribed to perjure themselves with false charges against Jesus, making him a bomb-throwing anarchist breathing threats to level the temple, just cannot get their stories straight. When their bought witnesses fail, Jesus himself hands them the trump card. Exasperated, the high priest asks him point blank (albeit using reverent euphemisms for God), "Are you the Christ, the son of the Blessed One?" Of course, he is not asking for the truth about Jesus, which he thinks he already knows, but rather what Jesus claims about himself. And he hits the jackpot! Jesus says, according to most manuscripts of Mark, "I am." A few manuscripts of Mark, together with Luke and Matthew, have him answer somewhat more equivocally, "You say so" or "You said it." Then, the evangelists put in his mouth the midrash on Ps. 110:1, Zech. 12:10, and Dan. 7:13: "You will see the Son of Man seated at the right hand of Power [God] and coming with the clouds of heaven." As Perrin showed, this is a Christian scribal compilation. It is nothing Jesus ever said.

The high priest realizes he will have a shorter night at this than he had thought! "Why do we need to bother with any more witnesses? You have heard his blasphemy! What is your decision?" The verdict, despite what we will later hear about Joseph of Arimathea (silently?) dissenting, is unanimous. He is guilty. Guilty, we might ask, of precisely *what*? From all we know about ancient Judaism, it was in no way blasphemy to make a claim, true or false, to the office of Messiah. For instance, in the first third of the second century C.E., the venerable Rabbi Akiba proclaimed the pious warrior Simon bar-Kochba as Messiah. The Son of the Star, for that is the meaning of his name, went on to win a very fleeting independence from Rome before being crushed. In the aftermath, Akiba realized he had backed the wrong horse, but no one charged him or his protégé with blasphemy. Why should they? Akiba's reputation was not even diminished! What we have here, manifestly, is another case of Mark's anachronistic misrepresentation of Judaism. What he surely has in mind is decades-later Hellenistic Christology that made of Jesus a demigod walking the earth, Son of God in the same sense as Pythagoras and Apollonius or, more to the point, like Hercules or Perseus. Jews of a later era did indeed view these beliefs as blasphemies against the unity of the Godhead. Mark has naively retrojected the later situation into the earlier, as so often. The Sanhedrin is depicted as condemning Christian Christology in the person of Jesus, just as Peter is elsewhere made the anachronistic mouthpiece for Mark's Christology (8:29).

False prophets don't get much respect, after they are exposed, that is. As their crime, deceiving Israel, is perceived as particularly heinous, they are entitled to a flood of contempt, directly proportional to the respect they once enjoyed. "And some began to spit on him, and to cover his face, and to strike him, saying to him, 'Prophesy!' And the guards gave him the salute of a pummeling" (Mark 14:65). Matt. 26:67 and Luke 22:64 both explain why they covered his head. "Who hit you?" He is blindfolded, but if he is a clairvoyant, a blindfold shouldn't stop him from telling which fist has struck him.

Where does this brutal scene come from? Not altogether from Mark's imagination. He has rewritten the story (1 Kings 22:24–27) of Micaiah ben-Imlah, summoned by the king of Israel to corroborate the hireling court prophets' rubber-stamp blessing of the planned expedition against Syria. He first pretends to bless the scheme, but the king knows he cannot mean it and admonishes him to give his true judgment, whereupon Micaiah says he overheard the heavenly council plotting to destroy the king of Israel by luring him into a military disaster. His prophets only went along with the idea because God sent a lying spirit into their mouths! This ill pleases the prophets, as might well be imagined. One of them, "Zedekiah the son of Chenaanah came near and struck Micaiah on the cheek, and said, 'How did the Spirit of Yahve abandon me to speak to you?' And Micaiah said, 'Behold, you shall see on that day when you go into an inner chamber to hide yourself!' And the king of Israel said, 'Seize Micaiah, and take him back to Amon the governor of the city and to Joash the king's son; and say, "Thus says the king: 'Put this fellow in prison, and feed him with scant fare of bread and water, until I come in peace.'"'"

Here are the elements of Mark's scene. The one true prophet is hauled before the wicked council, where he tells the truth at great cost. For this he is struck, abused as a false prophet (John 18:22 has Jesus slapped already while testifying), but he warns his tormentors that they will soon see the tables turned and his utterance vindicated. "You will see" is the great tip-off. Mark has rewritten 1 Kings 22:24–27 to provide the context for the Psalm 110/Daniel 7/Zechariah 12 midrash. That the trial hearing cannot be historical is evident enough from the sheer implausibility of the Sanhedrin convening (formally or informally) on Passover Eve! Again, Mark just does not know Judaism. Besides this, how would he have known what was said? He "knew" because he made it up.

The Sanhedrin, one might think, would have applied to Pilate for permission to have Jesus, as a blasphemer, stoned to death as the Torah required. That they instead ask Pilate to have Roman soldiers crucify him as a rebel king should make us think twice. Mark has mentioned more than once that the elders were afraid of a popular uprising against them should they dare act against Jesus publicly, or even let it be known that they thought him a false prophet (Mark 11:18–32, 12:12, 14:1–2). It would make sense, then, for them to try to avoid public responsibility for his execution, which they could hardly do if he died as a blasphemer by stoning. No one but the Sanhedrin could convict him of this. But if they could maneuver the Romans into doing their dirty work for them, persuading Pilate that Jesus' execution was in Rome's own best interests, whether or not the crowd liked it, then the Sanhedrin would be off the hook. Thus, the plan to translate a Jewish crime (an imagined one) into a Roman one: if Messiah meant king of the Jews, then Rome would condemn a would-be Messiah as a seditionist, as in fact they usually were.

They bring Jesus before the Roman procurator, who routinely interrogates him. Does he indeed claim to be the true king of the Jews? Jesus gives the same equivocal answer to Pilate as he had given to the high priest: "You say so." Pilate sees no reason to condemn Jesus and attempts to release him. Up to this point, the story might have had a degree of plausibility, if we supposed that Pilate suspected something was afoot, that he was being used (Mark 15:10). But then why does he not just refuse to condemn Jesus unless the priests can come up with something better? Why does he try, as if it is the only path open to him, to use a customary clemency gesture to free Jesus? He does, and it backfires. Pilate apparently assumed Jesus was quite popular with the crowds, that *they* called him king of the Jews (Mark 15:12), that he was their leader. So he sets up a choice: the crowd may pick either of two insurrectionists, Jesus or Barabbas, who is among the insurgents currently held. And they choose Barabbas, having been bought by the priests. Reluctantly, Pilate hands Jesus over to be crucified. Here we have a major problem of both narrative and historical probability: we have no other evidence of such a custom, and in any case, it is just inconceivable that Pilate would release known anti-Roman rebels! And if he thinks Jesus is popular with the crowds, that is what he is ready to do. Matthew saw the problem here. He knew there would have to be some extraordinary factor in play for Pilate to have behaved this way. So he supplied it: Mrs. Pilate heard her husband was to hear Jesus that day and panicked, having tossed and turned all night because of nightmares in which Jesus somehow loomed large. Feeling it is a bad omen, she has sent word to her husband: hands off the holy man! (Matt. 27:19). He tries repeatedly to persuade the crowds to have mercy on Jesus—as if it were up to them! Why doesn't he just let Jesus go? John sees the problem and has the crowd threaten Pilate; if he lets Jesus go, that will get him in hot water with Rome, because word will get back that he has freed a known enemy of Caesar—as if the assassin Barabbas were not a worse one! Matthew finally has Pilate make the public gesture of washing his hands, repudiating any responsibility for the execution, as if he is just looking the other way at what amounts to a mob lynching. But this will not do.

The best explanation for this halfway rehabilitation of Pilate is that it represents a rewriting of an earlier version of the story in which blame was placed exclusively on Rome, and in which Jesus died on a Roman cross as a matter of course. And as time went by, Christians felt the need to play up to the Romans and curry their favor, so they did what they could to shift the blame from Rome to Jewry. Pilate was too much a part of the story for his role to be completely expunged, but he was made at least to have declared Jesus innocent. But either way, the trial before Pilate, with the Jewish rulers standing by, filled as it is with fatal implausibilities, must be a fiction, and its origin is, again, not far to seek. Mark borrowed it from Josephus's story of another Jesus, Jesus ben-Ananias.

> An incident more alarming still had occurred four years before the war at a time of exceptional peace and prosperity for the City. One Jeshua, son of Ananias, a very ordinary yokel, came to the feast at which every Jew is supposed to set up a tabernacle for God. As he stood in the temple he suddenly began to shout: "A voice from the east, a voice from the west, a voice from the four winds, a voice against Jerusalem and the Sanctuary, a voice against bridegrooms and brides, a voice against the whole people." Day and night he uttered this cry as he went through all the streets. Some of the more prominent citizens, very annoyed at these ominous words, laid hold of the fellow and beat him savagely. Without saying a word in his own defence or for the private information of his persecutors, he persisted in shouting the same warning as before. The Jewish authorities, rightly concluding that some supernatural force was responsible for the man's behaviour, took him before the Roman procurator. There, though scourged till his flesh hung in ribbons, he neither begged for mercy nor shed a tear, but lowering his voice to the most mournful of tones answered every blow with "Woe to Jerusalem!" When Albinus—for that was the procurator's name—demanded to know who he was, where he came from and why he uttered such cries, he made no reply whatever to the questions but endlessly repeated his lament over the City, till Albinus decided he was a madman and released him (*The Jewish War* VI 302).[29]

Four years later, his prophecy was fulfilled by the Roman siege, during which Jesus ben-Ananias was killed. Can anyone fail to notice the parallels here? Jesus comes to Jerusalem for one of the great festivals and creates a prophetic disturbance in the temple. He preaches soon-coming judgment, the destruction of the temple, and he says it will spell the end of ordinary life, for example, weddings (Matt. 24:38). The elders of the people haul him before the Roman procurator, who interrogates him but gets only silence for an answer. Puzzled, the procurator asks him where he is from (John 19:9). He decides to have him flogged and let him go (Luke 23:22b). Which Jesus are we talking about here? Both. Yet again, Mark has retrojected the events of the subsequent generation into the time of Jesus.

Luke introduces a major complication, yet another trial, this time before Herod Antipas, whom he has already told us was looking for some opportunity to deal with Jesus as he had dealt with his pesky predecessor John the Baptist (Luke 13:31). In this he was perhaps motivated by the outrage of his steward Chuza's wife, Joanna, having left him to follow and support Jesus (Luke 8:3). I surmise that Luke derived all this from another source that shared the basic plot of the Apocryphal Acts of the Apostles, where a highborn woman hears the man of God preach the gospel of chastity, repents, and henceforth refuses to sleep with her pagan spouse, following the man of God instead. Enraged by this and suspecting his wife is having an affair with her guru, the husband entreats his friend the king or governor, who agrees to capture and kill the home wrecker. This he does, and the martyred apostle, in some of the texts, rises from the dead, while the converted woman goes on to preach the gospel. This pre-Lukan source must have eventuated with Herod seeing to the execution of Jesus, as Loisy proposed.[30] Luke felt compelled to harmonize this account with Mark's, so he decided to include both the Markan trial before Pilate and the other trial before Herod Antipas. He tilted toward Mark and gave Pilate the honor of having Jesus executed. So he sandwiches the Herod scene between halves of the Pilate trial scene. And he must needs change the original outcome of the Herodian trial. After telling us Herod wanted to kill him, Luke arbitrarily has Herod acquit Jesus! Had he really done so, would not Jesus have been free to go? Why send him back to Pilate? So Luke can continue with Mark! The whole point of Pilate remanding Jesus to Antipas was to rid himself of the need of seeing Jesus again, and yet here he is, and Pilate takes up the challenge of what to do with him once more—inexplicably, since Herod would seem to have settled the problem for him. Here Luke has become as incoherent as he was in the census sequence of chapter 2, with Joseph registering for a Roman taxation census in another province where a remote ancestor had lived a thousand years before!

At this point, we must indicate yet another source of the trial narratives. Jesus is displayed in mock finery as a burlesque king of the Jews, a scarecrow king, by Pilate's soldiers in Mark 15:16–20, Matt. 27:27–31, and John 19:2–5. Luke has Herod's soldiers engage in this mockery instead (23:11). Some have pointed to a possible precedent for this scene in the Saturnalia games of the Roman soldiers, who would choose a condemned criminal to be arrayed as a mock king and honored before his execution. And this ought to be considered. But it seems we must also reckon with a story told by Philo of Alexandria in his apologia *Flaccus*. He describes an elaborate prank played by Alexandrian ruffians to ridicule the visiting Herod Agrippa I (Acts 12), returning through Egypt from Rome, where he had just been created king of Judea, on his way back home.

> There was a certain madman named Carabbas . . . , the sport of idle children and wanton youths; and they, driving the poor wretch as far as the public gymnasium, and setting him up there on high that he might be seen by everybody, flattened out a leaf of papyrus and put it on his head instead of a diadem, and clothed the rest of his body with a common door mat instead of a cloak, and instead of a sceptre they put in his hand a small stick of . . . papyrus . . . and when he had been adorned like a king, the young men bearing sticks on their shoulders stood on each side of him instead of spear bearers . . . , and then others came up, some as if to salute him, and others as though they wished to plead their causes before him. . . . Then from the multitude . . . there arose a . . . shout of men calling out "*Maris!*" And this is the name by which it is said that

they call the kings among the Syrians; for they knew that Agrippa was by birth a Syrian, and also that he was possessed of a great district of Syria of which he was the sovereign (VI, 36–39).[31]

Do we really need to look further for the origin of Barabbas and the mockery of Jesus as king of the Jews? We can almost catch echoes of the Carabbas story in Luke's Herod trial, in that he has Herod dress Jesus up as a mock king and send him to Pilate. If it had been the other way around (as conceivably it was in the source), Pilate might have arrayed Jesus as a mock king of the Jews and sent him as an insult to Herod Antipas, who coveted the title for himself.

NOTES

1. Richard L. Tierney (author of *The Scroll of Thoth*, *The House of the Toad*, Drums of Chaos, etc.) made this waggish suggestion in a 1986 letter to the present writer.

2. J. K. Elliott, ed. and trans., *The Apocryphal New Testament: A Collection of Apocryphal Christian Literature in an English Translation* (Oxford: Clarendon Press, 1993), p. 95.

3. Ellis Nassour, *Rock Opera: The Creation of* Jesus Christ Superstar, *from Record Album to Broadway Show and Motion Picture* (New York: E. P. Dutton, 1973), p. 47.

4. Robert W. Funk and the Jesus Seminar, *The Acts of Jesus: The Search for the Authentic Deeds of Jesus*, A Polebridge Press Book (San Francisco: HarperSanFrancisco, 1998), p. 121.

5. S. G. F. Brandon, "The Markan Gospel: an *Apologia ad Christianos Romanos*," chap. 5 in *Jesus and the Zealots: A Study of the Political Factor in Primitive Christianity* (New York: Scribner, 1967), pp. 221–82.

6. Burton L. Mack, *A Myth of Innocence: Mark and Christian Origins* (Philadelphia: Fortress Press, 1988), pp. 291–92.

7. Josephus, *The Jewish War*, trans. G. A. Williamson (Baltimore: Penguin Books, 1959), p. 268.

8. Dale Miller and Patricia Miller, *The Gospel of Mark as Midrash on Earlier Jewish and New Testament Literature*, Studies in the Bible and Early Christianity 21 (Lewiston, N.Y.: Edwin Mellen Press, n.d.), p. 325; J. Duncan M. Derrett, *The Making of Mark: The Scriptural Bases of the Earliest Gospel* (Shipston-on-Star, U.K.: Peter Drinkwater, 1985), p. 187.

9. Annie Jaubert, *The Date of the Last Supper: The Biblical Calendar and Christian Liturgy*, trans. Isaac Rafferty (Staten Island: Alba House, 1965), pp. 95–102.

10. Albert Schweitzer, *The Problem of the Lord's Supper According to the Scholarly Research of the Nineteenth Century and the Historical Accounts*, trans. Andrew J. Mattill Jr. (Macon: Mercer University Press, 1982), pp. 131–34; Joachim Jeremias, *The Eucharistic Words of Jesus*, trans. Arnold Ehrhardt (Oxford: Basil Blackwell, 1955), pp. 118–31.

11. Solomon Schechter, *Some Aspects of Rabbinic Theology* (New York: Macmillan, 1910), p. 311.

12. Hyam Maccoby, *Paul and Hellenism* (Philadelphia: Trinity Press International, 1991), pp. 91–92.

13. Rudolf Bultmann, *The Gospel of John: A Commentary*, trans. G. R. Beasley-Murray, R. W. N. Hoare, and J. K. Riches (Philadelphia: Westminster Press, 1971), pp. 234–37.

14. Alfred Loisy, *The Birth of the Christian Religion*, trans. L. P. Jacks (London: George Allen and Unwin, 1948), p. 249.

15. I take very seriously the theory that Luke is the author of the Pastorals. You should, too. See Stephen G. Wilson, *Luke and the Pastoral Epistles* (London: SPCK, 1979).

16. Jacques Derrida, "Force and Signification," in *Writing and Difference*, trans. Alan Bass (Chicago: University of Chicago Press, 1978), pp. 24–25.

17. Robert M. Fowler, *Let the Reader Understand: Reader-Response Criticism and the Gospel of Mark* (Minneapolis: Fortress Press, 1991), pp. 76–77.

18. Dale Miller and Patricia Miller, *The Gospel of Mark as Midrash*, p. 332.

19. Three in the Septuagint; Hebrew: three or four, the text being unclear.

20. J. Duncan M. Derrett, "The Prayer in Gethsemane (Mark 4:35–36)," *Journal of Higher Criticism* 4, no. 1 (spring 1997): 78–88.

21. Neal Robinson, *Christ in Islam and Christianity* (Albany: State University of New York Press, 1991), p. 127.

22. Frank Kermode, *The Genesis of Secrecy: On the Interpretation of Narrative* (Cambridge: Harvard University Press, 1979), pp. 84–86; Hyam Maccoby, *Judas Iscariot and the Myth of Jewish Evil* (New York: Free Press/Macmillan, 1992), pp. 127–59.

23. Tzvetan Todorov, "Narrative-Men," *The Poetics of Prose*, trans. Richard Howard (Ithaca, N.Y.: Cornell University Press, 1992), pp. 66–79.

24. Joseph Gaer, *The Legend of the Wandering Jew* (New York: New American Library, 1961); George K. Anderson, *The Legend of the Wandering Jew* (Hanover: Brown University Press, 1965).

25. Philip R. Amidon, trans. and ed., *The Panarion of St. Epiphanius, Bishop of Salamis: Selected Passages* (New York: Oxford University Press, 1990), p.134.

26. E. A. Abbott, *Encyclopaedia Biblica* (London: Adam and Charles Black, 1914), s.v. "Gospels."

27. David Friedrich Strauss, *Life of Jesus Critically Examined*, trans. George Eliot, Lives of Jesus Series (1835; repr., Philadelphia: Fortress Press, 1972), pp. 665–66.

28. Erich Auerbach, *Mimesis: The Representation of Reality in Western Literature* (Garden City: Doubleday Anchor, 1957), p. 35–43.

29. Josephus, pp. 349–50.

30. Alfred Loisy, *The Origins of the New Testament*, trans. L. P. Jacks (London: George Allen and Unwin, 1950), p. 167.

31. C. D. Yonge, trans., *The Works of Philo* (Peabody: Hendrickson, 1993), p. 728.

CHAPTER THIRTEEN
CRUCIFIXION

DEAD MAN WALKING

Condemned to die by crucifixion, the ancient Phoenician torment adopted by Rome, Jesus embarks on the *Via Dolorosa*, the way of sorrows, out of the city to Golgotha, where there awaits him a reinforced hole in the ground and an upright beam, with which his tender back will soon become too familiar. Ordinarily the condemned man would hoist his own crossbeam and carry it to the site. According to the Synoptics, Jesus was spared this, and the Romans commandeered a Phoenician Jew, perhaps in Jerusalem for the festival, to carry the crossbeam for Jesus. We are not told why. Popular devotion has imagined Jesus too weak from the scourging to bear up under the weight. That may be the intent of Mark, followed by the others. But there is another very intriguing possibility. There may be some contamination of the Jesus narrative here by the mythos of Simon Magus (Acts 8:9–24), a notorious first- or second-century Gnostic mystagogue who claimed to have previously appeared as the Son of God among the Jews, at whose hands he suffered the Passion, albeit in docetic appearance only (Epiphanius *Panarion* 2:1). Simon was from the old Philistine town of Gitta, and our sources often seem to confuse Gitta with the Kittim, or Sea Peoples, ancient merchants who apparently included the Phoenicians and Philistines. Cyrene was an ancient Phoenician city, and thus Simon who carried the cross of Jesus may have been of the Kittim. And thus, he may have been Simon of Gitta, Simon Magus. Simon of Cyrene, who is identified as the father of the otherwise-unknown Alexander and Rufus (Mark 15:21), was said by early Gnostic teacher Basilides (who claimed to have been taught by one Glaukias, secretary of Peter) to have been crucified in place of Jesus. He may have been thinking of the fact that Simon's is the last name given (Mark 15:21), except for Alexander and Rufus, before we start hearing that "they brought *him* to the place called Golgotha. . . . And they offered *him* wine mingled with myrrh; but *he* did not take it. And they crucified *him*." Who? Simon of Cyrene? So thought Basilides. Perhaps Alexander and Rufus were earlier proponents of such a doctrine on behalf of Simon of Cyrene (or Simon Magus if they were not the same figure). Perhaps Mark has derived some of the colorful detail of the crucifixion story from their version of events, without meaning to assert that it was not Jesus who was crucified. But since Mark gives no mundane explanation for Simon carrying the cross of Jesus, a rather eye-opening oddity, it does seem as if we have here what was formerly a lead-in to a denouement we never get to follow up in the present state of the text.

John found the notion that Jesus did not or could not carry his own cross untoward, even offensive, perhaps thinking it made nonsense of any appeal for would-be disciples to take up their own crosses and follow Jesus. So he changed it. In John's version, there is no mention at all of Simon of Cyrene. From step one, it is Jesus who carries the crossbeam (John 19:17): "Jesus went out, bearing his own cross, to the place called the place of a skull." Apologists seek to harmonize the two accounts by simply splitting the difference, as if Jesus started out with the cross on his shoulder, then dropped it, whereupon the Romans yanked Simon out of the crowd and ordered him to take over. But this will not do. This is the one alternative excluded by both the Johannine and the Synoptic versions, each of which is quite clear.

Luke (23:27–31) has added a dialogue between Jesus and a group of mourning women. Elsewhere I have argued that this material originally constituted a resurrection appearance (note the "weep not for me" saying, as in John 20:13).[1] From this soil has grown a series of "stations of the cross" along the way, legendary embellishments including St. Veronica, who darts out of the crowd to wipe the sweating, bloody face of the savior and finds his image miraculously imprinted on the cloth.[2] Another is the legend of the Wandering Jew, no fan of Jesus, who curses or punches Jesus on his way to the cross, whereupon the savior, not in a very forgiving mood, turns to him and mutters, "Tarry thou till I come again." He is doomed to wander the world, witnessing all its catastrophes, especially those befalling fellow Jews, until the end of the age. He is clearly a symbol for Jews who have rejected Jesus. In this, as we have seen, he is a second Judas Iscariot.

WAS ANYONE THERE WHEN
THEY CRUCIFIED MY LORD?

Jesus is affixed to the cross, but how? People were sometimes tied at the wrists and nailed through the palms, sometimes nailed through the wrists, sometimes just tied. It is striking that no gospel crucifixion account tells us what they did to Jesus. We first and only hear of nailing in the subsequent Doubting Thomas resurrection story: "Unless I see in his hands the print of the nails . . ." (John 20:25). Nonetheless, as we shall soon see, Mark probably shared John's assumption, that Jesus was nailed to the cross, because of the implied reference to Ps. 22:16, "They have pierced my hands and feet."

When was Jesus crucified? According to the Synoptics, it was the day after Passover, but for John it was the Passover, since he understands Jesus as the Passover Lamb who takes away the sin of the world (John 1:29, 19:36, referring to Exod. 12:46). What time was it? According to Mark 15:25 it was "the third hour," nine in the morning. According to John 19:14, it was "the sixth hour," noon.

The narrative of Jesus on the cross is surprisingly brief. Even more surprising is that virtually every bit of that narrative seems to have come not from eyewitness memory, even indirectly, but rather from scripture exegesis. The crucifixion account of Mark, the basis for all the others, is simply a tacit rewrite of Psalm 22, with a few other texts thrown in. In what follows, please note that nothing at all is said of this or that happening in order to fulfill Scripture. John will add a bit of that, but Mark and the others conspicuously neglect to draw attention to the scriptural basis of the story. Nor should it be imagined that Psalm 22 is a prophecy of Jesus' death or of anything else. It is quite clearly what is called an Individual Lament psalm, a song sung by or on behalf of someone in extremity who feels himself forsaken by God, he knows not why, but still has faith and appeals to the Almighty to rescue him now, in the eleventh hour, promising to appear in the temple afterward with "a new song" (a Thanksgiving Psalm) and an offering to present, which he means to share with the poor invited for the occasion. He promises he will testify to all of them on that happy day how God finally rescued him from his undefined plight—undefined, as in all such psalms, so as to be applicable to anyone in trouble.[3]

Let us outline the crucifixion step by step. First, Jesus is attached to the cross, presumably with nails, based on Ps. 22:16, "They have pierced my hands and feet." Second, the soldiers divide his garments (Mark 15:24), a detail derived directly from Ps. 22:18, "They divide my garments among them, and for my raiment they cast lots." Third, the gloating mockers "wag their heads," an odd phrase, and one derived from Ps. 22:7: "All who see me mock at me, they make mouths at me, they wag their heads." Fourth, the very taunts of the priests ("Let the Christ, the king of Israel, come down from the cross, that we may see and believe!" Mark 15:32) echo those that stung the Psalmist: "'He committed his

cause to Yahve; let him deliver him, let him rescue him, for he delights in him!'"
(Ps. 22:8). Matt. 27:43 supplements the mockery here: "He trusts in God; let God
deliver him now, if he desires him; for he said, 'I am the son of God.'" Where
did Matthew get this? His own or others' memories of the event? No, from Wis.
of Sol. 2:12–20 (which he perforce condensed): "But let us lie in wait for the
righteous man, because he makes it hard for us, and opposes our works, and
upbraids us for sins against the law, and accuses us of sins against our training.
He professes to have knowledge of God, and calls himself the servant of the
Lord. He became to us a living reproof of our thoughts. He is grievous for us
even to behold because his life is unlike that of other men, and his ways are alien
to us. He disdains us as base metal, and he avoids our ways as unclean. The final
end of the righteous he calls happy, and he claims that God is his father. Let us
see if his words are true, and let us see what will happen at the end of his life!
For if the righteous man is God's son, he will uphold him, and he will rescue him
from the grasp of his adversaries. With outrage and torture let us put him to the
test, that we may see for ourselves his gentleness and prove his patience under
injustice. Let us condemn him to a shameful death; for surely God shall intervene
as this fellow said he would!"

Fifth, there is Jesus' cry of dereliction, "My God, my God, why have you
forsaken me?" which is of course the opening line of Psalm 22, only Mark does
not say so. Luke deems these words unbecoming, so he changes them—to something Luke knew Jesus had actually said on that occasion? No, he took it
("Father, into your hands I commit my spirit," Luke 23:46) from Ps. 31:5. John
explicitly cites Ps. 22:18 about the garments and tacitly uses Ps. 22:14 ("I am
poured out like water, and all my bones are dislocated; my heart is like wax, it is
melted within my breast") as the basis for his unique detail of the soldier stab-
bing Jesus' side, "and at once there came out blood and water" (John 19:34).
John also makes Jesus' thirst and its rough satisfaction with vinegar (John
19:28–29) a prophetic fulfillment, unwittingly pointing to Ps. 69:21 ("They gave
me poison for food, and for my thirst they gave me vinegar to drink") as the probable origin of the whole motif, which also appears in the Synoptics (Mark 15:36,
Matt. 27:34, Luke 23:36).

What are we to make of this very strange circumstance, that no memory of
the central saving event of the Christian religion survived, that when someone
first ventured to tell the story of the crucifixion of the Savior, the only building
blocks available for the task were various Scripture texts? It appears that the first
preaching of Christianity featured but "Christ crucified" (1 Cor. 2:2) with no historical setting or detail. 1 Cor. 2:8 has him crucified by the mythic Archons, the
archangelic servants of the Gnostic Demiurge. Similarly, Col. 2:14 says that by
the cross Jesus nullified the power of the Torah, wielded by the angelic Principalities and Powers, as in Gal. 3:19–20, where we learn that the Torah was given
to Moses, not by God but by the angels. It seems most natural to posit that, once
the saving death of Jesus was tied down to specific historical circumstances, the

first tellers of the tale sought to create their narrative from scriptural materials to give it scriptural gravity, just as Mark did when he composed the lines for the heavenly voice to say at the Jordan baptism.

HONOR AMONG THIEVES

Mark has Jesus crucified between two "thieves," a word that could denote actual pickpockets and muggers, but that was also used for rebels like Barabbas, John of Gischala, or Judas the Gaulonite. Thus Jesus, the king of the Jews, would have been executed along with fellow revolutionaries. We have already seen how Christian desires to offset Roman suspicions may have led to soft-pedaling Pilate's role in the death of Jesus. Luke seems to have the same concern, as he spins a new scene out of the presence of these other two criminals. From Mark he took the idea that the criminals crucified with Jesus joined in the derision (Mark 15:32). But Luke has only one of them make fun of Jesus: "Are you not the Christ? Save yourself—and us!" The other sharply rebukes him: "Have you no fear of God? You yourself are under the same death sentence! And we deserve it, but this man has done nothing!" (Luke 23:39–41). Then the "good thief" addresses Jesus, "Jesus, remember me when you come to your throne!"[4] This last is a verbatim quotation of a scene in Diodorus Siculus, where a nobleman mocks a slave who cherishes grandiose pretensions to royalty. We can only assume Luke took it over as a serious good wish, if not actually a confession of faith. But it would have made perfect sense as a piece of mockery, in which case Luke's version would parallel Mark's, only spelling out what both mocking criminals said. Jesus' reply, "Amen: I say to you, today you will be with me in Paradise" (Luke 23:43), is quite interesting in its own right. Jesus' remark does not anticipate that he will rise from dead in two or three days to ascend to a messianic throne at the right hand of the Father; it only posits that he will die and go to heaven, Paradise being the destination of the righteous dead. But does Luke misunderstand Paradise as the kingdom Jesus will enter that day? One wonders again if there was some lost layer between Mark and Luke. At any rate, Luke's apologetical agenda, trying to make Christianity look wholesome in Roman eyes, has dictated his rewriting the notice of the two thieves, having one defend Jesus from the other's mockery. It is important for Luke to differentiate Jesus from the bad company this scene finds him in. What better way than to have the expert's judgment? Here is a genuine criminal against Rome who ought to know a fellow criminal when he sees one, and he pronounces Jesus innocent. This is manifestly for Roman consumption, and the same agenda will explain another otherwise odd Lukan alteration.

Needless to say, the familiar notion that both thieves began mocking Jesus, but that then one thought better of it, is just one more lame harmonization. No text says this; it is the product of wishful thinking on the part of those who secretly wish they had but one gospel and did not rejoice, as critics do, in the variety of the four.

NIGHT OF THE LIVING DEAD

1 Cor. 1:22–23, "For Jews demand signs and Greeks seek wisdom, but we preach Christ crucified, a stumbling block to Jews and folly to Gentiles," would seem to envision a conspicuously nonsupernatural crucifixion scene; else why would miracle-hungry Jews be disappointed in the preaching of the cross? Would Paul have even put it this way if he had known of prodigies at the cross such as we read of in the Gospels? For Mark 15:33 and Matt. 27:45 lower a curtain of supernatural darkness over the scene for three hours, from noon to three in the afternoon. Luke 23:45 mitigates the miraculous character somewhat, making the darkness into an eclipse, despite the impossibility of having an eclipse of the sun at the time of the full moon. John has no darkness at the crucifixion. (Seneca and Pliny the Elder both recorded eclipses and suchlike in the Mediterranean world at this time, but neither records this one.)

At the same time, the great veil separating the Inner Sanctum of the temple from the Holy Place was ripped down the center (Mark 15:38, Matt. 27:51, Luke 23:45), a Christian etiological legend explaining the fact that the temple veil, when on display in Rome where it was taken by Titus after the sacking and destruction of Jerusalem in 70 C.E., was seen to be ripped. It was no doubt torn by the Romans taking it down. But it is a powerful theological symbol, implying that the death of Jesus has opened the way for people to come near to God, as in Heb. 10:19–20. Even this is not enough for Matthew, who pours on the marvels, including an earthquake, which causes even loose rocks to shatter (27:51b). Neither does it end here. "The tombs also were opened, and many bodies of the saints who had fallen asleep were raised, and coming out of their tombs after his resurrection they went into the holy city and appeared to many" (27:53–54). This bizarre enormity seems to be a confused version of the notion that the resurrection of Jesus was to be the firstfruits of the general resurrection of the dead, the beginning of a continuous process (1 Cor. 15:23). But Matthew's retrojection of this hoped-for event raises possibilities he no doubt did not anticipate, for who, reading this, could be blamed for concluding there had been a widespread outbreak of visions/hallucinations that weekend in Jerusalem, and that the disciples' visions of the dead Jesus were but part of a wider epidemic in which many claimed to have seen dead loved ones?

Mark writes as if the soldiers on duty at Golgotha saw all the aftermath of the crucifixion. Had any of it happened, they could have witnessed only the darkness, which would have been quite enough to throw a scare into them. The centurion exclaims in superstitious terror: "This man actually *was* the son of God!" (Mark 15:39). He says the same in Matt. 27:54, but Luke 23:47 changes the centurion's exclamation to "This man was innocent after all!" Compared with Matthew/Mark's confession of divine sonship, this may seem anticlimactic, but from Luke's standpoint it is more to the point: Christians are innocent of sedition just as their founder was. Even a Roman on the scene could tell what a frame-up, what a miscarriage of Roman justice, it was!

Portents filling the sky to mark the passing of a great leader or hero were nothing new. After Julius Caesar's death, a comet appeared in the sky for eleven straight days. And for an entire year the light and warmth of the sun were diminished. But there is one parallel account so startlingly similar that we must ask seriously if the legend recorded in it may not even have been the source of the portents at the cross of Jesus. It is Plutarch's life of Cleomenes, a radical Spartan king who was exiled for his land reform policies and was finally crucified (already dead, having killed himself in anticipation of arrest) by the Alexandrian authorities. "And a few days afterwards those who were keeping watch on the body of Cleomenes where it hung, saw a serpent of great size coiling itself about the head and hiding away the face so that no ravening bird of prey could light upon it. In consequence of this, the king was seized with superstitious fear, and thus gave the women occasion for various rites of purification, since they felt that a man had been taken off who was of a superior nature and beloved of the gods. And the Alexandrians actually worshipped him, coming frequently to the spot and addressing Cleomenes as a hero and a child of the gods" (*Agis and Cleomenes* 39).[5] Jesus, like Cleomenes, is a repudiated king. His body rests upon the cross. The theme of divine protection from the vultures finds its echo in Acts 2:27, 31, where Ps. 16:10 is applied to Jesus: "'You will not abandon my soul to Hades, nor let your Holy One see corruption.' . . . Nor did his flesh see corruption." The king's fear becomes, in Mark, that of the centurion. The ritually mourning women devotees of Cleomenes become Mary Magdalene and the others, resolving to return to his grave with anointing spices. The acclamation of Cleomenes as child of the gods has simply been transferred to Jesus.

WAS HE THERE WHEN THEY CRUCIFIED MY LORD?

There has been a stubborn belief going back at least to the second-century Gnostic Basilides that Jesus cheated death on the cross in some fashion. More Gnostic versions held that either the crucified form of Jesus was a mirage, just as it had been in life (*Acts of John*), or that the body, physically solid though it might be, was not the real Christ anyway, any more than anyone's physical form is his real self (Nag Hammadi *Apocalypse of Peter*). Less Gnostic versions (like "Separationism") had the man Jesus as the temporary "channeler" for the Christ Spirit, and posited that the latter fled Jesus on the cross (Gospel of Peter), or even that someone else had been substituted for Jesus on the cross, perhaps Simon of

Cyrene, as we have seen (Basilides). The most modest of these held that Jesus had been crucified but survived it and lived to teach again, outside Israel, a doctrine taught today by the Ahmadiyya sect of Islam.[6] Is there any possible basis for such a view in the Gospels? I believe there is. This is not the same as saying that Jesus did actually survive crucifixion, though there are certainly credible scholars who believe this.[7] Rather, the point is merely that it may still be possible for us to discern clear traces of a largely effaced version of the Passion in which Jesus cheated death on the cross. It need not be the fact underlying the fiction, rather an earlier or alternative fiction. What are the clues?

The Gethsemane prayer of Jesus is a request for God to allow Jesus to avoid the Socratic cup of martyrdom, reminding God (and the reader) that God is not bound to any plan; all things are possible for him. The fact that Jesus is humbly willing to accede to God's will, even should it entail death, does not need to mean that Jesus will necessarily die after all. In fact, it might well be intended as evidence of the very filial piety of Jesus that persuaded the Father to grant his request, even as Heb. 5:7 says, "In the days of his flesh, he offered up prayers and supplications, with loud cries and tears, to him who was able to save him from death, *and he was heard for his godly fear*." It had been the same with Abraham: once he had proven his obedient willingness to kill his son, God rescinded the order that he do so.

Jesus' detractors dare him to come down alive from the cross, which he ought to be able to do if he is really the messianic king of Israel (Mark 15:30, 32). And we readers know that he is, right? Surely we are to recognize the irony of their words: this is exactly what Jesus is going to do! Not die and appear alive again later, but descend the cross still alive!

On the cross, Jesus is given some sort of drug from a sponge on the lance tip (Mark 15:36). He is said to have expired in a surprisingly short time, as crucifixion was designed as a slow death by dehydration. It should ordinarily have taken days (during which time it was far from unheard of for the crucified to be rescued by loved ones who might bribe the soldiers). But when Joseph of Arimathea appears to request custody of the body, Pilate is surprised: "And Pilate wondered that he should be dead already; and summoning the centurion, he asked him whether he had been some time dead" (Mark 15:44). This should sound to us like one shoe falling, with the other to come.

Joseph of Arimathea provides another important piece of the puzzle. Like Judas, Joseph is a fictional character who grows in the telling. For one thing, as Dennis R. MacDonald has shown, he is based on King Priam, begging Agamemnon for the body of his son Hector. It is because he corresponds to the slain hero's father that he is called *Joseph*.[8] (Postbiblical legend seems to understand this, since it came close to making this explicit, casting Joseph of Arimathea as Jesus' great uncle,[9] taking the place of the elderly, then deceased Joseph, husband of Mary.) His town of origin, Arimathea, is made into a pun marking Joseph as another of Todorov's "narrative-men." Richard C. Carrier has broken the name down to the figurative "Best [Ari-] Disciple [mathai-] Town/Place [-a]."[10] Thus, he is a precursor to the equally fictive "Beloved Disciple" of John's gospel. Mark 15:43 introduces him as "a respected member of the council, who was also himself looking for the kingdom of God." Luke noticed the problem: hadn't Mark made the Sanhedrin's condemnation of Jesus unanimous? So Luke's Joseph is "a member of the council, a good and righteous man, who had not consented to their purpose and deed, and he was looking for the kingdom of God" (Luke 23:50b–51). For Matthew (27:57), Joseph is suddenly both a rich man and a disciple of Jesus, implied already, as we have just seen, in his very patronymic. John makes him a secret disciple, fearing (an anachronistic) excommunication from the synagogue (John 19:38). His wealth is also implicit in Mark, Luke, and John, since all make him a council member, an aristocrat. Again, Matt. 27:60 is only making explicit what must be implicit in the situation, that the tomb in which Joseph buries Jesus is his own. Mark 15:46 says the tomb is unoccupied, implying it is a new one, while Luke 23:53 and John 19:42 make it explicit that no corpse had ever been deposited in it. And Mark and Luke assume Joseph had the right to bury Jesus where he did, implying that he owned the sepulchre. It is only John who implies that Joseph may have placed the body there temporarily for reburial as soon as the sabbath should be over (John 19:42), in which case it might have been someone else's.

It is important that Joseph is rich and buries Jesus in his own, presumably opulent, tomb. This provides the narrative motivation for tomb robbers to move in and seek the rich funerary tokens they assume have been buried with Joseph, who they assume must be laid out inside. (Who's buried in Grant's tomb?) Instead, they discover someone coming out of a deathlike torpor—and flee! This is exactly what happens in various Hellenistic romance novels of the period, such as Chariton's *Chaireas and Callirhoe*, with the one exception that the robbers do not want witnesses and so kidnap the newly revived person. Mourners visiting the tomb are stunned to find it empty, in the novels as in the Gospels. Jesus has departed.

Luke's angels at the tomb rhetorically ask the mourning women why they expect to find the living in the place of the dead (24:5b). What is the nature of their error? That Jesus is no longer dead? Or that the report of his death is premature? Perhaps the latter. Luke has Jesus appear to his disciples, who naturally assume he is dead. They are wrong, but, again, wherein lies their error? Jesus says, "Why are you troubled? Why do doubts arise in your hearts? See my hands and feet, that it is I myself; handle me and see; for a spirit has not flesh and bones as you see that I have. . . . Have you anything here to eat?" (Luke 24:38–41). Is Jesus offering proof that he has risen from the dead, having been dead? We are in the habit of reading it that way. But there is another way to view it. After all, one might say that the disciples are in error precisely because they *do* believe he *has* returned from the dead: they think he is a *ghost*! Their error is not recognizing that the man they had given up for dead is *still alive*, having cheated death.

We are fortunate to be able to compare Luke's story with a close parallel in which it is absolutely clear that the hero, Apollonius of Tyana, is *still* alive, not alive *again*. Philostratus tells us how Apollonius was due to stand trial before the emperor Domitian, who would surely condemn him to death. The sage sent his disciples back east before the trial and, back home, they mourned him, sure that he must be dead. But Apollonius vanished from the courtroom to reappear immediately back east in the midst of his disciples (much as Acts has Philip miraculously transport from the road between Jerusalem and Gaza to Ashdod, Acts 8:39–40). They ask if he is a ghost risen up from Hades to bid them a last farewell. He laughs and extends his hands. "'Take hold of me, and if I evade you, then I am indeed a ghost come to you from the realm of Persephone, such as the gods of the underworld reveal to those who are dejected with much mourning. But if I resist your touch, then you shall persuade [the doubting disciple] Damis also that I am both alive and that I have not abandoned my body.' They were no longer able to disbelieve, but rose up and threw themselves on his neck and kissed him, and asked him about his defense" (*Life of Apollonius* 8.12).[11]

John seems to have been aware that, not only was it possible to read Luke 24:36–43 in this manner, but that some did, to his great distress. This is why he makes doubly certain that Jesus is shown to have truly died on the cross. Only in John does the soldier pierce Jesus' side with his spear, causing water and blood to flow (though, depending on whose medical expertise one accepts, flowing blood would prove the opposite, that he was still alive!). In light of this addition, John rewrites Luke 24:36–43. In John's version (20:20), Jesus shows not his (substantial) hands and feet, but his (wounded) hands *and side*. This Jesus definitely died and came back, in the flesh, from the dead.

What would the surviving Jesus have done next? How did anyone picture the "second life of Jesus" (Schleiermacher)?[12] They apparently pictured him leaving the Holy Land to preach elsewhere in the Mediterranean world. Again, John seems to want to rule out such a notion. In 7:35, Jesus' willfully obtuse opponents misunderstand his prediction that he will disappear and that their efforts to find him will be futile: "Where does this man intend to go, that we shall not be able to find him? Does he intend to go among the Diaspora [of Jews] among the Greeks and teach the Greeks?" Like Paul? In John 12:20–23, we have a sawed-off stump of a story that begins thusly: "Now among those who went up to worship at the feast were some Greeks. So these came to Philip, who was from Bethsaida in Galilee [hence a Greek speaker?], and said to him, 'Lord, we wish to see Jesus.' Philip went and told Andrew; Andrew went with Philip and they told Jesus. And Jesus answered them, 'The hour has come for the son of man to be glorified.'" This, I feel quite sure, is another version of Eusebius's story (*Ecclesiastical History* 1.13) of King Abgar of Edessa sending a letter to Jesus via the runner Ananias, inviting Jesus to escape his enemies and come to Edessa. "Abgarus Uchama the toparch to Jesus the good Saviour who has appeared in the region of Jerusalem, greeting. I have heard about you and your cures, that they are performed by you without drugs or herbs: for, as the report goes, you make blind men to see again, lame men to walk, and cleanse lepers, and cast out unclean spirits and devils, and those afflicted with long illness you heal, and raise the dead. And having heard all this about you, I had determined one of two things, either that you are God come down from heaven, and so do these things, or you are a son of God who does these things. Therefore now I have written to entreat you to trouble yourself to come to me and heal the affliction I have. For indeed I have heard that the Jews murmur against you and wish to do you harm. And I have a very little city, but quite nice, and it will be sufficient for us both."

To this Jesus answers, "Blessed are you who have believed in me, not having seen me. For it is written about me that those who have seen me shall not believe in me, and that those who have not seen me shall believe and live. But concerning that of which you have written me, to come to you; I must needs fulfill all things for which I was sent here, and after fulfilling them be taken up to him who sent me. But once I am taken up, I will send you one of my disciples to heal your affliction and to give life to you and to those who are with you." According to the foundation legend of the Edessan church, of which this spurious epistle is an integral part, Jesus did in fact send Addai (Thaddeus) to Edessa to heal and preach.

I suggest that originally, these Greeks invited Jesus to come and teach among them, and so to escape his enemies in Judea, which is exactly what Jesus' enemies speculate he will do in John 7:35. Much the same happened in the early career of Muhammad, when he was preaching in the streets of Mecca and gaining increasing hostility from the Quraiysh leadership. Having heard of his prophesying, a delegation from war-torn Yathrib (Medina) came to ask him to come to their city and use his prophetic clout to help them prevail. If it worked, they would make him theocratic ruler. Eventually he accepted the invitation, when things in Mecca got hotter, and he made the great flight (*Hegira* or *Hijra*) from Mecca to Medina and established his power base there.

As we now read Jesus' reply to the Greeks, it is abrupt and apparently off-topic, like that to Nicodemus in chapter 3—and for the same reason: John has omitted the question and given only the answer. It is a repudiation of the whole idea: Jesus' hour has come, and he will hear nothing about evading it by making a hasty escape to Greece (or Edessa). But was there a version in which Jesus remembered this offer, so much like that in the Abgar legend, and took them up on it? Having seen the extent of his enemies' wrath on the cross, he knew it was time to go elsewhere and shake the dust off his feet. It sounds to me like John knew of such a version of the Jesus story and sought to make it look ridiculous both by his rough editing of the story of the Greeks' embassy and his rewriting of Luke 24:36–43.

Is it possible for this palimpsest version of the Passion to have been earlier than the familiar version in which Jesus actually does die? Most scholars will say no; after all, isn't any docetic (merely apparent death) version by its very nature parasitic on and derivative from a real death version? Isn't a docetic version an attempt to mitigate the scandal, the stigma, of the cross? If so, then a real death version must have preceded it. But I think the crucifixion and survival can be shown to possess its own integrity and need not be viewed as a backpedaling from the "real thing." For one thing, as I have argued elsewhere,[13] the hero's narrow escape from crucifixion is a staple in the Hellenistic novels of the day. And then there is the kinship of the Passion, as all scholars now recognize, to the stereotype Jewish tale of the Suffering Righteous One, where a Jew's (Daniel, Joseph, Esther, Ahiqar, et al.) fidelity to God against all pagan threats and blandishments wins deliverance in the end. The existence of a Passion of Jesus in which he escaped the designs of the wicked would fit this pattern better than one in which he actually died and then rose from the dead. The latter motif, it seems to me, clearly fits in more naturally with an altogether different Hellenistic/ Middle Eastern mytheme, that of the dying and rising god. I judge that it was the influence of the latter (which we have already detected abundantly in the Words of Institution and the Anointing at Bethany) that eventually invaded the hero-story version in which Jesus had escaped the cross alive. Once this happened, the crucifixion and survival version turned into the death and resurrection version.

The consensus opinion that the Pauline Epistles are earlier than the emerging gospel tradition might demand that the real death version of the crucifixion be the earlier, as the epistles speak only of the death of Jesus on the cross. In fact, one can explain the composition of Mark 15 from Psalm 22, as we have suggested, on the supposition that Mark knew only the bare fact of Jesus' crucifixion from gospel preaching, to which was attached no historical account, and this is what would have necessitated Mark's having to go to scripture for what history and apostolic memory failed to provide him. But that is not the only possibility. It may be that the preached Christ was not originally the same as the hero Jesus who survived crucifixion. 2 Corinthians speaks intriguingly of "another Jesus than the one we preached" (2 Cor. 11:4), championed by triumphalistic "superapostles" (11:5) who shun the death of Jesus, whereas in the Paulinist view, it is precisely in the death of Jesus that God's power is most clearly shown. What perfect sense it would make of the position of Paul's Corinthian opponents if they had told the story of a Jesus who had triumphed by escaping the designs of his enemies! In fact, it would make little difference for our purpose whether the superapostles had spoken of a different figure altogether, also named Jesus ("savior"), or just had a very different version of the story of the same Jesus, one in which he escaped the cross. The point would stand: both versions of the Passion may have been circulating even in the time of the Pauline Epistles, even if one accepts their date as pregospel.

There is also our criterion that the more spectacular of two versions of a story must be the later, since, had it been the original, no one would have felt dissatisfied with it and wanted to improve on it. Here we have two versions of the Passion. In one a man escapes death on his cross because someone has drugged him, and he is taken down prematurely. In the other, a man dies and miraculously rises from the dead. Which is more probable by historical reckoning? Of course, even if we judge the hero-story version the earlier, that hardly means we have arrived at the truth concerning the historical Jesus. A variety of accounts of a historical figure's death, like that of Apollonius of Tyana, implies no one had any real information and that several sought to fill in the gap. We have seen that the astonishing uncertainty among Jewish and Christian writers as to the decade or even the century of Jesus' death, and over who condemned him to death (Pilate? Antipas? Alexander Jannaeus?), should make us wonder if there had been any historical memory of the "event," which may originally have been a timeless cosmic drama of salvation, like that of Purusha, Prometheus, or Mithras. Now in exactly the same way, we have to ask ourselves whether the different versions of his death (on the Golgotha cross, or years later outside the Holy Land) imply no one knew what had happened to Jesus, and that familiar mythemes and fictional motifs were drawn on to fill in the blank.

NOTES

1. Robert M. Price, *Widow Traditions in Luke-Acts: A Feminist-Critical Scrutiny*, Dissertation Series 155 (Atlanta: Scholars Press, 1997), p. 163.

2. Jacques Derrida expresses surprise that Veronica's veil is not actually mentioned in the Gospels! See Derrida, "Living On: *Border Lines*," in *Deconstruction and Criticism*, ed. Harold Bloom (New York: Continuum, 1979), p. 130.

3. Hermann Gunkel, "Individual Complaint Songs," chap. 6 in *Introduction to Psalms: The Genres of the Religious Lyric of Israel*, trans. James D. Nogalski, Mercer Library of Biblical Studies (Macon: Mercer University Press, 1998), pp. 121–98; Sigmund Mowinckel, "Personal (Private) Psalms of Lamentation," chap. 8 in *The Psalms in Israel's Worship*, trans. D. R. Ap-Thomas, one vol. ed. (Nashville: Abingdon, 1962), pp. 1–25.

4. Literally, "your kingdom."

5. Plutarch, *Agis and Cleomenes, Tiberius and Gaius Gracchus, Philopoemen and Flamininus*, trans. Beradotte Perrin, Loeb Classical Library 102 (Cambridge: Harvard University Press, 1921), p. 141.

6. Hazrat Mirza Ghulam Ahmad, *Jesus in India: Being an Account of Jesus' Escape from Death on the Cross and of His Journey to India* (Rabwah, Pakistan: Ahmadiyya Muslim Foreign Missions Department, 1962); Mumtaz Ahmad Faruqui, *The Crumbling of the Cross* (Lahore: Ahmadiyya Anjuman Isha'at-i-Islam, 1973); Khwaja Nazir Ahmad, *Jesus in Heaven on Earth* (Bombay: Dar-ul-Isha'at-Kutub-E-Islamia, 1988).

7. J. Duncan M. Derrett, *The Anastasis: The Resurrection of Jesus as an Historical Event* (Shipston-on-Stour, Warwickshire: Peter Drinkwater, 1982); Barbara Thiering, "A Death That Failed," chap. 25 in *Jesus and the Riddle of the Dead Sea Scrolls: Unlocking the Secrets of His Life Story* (San Francisco: HarperSanFrancisco, 1992), pp. 116–20. Many scholars dismiss Thiering as an eccentric, but while I do not hold with all her judgments, I am not persuaded that her critics are remotely competent to evaluate her work, based as it is on intricacies of ancient calendar lore and exegetical technique of which she seems to possess a unique mastery.

8. Dennis R. MacDonald, *Homeric Epics and the Gospel of Mark* (New Haven: Yale University Press, 2000), pp. 154–55.

9. C. C. Dobson, *Did Our Lord Visit Britain as They Say in Cornwall and Somerset?* (Merrimac: Destiny Publishers, 1944), p. 9.

10. E-mail dated February 7, 2001, to the present writer from Richard C. Carrier.

11. Philostratus, *The Life of Apollonius of Tyana*, trans. F. C. Conybeare, vol. 2 of Loeb Classical Library 16 (Cambridge, Mass.: Harvard University Press, 1912), p. 361.

12. Friedrich Schleiermacher, *The Life of Jesus*, trans. S. Maclean Gilmour, Lives of Jesus Series (Philadelphia: Fortress Press, 1975), pp. 471–72.

13. Robert M. Price, "The Cruci-Fiction?" chap. 7 in *Deconstructing Jesus* (Amherst, N.Y.: Prometheus Books, 2000), pp. 213–24.

CHAPTER FOURTEEN
RESURRECTION

THE EMPTY TOMB

Mark's story of the empty tomb (16:1–8) starts out with a stumble, since it is predicated on the women visiting the tomb of Jesus to anoint the body for preservation, despite the fact that the Middle Eastern climate pretty much rules out the viability of such an attempt two days after death. It is, of course, possible that Markan chronology is artificial and has produced the problem by accident. Perhaps in the first telling of the story, there was no attempt to keep the sabbath by waiting to prepare the corpse. It ends with a lurch, abruptly with no resurrection appearances. The young man at the empty tomb tells the mourning women to go and tell the disciples that their master is not dead, but has risen. He will meet them in Galilee. But the women disobey the order! They are pointedly said to have told nothing to anyone, out of fear. And on that note the Gospel of Mark ends! There are two reasons for this.

First, the evangelist knows his readers have never heard the story before, and they will find it suspicious for that reason. "Why haven't we heard about this till now?" This probably means the story was of fairly recent coinage. Who coined it? No doubt it was the product of a female mourning cult such as those who mourned for slain gods like Tammuz (Ezek. 8:14), Baal Haddad (Zech. 12:11), and Osiris.

They populated the story with devout women like themselves, based on the searching goddesses Cybele, Ishtar, Isis, Aphrodite, and Anat. It was the etiological legend for their group and its yearly rites. Mark decided to incorporate it into his story, but there were as yet no resurrection stories. He implied that the disciples would be seeing Jesus shortly in Galilee, provided they knew to go there, which they *didn't*, thanks to the women. If they somehow managed to get the message some other way, it is certainly strange that no New Testament writer even tries to tell us what transpired between Jesus and Peter on the occasion. Nor do there seem to have been other traditional accounts of resurrection appearances floating around, since, when Matthew and Luke added appearance stories onto the end of Mark, it is clear, as we shall shortly see, that they had to make up their own.

Second, an empty tomb story without any resurrection appearances is quite understandable, even natural, once we understand that the story falls neatly into a particular form of ancient literature, as Charles H. Talbert has shown.[1] It is an ancient *apotheosis* narrative, such as were frequently told about figures both ancient and contemporary. The basic outline has the hero suddenly turn up missing. His companions try to find him but cannot. There is no trace of his body or of his clothing. With the help of a heavenly voice or a remembered prophecy, they realize the hero has ascended to heaven to take his place among the gods. We can adduce ample instances from the Old Testament, Greek and Roman myth, and from Hellenistic-era hero biographies (the genre to which the Gospels belong).

Enoch, in the briefest of stories, really just a notice, is rewarded for a life of perfect righteousness by being translated to heaven (Gen. 5:24), or so the text was understood in antiquity. "He was not," that is, not to be found. Moses, too, ascended to heaven, according to ancient belief (which is why he returns with Elijah to visit Jesus at the Transfiguration—neither saint had died). Deut. 34:6 had said that no one knew where Moses was buried, which later writers took as a coy way of saying he *wasn't*—he hadn't died. Philo tells the tale in New Testament times: "He was about to depart from hence to heaven, to take up his abode there, and leaving this mortal life to become immortal, having been summoned by the Father, who now changed him, having previously been a double being, composed of soul and body, into the nature of a single body, transforming him wholly and entirely into a most sunlike mind. . . . For when he was now on the point of being taken away, and was standing at the very starting-place, as it were, that he might fly away and complete his journey to heaven, he was once more inspired and filled with the Holy Spirit, and while still alive he prophesied admirably what should happen to himself after his death, relating, that is, how he had died when he was not as yet dead, and how he was buried without anyone being present so as to know of his tomb, because in fact he was entombed not by mortal hands, but by immortal powers, so that he was not placed in the tomb of his forefathers, having met with particular grace that no man ever saw" (*Life of Moses* 39).[2]

Josephus is more explicit still: "All who accompanied him [Moses] were the senate [the seventy elders], and Eleazer the high priest, and Joshua their commander. Now as soon as they were come to the mountain called *Abarim* . . . he dismissed the senate; and as he was going to embrace Eleazer and Joshua, and was still discoursing with them, a cloud stood over him on the sudden, and he disappeared in a certain valley, although he wrote in the holy books that he died, which was done out of fear, lest they should venture to say, that because of his extraordinary virtue, he went to God" (*Antiquities* 5.1.48).[3] Though each seems to feel the need to be cagey about it, it is plain enough that both writers believed Moses did not really die but ascended into heaven. This was because no one could locate his body; no one knew where (or if) there was a grave.[4]

Elijah, too, skipped death, ascending to the zenith of heaven aboard a flaming chariot (2 Kings 2:11), which his disciples knew because, after an exhaustive search, they failed to find the body (2 Kings 2:15–18).

After Heracles, son of Zeus, died, men looked for his bones and found nary a one. Because they recalled a prior prophecy that he was destined for immortality, they concluded he must have been taken to heaven (Diodorus *Library of History* 4.38.4–5). Likewise, Apollo's son Aristaeus, after dwelling in the region of Mt. Haemus, was never seen again, and all men assumed he had been taken up (ibid., 4:81–82). Aeneas, son of Venus, was the survivor of Troy whose descendants founded Rome. After a certain battle, no one could find a trace of his body, so they concluded he had been translated to heaven (Dionysus of Halicarnassus *Roman Antiquities* 1.64.4–5). Likewise, Romulus, son of Mars, vanished from human sight after a battle in which the sun was momentarily darkened. Some claimed actually to have seen him ascending from the battlefield. He was deified as the god Quirinus (ibid., 1.77.2; Cicero *The Republic* 1.41; 2.2, 10; 6.21; Ovid *Metamorphoses* 14.805–28; 15.862–63; Livy *History of Rome* 1.16; Plutarch "Romulus" (27): "He disappeared on the Nones of July . . . leaving nothing of certainty to be related of his death: only the time . . . Romulus, when he vanished, left neither the least part of his body, nor any remnant of his clothes to be seen . . . the senators suffered them not to search, or busy themselves about the matter, but commanded them to honour and worship Romulus as one taken up to the gods."[5]

Empedocles the philosopher (484–424 B.C.E.) invited some friends to a sacrificial feast. "Then, after the feast, the remainder of the company dispersed and retired to rest . . . while Empedocles himself remained on the spot where he had reclined at table. At daybreak all got up, and he was the only one missing. A search was made, and they questioned the servants, who said they did not know where he was. Thereupon someone said that in the middle of the night he heard an exceedingly loud voice calling Empedocles. Then he got up and beheld a light in the heavens and a glitter of lamps, but nothing else. His hearers were amazed at what had occurred, and Pausanias came down and sent people to search for him. But later he bade them take no further trouble, for things beyond expectation had happened to him, and it was their duty to sacrifice to him since he was now a god" (Diogenes Laertius *Lives of Eminent Philosophers* 8.68).[6]

Apollonius of Tyana (a contemporary of Paul), son of Proteus, was said to have entered Dictynna's temple in Crete late one night, rousing the fearsome guard dogs. But "instead of barking, they approached him and fawned upon him. . . . The guardians of the temple arrested him in consequence, and threw him in bonds as a wizard and a robber, accusing him of having thrown to the dogs some charmed morsel. But about midnight he loosened his bonds, and after calling those who had bound him, in order that they might witness the spectacle, he ran to the doors of the temple, which opened wide to receive him; and when he had passed within they closed afresh, as they had been shut, and there was heard a chorus of maidens singing from within the temple, and their song was this. "Hasten thou from earth, hasten thou to Heaven, hasten!" He was no more seen on earth (Philostratus *Life of Apollonius of Tyana* 8.30).[7]

Talbert is surely right that any ancient reader of Mark's empty tomb story would at once understand what sort of story he was reading. He would not have needed any resurrection appearances to get the point. The words of the young man (likely an angel) at the empty tomb would have been enough of a climax to an apotheosis story, showing that Jesus, too, had risen from the grave and ascended into heaven.

APPARITIONS

We must not be content with observing (as one often reads) that Matthew and Luke simply "add resurrection appearances where Mark lacked them." It is important to keep in mind that the addition of resurrection appearances is ipso facto a secondary embellishment, like Matthew adding Peter's walk on the water or the earthquake and the rescusitations of the saints at the crucifixion. Again, remember, the more spectacular version is always to be judged the secondary, the less authentic. The less spectacular version was once deemed quite good enough by itself. Had there been something better already available, we may be sure the earlier author would have used it. If you knew Elijah had returned in person atop the mountain with Jesus, you would never bother cooking up an excuse such as that Elijah returned figuratively as John the Baptist. And in the same manner we must remind ourselves that, had there been any resurrection appearances circulating in Mark's time, he would have used them.

And once we realize, by examining Matthew's and Luke's redaction of Mark 16:1–8, that they had to *change* what ending Mark did provide to substitute a new one, the completely fictional character of their endeavor ought to become completely manifest. That is, they are not merely supplying "what came next." They are revising and improving the story. Luke 24:1–12 is a drastic rewrite of Mark's empty tomb story. For one thing, Luke has changed Mark's young man in white to a pair of angels in dazzling apparel. They speak (as one, a sign of fiction) to the women in a highly edited version of Mark 16:7. Instead of "He is going before you into Galilee," Luke's angels say, "Remember how he told you, *when he was still in Galilee*, that the Son of Man must be delivered into the hands of sinful men, and be crucified, and on the third day rise" (24:6–7). Why this change? Because Luke plans to restrict the resurrection appearances to Jerusalem (and close by) with none in Galilee. So he leaves "Galilee" in the sentence to make it sound as much like the original as he can, so it will ring true to the reader, but he changes the sense of it completely. More astonishing still is that he directly contradicts Mark by having the women report to Peter and his colleagues after all! The Apostles do not believe them, but, according to some manuscripts, Peter does at least visit the tomb himself to check out the story. Finding it empty of corpses and angels alike, he returns home more puzzled than ever. But all this is spurious. None of it is independent, parallel tradition or any such nonsense. It is all the historically spurious extension of Mark's story by a later writer.

The same may and must be said of Matthew's rewrite of Mark's empty tomb story in Matthew 28. Mark had the women discover that the stone door of the tomb was already opened and then see the young man in white. But Matthew ups the voltage considerably. For him, like Luke, the young man must be an angel (though only one of them), and, borrowing some special effects from Dan. 10:6, he gives the angel a visage like lightning. He has borrowed his snow-white vestments from the Ancient of Days in Dan. 7:9. In full view of the women, the angel swoops down from the sky and rolls the stone away, sitting atop it. This time, as in Luke, the women do obey the angelic direction and tell the disciples. But before they can even get back to them, the women are accosted by the Risen Christ himself! How did Mark neglect to inform us of this little tidbit? But Jesus' apparition to the women is superfluous: he does little but reiterate the instructions the angel had already given them. Why does Matthew go to the trouble to add an appearance of Jesus when he has nothing new for him to say? Simply because Matthew was not quite sure who Mark's "young man" was. Surely he was an angel, and so Matthew depicts him, but is it possible the man was the Risen Jesus himself? Just in case, Matthew repeats the character's appearance and his speech. First he is an angel, then he is Jesus. And from such cloth are the resurrection appearances cut!

But even this is not the most extravagant embellishment by Matthew. He hatches the notion of posting guards at the tomb to up the ante and so add to the glory of Jesus' triumph. He seems to have derived the idea from Dan. 3:20, where Nebuchadnezzar "ordered certain mighty men of his army to bind Shadrach, Meschach, and Abednego, and to throw them into the fiery furnace." So he has a delegation of chief priests and Pharisees petition Pilate for a contingent of guards to prevent the disciples from stealing Jesus' corpse and spreading the hoax that he had risen from the dead. Pilate agrees and assigns Roman soldiers to guard the tomb. To make certain, they seal the tomb (27:62–66), a detail Matthew derived from Dan. 6:17, "And a stone was brought and laid upon the mouth of the [lion's] den, and the king sealed it with his own signet and with the signet of his lords, that nothing might be changed concerning Daniel." Once the angel descends, the poor guards faint dead away (Matt. 28:4), as suggested by Dan. 3:22, "Because . . . the furnace was very hot, the flame of the fire slew those men who took up Shadrach, Meschach, and Abednego." The guards are waking back up about the time the women leave to carry their message, and they go report to the Jewish elders who, apparently unmoved by this definitive proof of the divine vindication of the Son of God, cook up a crazy scheme whereby the soldiers are to spread the tale that the disciples stole the body, which they are somehow supposed to know despite having been fast asleep at the time! This is just comedy. No one would have floated such a ridiculous excuse.

Matthew means to supply the Galilee reunion Mark's young man mentioned. The disciples gather at the mountain Matthew says Jesus had designated (Matt. 28:16), though he has not shown him designating any mountain. "And when they saw him, they bowed before him, though they doubted" (Matt. 28:17, which is usually not translated literally, since it would not sound good from the lectern on Easter). The doubt element ought to be, as it is in Luke's and John's resurrection appearance stories, preliminary to a convincing demonstration of the resurrection, but it is not. Is it possible that someone has abridged Matthew, cutting out that scene of proof as well as Jesus directing the disciples to a particular mountain? It sounds like it. Eusebius tells us there has been some tampering with the text, as we will see just below. The words of the Risen Jesus are all artificial. His brief speech is redolent of special Matthean vocabulary: "to disciple" (Matt. 13:52), "unto the consummation of the age" (Matt. 13:40, 49). But the meat of it comes from a conflation of two different Greek translations of Dan. 7:14. "Behold, all authority in heaven and on earth has been given to me" draws from the Septuagint version, "to him was given the rule . . . and his authority is an everlasting authority," and from Theodotion's version, "authority to hold all in the heaven and on the earth." The scope of the evangelistic mission is "all nations," and this comes from the same verse, where we read that "all peoples, nations, and languages should serve him."[8] He gives them a baptismal formula that sounds suspiciously Trinitarian, and indeed there is good reason to believe the text has been doctored at this point. Eusebius, himself a devout champion of Nicene Trinitarianism, admits that he had seen some copies of Matthew dating from before the Council of Nicea in which the text read simply, "baptizing them in my name."[9] No doubt that is the original text of Matthew.

At any rate, we can erase every bit of the forgoing as pure Matthean invention. If that were not clear from a close reading of the text itself, the mere facts that none of this appears in Mark and that all of it is predicated upon Matthew's changing the ending of Mark make it impossible to accept any of it. If any of this had been known (*Roman guards*, for God's sake!), Mark simply would never have written as he did. It is that simple.

TRAVELS WITH JESUS

Returning to Luke 24, we must consider the famous and beautiful story of the disciples on the road to Emmaus (verses 13–35). The basic premise of the story is a very ancient mytheme, whereby the gods test the mettle of mortals by walking among them incognito to see how they are treated. Gen. 18–19 is a prime example, as is the Greek myth of Baucis and Philemon (cf. Acts 14). But there is one example startlingly close to the Emmaus story. It is an old testimonial (fourth century B.C.E.) from the Epidaurus healing shrine of Asclepius. "Sostrata, a woman of Pherae, was pregnant with worms. Being in a very bad way, she was carried into the Temple and slept there. But when she saw no distinct dream she let herself be carried back home. Then, however, near a place called Kornoi, a man of fine appearance seemed to come upon her and her companions. When he had learned from them about their bad luck, he asked them to set down on the ground the litter in which they were carrying Sostrata. Then he cut open her abdomen and took out a great quantity of worms—two wash basins full. After having stitched her belly up again and made the woman well, Asclepius revealed to her his presence and enjoined her to send thank-offerings for her treatment to Epidaurus" (Stele 2.25).[10] As the two disciples had come to Jerusalem hoping for messianic deliverance, so Sostrata and her companions had journeyed to another holy city, Epidaurus, seeking a miracle of healing. Both parties are disappointed and head for home. Each party is accosted by a man who seems to be a simple traveler unknown to them. He sees their dismay and asks the reason for it. And then he works the miracle they had hoped for, reveals his identity, and vanishes. That is pretty close! It is certainly not impossible that Luke actually knew about this story and copied it. But it doesn't really matter. The point is that it is exactly the same kind of story, cut from the same cloth. No one could give a good reason for maintaining one is fiction while the other is history.

The speech of the Risen Jesus here is a Lukan creation, closely similar to other short Lukan speeches, for example, Luke 24:44–47, Acts 2:22–36, 13:27–31, 10:36–43. Why has Luke chosen the town of Emmaus for the destination of the disciples and thus for the site of the climax? My guess is that Luke intends a punning reference to a name from the *Odyssey*, that of *Eumaeus*, the faithful servant to whom Telemachus and Odysseus reveal their secret identities, as Jesus does to the Emmaus disciples.

We have already discussed Luke 24:36–43, suggesting that it may naturally be read as a miraculous translation of a still-living Jesus from Emmaus to Jerusalem, along the lines of the teleportations of Philip from Gaza to Ashdod and of Apollonius from Rome to Dicaearchia. But of course it may be intended as a resurrection story. But if it is, then it is a very confused one. Jesus means to convince the disciples that he is not a bodiless phantom, so he lets them touch his solid flesh and eats a bit of fish, something Jewish lore made impossible for angels and spirits. But, on the usual reading, he has just walked through a locked door like Jacob Marley! Well, which is it? Is he substantial or not? It is no divine mystery; if it were, then why would Jesus/Luke talk in terms of proving something, making something plain to those present? As old Hosea Ballou said, something passing as a "revelation" ought to elucidate things, not confuse them! The scene is just poorly thought out.[11] And the speech is more Lukan theology, plus marching orders. Luke makes little effort to hide this, as he actually has Jesus remind them of what he had said "when I was with you." Where does he think he is now? The words reflect Luke's retrospective viewpoint.

And again, absolutely all of this can be sponged away as secondary embellishment of Mark's simple apotheosis narrative. It is a complex story predicated upon an imaginary premise: as if Mark's story had ended differently than it did.

THE SYNOPTICON OF JOHN

John 20:1–18 is the fourth evangelist's version of the empty tomb story of Mark. He has rewritten it with great skill and great ingenuity, just as he has taken the perfunctory Synoptic scene of Pilate interrogating Jesus and made it into a suspenseful and stimulating dramatic dialogue. The same artist is at work here. He has narrowed the focus to Mary Magdalene, since the other women were superfluous anyway. He does leave a vestige of the earlier version in verse 2 ("*we* do not know where they have laid him"), but Mary is definitely the star of the show this time around. She visits the tomb (though not to anoint the corpse, since in this gospel Joseph of Arimathea and Nicodemus have already taken care of that, 19:39–40) and finds it empty, but there is no one to explain it to her—not yet, anyway. She reports the emptiness of the tomb to the disciples. John must have been reading the Western version of Luke, since he borrows from Luke 24:12 the notion of Peter checking out the tomb, but he pairs him with the Beloved Disciple, a creation of his, just as he teamed Joseph of Arimathea with his own character Nicodemus. Peter saw the graveclothes of Jesus lying by themselves and knew not what to think. John expands this scene and makes it much more vivid. And though some apologists contend that the vividness is a mark of eyewitness recollection, it is easier to understand it as novelistic detail, especially since we happen to possess an almost identical scene from an admitted fictional novel from the same period, *Chaireas and Callirhoe* by Chariton. "Chaireas was guarding and toward dawn he approached the tomb [cf. Luke 24:1; John 20:1a], supposedly to bring crowns and jewels, but really he had in mind to kill himself. For he did not admit that he was unbetrothed from Callirhoe, and he considered death to be the only healer of grief. When he came close, however, he found the stones moved away [cf. John 20:1b] and the entrance open. He looked in and was shocked, seized by a great perplexity [cf. Luke 24:4] at what had happened. Rumor made an immediate report to the Syracusans about the miracle. All then ran to the tomb; no one dared to enter until Hermocrates ordered it [cf. John 20:5b]. One was sent in [cf. John 20:8], and he reported everything accurately [cf. John 21:24]. It seemed incredible—the dead girl was not there. Then Chaireas thought he ought to see again the dead Callirhoe; but when he searched the tomb he was able to find nothing. Many came in after him, disbelieving. Amazement seized everyone, and some said as they stood there, 'The shroud has been stripped off [cf. John 20:6–7], this is the work of grave robbers, but where is the body?'" (*Chaireas and Callirhoe* 3.3).[12]

John next plugs in Luke 24:4–7, the revelation of the two angels, having traded places between it and Luke 24:9–12. Because the Lukan original had the angels appear to Mary during her first (and only) visit to the tomb, she is suddenly "back" there once the Johannine narrator returns to the first part of the Lukan text. Taking a leaf from Matthew's gospel, John introduces the Risen Jesus himself, only he is more skilled than Matthew: instead of having Jesus simply repeat the angels' message, he divides the message between them. Both ask, "Woman, why are you weeping?" but only Jesus tells her to relay a message to the disciples.

The next section, the scene between Jesus and Mary, appears to be based on the Book of Tobit, as Randel Helms has indicated.[13] Mary sees Jesus but does not know he is Jesus, as in Tob. 5:5, Tobit "went to seek a man and found Raphael, who was an angel, and he knew it not." Jesus reveals his identity, and Mary is abashed. She grasps his feet (borrowed from Matt. 28:9) in a gesture of devotion and supplication. Jesus warns her away: "Touch me not, for I have not yet ascended to the Father; but go to my brethren and say to them, 'Behold, I am ascending to my Father and your Father, to my God and your God'" (John 20:17). Jesus here plays the role of the angel Raphael, as he reveals his identity to Tobias and Sarah, "And they were both troubled, and fell upon their faces; for they were afraid. And he said to them, 'Be not afraid; ye shall have peace; but bless God forever. For not of any favor of mine, but by the will of your God I came. All these days did I appear unto you; and I did neither eat nor drink, but ye saw a vision. And now give God thanks: because I ascend to him that sent me'" (Tob. 12:16–20a). And this parallel even makes sense of the puzzling detail of Jesus not wanting to be touched: it appears to be a vague reflection of the "docetism," the merely apparent physical reality, of the angel.

We have already seen how John rewrote Luke 24:36–43 into John 20:19–20 in such a way as to close the door on the possibility that Jesus had survived the cross. Verses 21–22 constitute "the Johannine Pentecost," as well as John's version of Matt. 18:18, the granting of apostolic authority to bind and loose, that is, to make halakhic and penitential rulings.

DOUBTING DISCIPLES

Though John 20:19–20 clearly presupposes the presence of all the disciples at the appearance of the resurrected Jesus, John retroactively excepts Thomas because he next wants to use him as a symbol for his readers, who of course did not see the Risen Jesus and may feel themselves at a permanent and fatal disadvantage. The story is of a piece with Philostratus's story of how the ascended master Apollonius satisfied the doubts of a skeptical disciple. "The young man in question . . . would on no account allow the immortality of the soul, and said, 'I myself, gentlemen, have done nothing now for nine months but pray to Apollonius that he would reveal to me the truth about the soul; but he is so utterly dead that he will not appear to me in response to my entreaties, nor give me any reason to consider him immortal.' Such were the young man's words on that occasion, but on the fifth day following, after discussing the same subject, he fell asleep where he was talking with them, and . . . on a sudden, like one possessed, he leaped up, still in a half sleep, streaming with perspiration, and cried out, 'I believe thee.' And when those who were present asked him what was the matter; 'Do you not see,' said he, 'Apollonius the sage, how that he is present with us and is listening to our discussion, and is reciting wondrous verses about the soul?' 'But where is he?' they asked, 'For we cannot see him anywhere, although we would rather do so than possess all the blessings of mankind.' And the youth replied: 'It would seem that he is come to converse with myself alone concerning the tenets which I would not believe'" (*Life of Apollonius of Tyana* 8:31).[14] Form criticism does not require us to suppose that John somehow knew of this story and copied it. No, the point is that form criticism enables us to recognize what Robert Alter calls a type-scene, a literary stereotype with a common syntagm (plot logic) and interchangeable items from a common paradigm.[15] It is not a piece of history. It is rather formula fiction.

Again, we have already had occasion to note, not only the similarity of John 21:1–14 to, but its certain derivation from, a Pythagoras story in which the sage, a pious vegetarian, bets some fishermen that if he can correctly "guess" the number of fish they have just hauled in, they will free them. Of course Pythagoras knows the number and saves the fish, paying the fishermen the market price. The number of fish is irrelevant to the Johannine version since, Christians not being vegetarians, Jesus' miracle has to do with something else: it is he who makes the catch possible. Nor are the disciples said in John 21 to have bothered counting the fish, and yet the number occurs in the text, one hundred fifty-three fish, a vestige from the Pythagoras version where the number mattered. Not only that, but the number is a Pythagorean "triangular" number.

John 21:15–19 seems to take up Luke's promise of Peter's rehabilitation in Luke 22:31–32, with Jesus giving Peter as many opportunities to affirm his love as he had made denials previously. He charges Peter to shepherd his flock, namely, the disciples (as in Luke 12:32), just as Luke envisioned Peter "strengthening [his] brothers" (22:32). John also has Jesus predict Peter's eventual martyrdom by crucifixion (hands stretched out on the cross, waist looped with a leash, led to the place of execution).

We have seen how a broad promise attributed to Jesus, that his generation would live to see the coming of the kingdom of God (Mark 13:30), created more and more embarrassment as the years went by and more Christians died. What would happen to the ones who died in the meantime (cf. 1 Thess. 4:13)? And had the promise finally failed? Mark 9:1 comes from a time when some of that generation still lived. 2 Pet. 3:4 and John 21:20–24 come from some time later, when no one from that generation could still be alive.[16] John (desperately) reinterprets the promise, which by his time had been whittled down to the single Christian leader believed to have lived at the time of Jesus. "This is the disciple who [in this book] is bearing witness to these things, and who has written these things; and we know that his testimony is true" (verse 24). Who is this "we"? I suspect that we have here the first attestation of the legend that this gospel was written by John the son of Zebedee at the request of the other disciples, as in the Muratorian Canon fragment.[17] "We" might be intended as the other ten disciples plus Matthias, though it would be a piece of pseudepigraphy.

And, to risk monotony, let me reiterate that the whole collection of Johannine resurrection episodes, being a rewrite of all three Synoptics' empty tomb and resurrection stories, is thereby shown to be entirely secondary, literary in character, and historically spurious. None of this material is of any more value than the forged scribal endings of Mark. All of the resurrection appearance stories are attempts to improve the ending of the Markan original by contradicting it. It is as if one read Dickens's unfinished *The Mystery of Edwin Drood* and then sought out the various attempts by other authors to complete the work; would not the very existence of disparate endings demonstrate not only the fictive character of them all but that of Dickens's original as well?

CAVALRY COMING OVER CALVARY?

But do we not have more valuable information about the resurrection in 1 Corinthians 15? Most scholars point to the list of resurrection appearances in 1 Cor. 15:3–11 as prime real estate on which to build a historical case for the resurrection, at least for believing, as Bultmann did, that Christianity began with the Easter morning faith of the first disciples, or as Gordon Kaufman says, holy hallucinations.[18] That is, no matter how one evaluates it, mustn't the serious student of the text admit that this passage tells us someone early on saw something they deemed to be visions of the resurrected Jesus? As these scholars themselves are quick to point out, such an optimistic estimation depends on accepting the conventional dating, not of the epistle itself, but of the specific passage. That is, the appearance list has all the earmarks, as all agree, of a creedal formula. It may have been used as a list of credentialed apostles, or as evidence for the resurrection; it does not matter for our purpose. But Paul is said to be quoting it to the Corinthians to remind them that, whatever their differences, all the apostles agree on the doctrine of Jesus' resurrection. When would he have obtained this list? Gal. 1:18–19 makes Paul visit Cephas and James the Just in Jerusalem only three years after his conversion. It seems not unreasonable to posit that he learned this formula at that time, and that would make it quite old indeed. Except that, as far as I am concerned, the passage is not a quotation of earlier material but rather a subsequent interpolation into the text.[19]

First, the very notion that Paul received from the Jerusalem apostles this material as the very essence of the gospel he preached (1 Cor. 15:1) is impossible for Paul. Not only may one ask what Paul can have been preaching for three years before he would have received this material from Cephas and James; but it is just impossible to square the notion of Paul's very gospel being derivative from the Jerusalem apostles with the clear testimony of Gal. 1:11–17, where Paul is concerned precisely to assert his independence from them, his only sporadic contact with them, and the independent origin of his gospel from God himself. There is no way short of doublethink, the usual strategy, to harmonize these passages. Second, the list of appearances seems itself to have harmonized what must originally have been two rival apostolic lists, "Cephas and the Twelve" (verse 5) versus "James and all the apostles" (verse 7), reflecting sectarian strife within Jewish Christianity. The subsequent healing of the breach was sealed by simply juxtaposing the two overlapping lists as a compromise. This rapprochement presupposes a long period, first of factionalism, then of assimilation and unification, and this is impossible by the time Paul would have written 1 Corinthians (or anything else). Third, the appearance to more than five hundred followers of Jesus (verse 6) is so grandiose that it must be a later, apocryphal legend. If such a thing were known from the earliest times (and if it had happened, how could it *not* be?), why do we find no mention of it in the Gospels? Can we imagine any, much less all, of the evangelists would have been ignorant of it or omitted it had they known about it? Fourth, the postscript attempt to add Paul to the list in the first person (verse 8) seems to feature Gnostic terminology: "Last of all, as to the *ektroma*," the aborted fetus, "he appeared also to me." "As to one born out of time," implying a protracted pregnancy, the usual translation/interpretation, does not capture the point. What does? The only identifiable reference is to the Gnostic cosmology according to which Sophia, the last of the divine Aions (emanations from the Godhead), manages to effect a forbidden virgin birth, bringing forth a malformed monster, the Demiurge, the creator of the material world from which all Gnostic mystics hoped to be liberated through the secret teaching of the revealer Jesus. The Demiurge was called the *ektroma* because of his ill-starred, monstrous birth. For the Risen Christ to appear to him reflects the Gnostic myth that the Primal Man, the Man of Light, a kind of Proto-Christ, had appeared before the Demiurge and/or his henchmen, the Archons, who tore him apart and infused their creation with his light-essence, lending the creation a stability and life it had lacked. Why is Paul compared to the Demiurge? Obviously, because he had been the persecutor of the saints, the enemy of God, and the Antichrist, as Jewish Christians still viewed him. But all this is, again, too late for Paul. 1 Cor. 15:3–11 is an interpolation. It is no more helpful to the historian than the Gospels.

But what if it were somehow authentic? Would we have the valuable evidence that most think it affords us? Not really, for then we should have to account for the drastic difference in conception between the Gospels, where the Risen One has physical flesh (even though the stories are inconsistent), and 1 Cor. 15:44–50, where we are told the Risen One had become a vivifying *spirit*, having neither flesh nor blood, since these frail elements cannot endure eternity in the kingdom of God. Luke had Jesus say he could not be a spirit since he had flesh (24:39), whereas Paul says the Risen Jesus was a spirit lacking flesh (1 Cor. 15:45, 50). If we are to assign the list of appearances in 1 Corinthians 15 and the subsequent discussion of the resurrection to the same author, as most scholars do, then we must infer that the other appearances Paul lists were of the same sort as his discussion implies. And this means we have an earlier tradition, Paul's, derived from Jerusalem, that flatly rules out the kind of stories we read in the gospel Easter chapters. And what does 1 Corinthians 15 by itself give us? Only information that some people once had some sort of visions of Jesus after he died, "such as the gods of the underworld often grant to those who are distracted by mourning."

UPWARD FROM EARTH

Originally, it appears that the ascension and the resurrection were understood to be the same thing. This is apparent from the widespread New Testament use of Psalm 110 as a prooftext and model for picturing the resurrection of Jesus: "The Lord said to my lord, 'Sit at my right hand until I make your enemies a footstool for your feet.'"[20] For this text to be used to illustrate (or to understand) the resurrection means Jesus is pictured as rising directly to the right hand of the Father. It does not exactly preclude resurrection appearances, yet it is certainly sufficient without them. It may be instructive to refer to Stephen's vision of the Risen Christ in Acts 7:55–56, where the martyr gazes *into heaven* and spots the Son of man standing at the right hand of the Father. If there were in fact early resurrection appearances, something we certainly cannot afford to take for granted, we may wonder if they were not all heavenly glimpses of the enthroned Christ.

The idea of there having been a separate ascension subsequent to the resurrection is a later, concretizing development. It presupposes a material body that must rise physically into the sky to enter heaven, conceived in the manner of the ancients as a horizontal plane vertically above our own flat earth. Once the notion of the resurrection has been made into the resuscitation of a physical body, as is the case with Jesus in the Gospels (though, again, they are confused and inconsistent), it is possible to conceive of Jesus first rising from the dead, walking among mortals again, and only later rising into the sky. How do the Gospels handle this new mytheme? Luke is the most thorough. He has plainly borrowed from Josephus the ascension of Moses, which we have already reproduced above. In Luke 24 he makes it explicit that Jesus ascended on Easter evening; everything is said to have transpired on the same day. But in Acts, chapter 1, the same author has the ascension occurring a full forty days later! Luke has borrowed a Gnostic motif, the idea that Jesus remained on earth for an extended period (some said eighteen months, others as long as eleven years!) teaching the esoteric gnosis to the apostles. Luke has Jesus teaching the disciples all about the kingdom of God, while omitting any particulars. Why? He means to write the bishops of his day a blank check, so that they may claim whatever they teach goes back to the Risen Jesus and his unspecified instructions. But, as if we could not tell by the divergence of dates for the ascension between Luke 24 and Acts 1, the whole thing is shown to be artificial by Luke's addition of the old "misunderstanding of the disciples" device. It is the fortieth day. Jesus has spent all this time teaching these men what they will need to found the Christian religion. And then someone pipes up, "Lord, is now the time you will restore independence to Israel?" (Acts 1:6). One can imagine Jesus' eyes rolling, him slapping his forehead in exasperation! He tells them to forget apocalyptic date setting and dispensational chart making and to get down to business missionizing the world once the Holy Spirit comes. Of course, all this is aimed at Luke's readers, whose priorities he seeks to rearrange. It all makes good sense as a piece of didactic fiction, which is exactly what it is. And Jesus rises into the sky.

John seems to be referring to Luke 24:51 when he has Jesus ask ironically, "Do you take umbrage at this [that he claims he descended from heaven—John 6:42]? What if you saw the Son of man ascending to where he was before?" (John 6:62). But he takes it for granted and neglects to narrate the ascension. He does have Jesus anticipate it once he is resurrected (20:17), but it never happens on camera. Astonishingly, the gospel comes to an end focusing not on Jesus but on the Beloved Disciple as the late and lamented leader of the Johannine community—though this is not really so odd once one remembers that it is he who is the real "Jesus" in the fourth gospel, the origin of the words ascribed to Jesus.

Mark, of course, has no more an ascension than he does resurrection appearances. Matthew seems to be aware that the resurrection of Jesus meant that he had taken the heavenly throne of Daniel 7, and that all stories of him appearing on earth are mere midrash, edifying and instructional fiction such as he has created. An ascension scene did not even occur to him because he is quite aware that the Risen Jesus remained in heaven alongside the Ancient of Days, but that he remains in spirit forever among his disciples, wherever two or three of them may gather (18:20). This is why he has the Risen One assure his missionaries to the nations, "I am with you always, even unto the consummation of the age" (28:20).

MANY AROUND THE CISTERN
BUT NO ONE IN THE CISTERN

Did Jesus rise from the dead? The Gospels give us no reason to think so. Every single story bears the marks of fiction, with earlier versions ruling out later ones, with extrabiblical parallels providing abundant nonhistorical analogies, while current experience provides no historical parallel. The Gospels certainly do not put us in touch with the faith (whatever it may have been) of the earliest Christians. They do not tell us whether the resurrection of Jesus was even part of the first Christian faith(s). Everywhere we have looked, we have found naught but legend and myth, fiction and redaction. What we have found is a kind of empty tomb. What we can never tell is whether anyone was ever buried there.

NOTES

1. Charles H. Talbert, *What Is a Gospel? The Genre of the Canonical Gospels* (Philadelphia: Fortress Press, 1977).

2. Nahum N. Glatzer, ed., *The Essential Philo*, trans. C. D. Yonge (New York: Schocken Books, 1971) pp. 269, 270.

3. William Whiston, trans., *The Works of Flavius Josephus* (London: Ward, Lock & Co., n.d.), p. 123.

4. It is just as clear in the wonderful Charleton Heston movie *The Ten Commandments*, which is based partly on Philo and Josephus, that Moses is about to ascend into heaven, not to die. Dare we recognize that this is one of those cases, like *The Wizard of Oz* and *Frankenstein*, where the movie, not the original book, stands as the definitive version?

5. Plutarch, *The Lives of the Noble Grecians and Romans*, trans. John Dryden, rev. Arthur Hugh Clough (New York: Modern Library, n.d.), pp. 43–44.

6. Diogenes Laertius, *Lives of Eminent Philosophers*, trans. R. D. Hicks, vol. 2, rev. ed., Loeb Classical Library 184 (Cambridge: Harvard University Press, 1931), p. 383.

7. Philostratus, *The Life of Apollonius of Tyana*, Loeb Classical Library 16 (Cambridge, Mass.: Harvard University Press, 1912), p. 401.

8. Randel Helms, *Gospel Fictions* (Amherst, N.Y.: Prometheus Books, 1989), p. 141.

9. Arthur W. Wainwright, *The Trinity in the New Testament* (London: SPCK, 1962), pp. 238–39.

10. Emma J. Edelstein and Ludwig Edelstein, *Asclepius: A Collection and Interpretation of the Testimonies* (Baltimore: Johns Hopkins University Press, 1998), p. 234; also available in Mary R. Lefkowitz and Maureen B. Fant, eds., *Women's Life in Greece and Rome: A Source Book in Translation* (Baltimore: Johns Hopkins University Press, 1982), p. 122.

11. A. J. M. Wedderburn, "Historical Problems in the Resurrection Stories," chap. 2 in *Beyond Resurrection* (Peabody: Hendrickson Publishers, 1999), pp. 29–37.

12. David R. Cartlidge, trans., *Sourcebook of Texts for the Comparative Study of the Gospels*, ed. David L. Dungan and Cartlidge, Sources for Biblical Study 1, 4th ed. (Missoula, Mont.: Scholars Press, 1974), p. 157.

13. Helms, *Gospel Fictions*, pp. 146–47.

14. Conybeare, trans., Loeb ed., vol. 2, pp. 403, 404.

15. Robert Alter, "Biblical Type-Scenes and Uses of Convention," chap. 3 in *The Art of Biblical Narrative* (New York: Basic Books, 1981), pp. 47–62; see also Alter, *Genesis: Translation and Commentary* (New York: W. W. Norton, 1996), p. 52, where he defines a "type-scene in biblical narrative, in which the writer invokes a fixed sequence of narrative motifs, familiar as a convention to his audience, while pointedly modifying them in keeping with the needs of the immediate narrative context."

16. It seems to me it is worth exploring the possibility that this problem of the ever-receding Parousia might account for some of the uncertainty over when Jesus lived and died! One might have been inclined to carry the life and death of Jesus with one as a "recent past," the further one went on in history, from Alexander Jannaeus to Claudius Caesar.

17. Of course, it is at least as likely that the notion of the other apostles suggesting John write the gospel is based on this passage!

18. Rudolf Bultmann, "New Testament and Mythology," in *Kerygma and Myth: A Theological Debate,* ed. and trans. Hans Werner Bartsch, trans. rev. Reginald H. Fuller (New York: Harper & Row Torchbooks/Cloister Library, 1961), p. 42; Gordon D. Kaufman, *Systematic Theology: A Historicist Perspective* (New York: Scribner, 1968), pp. 422–25.

19. Robert M. Price, "Apocryphal Apparitions: 1 Corinthians 15:3–11 as a Post-Pauline Interpolation," *Journal of Higher Criticism* 2, no. 2 (fall 1995): 69–99.

20. David M. Hay, *Glory at the Right Hand: Psalm 110 in Early Christianity*, Society of Biblical Literature Monograph Series 18 (New York: Abingdon, 1973).

CONCLUSION
THE NAME
OF THE LORD

THE FINAL DOOR

Thus far we have traced a consistent pattern. We found we were able to identify earlier and later layers of the gospel tradition, places where one oral tradition has superceded another, where one evangelist has edited or censored another's work. Again and again we have found that earlier material negated later material and then wound up being negated in turn by criteria including that of the more spectacular being secondary to the less spectacular, and of this saying or that story being redundant to Judaism or Hellenistic Christianity and thus liable to have been derivative from these sources. We have arrived at the conclusion that the gospel tradition seems completely unreliable. That is, most of the sayings and stories alike seem to be historically spurious. If any of them should chance to be genuine, we can no longer tell. We cannot render their possible authenticity probable, so they fall to the cutting-room floor. It is not that the material thus eliminated is somehow distasteful or objectionable. Most of it is still worth admiring and cherishing. But if our goal is that of the historian striving to establish the facts of Jesus and Christian origins, we must admit there is precious little help for us in the Gospels.

Among our pathmarks are Mark 12:35–37, which repudiates the Davidic descent of the Messiah. If Jesus was thought to have ever said that, then we can dismiss Matthew's and Luke's genealogies tracing Jesus back to David. If Jesus was ever thought to have spoken the words of Mark 8:11–12, "I tell you, no sign shall be given to this generation," then we must reject all the stories in which he does supply miracles. If, as Rom. 1:4; Acts 2:36, 3:26 preserve, Christians once believed Jesus had become the Messiah as of his resurrection, then all passages that have him claiming messiahship during his ministry must be judged spurious. If Mark 16:1–8 rules out any resurrection appearances, then the embellishments of Matthew, John, and Luke cannot be accepted. If Jesus was believed to have renounced all apocalyptic speculation ("The kingdom of God is not coming with signs to be observed," Luke 17:20), then the Olivet Discourse is someone else's. If the coast was clear even to *pretend* that Jesus said, "Go nowhere among the Gentiles, and set foot in no village of the Samaritans" (Matt. 10:5), then how can we credit the parable of the Good Samaritan to the historical Jesus? If the earliest known version of resurrection faith had Jesus raised as a spirit (1 Cor. 15:45, 50), then all the gospel tales of his physical resurrection must be dismissed.

This astonishingly complete absence of reliable gospel material begins to coincide, along its own authentic trajectory, and not as an implication of some other theory, with another minimalist approach to the historical Jesus, namely, that there never was one. Most of the Dutch Radical scholars, following Bruno Bauer, argued that all of the gospel tradition was fabricated to historicize an originally bare datum of a savior, perhaps derived from the Mystery Religions or Gnosticism or even further afield. The basic argument offered for this position, it seems to me, is that of analogy, the resemblances between Jesus and Gnostic and Mystery Religion saviors being just too numerous and close to dismiss. And that is a strong argument. Any attempt to avoid it is, I fear, special pleading. And yet that does not prove the point. Bultmann acknowledged all these parallels and explained their occurrence in Christian mythology as straight borrowings. He was quite willing to admit that New Testament Christology was derived in whole and in part from contemporary mythico-religious categories. But there was always the possibility that there had truly been a historical Jesus at the root of the thing, that he had been lost behind the mythology, as almost happened in the case of Caesar Augustus or the myth-encrusted Alexander the Great.

Nor was Bultmann especially optimistic about how much gospel teaching or narrative could be claimed for the historical Jesus. He often said virtually nothing could be known of Jesus. But many of his students, the "Post-Bultmannians," like Ernst Käsemann, Günther Bornkamm, Gerhard Ebeling, Ernst Fuchs, and James M. Robinson, persuaded him that he had gone overboard, that he had ventured too close to theological docetism, confessing the church's Christ of faith and letting the historical Jesus practically disappear. The Post-Bultmannians thus embarked on a "new quest of the historical Jesus," striving to find some insight into Jesus' existential self-understanding that would be continuous, compatible, with the existential self-understanding of the gospel as Bultmann, following Heidegger, described it, a total openness toward the future as the gift of God. At one point Bultmann was willing to go no further than the admission that Christian faith would be in trouble, shown up as based on illusion, if it were to be discovered that Jesus was dragged kicking and screaming to the cross. We must posit, Bultmann said, that Jesus accepted his fate from the hand of God. Afterward, Bultmann went on to write a book on the historical Jesus and his teaching, *Jesus and the Word*,[1] implying that Bultmann had allowed himself to be convinced by his students,[2] many of whom wrote their own historical Jesus books. All alike were based on a predictable core of sayings that allowed them to depict Jesus as a radical social and/or religious innovator, and a prophet of a kingdom of God that had already been inaugurated through the agency of his ministry, though with a future consummation to come. All these texts we have found to be highly dubious or outright spurious.

More recent treatments of the historical Jesus by Richard A. Horsley, John Dominic Crossan, the Jesus Seminar, and others[3] are also insufficiently critical, in many cases welcoming back a whole host of texts that Bultmann wouldn't have touched with a ten-foot pole. But in my judgment, even this supposed arch-skeptic did not go nearly far enough, and Norman Perrin, who contributed the most explicit discussion of the criterion of dissimilarity, seems to me to have been surprisingly lenient in its application. One wonders if all these scholars came to a certain point and stopped, their assumption being, "If Jesus was a historical figure, he must have done and said *something*!" But their own criteria and critical tools, which we have sought to apply here with ruthless consistency, ought to have left them with complete agnosticism, which is where we have ended up. But even at that, there may yet be one more step for us to take. There may be yet one more key text that will provide the fulcrum with which we must, like it or not, overthrow the last bit of the historical Jesus tradition.

THE NAME ABOVE ALL NAMES

Paul L. Couchoud made an observation that fell like a tree in an empty forest. He pointed out a neglected detail of the important text Phil. 2:6–11, a hymn fragment about the suffering and exaltation of the Christ:

> Who, though he was in the form of God,
> Did not count equality with God a thing to be grasped,
> But emptied himself, taking the form of a slave,
> Being born in the likeness of men.
> And being found in human form, he humbled himself
> And became obedient unto death [even death on a cross].
> Therefore God has highly exalted him,
> And bestowed on him the *name* that is above every name,

> That at the *name* of Jesus, every knee should bow,
> In heaven and on earth, and under the earth,
> And every tongue confess that Jesus Christ is Lord
> To the glory of God the Father.

Scholars agree[4] that the bracketed phrase, "even death on a cross" is secondary, as it interrupts the meter of the rest. All agree as well that the hymn text is based ultimately on Isa. 45:22–23:

> Turn to me and be saved,
> All the ends of the earth!
> For I am God, and there is no other.
> By myself I have sworn,
> From my mouth has gone forth in righteousness
> A word that shall not return:
> "To me every knee shall bow,
> Every tongue shall swear."

The Philippians hymn thus delegates what was originally conceived as the exclusive divine dominion of Yahve to his glorified Christ after his suffering, in accord with the ancient mytheme glimpsed in Dan. 7:13–14 of Baal assuming coregency with his Father El following his resurrection victory over Mot the death monster. In Jewish visionary texts the pattern repeats, for example, in 3 Enoch, where the undying patriarch is not only assumed bodily into heaven but is even made to occupy a throne beside that of God himself. He is thereafter to be known, astonishingly, as the Lesser Yahve! Other entities were delegated divine power and honor, such as Yahoel, the angel of the divine name.[5] Though some scholars do not exactly relish these history-of-religions parallels, all agree that the Philippians hymn does depict the divine enthronement of the vindicated Christ. But they invariably read the text as if God had bestowed on someone already called Jesus the divine title *Kurios*, "Lord," equivalent to Adonai in the Old Testament, often substituted in Jewish liturgy for Yahve, the divine name itself.[6] Couchoud noticed that this is not quite what the text says. Instead, what we read is that, because of his humiliating self-sacrifice, an unnamed heavenly being has been granted a mighty name that henceforth should call forth confessions of fealty from all beings in the cosmos. At the name "Jesus" every knee should bow, every tongue acknowledging his Lordship.

Note the parallelism of the hymn; several lines are obviously paraphrases of one another. One such pair, equivalent in meaning, would be: "at the name of Jesus every knee should bow" and "every tongue [should] confess that Jesus is Lord." To break it down further, "bowing to the name of" is equivalent in meaning to "confessing the lordship of." Both are parallel predicates of "Jesus."

But, Couchoud reasoned with ineluctable logic, does not this piece of early Christian tradition presuppose a theology of the savior whereby he received the name Jesus only after his death struggle, even as Jacob received the honorific name Israel only after wrestling with God (Gen. 32:24–28)? According to such an understanding, there can have been no Galilean adventures of an itinerant teacher and healer named Jesus. Rather, these stories must necessarily have arisen only at a subsequent stage of belief when the savior's glorification, along with his honorific name Jesus, had been retrojected back before his death. I would suggest that only such a scenario of early Christological development can account for, first, the utter absence of the gospel-story tradition from most of the New Testament epistles, and second, the fictive, nonhistorical character of story after story in the Gospels.[7]

And this in turn implies that the name of Jesus, once it came to be taken for granted as the name of the character, was unwittingly retrojected into the past history of the character. (And then stories began to be told of what "Jesus" had done on earth, in Galilee and Jerusalem. The Archons who crucified him, as Zeus had crucified Prometheus, became Pilate and Herod and Alexander Jannaeus.) We have two very close parallels to the process Couchoud envisions. First, there is the process whereby the title Messiah was first believed to have been bestowed only on the Risen Christ, but was eventually retrojected into his earthly life, first at the baptism, then the nativity, as we have seen. And this title soon became a name, as in the epistles, where it seems never to denote "Davidic heir" but only "Mr. Christ." Second, think of the confusion among the Pentateuchal sources over when the name Yahve was revealed to mankind. The Elohist and the Priestly writer are crystal clear on the point: "God also said to Moses, 'Say this to the people of Israel, "Yahve, the God of your fathers, the God of Abraham, the God of Isaac, and the God of Jacob, has sent me to you." This is my name forever, and thus I am to be remembered throughout all generations'" (Exod. 3:15, E). "And God said to Moses, 'I am Yahve. I appeared to Abraham, to Isaac, and to Jacob, as El Shaddai, but by my name Yahve I did not make myself known to them'" (Exod. 6:2–3, P). And yet, according to the Yahvist, or J, source, people knew the name Yahve almost from the start: "To Seth also a son was born, and he called his name Enosh. At that time men began to invoke the name of Yahve" (Gen. 4:26, J). Apparently, the name became so familiar that people just naturally came to assume it had always been in use. The same thing happened, if Couchoud is right, with the name "Jesus."

Couchoud was blunt: if we have another of these strategic "class action" texts that, in this case, attests a time when the Christian savior was not yet called Jesus during his earthly sojourn, then we can wash away every single gospel story in a great tidal wave. All of them are predicated on the secondary assumption that the savior was named Jesus from the first. In one sense this should not surprise us. For have we not seen, time after time, that this saying or that story already presupposes the divine glory, the messianic dignity, and the retrospective knowledge of the cross that make them plainly anachronistic?

BID ME COME TO YOU, WALKING ON THE WATER

Couchoud's insight, if we accept it, might enable us to make a whole new sense out of the Nag Hammadi Gnostic texts that feature a beloved savior, whether Mechizedek, Seth, Derdekas, or Zoroaster, who is only late in the day identified with Jesus. We need some sort of new key to unlock the meaning of these enigmatic texts and the mystery of where and how they fit into the evolution of early Christianity. Couchoud's theory might provide it. What did the unquoted portion of the Philippians hymn call its Christ figure before his exaltation and possession of the throne-name "Jesus"? Could it perhaps have been one of these names? It would imply that the Christian Jesus was merely a more recent stage in the development of a much more ancient mythic character, just like Seth, Enosh, and the other ancient figures venerated by the Gnostics despite an utter lack, in the nature of the case, of any biographical or historical data about them.

Couchoud has indicated the final door we must pass through if we are to be consistent with the methodology that has served us so well thus far. Dare we step through that door to what Schweitzer called "thoroughgoing skepticism"? Even if doing so will mean that the historical Jesus will have shrunk to the vanishing point?

NOTES

1. Rudolf Bultmann, *Jesus and the Word*, trans. Louise Pettibone Smith and Erminie Huntress Lantero (New York: Scribner, 1958).

2. Works stemming from this circle included Günther Bornkamm, *Jesus of Nazareth*, trans. Irene and Fraser McLuskey with James M. Robinson (New York: Harper & Row, 1960); Ernst Fuchs, *Studies in the Historical Jesus*, trans. Andrew Scobie, Studies in Biblical Theology 42 (London: SCM Press, 1964); James M. Robinson, *A New Quest of the Historical Jesus*, Studies in Biblical Theology 25 (London: SCM Press, 1959); Hans Conzelmann, *Jesus*, trans. J. Raymond Lord (Philadelphia: Fortress Press, 1973); Norman Perrin, *The Kingdom of God in the Teaching of Jesus* (London: SCM Press, 1963); ibid., *Rediscovering the Teaching of Jesus* (New York: Harper & Row, 1976); Herbert Braun, *Jesus of Nazareth: the Man and His Time*, trans. Everett R. Kalin (Philadelphia: Fortress Press, 1979); Ernst Käsemann, "The Problem of the Historical Jesus," in *Essays on New Testament Themes*, trans. W. J. Montague, Studies in Biblical Theology 41 (London: SCM Press, 1964), pp. 15–47; ibid., "Blind Alleys in the 'Jesus of History' Controversy," in *New Testament Questions of Today*, trans. W. J. Montague (Philadelphia: Fortress Press, 1969), pp. 23–65; Gerhard Ebeling, "The Question of the Historical Jesus and the Problem of Christology," in *Word and Faith*, trans. James W. Leitch (Philadelphia: Fortress Press, 1963), pp. 288–304; James M. Robinson, ed., *The Bultmann School of Biblical Interpretation: New Directions?* Journal for Theology and Church 1 (New York: Harper & Row Torchbooks/Cloister Library, 1965). Van A. Harvey leveled a devastating criticism of the whole approach in his "The Morality of Historical Knowledge and the

New Quest of the Historical Jesus," chap. 6 in *The Historian & the Believer: The Morality of Historical Knowledge and Christian Belief* (New York: Macmillan, 1966), pp. 164–203.

3. Richard A. Horsley, *Jesus and the Spiral of Violence: Popular Jewish Resistence in Roman Palestine* (Minneapolis: Fortress Press, 1993); John Dominic Crossan, *In Parables: The Challenge of the Historical Jesus* (New York: Harper & Row, 1973); ibid., *The Historical Jesus: The Life of a Mediterranean Jewish Peasant* (New York: HarperCollins, 1991); Bernard Brandon Scott, *Jesus, Symbol-Maker for the Kingdom* (Philadelphia: Fortress Press, 1981); ibid., *Hear Then the Parable: A Commentary on the Parables of Jesus* (Minneapolis: Fortress Press, 1989); James Breech, *The Silence of Jesus: The Authentic Voice of the Historical Man* (Philadelphia: Fortress Press, 1983); Marcus Borg, *Conflict, Holiness and Politics in the Teaching of Jesus*, Studies in the Bible and Early Christianity 5 (New York: Edwin Mellen Press, 1984); Robert W. Funk, *Parables and Presence: Forms of the New Testament Tradition* (Philadelphia: Fortress Press, 1982); Robert W. Funk, Roy W. Hoover, and Robert J. Miller, eds., *The Five Gospels: The Search for the Authentic Words of Jesus* (New York: Free Press/Macmillan, 1993); Robert Funk and the Jesus Seminar, *The Acts of Jesus: The Search for the Authentic Deeds of Jesus* (San Francisco: HarperSanFrancisco, 1998).

4. Ralph P. Martin, *Carmen Christi: Philippians 2:5–11 in Recent Scholarship and in the Setting of Early Christian Worship*, rev. ed. (Grand Rapids: William B. Eerdmans, 1983) pp. ixxxvii–xxxviii, 314–15; Joachim Jeremias, *The Central Message of the New Testament* (New York: Scribner, 1965), p. 74; Reginald H. Fuller, *The Foundations of New Testament Christology* (New York: Scribner, 1965), p. 204.

5. Gershom Scholem, *Major Trends in Jewish Mysticism* (New York: Schocken Books, 1973), pp. 67–68; Alan F. Segal, *Two Powers in Heaven: Early Rabbinic Reports about Christianity and Gnosticism*, Studies in Judaism in Late Antiquity 25 (Leiden: E. J. Brill, 1977), p. 65.

6. J. H. Houlden, *Paul's Letters from Prison: Philippians, Colossians, Philemon, and Ephesians*, Pelican New Testament Commentaries (Baltimore: Penguin Books, 1970), p. 84, is typical: "The name in question is *Kyrios* (*Lord*)."

7. Paul L. Couchoud, *The Creation of Christ: An Outline of the Beginnings of Christianity*, trans. C. Bradlaugh Bonner (London: Watts & Co., 1939), p. 438: "*The God-Man does not receive the name of Jesus till after his crucifixion.* That alone, in my judgment, is fatal to the historicity of Jesus."

INDEX

SCRIPTURE
INDEX

John

Acts

Romans

1 Corinthians